THE RASHNESS OF THAT HOUR

UNEDITED

ADVANCE GALLEY

THE RASHNESS

Robert J. Wynstra

Forney Field, Gettysburg. *Photo by Steven Stanley*

OF THAT HOUR

Politics, Gettysburg, and the Downfall of
Confederate Brigadier General Alfred Iverson

SB
Savas Beatie
New York and California

© 2010 by Robert J. Wynstra

All rights reserved. No part of this publication may be reproduced, stored in a retrieval system, or transmitted, in any form or by any means, electronic, mechanical, photocopying, recording, or otherwise, without the prior written permission of the publisher. Printed in the United States of America.

Cataloging-in-Publication Data is available from the Library of Congress.

ISBN 978-1-932714-88-3

05 04 03 02 01   5 4 3 2 1
First edition, first printing

SB

Published by
Savas Beatie LLC
521 Fifth Avenue, Suite 1700
New York, NY 10175

Editorial Offices:

Savas Beatie LLC
P.O. Box 4527
El Dorado Hills, CA 95762
Phone: 916-941-6896
(E-mail) sales@savasbeatie.com

Savas Beatie titles are available at special discounts for bulk purchases in the United States by corporations, institutions, and other organizations. For more details, please contact Special Sales, P.O. Box 4527, El Dorado Hills, CA 95762, or you may e-mail us at sales@savasbeatie.com, or visit our website at www.savasbeatie.com for additional information.

To Anita,
without you none of this would have been possible

The Union view from Oak Ridge across the Forney farm field. *Photo by Steven Stanley*

Contents

Acknowledgments
x

Introduction
The Horrors of That Day
xiii

Chapter 1
At Liberty to Tender My Services
1

Chapter 2
All the Devils are Here
30

Chapter 3
An Earnest Protest Against This Injustice
52

Chapter 4
There is Quite a Stir in Our Regiment
78

Chapter 5
I Did Not Think to Look in the Rear
101

Chapter 6
We Have No Doubt Succeeded in Deceiving Hooker
124

Chapter 7
A Perfect Triumphal March
143

Chapter 8
He That Soweth of the Flesh
175

Contents (continued)

Chapter 9
We are Brought in Hearing of Artillery
198

Chapter 10
The Yankees Crossed Fired on Us a Good While
225

Chapter 11
For a Few Minutes the Fighting was Terrific
247

Chapter 12
I Told Him it was Then Too Late
271

Chapter 13
We Have an Awful Night of It
300

Epilogue
The Glory it had is Now Passed Away
325

Appendix 1
Order of Battle: Iverson's Brigade, July 1, 1863
347

Appendix 2
Numbers and Losses in Iverson's Brigade
350

Bibliography
359

Index
381

Maps

Map 1: Lower Cape Fear, 1861-1862
16

Map 2: Route to Gettysburg, June 10-21, 1863
144

Map 3: Route to Gettysburg, June 22-July 1, 1863
174

Map 4: Iverson's Initial Contact at Gettysburg, July 1, 1863
205

Map 5: O'Neal's Attack at Gettysburg, July 1, 1863
218

Map 6: Iverson's Attack at Gettysburg, July 1, 183
228

Map 7: Ramseur's Attack at Gettysburg, July 1, 1863
249

Map 8: Night Attack on West Cemetery Hill, July 2, 1863
275

Map 9: Ewell's Wagon Train, July 4-7, 1863
302

Map 10: The Battle for Hagerstown, July 6, 1863
317

Illustrations appear throughout the book
for the convenience of the reader

Acknowledgments

This book would not have been possible without the help of those individuals listed herein. The assistance of Gary Kross, Gettysburg licensed battlefield guide, proved especially crucial. He generously provided me with unlimited access to his trove of Iverson family papers and photographs. He also accompanied me on several walks of the Gettysburg battle sites associated with Iverson's Brigade and helped shape my understanding of the events that took place there. Without his help and encouragement, my task would have been much more difficult.

The contributions by Henry Mintz of Shelby, North Carolina, were just as essential. His determined sleuthing through the archives located in North Carolina and the South provided much of the source material used in this book. Time after time, he uncovered previously unknown documents that led to new avenues of inquiry regarding the political feuds that dominated Iverson's Brigade. He proved equally adept at locating important period photographs. In many ways, this book is as much his as it is mine.

Steve French from Hedgesville, West Virginia, generously perused several manuscript versions and provided me invaluable documents and pieces of information. His help throughout the long hours of research and writing is greatly appreciated. Gregory White provided similar encouragement and went the extra distance to provide me with several newspaper accounts and other important documents from his home state of Georgia. Charles Teague from Gettysburg kindly reviewed my manuscript and helped me obtain several elusive documents. But even greater was his enthusiasm for my efforts; he helped me move ahead whenever my spirits flagged.

Thanks are also due to Eric J. Wittenberg for his early interest in my project and his kind assistance over the years. J. David Petruzzi also deserves special thanks for his encouragement and interest in my manuscript. Without their help, this book would have suffered many more delays in getting published. In addition, Scott Mingus willingly shared information on Confederate activities in the area outside of Gettysburg. I would also like to acknowledge Robert deButts for granting me permission to quote material from the Lee Family Papers at the

Virginia Historical Society. Raymond J. DeStefano generously allowed me to quote from an important Gettysburg letter in his collection.

Greg Mast was extremely helpful in securing several photographs for use in this book. His kind assistance is greatly appreciated. Garry Adelman provided invaluable help in obtaining photographs of the Gettysburg battlefield. Thanks also to R. Carol McLean from Rockingham, North Carolina, for granting me permission to use the photograph of his relative, Pvt. Solomon McLean of the 23rd North Carolina, and to Lindsey Lambert from the Brock Historical Museum at Greensboro College for providing an image of Charles Force Deems. Gary Beaumont and L. Brian Stauffer provided invaluable assistance in scanning and preparing my photographs.

Without exception, the staff from the public and private archives and other institutions that provided source material for this book were remarkably helpful. Special appreciation for their assistance is due to John Coski from the Museum of the Confederacy and Sion Harrington III from the North Carolina Office of Archives and History. Bev Tetterton from the North Carolina Room at the New Hanover County Library in Wilmington, North Carolina, displayed unparalleled efficiency in providing me with material from the Cowan and Denson Family Papers.

Maps play an essential role in any book of military history. In this case, George Skoch masterfully handled the task of preparing those that appear in this book. His professionalism and skill shine through on each of them.

I am especially honored that historian Robert K. Krick, whose knowledge of the Army of Northern Virginia is unsurpassed, took the time to review the manuscript and offer important suggestions I endeavored to incorporate.

Without Theodore P. Savas, the managing director of Savas Beatie, this book would not have been possible. His enthusiasm and unmatched professionalism made every step in the process remarkably enjoyable. In all respects, he is truly a "dream publisher." I would also like to thank Kimberly Largent-Christopher, who helped with an early draft of my manuscript.

Lastly, I would like to thank Anita Povich for enduring several years of talk about someone named Alfred Iverson. Every time I faltered, she was there to pick me up and prod me forward. Many times, she possessed more faith in my ability to pull off this project than I did. Without her support and encouragement, I certainly would still be struggling to write this book.

Robert J. Wynstra

INTRODUCTION

The Horrors of That Day

Arguably, no commander in the Army of Northern Virginia suffered more damage to his reputation at Gettysburg than did Brig. Gen. Alfred Holt Iverson of Georgia. In little more than an hour during the early afternoon of July 1, 1863, much of his North Carolina brigade was slaughtered just north of the town in front of a stone wall on Oak Ridge. Amid widespread rumors that he was a drunk and a coward who had slandered his own troops, Iverson was stripped of his command in Maj. Gen. Robert E. Rodes' Division less than a week after the end of the battle.[1]

By that point, however, a series of bitter feuds in the brigade had made Iverson's downfall nearly inevitable. The most well-known dispute took place in the 20th North Carolina over who would succeed him as colonel following his promotion to general in the fall of 1862. Equally nasty disagreements over promotions erupted at about the same time in the 5th North Carolina and the 12th North Carolina. Governor Zebulon Baird Vance and other major political figures in North Carolina directly opposed Iverson and even worked behind the

---

1 Gary Kross, That One Error Fills Him With Faults: General Iverson and His Brigade at Gettysburg," *Blue and Gray Magazine*, 12, Issue 3 (February 1995), 22-24, 48-53.

scenes to have his promotion blocked in the Confederate Senate. As his list of enemies continued to grow, Iverson entered the fighting at Gettysburg with hardly a friend in the brigade.[2]

Despite those problems, no one could have anticipated the extent of the disaster that struck his men that day. After forming his regiments along the Mummasburg Road, near the John S. Forney farmhouse, Iverson remained in the rear as his North Carolina troops marched in perfect formation across a field of ripening timothy. "Along the path or eastern side of the field and on a ridge ran a stone fence which formed part of the enemy's line," one officer from the 23rd North Carolina recalled. "Behind this fence, alone, lay hidden from view, more men than our assaulting column contained."[3]

As they approached within point-blank range, a blast of gunfire from Brig. Gen. Henry Baxter's Federal brigade, most of which had remained hidden behind the wall, tore a swath of destruction through the ranks of the Tar Heel soldiers. "Hundred of the Confederates fell at that first volley, plainly marking their line with the ghastly row of dead and wounded men, whose blood trailed the course of their line with a crimson stain clearly discernable for several days after the battle, until the rain washed the gory record away," one soldier from the 88th Pennsylvania in Baxter's brigade recounted.[4]

Men throughout Iverson's Brigade expressed shock at the carnage they witnessed along the stone wall and in a nearby hollow where many of them sought refuge. Private James D. Ireland from the 20th North Carolina insisted that "our brigade was almost annihilated." Captain Benjamin Robinson from the 5th North Carolina proclaimed in a letter to Governor Vance that the ranks of his regiment "were decimated by the terrific fire to which they were subjected." He further claimed that the men had "suffered such a loss as no

---

2 Robert K. Krick, "Three Confederate Disasters on Oak Ridge: Failures of Brigade Leadership on the First Day at Gettysburg," in Gary W. Gallagher, ed., *The First Day at Gettysburg: Essays on Confederate and Union Leadership* (Kent, OH: Kent State University Press, 1992), 129-137; Walter A. Montgomery, "Twelfth Regiment," in Walter Clark, *Histories of the Several Regiments and Battalions from North Carolina in the Great War 1861-'65*, 5 Vols. (Goldsboro, NC: Nash Brothers, 1901), 1:642, hereafter Clark, *NC Regiments*); Daniel Harvey Christie to Zebulon B. Vance, March 31, 1863, Zebulon Baird Vance Papers, Private Collection, North Carolina Office of Archives and History, Raleigh, North Carolina (hereafter cited as NCOAH).

3 V. E. Turner and H. C. Wall, "Twenty-Third Regiment," included in Clark, *NC Regiments*, 2:235. Of the two authors, only Turner was present at Gettysburg.

4 John D. Vautier, *History of the Eighty-Eighth Pennsylvania Volunteers in the War for the Union, 1861-1865* (Philadelphia: J.B. Lippincott Company, 1894), 135.

other troops have sustained in this or any other war." Assistant Surgeon William W. Marston from the 12th North Carolina declared in his diary that "our brigade suffers terribly."[5]

Compiled casualty lists for the Tar Heel troops support these firsthand accounts of the devastation. Including the sharpshooter detachment, which operated as a separate unit guarding the left flank, an estimated 100 officers and 1,238 enlisted men were engaged on the field that day. Of that number, about 860 officers and enlisted men were killed, wounded, or captured, which is a casualty rate of 65 percent for the entire brigade. That total included more than 180 men, who were killed or mortally wounded in the attack along Oak Ridge. A private from the 5th North Carolina named Daniel M. Moose lamented in a letter home that "the whole brigade looks like two small regiments."[6]

On the right of the line, two companies from the 12th North Carolina lost more than half of the four officers and 41 enlisted men engaged in front of the stone wall. Largely because of the luck of position and a roll in the terrain, the remaining eight companies from that regiment escaped the worst of the slaughter, losing only about 40 men in the fighting. The casualties proved much more extensive among the men of the 5th North Carolina on the left of the line. An estimated 28 officers and 387 enlisted men from the regiment entered the fight that day. Only 22 officers and 238 enlisted men emerged unscathed.

The outcome of the bloody Forney field fiasco proved even worse for the two regiments at the center of the line of attack. The 20th North Carolina carried approximately 23 officers and 263 enlisted men into the fight in front of the stone wall. Only two officers and fewer than 40 enlisted men from the regiment escaped unharmed from the field that day, which is a stunning 84 percent casualty rate. Lieutenant Joseph B. Oliver from that regiment, who was captured in the nearby hollow, exaggerated just slightly when he claimed that "only those escaped who were on the skirmish line or on detached duty."[7]

---

5 J. D. Ireland, "Memoirs," Military Collection, NCOAH; Benjamin Robinson to Zebulon Baird Vance, July 9, 1863, *Raleigh Daily Progress*, July 24, 1863; William W. Marston diary, entry for July 1, 1863, Confederate Miscellany b, Robert W. Woodruff Library, Emory University, Atlanta, Georgia (hereafter cited as Emory).

6 Daniel M. Moose to Dear Father-in-law, Aug. 20, 1863, in Beverly Barrier Troxler and Billy Dawn Barrier Auciello, eds., *Dear Father: Confederate Letters Never Before Published* (North Billerica, MA: Auciello Publishers, 1989), 138.

7 Joseph B. Oliver, "My Recollections of the Battle of Gettysburg," 2, Military Collection, NCOAH.

Lieutenant George B. Bullock was the lone officer from the 23rd North Carolina to emerge unscathed from the Forney field on July 1, 1863.

North Carolina Office of Archives and History

The troops from the 23rd North Carolina sustained even heavier losses during the fighting along Oak Ridge. Of its estimated 22 officers and 262 enlisted men on that part of the field, only one officer and about 16 enlisted men made it out unscathed. The casualty rate of 94 percent for the troops engaged along the wall ranks as one of the highest for any regiment during the entire war. Lieutenant George B. Bullock, the lone officer in the regiment to emerge unharmed, summed up the extent of the devastation with the statement that it was the only battle he witnessed during the entire war "where the blood ran like a branch."[8]

Few, if any, of the men from the ill-fated brigade would have disagreed with Pvt. John F. Coghill of the 23rd North Carolina when he declared to his family soon after the battle that "toungs cannot tell the horrows of that day." After months of internal feuding and political maneuvering behind the scenes, the survivors had no doubt about who was to blame for the unspeakable disaster. Almost to the man, they placed the fault directly on the failed leadership displayed by their commanding general. What remained much more difficult to answer was the lingering question of exactly how such a thing could have happened at all.[9]

---

8 Clement A. Evans, ed., *Confederate Military History: Expanded Edition*, 14 vols. (Wilmington, NC: Broadfoot Publishing Company, 1987), 5:440; Turner and Wall, "Twenty-Third Regiment," in Clark, *NC Regiments*, 2:238.

9 John F. Coghill to Dear Pappy, Ma and Mit, July 17, 1863, John Fuller Coghill Letters, Southern Historical Collection, Wilson Library, University of North Carolina at Chapel Hill, Chapel Hill, North Carolina (hereafter cited as SHC).

CHAPTER ONE

At Liberty to Tender My Services

Despite the ordeal that his men endured at Gettysburg, Alfred Iverson's background and pre-war military experience seemed to make him ideally suited as a brigade commander in the Army of Northern Virginia.

Born in Clinton, Georgia, on February 14, 1829, young Alfred grew up in a family of wealth and political influence. His father, Alfred Iverson Sr., held office as both a congressman and U.S. senator from Georgia. His family was connected by marriage to the highest levels of the Democratic Party in the nation's capital. The younger Iverson also boasted military credentials. He dropped out of military school at just 18 to serve as a lieutenant in the Mexican War with a Georgia outfit his father helped fund. Mustered out in 1848, he searched for a fruitful career for seven years before finally being commissioned into the 1st U.S. Cavalry. Iverson served on the western frontier for several years, with stints in Kansas and during the Indian wars in the late 1850s. All of this would suddenly change when war came in 1861.

* * *

Iverson's influential father played a major role in shaping the future Confederate general's character. The senior Iverson was born in 1798 and grew up in Liberty County, Georgia. He attended Princeton College, which was then known as the College of New Jersey. Following his graduation in 1820, he returned to his home state and opened a law office in Jones County. Before too long, he was one of the most prominent citizens in the town of Clinton. Turning to politics, the elder Iverson represented the county in the lower house of the General Assembly from 1827 to 1830.[1]

The senior Iverson prospered equally well in his personal life. He married Caroline Goode Holt in 1822. She was 22 years old and came from a wealthy family in nearby Baldwin County, where they owned more than 4,000 acres of land, a ferry business, several lumber mills, and numerous slaves. Her father, Thaddeus Holt, had served for a short time in the state legislature and as a lieutenant colonel in the militia during the War of 1812. He participated in several duels during his life and was eventually murdered in October of 1813. Her older brother, Thaddeus Goode Holt, became an important lawyer and judge in the town of Macon.[2]

Iverson's fortunes took a major turn for the worse over the following years. The young couple's first child, Martha Ann, was born in 1823 but died suddenly only a few months later. In 1826, their family finally grew to include a healthy daughter named Julia. She was followed by young Alfred, who was born in 1829. About a year later, the senior Iverson lost his wife to a lingering illness. Her death left him devastated. A friend reported to one of his wife's relatives that he had "seldom seen any one more deeply afflicted than Mr. Iverson."[3]

Iverson responded by moving with his two young children and eight slaves to the town of Columbus, along the Chattahoochee River in a section of

---

[1] American Council of Learned Societies, *Dictionary of American Biography*, 9 Vols. (New York: C. Scribner's Sons, 1928), 9:517-518; Kenneth Coleman and Charles Stephen Gurr, eds., *Dictionary of Georgia Biography*, 2 Vols. (Athens: University of Georgia Press, 1983), 1:509-510; David Stephen Heidler, Jeanne T. Heidler, and David J. Coles, eds., *Encyclopedia of the American Civil War: A Political, Social, and Military History* (New York: W. W. Norton and Company, 2002), 1052-1053.

[2] Woodland G. Shockley, "A Brief History of the Families of Richard Holt, Simon Holt, Singleton Holt, And Their Descendants," http://freepages.Genealogy.Rootsweb.com/~caseytexas/Holt-White/Richholt.doc. For details on the murder, see *Daily National Intelligencer*, October 22, 1813.

[3] Nancy L. Jordan, "Iverson-Haynes Connection," http://wc.rootsweb.ancestry. Com/cgi-bin/igm.cgi?op=REG&db=:2469703&id=I524349733; Maria Bryan to Julia Ann Bryan Cummings, March 20, 1830, in Carol Bleser, ed., *Tokens of Affection: The Letters of a Planter's Daughter in the Old South* (Athens: University of Georgia Press, 1996), 113.

western Georgia that had been ceded by the Creek Indians only four years earlier. In late 1827, the legislature had established a major trading post there. Soon afterward, the state offered more than 500 half-acre residential lots for sale through a public lottery. As a leading figure in this frontier boomtown, Iverson established a thriving law practice. He also succeeded at numerous business ventures, from banking to horse racing.[4]

Iverson's social position in the community received a major boost on April 7, 1831, when he married 28-year-old Julia Forsyth, the eldest daughter of former Georgia governor and current U.S. senator John Forsyth. Her father had served as a congressman and as U.S. minister to Spain, where he played a key role in negotiating the transfer of Florida to the United States. Her mother, Clara Meigs Forsyth, was the daughter of the first president of Franklin College, which would later become the University of Georgia. Despite spending most of her life in Washington, D.C., and Madrid, Spain, Iverson's wife settled in Columbus and bore him a daughter named Clara in 1833 and a son named John in 1837.

His new father-in-law, meanwhile, took an increasingly important role on the national political scene as a major ally of President Andrew Jackson. He served as chairman of the powerful Senate Commerce Committee and as a member of the Foreign Relations Committee and the Finance Committee. Forsyth remained in the U.S. Senate until 1834, when he was appointed as secretary of state in the Jackson administration. He was reappointed by President Martin Van Buren and held that important position until just before his death in 1841 at the age of 60.[5]

With strong encouragement from his wife's family, Iverson continued to pursue his own influential political career. He served as the state senator for Muscogee County from 1843 to 1844 and as an elector for President James K. Polk. In 1847, Iverson won election to the U.S. House of Representatives. Following a single term in Congress, he decided to return to the legal profession and served as a superior court judge in the town of Columbus. The senior

---

4 Kross, "That One Error," 48; Richard Harrison Shyrock, *Georgia and the Union in 1850* (Durham, NC: Duke University Press, 1926), 14; John H. Martin, ed., *Columbus Georgia, From Its Selection as a "Trading Town" in 1827 to Its Partial Destruction by Wilson's Raid in 1865* (Columbus, GA: Thomas Gilbert Printers, 1874), 1-22.

5 Coleman and Gurr, *Dictionary of GA Biography*, 1:316-318; Martin, *Columbus Georgia*, 31. For details on Forsyth's career, see Alvin Laroy Duckett, *John Forsyth: Political Tactician* (Athens: University of Georgia Press, 1962).

Alfred Iverson Sr. from Georgia emerged as a leading advocate of secession in the U.S. Senate during the late 1850s. *Library of Congress*

Iverson reached the pinnacle of his political fortunes in late 1854, when he was selected by the legislature on the 16th ballot to serve as a U.S. senator from Georgia.[6]

During those years, young Alfred enjoyed the advantages available to one of the most prominent families in the state. After receiving his early education at private schools in Columbus, he followed the lead of his father, who once held a commission in a Georgia militia company, by taking up studies at the Alabama Military and Scientific Institute in Tuskegee. The school was founded in 1843 under a former major from the U.S. Army. Arnoldus V. Brumby, a West Point graduate and an accomplished civil engineer, took over as head of the institute about three years later.[7]

The campus was located about a mile outside of town. Charles Hentz, who taught there while Iverson was in attendance, described it "as an imposing looking establishment, with a U.S. flag floating from the turret over the Sally port." The school had more than 90 students, with about 20 boys in each of the four upper classes. They ranged in age from "little A.B.C. children" to cadets in their late teenage years. The curriculum was modeled after that in use at West Point and included instruction in military tactics and engineering, as well as daily drilling on the parade grounds in the main compound.

When war broke out with Mexico in 1846, Tuskegee became a hotbed of patriotic fervor. Hentz recalled that "volunteers went off in numbers" from the surrounding area throughout that spring. Although too young to join the first wave of recruits, Iverson eventually took up arms for his country through the influence of his father. On July 24, 1847, he received an appointment as second lieutenant in a battalion of Georgia infantry volunteers that had been partially raised and equipped by the senior Iverson. According to one of his relatives, he "was so eager to go to the war that his father allowed him to leave school."[8]

---

6 American Council of Learned Societies, *Dictionary of American Biography*, 9:517-518; Coleman and Gurr, *Dictionary of GA Biography*, 1:509-510; Heidler, et al., *Encyclopedia of the American Civil War*, 1,053-1,054.

7 Kross, "That One Error," 48; Coleman and Gurr, *Dictionary of GA Biography*, 1:510-511; John Hope Franklin, *The Militant South, 1800-1861* (Urbana: University of Illinois Press, 2002), 153-154; George W. Cullum, *Biographical Register of the Officers and Graduates of the U.S. Military Academy at West Point, N.Y.*, 2 Vols. (Boston: Houghton, Mifflin and Company, 1891), 1:591.

8 Charles A. Hentz, "My Autobiography," in Steven M. Stowe, ed., *Southern Practice: The Diary and Autobiography of Charles A. Hentz, MD* (Charlottesville: University of Virginia Press, 2000),

The five companies in the battalion were organized as replacements for the men from the Georgia Volunteer Regiment, whose one-year term of enlistment was due to expire in mid-1847. Iverson initially worked to gather volunteers for service with Company D. Along with their normal pay, the men were promised 160 acres of land or $100 in cash upon completion of their service. "But the greatest inducement to ambitious youth, is the surpassing beauty and richness of the country through which we are to march; the manly excitement of honorable war; the conquest of the finest country, and richest city in the world," the younger Iverson declared in an open letter to the people of Columbus.[9]

The recruiting efforts proved so successful that the first four companies were completely filled by early September and placed under the temporary command of Capt. William N. Nelson. After rendezvousing at Mobile, Alabama, Lt. Iverson and nearly 400 other men from those companies left for Mexico by ship on October 11. "These were stout 'tall fellows,' men enured to fatigue by constant manual labor, and capable, we thought, of combating successfully, not only the enemy, but the hardship and exposure incident to the soldier's duties," one of the men remarked in a letter to a Columbus newspaper.

Iverson and his fellow volunteers began their operations in Mexico by going into camp just outside of Vera Cruz. On November 2, they moved 13 miles inland to the town of San Juan, where many of them began to show signs of disease. "From that time until the 18th of November, we had never more than one hundred and twenty men on Dress Parade," one member of the battalion remarked. "Every officer and man had been sick of Diarrhea and Intermittent Fever." He admitted that "here were sown the seeds of death in our ranks, which have since produced such an awful harvest."

In late November, the troops escorted a train of 200 wagons through the mountain pass at La Hoya to the town of Perote. Only about 40 men were still "able to march" by the time they reached their destination. "Being furnished with quarters, our troops would here, we hoped be restored to health by rest and care," one soldier reported to his hometown newspaper. "Unfortunately,

---

448-450; Charles A. Hentz Diary, Entry for May 8, 1847, in *ibid*, 160; Handwritten note on Mexican War, Iverson Family Papers, Emory.

9   Joe Griffith, "Georgians in the War with Mexico, 1846-1848," *Journal of the Historical Society of the Georgia National Guard*, 6 (1997), 3, 12; Alfred Iverson Jr., Mexican War Pension Record, Adjutant General's Office, Record Group 94, National Archives, Washington, D.C. (hereafter cited as NA); "Another Call for Georgia Volunteers," *Albany Patriot*, May 5, 1847; "Volunteers for Mexico," July 27, 1847, *Columbus Enquirer*, Aug. 24, 1847.

disease nourished by fatigue and exposure, had taken strong hold on the men." Although he was only 18 years old, Lt. Iverson served as acting commander of his company during much of this time.[10]

The battalion commander, Lt. Col. Isaac G. Seymour, finally arrived in Perote with the fifth company in early January. He immediately adopted "such sanatory measures as circumstances suggested" to stem the tide of illness among his troops. Despite those efforts, the disease outbreak soon worsened. The impact on the men in the ranks proved devastating. "Just at this time Typhus Fever made its appearance, and attacking the debilitated constitution of the men, defied the power of medicine," one member of the battalion remarked. "Our men died by scores."[11]

The soldiers in Iverson's company suffered so severely from diseases that "not a dozen" were present for duty by the time Seymour joined the battalion. Twenty-nine men from that company alone had already died from disease. Iverson himself became so sick in mid-January that he was sent to recover in Georgia. A handful of men stayed behind at Perote until June, when they began returning home. By then, only 34 men from the five companies were reported as still "fit for duty." During their stay, the men from the battalion failed to fire a single shot in anger.[12]

The only event of note during Iverson's absence came when Lt. Col. Seymour accepted the prearranged surrender of the deposed Mexican leader

---

10 "Correspondence of the Times," March 13, 1848, *Columbus Times*, April 25, 1848; Alfred Iverson Jr., Compiled Service Record, Mexican War, Adjutant General's Office, Record Group 94, NA.

11 "Lieut. Col. Isaac G. Seymour," *Columbus Enquirer*, Oct. 19, 1847; "Lt. Col. Seymour," *Georgia Telegraph and Republic*, Nov. 12, 1847; "Correspondence of the Times," March 13, 1848, *Columbus Times,* April 25, 1848. Seymour was a former mayor of Macon, Georgia. His only prior military experience came when he commanded a volunteer company against the Seminole Indians in Florida. Following the Mexican War, he moved to New Orleans, where he became a prominent newspaper editor. He later served as colonel of the 6th Louisiana in the Civil War and was mortally wounded at Gaines' Mill on June 27, 1862. For additional details on his career, see Terry L. Jones, ed., *The Civil War Memoirs of Captain William J. Seymour* (Baton Rouge: Louisiana State University Press, 1991), 2; Robert K. Krick, *Lee's Colonels: A Biographical Registry of the Field Officers of the Army of Northern Virginia* (Dayton, OH: Morningside Press, 1991), 339.

12 "Correspondence of the Enquirer," December 14, 1847, *Columbus Enquirer*, Jan. 24, 1848; "Correspondence of the Times," March 13, 1848, *Columbus Times*, April 25, 1848; "Letter of Col. Seymour," Dec. 3, 1847, *Columbus Enquirer*, Feb. 8, 1848; "Correspondence of the Times," Jan. 11, 1848, *Columbus Times*, Feb. 29, 1848; Iverson Jr., Compiled Service Record, Mexican War, NA; Jones, *Civil War Memoirs*, 339; "Correspondence of the Enquirer," Jan. 16, 1848, *Columbus Enquirer,* Feb. 22, 1848.

Antonio Lopez de Santa Anna at Perote. Captain Nelson recalled that this incident provided one of the few major breaks from "the monotony of garrison life." Seymour was later assigned the duty of escorting the former general into exile on the island of Jamaica. Lieutenant Iverson's term of service, meanwhile, finally ended on July 11, 1848, when he was mustered out with the other members of the battalion.[13]

Following the war, the young veteran spent several frustrating years trying to find a suitable career. He first read law in his father's office and then worked for a brief period as a railroad contractor in Georgia. His seeming lack of direction changed abruptly on March 3, 1855, when he was commissioned as a first lieutenant in Company C of the 1st U.S. Cavalry. This was one of two new cavalry regiments formed under the direction of his father's political ally, Jefferson Davis, who was serving as secretary of war in the administration of President Franklin Pierce.[14]

According to the administration plan, half the officers in the two new regiments would come from the Regular Army, with the other half appointed directly from civilian life. "This arrangement was probably adopted in order to propitiate the politicians, and insure the passage of the bill through Congress," one former officer explained. Almost certainly, Iverson's political connections played a major role in his selection from among the 1,300 civilian applications for the 31 available commissions. His father, in fact, openly lobbied for his son's selection as an officer in the new regiment.[15]

In late February, the senator-elect wrote to Secretary of War Davis requesting information about a direct commission for young Alfred. As would be repeated throughout much of his son's life, the senior Iverson's influence apparently had the desired effect. Little more than a week later, his old friend Jefferson Davis responded with the strong assurance that his application "will receive due consideration." As it turned out, the younger Iverson received his

---

13 William N. Nelson, "Capturing an Ex-Dictator," *The Southern Magazine*, 10 (1872), 241-245; "Statistics of War," *Georgia Telegraph and Republic*, Aug. 15, 1848; Alfred Iverson Jr., Compiled Service Record, Mexican War, NA.

14 Coleman and Gurr, *Dictionary of GA Biography*, 1:510-511; Kross, "That One Error," 48; Alfred Iverson Sr. to Jefferson Davis, March 6, 1861, Compiled Service Record of Alfred Iverson Jr., Microform 270, Roll 273, Record Group 109, NA (hereafter cited as Service Record followed by appropriate microform and roll numbers).

15 Jubal A. Early, "Comments on the First Volume of Count of Paris' Civil War in America," *Southern Historical Society Papers*, 3 (1876), 140-142 (hereafter cited as *SHSP*).

commission as a lieutenant in the new army regiment on the day before his father assumed office as a U.S. senator from Georgia.[16]

After reporting for duty at Jefferson Barracks, Missouri, Iverson settled quickly into military life. He served with a group of officers destined to become household names during the next decade. Colonel Edwin V. Sumner commanded the regiment, with field officers Lt. Col. Joseph E. Johnston, Maj. William H. Emory, and Maj. John S. Sedgwick. Captain George B. McClellan served as one of the senior captains. The junior officers included future Confederate generals James Ewell Brown Stuart, William S. Walker, George T. "Tige" Anderson, Robert S. Garnett, William N. R. Beale, George H. "Maryland" Steuart, James McIntosh, Robert Ransom, and Lunsford L. Lomax.[17]

The regiment soon transferred to Fort Leavenworth, Kansas, which occupied a strategic position along the Missouri River in the eastern part of the territory. The men from the 1st U.S. Cavalry assumed the task of policing the bitter sectional clashes that were ripping the Kansas Territory apart. From November 1855 to December 1856, more than 200 people died in the increasingly brutal fighting between the two warring factions. During the spring of 1856, a small detachment from the regiment led by Lt. Stuart even helped free several pro-slavery prisoners being held by John Brown and a band of his followers.[18]

Later that year, Lt. Iverson took on recruiting duties at Carlisle Barracks in Pennsylvania. Carlisle originally served as an important encampment for the British Army during the French and Indian War and was first established as a permanent military facility by the Continental Congress in 1776. During the following years, it mainly operated as a recruiting depot. The U.S. Army finally converted the post into the School of Cavalry Practice in 1838. Except for a

---

16 Lynda Lasswell Crist, ed., *The Papers of Jefferson Davis,* 10 Vols. (Baton Rouge: Louisiana State University Press, 1981-1997), 5:406; Ezra J. Warner, *Generals in Gray: Lives of the Confederate Commanders* (Baton Rouge: Louisiana State University Press, 1988), 268-269.

17 Kross, "That One Error," 48; "The New Regiments: The Appointments Completed," *New York Times,* March 21, 1855; Francis B. Heitman, *Historical Register and Dictionary of the United States Army,* 2 Vols. (Washington: U.S. Government Printing Office, 1903), 1:565, 578, 656, 872, 933, 936; Early, "Comments on First Volume," 143.

18 Robert Morris Peck, "Recollections of Early Times in Kansas Territory: From the Standpoint of a Regular Cavalryman," *Collections of the Kansas State Historical Society,* 8 (1904), 485-486; Emory H. Thomas, *Bold Dragoon: The Life of J. E. B. Stuart* (Norman: University of Oklahoma Press, 1999), 46.

brief period during the Mexican War, the barracks served from then on as the primary location for recruiting and training cavalrymen and dragoons for service on the western frontier.[19]

The relaxed pace of duty at the barracks provided Iverson with ample opportunity to pursue a budding romance with his 19-year-old cousin, Harriet Harris Hutchins. She was one of 10 children of Nathan L. and Mary Dixon Holt Hutchins. Iverson was related to her through the Holt line on his mother's side of the family. Her father was a prominent lawyer and judge in Gwinnett County and owned a plantation of nearly 2,300 acres with about 65 slaves. He also took an active part in politics, serving five terms as a state senator before being appointed as the justice of Georgia's Western Judicial Circuit.

The young couple married in her hometown of Lawrenceville, Georgia, on October 23, 1856. Except for a few short periods, Iverson would be away from his growing family for most of the next four years. After briefly living with him in the married officers' quarters at Carlisle Barracks, Harriet returned to her family's home in Georgia for the birth of their first child, Julia, in September of 1857. A second daughter named Minnie was born two years later in August of 1859. With two young children to take care of, she remained behind at their newly purchased home in Columbus throughout much of his tour of duty in the army.[20]

After more than a year and a half at Carlisle, Iverson finally rejoined his regiment in early 1858. His regiment was part of the 2,500 U.S. troops organized at Fort Leavenworth to accompany the newly appointed governor for the Mormon Territory on the trip to Utah. Late in the previous year, President James Buchanan had prompted a crisis when he appointed a new governor to replace the Mormon leader Brigham Young. In response, Young declared martial law in the territory and deployed the local Mormon militia. The dispute threatened to get out of hand but was peacefully settled soon after Iverson's return to Kansas.[21]

---

19 Samuel P. Bates, *History of Cumberland and Adams Counties Pennsylvania* (Chicago: Warner, Beers and Company, 1886), 109; James M. Merrill, *Spurs to Glory: The Story of the United States Cavalry* (Chicago: Rand McNally, 1966), 80-81; Merrill J. Mattes, ed., "Patrolling the Santa Fe Trail: Reminiscences of John S. Kirwin," *Kansas Historical Quarterly*, 21 (1955), 577.

20 Bill Arp, *Bill Arp from the Uncivil War to Date, 1861-1903* (Atlanta: Hudgins Publishing Company, 1903), 29; David B. Parker, *Alias Bill Arp: Charles Henry Smith and the South's "Goodly Heritage"* (Athens: University of Georgia Press, 1991), 6.

21 Kross, "That One Error," 48.

Harriett Harris Hutchins, who married Alfred Iverson Jr. in 1856, came from a prominent family in Gwinnett County, Georgia. *Gary Kross*

In November of 1858, the regiment moved to Fort Riley along the banks of the Kansas River in the western part of the territory. Less than a month later, Capt. Thomas J. Wood's Second Squadron, which consisted of Company I and Iverson's Company C, was detached for duty at Fort Washita in the Indian Territory. This change came in response to increased lawlessness and the threat from hostile Indians in the southern area of the sprawling territory. "Crime prevails to a great extent in this part of the country," was how one soldier explained the region. "Not a day passes but what we hear of someone being killed." He noted that "justice is slack and but rarely administered even if the rogues are caught."[22]

The fort stood about 18 miles north of where the Washita River flows into the Red River. Despite its remote location, Fort Washita proved ideal for the newly arrived companies to carry out their mission. "This post has a very fine situation—elevated on a hill, it commands a superb view for many miles around the country," one soldier from Iverson's company commented soon after their arrival. He further noted that there was "not much" to fear from hostile Indians in the immediate vicinity of the fort. Another trooper described it as "one of the handsomest posts in the West." [23]

Although commissioned as a line officer, Iverson spent much of his time there in the quartermaster and commissary departments. Most of the officers, in fact, found duty at the fort far from arduous. Frequent horse races served as some of the most enjoyable distractions from daily duties. "Horse racing is all the excitement at our camp for the present, giving pleasant faces to all the winners, and sour ones to the losers," one trooper reported. He noted that those contests were often "closed by trying the speed of several mules, who threw their riders, which occasioned a great deal of mirth."[24]

The one constant for Iverson and the other officers was the unrelenting discipline that they imposed on the men in the ranks. The most common form of punishment was known as "bucking and gagging," in which the man's mouth was gagged and his wrists were tied to his ankles while a thin log was thrust behind his knees and over his elbows. The men endured this punishment so often that they actually turned their ordeal into a song. "The treatment they give us, as all of us know, Is bucking and gagging for whipping the foe," one trooper

---

22 Unsigned letter to Leavenworth *Daily Times*, Oct. 18, 1859, in Louise Barry, ed., "With the First U.S. Cavalry in Indian Country, 1859-1861: Letters to the Daily Times, Leavenworth," *Kansas Historical Quarterly*, 24, No. 3 (1958), 278.

23 J. W. Reeder to Editors of the Daily Times, Jan. 17, 1859, in Barry, "With the First U.S. Cavalry," 261-262; "Cato" to Editor of the Times, Feb. 2, 1859, in *ibid.*, 263. For further details on Fort Washita, see W. B. Morrison, "Fort Washita," *Chronicles of Oklahoma*, 5 (1927), 251-256; Rodney Glisan, *Journal of Army Life* (San Francisco: A. L. Bancroft, 1874), 46; Randolph B. Marcy, *Prairie Traveler: A Handbook for Overland Expeditions* (Washington: United States War Department, 1859), 263-264; and Muriel H. Wright, "Old Boggy Depot," *Chronicles of Oklahoma*, 5 (1927), 4-9.

24 Iverson Sr. to Davis, March 6, 1861, Iverson Jr. Service Record; "Cato" to Editor of the Times, Feb. 2, 1859, in Barry, "With the First U.S. Cavalry," 263; "Cato" to Editor of the Times, June 29, 1859, in *ibid.*, 269-270.

from his regiment reported as the lyrics. "They buck us and they gag us for malice or for spite, But they are glad to release us when going to fight."[25]

Iverson's only combat came during the campaign against the Comanches and Kiowas along the Arkansas River in the spring of 1860. The troopers from the 1st U.S. Cavalry set out in two columns, one operating from the forts in Arkansas and the Indian Territory and the other from Fort Riley. They eventually "struck the trail of a band of the Kiowas" in the Colorado Territory. The cavalrymen killed approximately 20 Indians during the ensuing fight. The expedition ended on August 11, following a few other minor engagements. By then, the men had marched 1,404 miles and claimed to have killed 29 Indians.[26]

During most of his stay on the frontier, Iverson's wife remained behind at their home in Columbus. Although he often wrote to her, she found their time apart nearly unbearable. "The care of my children & the house does not dissipate the pain of his absence," Harriet confided to her father in early 1860. She acknowledged that "being away from Alfred grows heavier on my spirits every day." At the same time, she had become "more opposed to Alfred's resignation than I have formerly been because I do not think he will ever become reconciled to any occupation in civil life."[27]

Despite being of average height and build, Iverson certainly fit the image of a professional soldier. Family members described him as "reserved and dignified, congenial but of erect military bearing." They further reported that he was a fine horseman. Iverson was also a hopeless romantic, with a special fondness for writing poetry and reading Shakespeare's plays and sonnets. Although he shared his first name with his father, he disdained being referred to as "Junior." He was a practicing Freemason and remained a member of Colombian Lodge 108 in his hometown of Columbus throughout his military service.[28]

---

25 Lambert Bowman Wolf Diary, Entry for Nov. 30, 1858, in George A. Root, ed., "Extracts from Diary of Captain Lambert Bowman Wolf," *Kansas Historical Quarterly*, 1 (1932), 198. Although Wolf later became an officer, he served as an enlisted man during that time period.

26 Mattes, "Patrolling the Santa Fe Trail," 585-586; Kross, "That One Error," 48; W. Stitt Robinson, ed., "The Kiowa and Comanche Campaign of 1860 as Recorded in the Personal Diary of Lt. J. E. B. Stuart," *Kansas Historical Quarterly*, 23 (1957), 382-400.

27 Harriet Hutchins Iverson to Nathan L. Hutchins, Jan. 10, 1860, Iverson Family Papers, Gary Kross Private Collection, Gettysburg, Pennsylvania.

28 Kross, "That One Error," 48; Iverson Family Papers, Kross Collection.

He took special interest in the political events that were pushing the country toward a breakup. While home on a rare leave in 1858, Iverson addressed those issues at a meeting of the Athens Guard Militia. Describing the volunteer companies as "the gymnasia in which those enter, as pupils, who in the hour of danger may show themselves masters of military science," he emphasized the need for strict discipline as war approached. "The lessons taught on parade are to be borne in mind when we may be called to repel an invading army," the young lieutenant told the crowd. "The evolutions learned in the drill room are to be of service in the hour of stern conflict with veteran troops." He noted that "the subordination required by our rules is to preserve order in the camp."[29]

His father, who had emerged as a leading state-rights Democrat, remained equally convinced that a crisis over dissolution of the Union was inevitable. In January of 1859, he argued on the Senate floor that "there is but one path of safety for the institution of slavery in the South, when this mighty Northern avalanche of fanaticism and folly shall press upon us." Senator Iverson insisted that this "path lies through separation and to a southern confederacy." He expressed similar views in a widely publicized address at Griffin, Georgia, on July 14 of the same year. His numerous fiery speeches on Southern rights proved too radical even for fellow Georgia Sen. Robert Toombs and so injured him politically that he was not reelected to the Senate in 1860.[30]

With only a few weeks left in his term, the senior Iverson vacated his senate seat when Georgia seceded in January of 1861. Based on his outspoken support for secession, he became a prime candidate for election to the Confederate Senate in November of that year. After leading on several early ballots in the Georgia legislature, Iverson finally withdrew his name following the fifth round of voting, resulting in the election of Robert Toombs. When Toombs refused to take the seat, Iverson publicly declined all efforts to have his own name put forward for appointment by Governor Joe Brown. Instead, he resumed the practice of law in Columbus and took no further direct part in Confederate military or political affairs.[31]

---

29 Address to Athens Guard Militia, Iverson Family Papers, Emory.

30 United States Congress, *The Congressional Globe, 35th Congress, 2nd Session* (Washington: Globe Printing Office, 1859), 243.

31 American Council of Learned Societies, *Dictionary of American Biography*, 9:517-518; T. Conn Bryan, *Confederate Georgia* (Athens: University of Georgia Press, 1953), 37. For details on

Throughout that time, however, the former senator used his considerable political influence to promote the careers of his family members. As early as January, he wrote directly to Governor Brown requesting an appointment for his eldest son in any Georgia military organization that might be formed. He emphasized that young Alfred's experience in the U.S. Army would "make him an important acquisition" for the cavalry service. "I am authorized by older officers of the army to say that no officer of his grade and age occupies a higher position in the opinion of his brother officers," he wrote.[32]

Following his return to Columbus in February, the senior Iverson continued to press the adjutant general of Georgia for his son's immediate appointment. "It seems to me that his age, experience & present position should entitle him to a captaincy at least in the southern army," he declared. In early March, young Iverson notified Adjt. Gen. H. C. Wayne that he "was now at liberty to tender my services to the governor." His father also wrote to his old friend President Davis on the following day, requesting an appointment for his son as an assistant adjutant general in the fledgling Confederate army. With a commission in hand a little more than two weeks later, Lt. Iverson took the final step by formally resigning from the U.S. Army on March 21, 1861.[33]

Rather than receiving a staff position, Iverson was appointed as an infantry captain in the Confederate States Provisional Army. In May of 1861, he was assigned to recruiting duties in North Carolina. He soon began organizing several companies into what would become the 10th Regiment North Carolina Volunteers. The men in these companies signed up for a 12-month term of service. The enlisted men were allowed to vote for their own company officers. The three field officers would be selected in balloting by their fellow officers once the organization was completed.[34]

Toombs' decision not to accept the senate seat, see William C. Davis, *The Union That Shaped the Confederacy: Robert Toombs & Alexander H. Stephens* (Lawrence: University of Kansas Press, 2001), 149-151 and Ulrich Bonnell Phillips, *The Life of Robert Toombs* (New York: The MacMillan Company, 1913), 240-241.

32 Alfred Iverson Sr. to Joseph Brown, Jan. 23, 1861, Iverson Family Papers, Kross Collection.

33 Alfred Iverson Sr. to H. C. Wayne, Feb. 10, 1861, *ibid.*; Alfred Iverson Jr. to H. C. Wayne, March 5, 1861, Iverson Family Papers, Emory; Iverson Sr. to Davis, March 6, 1861, Iverson Jr. Service Record; Heitman, *Historical Register*, 1:565.

34 Kross, "That One Error," 48; Greg Mast, *State Troops and Volunteers: A Photographic Record of North Carolina's Civil War Soldiers* (Raleigh: North Carolina Department of Cultural Resources, 1995), 24.

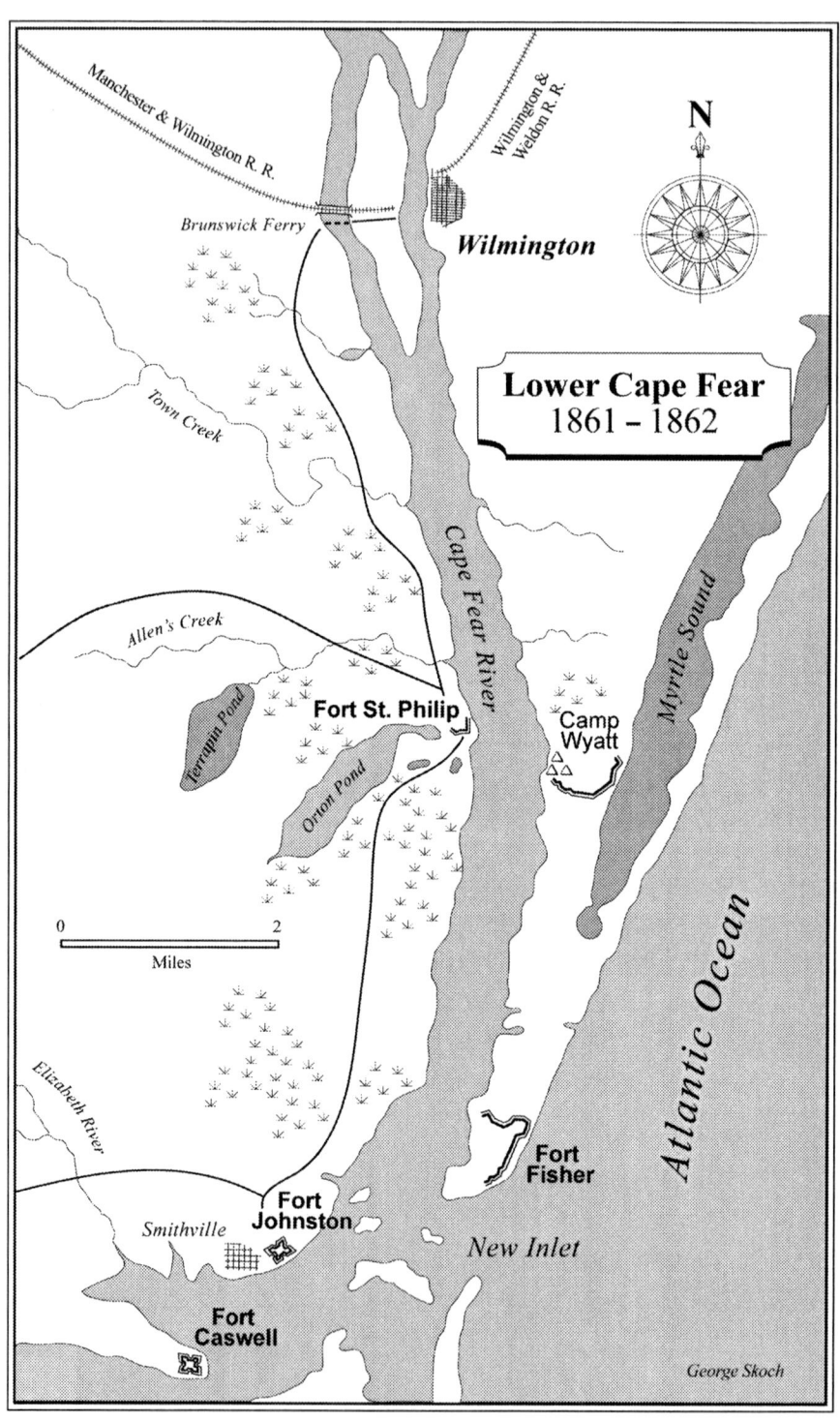

The camp of instruction for the new troops was located at Fort Johnston, along the lower Cape Fear River just south of Wilmington. The British originally built the fort in 1748. Following the Revolutionary War, the U.S. government expanded it into an imposing masonry structure with numerous gun emplacements and a dry moat. By the time Iverson took on duty there, the fort had fallen into a state of disrepair. All that remained intact were a barracks, a hospital building, and several sand earthworks and sod-covered mounds with two ammunition magazines and four artillery pieces.[35]

Even before North Carolina passed its formal ordinance of secession on May 20, local companies from around the state began arriving there for military training. Two of the companies assigned to the camp came from the surrounding area in Brunswick County. Two others were raised in Columbus County, just to the west of Wilmington. Another company was organized in Duplin County, directly north of Wilmington along the upper part of the Cape Fear River. Three other companies joined the service from Sampson County, which was located east of Fayetteville. The remaining two companies enlisted in Cabarrus County, just to the northeast of Charlotte.[36]

Although the state came late to secession, much of the population in North Carolina quickly rallied to the Southern cause. Typical of the send-off the volunteers received was that which greeted the two companies from Cabarrus County during their departure for the training camp. "At the depot practically the entire adult and adolescent population of the county was assembled to bid us God Speed," Pvt. Fred C. Foard recalled. He also noted that "both companies were formed in one rank for convenience in leave taking and everybody went around shaking hands with everybody else, the whole mass, men and women, old and young weeping in an ecastacy of mingled enthusiasm and grief."[37]

---

35 James Sprunt, *Chronicles of the Cape Fear River, 1660-1916* (Raleigh: Edwards and Broughton Printing Company, 1916), 52-55. Fort Johnston first fell into state hands on Jan. 9, 1861, when a group of armed citizens seized the compound from the single enlisted man, who served as the caretaker. To avoid a major confrontation, Governor John W. Ellis soon ordered the men to return control to the Federal government. Only a day after the attack on Fort Sumter in mid-April, the governor finally instructed several companies of militiamen from Wilmington to take permanent command of the fort. For details, see John L. Cantwell, "A Capture Before the War," included in Clark, *North Carolina Regiments*, 5:24, 27.

36 Thomas F. Toon, "Twentieth Regiment," included in Clark, *NC Regiments*, 2:111-112.

37 Fred C. Foard, "Reminiscences," Fred C. Foard Papers, NCOAH.

A young resident named William Franklin Elkins also witnessed the stirring scene at the county seat in Concord. He was especially struck by the splendor of the militia uniforms that the men from the "Cabarrus Guards" wore during the going-away ceremonies. Elkins described the outfits as "the most attractive I have ever seen." He reported that the uniforms included "dark blue dress coats, with light blue pants, all belt trimmings white, and caps that were topped with red, white and blue plumes." Elkins recalled that "each man looked full six feet tall with his plumes."[38]

The huge outpouring of support that the grateful troops received there was repeated throughout the trip all the way to the camp of instruction. Large crowds continued to form as the soldiers rode the rails east through the largely pro-secessionist Piedmont and Tidewater sections of the state. "The telegraph had sped the news of our coming and at every railroad station for three hundred miles to Wilmington by way of Raleigh and Goldsborough, we were greeted by great masses of people in wild frenzy of excitement," Pvt. Foard later remembered. He went on to describe the event as nothing less than "a wonderful day big with fate."[39]

Patriotic fervor proved equally strong among the cadets from the Franklin Scientific and Military Institute, located about 70 miles north of Wilmington in Duplin County. As war approached, the young cadets flocked to join the local company known as the "Confederate Grays." An influx of volunteers from the county seat at Faison and the surrounding farms and small towns quickly filled out the ranks. The new recruits soon went into camp on the school's grounds, where they began an intensive course of training in military tactics. During the final organization in mid-April, they elected the school's commandant, Claudius B. Denson, as captain of the company.

The enthusiasm for the Southern cause also ran deep among the local populace. Several rich patrons soon stepped forward to donate the equipment necessary for them to continue their training. "During this time the ladies in the vicinity of Franklin and Faison with patriotic zeal labored in the school building early and late to equip the company with uniforms, underwear, blankets, and camp equipage," one member of the company recalled. He noted that all the

---

38 William Franklin Elkins, "In the Junior Reserves," *Confederate Veteran*, 40 (1932), 171 (hereafter cited as CV).

39 Foard, "Reminiscences," Foard Papers.

Capt. Claudius B. Denson of the 20th North Carolina served as a leading figure in military education prior to the war as commandant of the Franklin Scientific and Military Institute in Duplin County.

Greensboro Historical Museum

equipment came "without cost to the State, the funds to supply the same being donated by the citizens of the Franklin and Faison communities."⁴⁰

In early May, the men in the company finally transferred to the main camp of instruction at Fort Johnston. One resident recalled that their departure prompted open celebration in the surrounding community. "The day the company left Faison, they were given a big farewell dinner," she remarked. "A long table was spread with every imaginable good thing to eat, that the ladies could prepare." She noted that "after the dinner the soldiers stood in line and Miss Rachel McIver presented the company with a handsome silk Confederate flag she made [for] the Flag bearer."⁴¹

At that point, the chance for glory far outweighed any thoughts about the realities of military service. Even the relatively well-drilled cadets had no real concept of what war would actually be like. "My idea of fighting was demonstrated in Wilmington 'en route' to our destination by purchasing a dirk which I added to my other weapons of offensive and defensive warfare," remarked Pvt. E. Faison Hicks, who was only 16 years old at the time he

---

40 William S. Powell, ed., *Dictionary of North Carolina Biography*, 6 Vols. (Raleigh: University of North Carolina Press, 1986), 2:55; C. B. Denson, "The Corps of Engineers and Engineering Troops," included in Clark, *NC Regiments*, 4:420; J. B. Oliver, E. F. Hicks, and B. B. Carr, *History of Co. E, 20th N.C. Regiment* (Goldsboro, NC: Nash Brothers, 1905), 3.

41 Georgia Hicks, "Memoirs," Anna Pierce Stafford Collection, NCOAH.

enlisted in the company. "When I explained my strategy for its use to my comrades it caused considerable amusement."[42]

The force assembled at Fort Johnston initially included another company from Sampson County, under the command of Capt. Franklin J. Faison. The 37-year-old Faison came from one of the wealthiest families in the state. His father owned a plantation of nearly 30,000 acres and ranked as the largest slaveholder in the county. Just as for the other companies, the local residents greeted the departure of the "Sampson Rangers" with outright enthusiasm. "The whole town was in excitement," one of the men recalled. He noted that their "mothers, wives, sisters, and sweethearts" were all present that day "encouraging their loved ones to go forth and do their duty."[43]

Captain Iverson, meanwhile, established his headquarters adjacent to the fort in the town of Smithville, which served as a popular summer resort and a center for the fishing industry. This prosperous seaside community had about 750 white residents, including seven teachers, three doctors, and 24 experienced river pilots. One visitor described it as "a pretty considerable village, having a Court House, church, and hotel." He further noted that Smithville was "a quite handsome settlement, abounding in a glorious growth of live oak and other shade trees."[44]

Any semblance of peace and quiet in the town quickly disappeared with the opening of the training camp. "Smithville was now full of soldiers, and the town presented the appearance of a military camp," a local doctor explained. "Patrols were ordered to patrol the streets, and sentinels at the corners of the streets, and the work of drilling commenced." He pointed out that "the sound 'hep, hep,' was continual and was the only music except for that of the drums." The worst disruptions resulted from the constant flow of steamships "bringing recruits, Commissary and Quartermaster stores, [and] the wives and children of soldiers in the camp who came to see their husbands and sweethearts before final parting."

---

42 E. Faison Hicks, "My War Reminiscences 1861-1865," Robert L. Brake Collection, United States Army Heritage and Education Center, Carlisle, Pennsylvania (hereafter cited as USAHEC).

43 Quoted in Sprunt, *Chronicles of Cape Fear*, 355; J. D. Hufham, "The Faison Family and the Kenan Family Honored by Duplin County," *Raleigh News and Observer*, Jan. 16, 1898.

44 Quoted in Jim McNeil, *Masters of the Shoals: Tales of the Cape Fear Pilots Who Ran the Union Blockade* (Cambridge, MA: De Capo Press, 2003), xiv. For additional details on the history of Smithville, see Sprunt, *Chronicles of Cape Fear*, 543-547. The town today is known as Southport.

The newly arrived troops soon took up quarters all over Smithville. One of Cabarrus County's two companies moved into the barracks at the fort, while the other settled into the hospital building. The doctor recalled that the men in Capt. Denson's company from Duplin County "pitched their camp alongside the brick walk in the Garrison and in the shade of the beautiful cedars which had been planted many years ago by Col. Churchill of the United States Army." He noted that two of the Columbus County companies also "found quarters in the Garrison enclosure." The remaining troops were forced into accommodations at various locations inside the town.[45]

During that time, Iverson continued as commandant at Fort Johnston while patiently waiting his turn at promotion. Under his supervision, the drill instructors maintained a relentless pace of instruction for the raw recruits. Despite their proximity to town, the men there found few chances for a break from their duties. Private Foard noted that "little occurred" during the following weeks "to disturb the routine of tattoo, taps, and reveille, guard mounting, drill and dress parade, while we were being licked into shape as trained soldiers."[46]

The final step in organizing the 10th Regiment North Carolina Volunteers arrived in the middle of July, when the company officers assembled to select the organization's three field officers. As one of the few professional soldiers in the camp, Iverson easily won election as the regiment's colonel, garnering 32 of the 38 votes cast. Captain Faison from Sampson County was selected as lieutenant colonel in a separate ballot. Soon after his election, Faison's former company transferred out of the regiment. The position of major went to 29-year-old Capt. William H. Toon from Columbus County. The regimental staff was filled out with the appointment of Lt. Robert Pryor James from Duplin County as adjutant.[47]

Less than two weeks later, Iverson received the devastating news that his 24-year-old wife had died at her father's home in Georgia on July 29. With that, he was left alone to provide for his young daughters, three-year-old Julia and nearly two-year-old Minnie. Even with support from his sister-in-law in caring for the children, his wife's death left him so forlorn that he kept a notebook

---

45 Walter Gilman Curtis, *Reminiscences of Wilmington and Smithville–Southport, 1848-1900* (Southport, NC: Herald Job Office, 1905), 22-23.

46 Foard, "Reminiscences," Foard Papers.

47 "Election of Field Officers," *Wilmington Journal*, July 25, 1861; Krick, *Lee's Colonels*, 134, 374.

Captain Claudius B. Denson leads the Confederate Grays from Duplin County in drills on the parade grounds at Ft. Johnston during June of 1861.
North Carolina Museum of History

---

throughout the war overflowing with nothing but page after page of love poems to her. "My lips no more her loving kisses draw," he wrote in one of the poems. "Her heaving bosom to mine no longer strain. Extasy remembered; Bliss no more to be. Ah! what is life or what is death to me."[48]

Putting aside the tragedy as best he could, Iverson soon assumed command at Fort Johnston, where most of his men had been assigned following the end of their training. By this time, these troops were being ravaged by major outbreaks of disease, and especially measles and mumps. "We have about 30 men with mumps now," Lt. Oliver E. Mercer explained to his mother in August. "In fact," he continued, "all of our company are sick. Only about 10 or 20 men for duty." He reported in September that "another camp was taken the

---

[48] Arp, *The Uncivil War*, 10; Parker, *Alias Bill Arp*, 10; "Iverson Notebook," Iverson Family Papers, Kross Collection.

same way, mumps, bilious and two congestive fevers are the principal complaints."[49]

Adjutant James noted in the official record of events for October that "a great deal of sickness has occurred in the regiment, thereby impairing their efficiency." As late as the following spring, sporadic outbreaks of disease still plagued many of the men in the regiment. Although fewer soldiers were getting sick by that point, the cases were generally more severe, with many dying as a result. "Our boys who are sick are quite ill," Capt. Denson remarked in a letter to his fiancée. He even described one of his former cadets as being so debilitated from an attack of fever that he appeared "like a shadow—his face almost has the imprint of death upon it."[50]

The harsh conditions for the troops, who were forced into temporary accommodations on the beach outside the fort, no doubt exacerbated the disease problems they were suffering. All that rough living drew sharp complaints throughout the regiment. "We were quartered in tents and our pallets were a board thickness above the sand, and every morning my hair was s[t]uccoed with sand, and my body from flea bites would pass for a well developed case of measles," Pvt. Hicks recalled. He further noted that "our food was abundant, but the manner of its preparation by amateur caterers was not very inviting."[51]

Even worse was the appalling lack of care at the camp hospital. Captain Denson complained to his fiancée in late October that there were "no nurses for their sick." He pointed out that there was "no attention paid to them, and the consequence is that they are broken spirited and gloomy." Denson eventually approached Iverson with his concerns that there was "no fireplace whatever" in the hospital. The colonel replied that he had "sent to Raleigh, but hasn't received any authority to purchase stoves for the sick rooms." That response came even though the doctor reported to Denson that "several of

---

49 Oliver E. Mercer to Dear Mother, Aug. 23, 1861, in Lillian Reeves Wyatt, ed., *The Reeves, Mercer, Newkirk Families: A Compilation* (Jacksonville, FL: The Cooper Press, 1956), 242; Oliver E. Mercer to Dear Father, Sept. 17, 1861, in *ibid.*, 243.

50 Record of Events, October 1861, 20th North Carolina, in Janet B. Hewitt *et al.*, eds., *The Supplement to the Official Records of the Union and Confederate Armies*, 95 Vols. (Wilmington, NC: Broadfoot Publishing Company, 1995-2000), Part 2, 48:738 (hereafter cited as *OR Supplement*); Claudius Denson to My Darling, April 7, 1862, *Civil War Times Illustrated* Collection, USAHEC.

51 Hicks, "Reminiscences," Brake Collection.

those upstairs are in danger of their lives if they remain in a room without heat."[52]

Despite the widespread outbreak of disease, Iverson remained determined to impose a strict code of discipline on his raw troops. In late August, he presided over a general court-martial that heard several apparently petty cases against four soldiers from his regiment. Although two of them were cleared in the trial, the other two received harsh sentences. One man was ordered "to be confined in charge of the guard for six months, with a twelve pound ball and chain attached to his left leg." The other soldier received a 90-day sentence while shackled to a six-pound ball. The punishments that he imposed proved so extreme that Brig. Gen. Richard S. Gatlin, who commanded the Department of North Carolina, eventually ordered Col. Iverson to remit the sentences.[53]

As officer of the day, Capt. Denson was forced to participate in another major round of punishments at Fort Johnston during mid-November. His duties that day required him "to place two men on barrels, standing two hours each without rest." Denson also helped assemble the entire garrison to witness the public whipping of another soldier from the regiment. "The man was tied to one of the cedar trees—the flogging performed by a drummer, [who] seemed to delight in his calling," he remarked in a letter to his fiancée. "It was my cruel [fate] to be forced, as executive officer, to stand by and count every lash, that all might know the sentence was carried out."[54]

Equally upsetting for morale was a "terrible accident" that occurred along the picket line outside their camp in September. While on guard duty, one of Iverson's men encountered a soldier who was returning from a stay in the hospital. "They passed some few words and the man started on," Lt. Mercer remarked in a letter home. "The Cent said look out, I am going to shoot you." Mercer noted that the man then "cocked his gun, took deliberate aim, resting the piece against the Center Box, and fired, the ball passed through and through his breast, killing him almost instantly."[55]

---

52 Claudius B. Denson to Dear Matilda, Oct. 29, 1861, Cowan and Denson Family Papers, North Carolina Room, New Hanover County Library, Wilmington, North Carolina.

53 General Order No. 3, Department of North Carolina, Sept. 11, 1861, Orders and Circulars, Department of North Carolina, 1861-1865, Record Group 109, NA.

54 Claudius B. Denson to Dear Matilda, Nov. 20, 1861, Cowan and Denson Papers.

55 Mercer to Father, Sept. 17, 1861, in Wyatt, *The Reeves, Mercer, Newkirk Families*, 243. According to an account in a Raleigh newspaper, the soldier on guard used a loaded gun but

The mood reached such a low point that drunkenness soon became commonplace among the troops. Captain Denson observed in early January that "the men use so much intoxicating liquor that many arrests have to be made." The problem even extended to many of the company officers. Denson reported to his fiancée that one officer "was so intoxicated upon dress parade that he came near falling." The captain went on to point out that several other officers "had been in that condition for several days." The drinking among the officers grew so far out of control that Iverson "threatened some of them with arrest."[56]

Iverson faced another family crisis in early October of 1861 when his stepmother suffered an attack of "bilious fever" and paralysis, the result of an apparent stroke. His half brother, Capt. John F. Iverson of the 5th Georgia, submitted his resignation so that he could return home to be with his mother. When the resignation was turned down by his superiors, the senior Iverson again used his considerable influence by contacting President Davis and Secretary of War Judah P. Benjamin for assistance. By the time they responded with their sympathies and offers of help, the former senator's wife had already died, and his son John had withdrawn his resignation.[57]

Soon after the death of his stepmother, Col. Iverson's command was re-designated as the 20th Regiment North Carolina State Troops. This change was necessitated by the extensive confusion caused from the dual system for numbering regiments that had been in use since the beginning of the war. The state initially enrolled 10 regiments, numbered one through 10, as state troops. Fourteen other regiments designated as volunteer troops were formed soon afterward, some of which had unit numbers that duplicated those of the state troops. Under the new plan, the volunteer regiments were all reassigned as state troops by adding 10 to their original numbers.[58]

---

had removed the percussion cap. He "playfully" halted the man and "raised his gun pulling the trigger." To his surprise, the gun accidentally discharged. The bullet struck the victim in the chest, killing him instantly. For additional details, see "Melancholy Accident.—A Soldier Shot," *North Carolina Standard*, Sept. 18, 1861.

56 Claudius B. Denson to Dear Matilda, Jan. 6, 1862, Cowan and Denson Papers; Claudius B. Denson to Dear Matilda, Dec. 1, 1861, *ibid*.

57 Alfred Iverson Sr. to Judah P. Benjamin, Oct. 28, 1861, Letters Received, Confederate Secretary of War, Record Group 109, NA; Alfred Iverson Sr. to Judah P. Benjamin, Nov. 15, 1861, *ibid*.

58 Mast, *Photographic Record*, 25.

More important for boosting spirits at Fort Johnston was the chance for the men to unwind during the upcoming Christmas season with a series of celebrations. Lieutenant Mercer reported to his sister that he went "to several egg-nog parties, and to one or two balls" during the holidays. Private Robert H. Galloway from their regiment proved much more forthcoming about the extent of the celebrations in a letter penned to his cousin on Christmas Day. He openly admitted that "we have been drinking egg nog all morning and the drunk folks you never seen the like in your life."[59]

Any semblance of regimental cohesion began to fall apart over the following months as many of the men were scattered across the lower Cape Fear area. Early in the year, several companies were assigned the chore of leveling the sand hills around Fort Caswell on nearby Oak Island. Private Foard recalled that the fortifications in the area included "a sand battery mounting two 24 pounder, smooth bore guns, on the beach below Fort Caswell at the point of debouchment of the Cape Fear River into the Atlantic Ocean." He pointed out that the heaviest guns at the fort itself were "8 inch Columbieds, smooth bore, with an extreme range of four miles and effective range of much less."

Two of those companies moved to an inlet 35 miles from Wilmington in order to protect the cargoes from ships that had run the Federal blockade. "While we were there the blockade runner Nashville, her pilot miscalculating the draft of his vessel and the depth of the water, stranded just beyond the range of the guns of Fort Fisher, and in full view of three of the enemies blockading vessels," wrote Pvt. Foard. "She had to remain there over night until some light draft vessels could be brought down from Wilmington to take off part of her cargo."[60]

The hardest duty fell to the men in the companies transferred in early April to Camp Wyatt, located just north of Fort Fisher on the opposite side of the Cape Fear River. "It is one of the last places on the earth, I do think," Lt. Mercer

---

59 Oliver E. Mercer to Dear Sister, Dec. 29, 1861, in Wyatt, *The Reeves, Mercer, Newkirk Families*, 249; Robert H. Galloway to My Dear Cousin, Dec. 25, 1861, Liebermann Family Papers, Virginia Historical Society, Richmond, Virginia (hereafter cited as VHS).

60 Record of Events, May 1862, 20th North Carolina, in Hewitt, *OR Supplement*, pt. 2, 48:737-738; Foard, "Reminiscences," Foard Papers. The complaints about separating the men began as early as May of 1861, when one of the companies from Cabarrus County was ordered on detached duty at Fort Caswell. For details, see Richard F. Harris to John W. Ellis, May 14, 1861, in Noble J. Tolbert, ed., *The Papers of John Willis Ellis*, 2 Vols. (Raleigh: North Carolina Department of Archives and History, 1964), 2:751.

openly complained in a letter to his sister. "And it was left in the worst fix I ever saw; I think the 30 Reg. must have been lousey from the way their quarters were left." He pointed out they "had expected to go to Maison Borrough Sound but the order was countermanded and we were sent to this hole."[61]

A soldier from another regiment, who was stationed at Camp Wyatt about two months later, echoed similar sentiments about the terrible conditions found at the camp along the Cape Fear River. William Means insisted that it was "the hardest camp" he had ever seen. "You can take a peck of sand, & sift it, & you will have a quart of flees," he griped in a letter home to his father. "The way they do bite." The situation there became so bad that he could hardly wait for the chance to leave. Means reported hearing one of the men from his company complain that "he would rather go to hell, & stay twelve hours, as to go to that camp."[62]

During that time, Iverson remained busy supervising routine inspections of the coastal fortifications in the Wilmington area. "I received . . . an order from Col. Iverson . . . to proceed to Zeek's Island, to examine the Battery there, which was being washed away by the sea, to report whether it was tenable & if not what works were necessary to make it so," Thomas Rowland, who served as a volunteer aide on Iverson's staff, commented to his mother in late March. On the following day, he again was "ordered down the river" to examine the defenses on the Cape Fear. Soon afterward, he began supervising construction of a battery emplacement outside of Wilmington.[63]

The only breaks in the tedium came amid unfounded rumors of a Federal landing along the lower Cape Fear River. "We have been in daily expectation here of a visit from the Burnside naval expedition," Rowland observed in a January letter. "During the past week the weather has been foggy & stormy, which may have detained them." Lieutenant Mercer noted during late May that

---

61 Oliver E. Mercer to Dear Sister, April 4, 1862, in Wyatt, *The Reeves, Mercer, Newkirk Families*, 250. For similar comments about Camp Wyatt from another officer in his company, see John S. Brooks to Dear Sister, April 2, 1862, John Stanley Brooks Letters, SHC.

62 William N. M. Means to John S. Means, June 20, 1862, Papers of the Means and McFadden Families, Manuscript Division, South Caroliniana Library, University of South Carolina, Columbia, South Carolina (hereafter cited as SC).

63 Thomas Rowland to My Dear Mother, March 25, 1862, Kate Mason Rowland Collection, Eleanor S. Brockenbrough Library, Museum of the Confederacy, Richmond, VA (hereafter cited as MOC). These were published in Kate Mason Rowland, ed., "Letters of Major Thomas Rowland, C.S.A.," *William and Mary College Quarterly Historical Magazine*, 26 (1917), 225-235.

there was still "much talk" of Gen. Burnside's fleet making an attack. "The enemy fired several shells at Fort Fisher a few days ago, but done no damages," he told his sister. "We retaliated, but our shots fell short, much more so than the enemys."[64]

This garrison duty soon proved intolerable for the men who had joined the army for the sole purpose of fighting the Yankees. "The duties were neither dangerous or burdensome, in fact, the men of the regiment became restless under their inaction and urged to be sent where they could take part in the glorious triumphs which made famous the Army of Virginia," one veteran recalled. He further declared that they "longed to snatch from the shock of battle, the clash of resounding arms, the sulphurous canopy and din of courageous conflict, glimpses of the bright laurels the future historians would weave around the ensanguined brow of those who for country 'dare to do or die.'"[65]

As they waited anxiously for the opportunity to join the main fighting in Virginia, the soldiers from the 20th North Carolina took part in the major reorganization mandated by the passage of the Conscription Act in mid-April and the resulting changes in their terms of enlistment from 12 months to three years or the duration of the war. The process involved new elections for all of the company and field officers in the regiment. Although all three field officers eventually held on to their positions, several company officers were defeated for reelection.

Even Iverson's tenure as commander had initially seemed far from secure. His chances for reelection received a major boost in mid-April when Lt. Col. Faison declined to put himself forward in the balloting for colonel. Faison, who was extremely popular with his fellow officers, reported to Capt. Denson that he "would be glad to have his present position but did not wish the Colonelcy on account of the responsibility." The officers relieved from duty, however, included Capt. Denson, who was unseated by one of his former cadets from the Franklin Military Institute.[66]

---

64 Thomas Rowland to My Dear Aunt, Jan. 20, 1862, Rowland Collection; Oliver E. Mercer to Dear Sister, May 20, 1862, in Wyatt, *The Reeves, Mercer, Newkirk Families*, 251-252.

65 Toon, "Twentieth Regiment," in Clark, *NC Regiments*, 2:113.

66 Mast, *State Troops and Volunteers*, 241; Weymouth T. Jordan Jr. and Louis H. Manarin, *North Carolina Troops, 1861-1865: A Roster*, 14 Vols. (Raleigh: North Carolina Division of Archives and

The reorganization proved just as frustrating for some of the enlisted men who had mistakenly assumed that the expiration of their 12-month term of enlistment would allow them to transfer out of Iverson's command. About 20 men from Company A even complained directly to the Confederate secretary of war about their predicament. "We do not wish to be misunderstood in this particular," they wrote. "It is not because we wish to get out of the service by any means that we make this application, but because . . . we wish to leave the present company and Regt. in order to enter for the war elsewhere." Despite their plea, the request for a transfer was eventually turned down.[67]

History, 1966-1998), 6:509; Claudius B. Denson to My Darling, April 9, 1862, Cowan and Denson Paper.

67 Josiah W. Rogers et al., to Judah P. Benjamin, April 16, 1862, Letters Received, Confederate Secretary of War.

CHAPTER TWO

All the Devils are Here

With the reorganization out of the way, Col. Iverson finally received orders for the 20th North Carolina to join the main Confederate army in Virginia under its newly appointed commander, Gen. Robert E. Lee. After departing from Wilmington early in the morning on June 16, the men reached the railroad depot in Richmond the following evening. Lieutenant Oliver Mercer reported that they "marched through the city into an open field and there turned in for night in the open air." The regiment numbered more than 1,000 men ready to defend the beleaguered capital.

The sight of the arriving troops attracted throngs of well-wishers along their route. "They praise our Reg. very highly as we pass, say it is equal to a Brigade," Mercer remarked to his sister. "There was crowds in R[ichmond] and Petersburg to see us as we marched through. Ladies threw flowers and waived Hdkfs at us." Their reception proved just as heartening for Pvt. Fred Foard. He recalled that "the citizens turned out in great numbers, the ladies marching along side of us pressing upon us at every step, refreshments and delicacies."[1]

---

1 Oliver, Hicks, and Carr, *History of Company E*, 5; Oliver E. Mercer to Dear Sister, June 18, 1862, in Wyatt, *The Reeves, Mercer, Newkirk Families*, 254; Foard, "Reminiscences," Foard Papers.

On the following day, the men from the 20th North Carolina moved on to the main camp just outside the capital. They were immediately assigned to one of the new single-state brigades that had been formed throughout the army in mid-June. The other regiments in the brigade included the 5th, 12th, 13th, and 23rd North Carolina regiments. Rather than serving under a Tar Heel general, however, the troops from this newly reorganized brigade in Maj. Gen. Daniel Harvey Hill's Division were commanded by Brig. Gen. Samuel Garland Jr., who came from Virginia.

At the age of 31, Garland was considered one of the rising stars in the army. He graduated from the Virginia Military Institute (VMI) in 1849, where he ranked third in his class. Garland later studied law at the University of Virginia. He became a prominent attorney in his hometown of Lynchburg, Virginia, where he helped organize a militia company. Garland entered military service as colonel in the 11th Virginia. Following conspicuous displays of gallantry in the fighting on the peninsula, he received a well-earned promotion to brigadier general on May 23, 1862.[2]

Garland assumed command as the replacement for Brig. Gen. Jubal A. Early, who had been severely wounded during the Battle of Williamsburg. The brigade he took over included the 5th and 23rd North Carolina, the 24th and 38th Virginia, the 2nd Florida, and the 2nd Mississippi Battalion. Garland led those troops with distinction at Seven Pines about one week after his appointment. On June 17, Garland's Brigade was reorganized into an all-Tar Heel command by replacing the Virginia, Florida, and Mississippi soldiers with the troops from the 12th, 13th, and 20th North Carolina.

The three new regiments differed considerably in their experience. Like those in the 5th and 23rd North Carolina, the men from the 13th North Carolina were veterans of the battles at Williamsburg and Seven Pines. The troops from the 12th North Carolina saw their first action during the recent fighting at Hanover Court House. Because they had never been in a battle, Iverson's men initially served on picket duty. "An advance by the enemy was momentarily expected, so we were ready at all hours to give them a welcome," Pvt. E. Faison Hicks recalled. "We were relieved every alternate night for about two weeks." He noted that they "were under a heavy cannonade so that the

---

2 Warner, *Generals in Gray*, 98-99; Lyon Gardiner Tyler, ed., *Encyclopedia of Virginia Biography*, 3 Vols. (New York: Lewis Historical Publishing Company, 1915), 3:53.

danger of falling limbs and tree-tops made no small factor in the casualties of the regiment."³

The green soldiers from the 20th North Carolina eventually got their first taste of combat on June 25 at King's School House, where they sustained only a handful of casualties. "Having been posted in reserve in the edge of a skirt of woods, the regiment was exposed for about an hour to a very heavy fire of shell from the enemy's batteries, by which we had 2 men wounded, but without the opportunity of taking any active part in the severe skirmishing in front," Maj. William H. Toon wrote in his official report. The action provided but a foretaste of what would soon come.

During the fierce fighting that took place two days later at Gaines' Mill, the regiment received orders to launch a near-suicidal assault across an open field against a federal battery. Major Toon reported that the men "advanced rapidly, amid a storm of grape, canister, and musketry, and charged the battery with a yell." General Garland noted that the attack was led by Col. Iverson, who immediately rushed to the front of the regiment but was "seriously wounded at an early period." The final push toward the enemy battery was headed by Lt. Col. Franklin Faison, who sustained a mortal wound while "in the very act of turning one of the captured pieces upon the fleeing foe."⁴

Both Iverson and Faison earned numerous accolades for their bravery during the action at Gaines' Mill. Iverson's conduct drew special praise from one gunner who witnessed the entire attack while serving with a nearby Confederate artillery battery. "Col. Alfred Iverson, of the 20th North Carolina, acted very gallantly," he wrote in a letter to his hometown newspaper. "The only men lying up to the guns of the Federal battery at Cold Harbor belonged to his regiment. I saw them identified and buried." He went on to note that "Col. Iverson was wounded in the hip."⁵

Despite the loss of their two top officers, the men from the 20th North Carolina quickly overran the Federal position. "The enemy were driven off and

---

3   Hicks, "Reminiscences," Brake Collection.

4   "Report of William H. Toon," July 13, 1862, *Wilmington Journal*, Sept. 21, 1862; United States War Department, *The War of the Rebellion: A Compilation of the Official Records of the Union and Confederate Armies*, 70 Vols. in 128 parts (Washington: Government Printing Office, 1880-1901), 11, Part 2, Series 1, 644, hereafter cited as *OR*, followed by the appropriate volume and part; all references are to Series 1 unless otherwise noted.

5   "Hardaway's Rifle Battery," *Atlanta Southern Confederacy*, July 14, 1862.

Lieutenant Colonel Franklin J. Faison of the 20th North Carolina performed gallantly and was mortally wounded at Gaines' Mill on June 27, 1862.
Sampson County History Museum

the battle flag of the regiment waved over their guns," declared Maj. Toon. "One of these was turned upon their retreating columns, but the caissons having been removed no munitions could be found." Toon, who took over command soon after they seized the enemy guns, pointed out that "a constant and rapid fire of musketry was kept up against the enemy during their retreat, and the battery was held by us I think full ten minutes."

During that time, the remaining troops in the assault came under heavy enemy fire and halted well short of the main Federal line. Major Toon reported that his men "were about to be flanked by a large force of the enemy, and seeing no appearance of reinforcements from other regiments of the Brigade, we were reluctantly compelled to abandon the guns and return to a position in the woods." He further noted that their final withdrawal that day "was not effected without loss, as the enemy reached the battery in force very soon after we had commenced to retreat."[6]

Private Hicks recalled that the order to fall back occurred so suddenly that he was almost left behind on the field. "Knowing there had been no forward movement on the part of our boys, I looked and saw our whole line had fallen back," he remarked. "And, the smoke having risen in my front and right saw the enemy charge in a run towards the battery." Their appearance left him no other choice than to retreat. Hicks noted that "they commanded me to halt, and, as I could not fly, I ran back and joined our lines at the charging point, at which position the regiment continued to fire."[7]

Just before sundown, the rest of the brigade finally launched another assault against the battery. Lieutenant Vines E. Turner, the adjutant of the 23rd North Carolina, reported that his regiment was one of the first to emerge from the thick undergrowth that had obstructed their earlier advance. "This brought us in full view of a battery on our left, which opened upon us, as we went forward at the double quick down a little slope," he remarked. From there, the men continued to press forward up the hill until "the enemy . . . broke and fled in great disorder through a dense swamp in their rear."[8]

Although the day ended in a stunning Confederate victory, the cost to the 20th North Carolina was appalling, with more than 100 men killed or mortally wounded among its nearly 300 casualties. "Heavy as was this loss, no doubt a greater loss was saved to the division in its advance by this gallant attack," Gen. D. H. Hill stated in his official report. "The temporary silence of the battery enabled the division to move up in fine style and turn the tide of battle in our favor." General Garland noted that the enemy troops "broke and retreated,

---

6 "Report of William H. Toon," July 13, 1862, *Wilmington Journal*, Sept. 21, 1862.

7 E. Faison Hicks to Newton M. Curtis, Dec. 21, 1904, in Newton Martin Curtis, *From Bull Run to Chancellorsville: The Story of the Sixteenth New York Infantry Together With Personal Reminiscences* (New York: G. P. Putnam's Sons, 1906), 123.

8 Turner and Wall, "Twenty-Third Regiment," in Clark, *NC Regiments*, 2:211.

made a second brief stand, which induced my immediate command to halt under good cover of the road-side and return their fire, when, charging forward again, we broke and scattered them in every direction."[9]

Following the battle, Iverson returned to convalesce at Wilmington where he was greeted as a hero. "Col. Iverson of the 20th is in town," his former volunteer aide Thomas Rowland remarked in a letter to his mother. "He was wounded in the fight near Richmond. His regiment behaved with great gallantry. Lieutenant Colonel Faison of the same regiment was killed in a desperate charge." Rowland described Faison "as a noble fellow & a universal favorite." The fighting, though, was still far from over. "What a closely contested battle it has been & it seems not yet to be decided," Rowland concluded.[10]

During Iverson's absence, the 20th North Carolina once again sustained severe casualties in the futile attack on the Federal army along the James River at Malvern Hill on July 1. "My command was here ordered to charge battery, distant more than half a mile, through an open field, and fully exposed to a fire that seemed to sweep its surface with destructive missiles of every sort," Maj. Toon wrote in his official report. After advancing about 300 yards across the field, the men from his regiment halted and fired on the enemy for nearly an hour before retreating. Toon reported that his command lost an additional "25 privates killed, 4 officers and 94 privates wounded."[11]

According to Pvt. Hicks, he and his comrades were shelled by several "massed batteries" and fired on from entrenched lines of infantry during the fighting there. Within minutes, the enemy fire cut down soldiers all along the line. "How any of us escaped alive is a mystery," wrote the North Carolina private. "I witnessed full a score or more of my comrades fall quite near me, before we got near enough the Yankee lines to use our guns. We were repulsed, but the Yankees made no move to follow." Hicks noted that "our loss in this engagement was fifty per cent."[12]

For men who had only recently been on coastal duty in their home state, the long week of fighting outside Richmond provided a frightful introduction to

---

9   Mast, *Photographic Record*, 123; OR 11, pt. 2, 625-626, 640-642.

10 Thomas Rowland to My Dear Mother, July 7, 1862, Rowland Collection.

11 "Report of William H. Toon," July 13, 1862, *Wilmington Journal*, Sept. 21, 1862.

12 Hicks, "Reminiscences," Brake Collection.

the harsh realities of combat. Lieutenant Mercer insisted that "the horrors of war" he encountered during that time were beyond his ability to express in words. "My God may I never see such sights as I seen since I saw you," he exclaimed in a letter to his sister. Mercer was struck most of all by the plight of his injured comrades. "The hospitals are crowded with wounded men," he declared. "It is enough to shock the strongest heart on earth." He openly admitted that he had "never expected to see such sights."[13]

For Pvt. Foard, the most distressing moments on the Virginia peninsula came when the division's "burial corps" began digging graves in the hours after the fighting ended at Gaines' Mill. "I counted 255 dead bodies and the men engaged in the work told me they had buried 280," he said. "At Cold Harbor at a little church near our line of battle converted into a field hospital," continued the private, "I saw arms and legs and hands and feet that had been amputated and cast into a pile for burial which would have made a large wagon load." Foard went on to note that even "the air was tainted everywhere with the scent of human blood."

The exceedingly poor quality of the medical treatment the men received on the battlefield made the overall death toll in the regiment even worse. Private Foard marveled that anyone with a serious wound could survive. "The mortality among the wounded in the hospitals was immense," he recalled. "The sultry July weather, the need of antiseptics, the inadequate sanitation and the insufficiency of the medical corps to meet the great demands upon them all conspired to that result." Foard also discovered that even slight injuries could turn deadly when he observed that "Piemia carried off hundreds of strong men with only flesh wounds."[14]

The men from the other four regiments in Garland's Brigade also endured significant losses in the fighting that week. Some of the fiercest action took place at Malvern Hill. Private Leonidas Torrence from the 23rd North Carolina reported to his parents that it "was as hard a Battle as ever was Fought." He pointed out that "the Balls fell around me as thick as hail for 2 or 3 hours." Another private, Franklin L. Stuard of the same regiment, noted in a letter to his father that eight or nine men were killed there in his company alone. Worst of all was the aftermath of the battle, where he "saw a lot of men dead and a lot of

---

13 Oliver E. Mercer to Dear Sister, July 10, 1862, in Wyatt, *The Reeves, Mercer, Newkirk Families*, 253.

14 Foard, "Reminiscences," Foard Papers.

them hurt, there arms and legs off and some of them dying while the doctor is operating on it."[15]

Despite the heavy casualties, the bloody Seven Days' fighting prevented the Federals from capturing Richmond and forced the Army of the Potomac many miles away to the James River and the protection offered there by the Federal navy. In response to unfounded rumors that the enemy was preparing to renew the attack, Pvt. Solomon McLean from the 23rd North Carolina boasted to his cousin that the outcome would certainly be the same if the enemy tried taking the city again. "They say They will have richmond or Hell is their home," he proclaimed. "I fear Hell will be their home before they ever get it. God grant them a better place for it will be bad for them to miss richmond & get Hell both."[16]

While its colonel recuperated from his wound, the 20th North Carolina remained in camp—just below Richmond along the York River—as part of the force assigned to keep watch on McClellan's army at Harrison's Landing. The troops there suffered from a renewed outbreak of disease, which was most likely aggravated by poor sanitation and the endless clouds of buzzing and biting mosquitoes in the swampy areas on the peninsula. One veteran from the regiment recalled that they "had a great deal of sickness from a very malignant type of camp fever." He also noted that nine men in the regiment died in the hospital from disease during that period. "In addition," he continued, "there were several in the hospital sick from fever who eventually recovered and returned to duty."[17]

In late August, Garland's entire brigade began moving north to rejoin the main part of Lee's army for an expected engagement with the new Federal Army of Virginia led by Maj. Gen. John Pope. The North Carolinians, however, experienced numerous delays during their long trip. One veteran from the 23rd North Carolina recalled that the troops from their brigade reached the area where the Battle of Second Manassas took place "in time only to view the green

---

15 Leonidas Torrence to Dear Pa & Ma, July 14, 1862, in Haskell Monroe, ed., "The Road to Gettysburg: The Diary and Letters of Leonidas Torrence of the Gaston Guards," *North Carolina Historical Review*, 36 (1959), 497; Franklin S. Stuard to Dear Father, July 18, 1862, Lewis Leigh Collection, USAHEC.

16 Solomon McLean to Dear Cousin, July 25, 1862, Civil War Miscellaneous Collection, USAHEC.

17 Oliver, Hicks, and Carr, *History of Company E*, 6.

plains strewn with the blue-coated dead, the living Yankees having fled in confusion in the direction of Washington."[18]

By then, most of the bodies had already been gathered in large piles on the field in preparation for burial. "To that end they had collected from all parts of the battlefield and strewn along the road upon which we marched so that without extravagance one could have walked a mile and a half stepping from one dead body to another without touching the ground," Pvt. Foard of the 20th North Carolina explained. "It was a horrible spectacle." He vividly recalled that "under the hot sultry August weather they were in an advanced state of decomposition."[19]

Lieutenant Turner of the 23rd North Carolina was also struck by the terrible sights he encountered on their arrival at Manassas. According to Turner, many of the corpses had been "crushed and mangled by the cannon wheels, which in the urgency of that fierce and prolonged combat had passed over them." Private John Coghill from the same regiment reported in a letter home that the dead Yankees were strewn "all along for about 5 miles" across the battlefield. "I saw more ded men than I ever saw before," he declared. "They smelt awfull bad."[20]

Despite the condition of the corpses, most of them were quickly stripped of all usable clothing and valuables. "Every single body had been denuded of its outer garments by negroes and camp followers," Pvt. Foard observed. "And among them all I only saw one foot that was shod and that belonged to a poor wretch whose leg had been nearly severed above the knee by a cannon ball remaining attached to the body only by a small shred of flesh." He noted with disgust that "the cavalry boot that was on it could not be taken off without taking the leg with it."[21]

By the end of August, Col. Iverson had finally recovered enough from his wound to rejoin his regiment. Within days of his return, the troops from the Army of Northern Virginia began moving forward across the Potomac River into Maryland. While Lt. Gen. Thomas J. "Stonewall" Jackson captured

---

18 H. C. Wall, *Historical Sketch of the Pee Dee Guards, From 1861 to 1865* (Raleigh: Edward Broughton and Company, 1876), 42.

19 Foard, "Reminiscences," Foard Papers.

20 Turner and Wall, "Twenty-Third Regiment," in Clark, *NC Regiments*, 2:216; John F. Coghill to Dear Pappy, Ma, and Mit, Sept. 9, 1862, James O. Coghill Papers.

21 Foard, "Reminiscences," Foard Papers.

Harpers Ferry, Virginia, the rest of Lee's army advanced north toward Hagerstown. Following a brief halt near Frederick, Maryland, the men from D. H. Hill's Division deployed along the gaps in the South Mountain range and served as the rearguard of the army.

On the morning of September 14, the mountain gaps held by Hill's troops were attacked. As the shooting began, Hill sought out Garland's Brigade, which was being held in reserve at Turner's Gap. "The firing had aroused that prompt and gallant soldier, General Garland, and his men were under arms when I reached the pike," Hill recalled. "I explained the situation briefly to him, directed him to sweep through the woods, reach the road, and hold it at all hazards, as the safety of Lee's large train depended upon its being held."[22]

Under Garland's direction, the troops from the brigade quickly moved into place along Fox's Gap near the point where a country lane intersected the Old Sharpsburg Road. Their line of battle extended along the dirt lane as it curved to the southwest across the top of a steep ridge. To the rear of their position, the terrain sloped off sharply into a deep ravine. The surrounding area on the Daniel Wise farm consisted of thick laurel woods interspersed with small farm fields. A large force of enemy troops remained mostly out of view in the heavy forest directly opposite their position.[23]

The fighting began about nine o'clock in the morning when the 5th North Carolina, located on the right of the line, pushed forward from the south edge of a cornfield directly into Federal troops posted in the woods on the side of the hill. "We found the growth very thick, so much so that it was impossible to advance in line of battle," the 5th's Col. Duncan K. McRae wrote in his official report. He noted that "the enemy's skirmishers had advanced almost to the very edge of the woods nearest us, and, as we appeared at the edge, a sharp skirmish fire ensued."[24]

Captain Isaac E. Pearce, also a member of the 5th North Carolina, reported that the men in his company, which had been deployed as skirmishers, proceeded only a short distance into the woods before encountering "a strong

---

22 Daniel H. Hill, "The Battle for South Mountain, or Boonsboro," included in Robert U. Johnson and Clarence C. Buel, eds., *Battles and Leaders of the Civil War*, 4 Vols. (New York: Castle Books, 1956), 2:563.

23 For a detailed account of the morning action at Fox's Gap, see John Michael Priest, *Before Antietam: The Battle of South Mountain* (New York: Oxford University Press, 1992), 129-173.

24 *OR* 19, pt. 1, 1,041.

force" of enemy soldiers on their flanks. The sudden appearance of the Federal troops brought the skirmishers from the 5th North Carolina to an immediate halt. "My men fired into the enemy who had gotten partly in my rear, the woods being so dense I could not see far," he explained in a letter to his sister. Pearce noted that he immediately ordered his men "to retreat & rally upon the regt. which they did."[25]

While all that was going on, Iverson remained busy deploying the troops from the 20th North Carolina on the opposite end of the main ridge line near the intersection of the two roads. Within minutes, he began to hear the sounds of heavy gunfire on their right. The signs that a major fight was underway drew an immediate response from Garland. "At that time I was ordered by Gen Garland to move rapidly with my regiment toward that point," Iverson recalled years later. He noted that "the firing seemed to be from Sharpshooters on a wooded mountain or hill on our right front."[26]

After directing Iverson' troops to the front, Garland moved farther to the left along the main ridge line, where he held a hurried conference with several field officers from the brigade. As enemy fire began pouring into their exposed position, Lt. Col. Thomas Ruffin Jr. from the 13th North Carolina urged Garland to move to a safer position. "Just then I was shot in the hip, and as there was no field-officer then with the regiment, other than myself, I told him of my wound, and that it might disable me, and in that case I wished a field-officer to take my place," recalled Ruffin. "He turned and gave me some order, which I have forgotten." At that moment, Ruffin heard a loud groan and found Garland "mortally wounded and writhing in pain."[27]

Colonel McRae from the 5th North Carolina, whose troops were already heavily engaged with the enemy, quickly assumed command of the brigade. The first sign of trouble came when the 12th North Carolina on the far right of the line moved forward to join in the fight. That regiment numbered fewer than 100 men, many of whom were recent conscripts, under the command of an inexperienced captain. "At this moment I found that the raw troops on my right who had never been under fire, had had no drill, and had but few officers, were

---

25 Isaac E. Pearce to Dear Sister, Sept. 22, 1862, Isaac E. Pearce Papers, NCOAH.

26 Alfred Iverson Jr. to Daniel Harvey Hill, Aug. 23, 1885, Daniel Harvey Hill Papers, NCOAH.

27 Quoted in Hill, "Battle of South Mountain," in Johnson and Buel, *Battles and Leaders*, 2:563-564.

breaking in some confusion, the rest of the line remaining firm," McRae reported. "I immediately hastened back and rallied those retreating at our first position."[28]

General Hill later insisted that this "badly trained regiment" actually deserted from its position along the front lines. One soldier from the 12th North Carolina reported, however, that the troops left the field in response to a direct order that called for them to fire at the enemy and then fall back. "The order was obeyed, but the fire was returned so promptly, at close range, that the withdrawal was attended with confusion," he explained. He noted that "thirty or forty" men from his regiment eventually reformed and moved into place directly alongside the 13th North Carolina.[29]

About that time, some of the new recruits from the 5th North Carolina also began to falter and run to the rear. Their retreat down the steep ridge soon swept up nearly the entire regiment. "When the enemy came down upon us in force, our conscripts, being unused to the noise of musketry, became . . . panic stricken and broke into confusion (my Co. being on the left of our Regt and the last to break) and retreated back in a perfect rout with the enemy pressuring and harassing the back upon us," Capt. Jacob Brookfield from that regiment openly admitted in his diary.[30]

The situation proved just as desperate for the men in the 20th North Carolina on the left center of the brigade line. Iverson recalled that their position extended across a "level plateau" with a field in front that sloped down so steeply that he could not see the bottom. "I knew it was a bad position for we had no range and could not kill a man till he was within sixty yards," he wrote. "I knew that my left would be enveloped unless some of our troops came into the interval." Still, Iverson decided to fight right where he stood. "I knew I was going to catch it, as I had crept to the front on my hands and knees and seen the Federal army at the foot of the hills getting ready for the charge," he explained.

As they awaited an attack, the regiment came under "a fierce fire" from a Federal battery along their front. Iverson responded by dispatching skirmishers under Capt. James B. Atwell in an attempt to flank the battery. The men quickly moved forward "in gallant style" and killed several of the enemy manning the

---

28 OR 19, pt. 1, 1,041.

29 Hill, "Battle of South Mountain," in Johnson and Buel, *Battles and Leaders*, 2:565-566.

30 Jacob Brookfield Diary, Entry for Sept. 30, 1862, Record Group 109, NA.

guns. "The gunners were destroyed, and there is but little doubt that this battery of four pieces was for the day abandoned," Col. McRae reported. Captain Atwell's skirmishers, however, were forced back to the main battle line.

Within minutes of their return, Iverson's troops along the ridge faced an overwhelming enemy assault. "In silence we waited with guns leveled over the low rail fence for the charge," Iverson recalled after the war. "It came, the Yankees shouting as they advanced." The men from his regiment quickly responded with a barrage of gunfire. "When I saw them, I gave the order to fire and the line in front went down," Iverson explained. "Before the men could reload, the woods on my left when there was no fire swarmed with them." He noted that "there was nothing to do but to get away or surrender."[31]

The final attack against their position came so suddenly that most of the men from the 20th North Carolina got off only a single volley before they were overrun. Private Foard described the scene along their front as resembling something out of a dream. "As I pulled my trigger with careful aim, throwing a musket ball and three buck shot into them at not more than 20 yards distance, I could see dimly through the dense sulphurous battle smoke and the line from Shakespeare's Tempest flitted across my brain: 'Hell is empty and all the devils are here,'" he declared.

During that time, the enemy continued to press forward in a three-deep line of battle against both flanks of Iverson's embattled regiment. "We resisted stubbornly retarding their progress in our front," Pvt. Foard recalled. Even so, their line soon began to crumble under the weight of the Federal attack. "But being unopposed in the intervals between the regiments they advanced more rapidly and got around both of our flanks and were about to completely surround us, which compelled a hasty and precipitate retreat with the sure alternative of death or capture," concluded Foard.[32]

After a brief stand, a large part of the 23rd North Carolina on Iverson's immediate right also broke into a full retreat from its position on the top of the ridge. "We stood the charge with coolness two successive times, but the third was too strong for us, and we were compelled to give way to their odds," one soldier from the regiment explained in a letter to his hometown newspaper. He noted that they "scampered over the rough and rugged mountain the best we

---

31 Iverson Jr. to D. H. Hill, Aug. 23, 1885, Hill Papers; OR 19, pt. 1, 1,042.

32 Foard, "Reminiscences," Foard Papers.

could and formed but did not again during the day engage in the fight, having lost some of our field officers."³³

The Federal attack proved so devastating that almost the entire line was forced back in a near rout from behind the stone wall along the dirt road. "The enemy's strength was overpowering and could not be resisted," Col. McRae explained in his official report. "The Twentieth and a portion of the Twenty-third, finding themselves surrounded, were compelled to retreat, and this they did, under a severe fire, down the mountain side." The losses in the brigade totaled 37 killed, 168 wounded, and 154 captured. Only the men from the 13th North Carolina on the far left of the line somehow escaped from the ridge in relatively good order.³⁴

With the enemy close on their heels, the withdrawal by the troops from the 20th North Carolina quickly turned into a mad scramble for safety as they descended the steep slope in their rear. Private Foard recalled that "it was a sharp run until we had extracted ourselves from the flanking columns." Private James Ireland noted that the men "ran down that mountain or rather we went down it in leaps of forty feet or more" at a time. "We could hear that the Yankees were following us but they were not fast enough to catch up," he commented. "Quite a number of us were lost from our proper commands."

The panic soon spread to soldiers throughout the entire brigade. According to Pvt. Foard, the crowd of men fleeing from the crest of the ridge even included one of their chaplains. He could be easily spotted by the bearskin leggings he always wore. "The parson with a prescience born of more than mortal wisdom quickly discerned it was impossible for us to with stand the enemy's onslaught, insured his own safety by flight," Foard remarked. He noted that "those bear skin leggens could be seen bounding over the tops of the lauerl bushes like a kangaroo."³⁵

Although his own men ran from the field, Iverson refused any responsibility for what had befallen his command. Instead, he placed the blame

---

33 "History of the Montgomery Volunteers, Company C, 23rd N.C. Regiment (March 8, 1862 to March 4, 1863)," *Fayetteville Observer*, March 16, 1863.

34 *OR* 19, pt. 1, 1,042. Thomas G. Clemens, ed., Ezra A. Carman, *The Maryland Campaign of September 1862, Volume 1: South Mountain* (New York: Savas Beatie, 2010), 376. This is the first of two volumes of Carman's magisterial Maryland campaign history. Editor Clemens is one of the leading scholars of the campaign, and his detailed annotations and explanatory notes are required reading for a full understanding of this critical operation.

35 Foard, "Reminiscences," Foard Papers; Ireland, "Memoirs."

directly on the lack of leadership by Col. McRae after Garland was killed. "I ascribed the disaster to Garland's death," he wrote to D. H. Hill after the war. "For had he been alive, he would have known where to put and how to handle his troops." He pointedly recalled that McRae was fleeing far ahead of him during the retreat. "I must have been the fastest runner for I caught up with him and together we went to the foot of the mountain," Iverson said. "My regiment was scattered in every direction and it took the balance of the day to get them together."[36]

Similar events were repeated only three days later on September 17 at Sharpsburg, where the dispirited brigade once again faltered under the weight of a Federal attack. The problems began just as the enemy approached their position in the East Woods, directly north of a sunken road that later became known as "Bloody Lane."

"The Federals advanced against us in dense lines through a corn field, which concealed the uniforms, though their flags and mounted officers could be seen plainly above the corn tassels," Adjt. Turner from the 23rd North Carolina vividly recalled years later. He noted that "as the blue line became more distinct, approaching the edge of the corn field, which brought it in our range, we commenced to fire, and effectively held it in check."[37]

Although they had caught the Federal troops by surprise, the men stopped shooting almost immediately in response to a false report that they were firing into their own soldiers. That moment of hesitation resulted in disastrous consequences for the troops in the brigade. "Coming in sight of the enemy, the firing was commenced steadily and with good will, and from an excellent position, but, unaccountably to me, an order was given to cease firing—that General Ripley's brigade was in front," Col. McRae reported in his official account of the battle. "This produced great confusion."[38]

The first break in the line came soon afterward. Captain Thomas M. Garrett from the 5th North Carolina reported that, just as an enemy regiment approached from the flank, a company commander "came up to me, and in a very excited manner and tone cried out to me, 'They are flanking us! See, yonder's a whole brigade!'" Garrett immediately ordered him to keep silent and

---

36 Iverson Jr. to D. H. Hill, Aug. 23, 1885, Hill Papers.

37 Turner and Wall, "Twenty-Third Regiment," in Clark, *NC Regiments*, 223.

38 *OR* 19, pt. 1, 1,042.

return to his post. "The men before this were far from being cool, but, when this act of indiscretion occurred, a panic ensued, and, despite the efforts of file-closers and officers, they began to break and run," he said.[39]

In a matter of minutes, the situation spiraled completely out of control. Captain Brookfield from the same regiment noted in his diary that the men were soon "thrown into confusion" and began to run from the field. Leading the way in the retreat were some of the conscripts from his own regiment. They were followed by many of the veteran soldiers. While admitting that "a greatest portion of our Regt acted cowardly and straggled off," Brookfield insisted that there also "were a good many officers & men who joined other forces and fought gallantly all day."[40]

With about 10 men, Capt. Garrett attempted to make a last-ditch stand behind a nearby stone fence. "I observed, however, immediately, that all the brigade on the left was retreating in disorder, and had already passed the fence without halting," he observed. "I retired with the few men behind the fence toward town. I could see no body of men of my regiment on the way." After forming a group of stragglers into another line of battle, Garrett watched as the entire left of his line once more gave way. Only later in the day was he finally able to establish a stable line of defense.[41]

The unseemly race for safety in the rear quickly encompassed the rest of the brigade, including many of the men from the 20th North Carolina. "A force of the enemy appearing on the right, it commenced to break and a general panic ensued," McRae acknowledged in his official report. "It was in vain that the field and most of the company officers exerted themselves to rally it." Even those efforts failed to hold back the soldiers fleeing from the front lines. McRae admitted that "the troops left the field in confusion, the field officers, company officers, and myself bringing up the rear." They fled from the field so quickly that the brigade lost only nine men killed, 42 wounded, and 33 captured. Some of the men reformed and moved into place in the rear along Bloody Lane.[42]

Following their return to Virginia, the troops from the 13th North Carolina transferred to the brigade commanded by Brig. Gen. William Dorsey Pender.

---

39 *Ibid.*, 1,044.

40 Brookfield Diary, Entry for Sept. 30, 1862, NA.

41 *OR* 19, pt. 1, 1,044.

42 *Ibid.*, 1,043.

This change took place in mid-October after repeated requests from the regimental officers. The problems were largely fueled by friction with Col. McRae, the acting brigade commander since the fighting at South Mountain. The transfer further reflected the strong desire by the men to serve under Pender, who had begun the war as colonel of their regiment. One veteran recalled that "then the boys were happy, as we were again with our first colonel."[43]

Throughout that time, the soldiers from the other four regiments waited anxiously to see who would be selected to lead them as their new general. Although Garland hailed from Virginia, he had earned their devotion on the hard-fought battlefields of Gaines' Mill, Malvern Hill, and South Mountain. Months after his death, an enlisted man from the 12th North Carolina still lamented that the "brigade misses him as much as a child misses his parent." Another soldier in the brigade insisted that "a nobler man, braver patriot, or more beloved commander has not offered up his life on the altar of Southern liberty."[44]

The final decision on Garland's successor was not long in coming. Although D. H. Hill recommended McRae and three other colonels for promotion along with Iverson, he closed with an "emphatic" statement that "Colonel Iverson is in my opinion the best qualified by education, courage, and character of any colonel in the service for appointment of brigadier-general." Stonewall Jackson added a recommendation that "Colonel Iverson be the first promotion." Lee forwarded the nomination to Richmond with a request for its "favorable consideration."[45]

Iverson's appointment also attracted strong support from Confederate President Jefferson Davis. While the military commanders were largely influenced in their choice by McRae's poor performance during the Maryland Campaign, President Davis was more than willing to provide full backing for the son of his longtime friend and political ally regardless of the circumstances. Taking no chances, however, the senior Iverson once again penned a letter to the president in which he urged favorable consideration for his son. With President Davis' concurrence, young Alfred was formally appointed brigadier

---

43 R. S. Williams, "Thirteenth Regiment," included in Clark, *NC Regiments*, 1:653.

44 "From the Rappahannock," April 14, 1863, *North Carolina Standard*, April 24, 1863; A North Carolinian to the Editor, May 28, 1863, *Raleigh Daily Progress*, June 8, 1863.

45 *OR* 51, pt. 2, 844.

Captain Don Peters Halsey from Virginia, who served as assistant adjutant general of Iverson's Brigade, was acknowledged as one of the most brilliant men in Lee's army.

Virginia Historical Society

general on November 1, subject only to confirmation by the Confederate Senate.[46]

Despite the endorsement of his superior officers, Iverson's promotion was greeted with widespread discontent within the ranks of the North Carolina troops, who resented serving under a general from another state. Those concerns first arose during the time that Garland commanded the brigade. The complaints remained largely muted because of Garland's leadership abilities and his undoubted courage in battle. The reaction to Iverson's appointment proved much worse. For many of the men in the brigade, his selection over Col. McRae and other qualified Tar Heel officers was seen as a major affront to their honor and state pride.[47]

Iverson compounded the problem by retaining Asst. Adjt. Gen. Don Peters Halsey and most of the other Virginia officers that staffed Garland's Brigade. In terms of ability, there was certainly no room for complaints about Capt. Halsey. He was born in Lynchburg, Virginia, in 1836 and graduated with distinction from Emory and Henry College in Virginia at the age of 19. After briefly attending the University of Virginia, Halsey spent several more years studying law and ancient languages at major German universities in Bonn, Berlin, and Heidelberg. He also spoke French, German, Spanish, and Italian with virtually no trace of an accent.

---

46 Alfred Iverson Sr. to Jefferson Davis, Oct. 24, 1862, Index of Letters Received, Confederate Adjutant and Inspector General's Office, RG109, NA.

47 Montgomery, "Twelfth Regiment," in Clark, *NC Regiments*, 1:610.

As the crisis over the Union began to build, Halsey returned from Europe and worked openly for the election of Union delegates to the State Convention. Like many other pro-Union Virginians, Halsey remained loyal to his home state at the outbreak of war and joined the Confederate army. He served first as a lieutenant in the 2nd Virginia Cavalry. Following the reorganization of his regiment, Halsey joined the staff of Maj. Gen. James Longstreet, where he served as a volunteer aide. Soon afterward, he assumed a permanent position on Samuel Garland's staff as an aide-de-camp and later as assistant adjutant general.

Besides being one of the most brilliant men in the army, at nearly six foot two Halsey was also an imposing figure. His physical presence was matched by his acknowledged bravery in battle. In his report on the action at Seven Pines, Garland noted that Halsey, "having attracted universal applause throughout my entire command by his handsome behavior, was rallying a disorganized regiment and leading it forward with their colors in his hand when he received a dangerous wound in the head." Although the injury left him blind in one eye, he soon returned to duty and was standing by Garland's side when he received his fatal wound at South Mountain.[48]

In addition to Halsey, the Virginia officers on Iverson's staff included Maj. Alexander B. Garland as brigade commissary and Maj. William M. Payne as brigade quartermaster. The only immediate changes were the appointments of 31-year-old Lt. John T. Ector from Iverson's hometown of Columbus as aide-de-camp and Lt. Waller Holladay from Virginia as the new brigade ordnance officer. Rather than filling the vacant position of brigade inspector, the newly promoted Iverson temporarily took on the duties himself. He also retained Dr. Robert I. Hicks from the 23rd North Carolina as the brigade surgeon. The fact that Hicks served as the lone Tar Heel officer on the staff only fueled the growing discontent over the selection of a Georgian to head the brigade.[49]

---

48 "Speech of Captain Robert D. Yancey Presenting the Portrait of Major Don P. Halsey," Confederate Memorial Association Collection, VHS; Don P. Halsey Jr., "A Sketch of Capt. Don P. Halsey," *SHSP*, 31 (1903), 193-197; Rosa Faulkner Yancey, *Lynchburg and Its Neighbors* (Richmond: J. W. Fergusson and Sons, 1935), 116-118; *OR* 11, pt. 1, 966.

49 James F. Johnston, "The Garland–Iverson–Johnston Brigade," included in Clark, *NC Regiments*, 4:522-523; Robert E. L. Krick, *Staff Officers in Gray: A Biographical Register of the Staff Officers in the Army of Northern Virginia* (Chapel Hill: University of North Carolina Press, 2003), 119-120, 135, 239.

Iverson responded to those concerns by striking a conciliatory note in the first general order to the troops. "He is deeply sensible of the great responsibility that develops upon him to supply to them the place of their beloved and lamented Garland," wrote Iverson, referring to himself in the third person. "But he hopes to receive the cordial cooperation of every officer and soldier in sustaining him in an earnest endeavor to promote the efficiency of the brigade." Iverson went on to further pledge that "no effort shall be wanting on his part to administer to your comfort and to subserve the interest of the service."[50]

Despite those remarks, Iverson soon made it clear that he was determined to impose strict rules of discipline. Only three days after taking command, he ordered regimental and company commanders to review the army regulations on military courtesy. "Courtesy among military men is indispensable to discipline," he emphasized. "Respect to superiors will not be confined to obedience on duty, but will be extended to all occasions." He declared that "it is always the duty of the inferior to accost or to offer first the customary salutations, and of the superior to return such complimentary notice."[51]

In addition, their new brigade commander called for all officers elected since the reorganization in May and all others of "doubtful" qualifications who had been promoted during that period to appear before a board of examination. He further required officers "to wear at all times their appropriate marks of rank on their collars and cuff." Noncommissioned officers were instructed "to wear their proper chevrons." Iverson also ordered the regimental commanders to read the articles of war regarding discipline to their commands on the last Sunday of every month.[52]

Because of his experience with disease problems in Mexico and along the lower Cape Fear River, Iverson placed special emphasis on maintaining "cleanliness in quarters, clothing, & persons." He insisted that "no excuse can exist for allowing men to wear filthy clothing." He declared that "dirtyness and filthiness in any company or regiment" would be considered negligence of duty by its commander and "will be sufficient cause for calling officers before a

---

50 Iverson's Brigade, General Order No. 1, Nov. 15, 1862, General and Special Orders, 23rd North Carolina, Record Group 109, NA.

51 Iverson's Brigade, General Order No. 2, Nov. 18, 1862, *ibid.*

52 Iverson's Brigade, Special Order No. 2, Nov. 17, 1862, *ibid.*; Iverson's Brigade, General Order No. 3, Nov. 20, 1862, *ibid.*

board of examination." He further ordered that "commanding officers will observe every Saturday as a day of police and will cause all clothing to be aired and the inside of tents and huts to be exposed in a thorough manner."[53]

Just as he had throughout his career in the military, Iverson called for all the orders on the books to be interpreted in the strictest possible manner. Especially meanspirited was his reaction to the common practice among enlisted men on the march of paying teamsters to carry their haversacks on the brigade wagons. "This is expressly forbidden and the brigade inspector is charged with the duty of having all such baggage thrown out and of reporting the teamster for dismissal from extra duty who [carries] any but the authorized baggage," declared the new brigade commander.[54]

After two months in command, the general continued to find fault with his subordinates for not properly respecting the line between officers and enlisted men. "The earnest attention of all officers is called to the necessity of introducing more effective discipline in their commands," he wrote in one of his general orders. "In the opinion of the Brig. Genl. Comdg., the chief cause of the want of discipline is found in the familiarity and companionship of officers with soldiers." He emphasized that from "a military point of view the private is certainly the inferior and must so be regarded."

Iverson allowed no exceptions to this policy for anyone under his command. He declared that "the harder the line is drawn between the officer and his men provided it is not done with self complacency and with contempt toward the inferior the better and more easily can discipline be enforced." He also demanded that the officers in the brigade "drop the home familiarity and properly appreciate the dignity of their ranks not by an unbecoming pride but with a course of conduct that will secure the prompt respect and obedience of their men."[55]

Despite his penchant for strict discipline, Iverson did not always take well to orders from his superiors. Soon after assuming command of the brigade, he sent in a routine request for a furlough. When Stonewall Jackson turned him down, Iverson threatened to resign in protest. "No one can tell what day a battle may be fought," Jackson wrote to Gen. Robert Rodes, who was temporarily

---

53 Iverson's Brigade, General Order No. 10, May 26, 1863, *ibid.*

54 Iverson's Brigade, General Order No. 6, April 25, 1863, *ibid.*

55 Iverson's Brigade, General Order No. 4, Jan. 6, 1863, *ibid.*

commanding the division. "Whilst I would regret to see General Iverson resign yet I would rather see him do so than to approve of his furlough under present circumstances." Rather than risk a showdown with his corps commander, Iverson backed down from his threat.[56]

By the early spring of 1863, Iverson had alienated nearly everyone in the brigade. The situation became so bad that many officers privately expressed outright contempt for their new commander. "I think our brigadier a very slow coach (*entre nous*)," Adjt. Fabius J. Haywood from the 5th North Carolina confided to Col. McRae's brother at the end of March. On the same day, Col. Daniel Harvey Christie from the 23rd North Carolina complained in a confidential letter to Governor Vance that Iverson "has been in camp nearly four months, & the organization of the Brigade is yet incomplete & what has been done has been mainly through the energy of subordinate officers."[57]

The few public comments focused on Iverson's position as a Georgian commanding a Tar Heel brigade. "Every man belonging to it is a North Carolinian," an unidentified private observed in a letter to a Raleigh newspaper. "And, still *let it be proclaimed throughout the state* that our Brigadier General (Iverson) is a *Georgian*, our Brigade Quartermaster and Commissary and Adjutant General *are all Virginians*, and many of our surgeons and other officers are from other states." The private openly wondered how such a situation had been allowed to happen when they had so many North Carolina officers capable of commanding them.[58]

---

[56] Stonewall Jackson Notebook, Entry for Feb. 10, 1863, Jedediah Hotchkiss Papers, Manuscript Division, Library of Congress, Washington, DC (hereafter cited as LOC).

[57] Fabius J. Haywood to James C. McRae, March 31, 1863, John McRae Papers, SHC; Christie to Vance, March 31, 1863, Zebulon Baird Vance Papers.

[58] A Private to W. W. Holden, May 26, 1863, *North Carolina Standard*, June 2, 1863. Italics as in original.

CHAPTER THREE

An Earnest Protest Against This Injustice

Iverson's problems continued to mount in the months after his promotion, when he became embroiled in a series of bitter disputes over the issues of rank, honor, and recognition of North Carolina's contributions to the war effort. At the center of the first fight was the 5th North Carolina's Col. Duncan McRae, who served as the acting brigade commander after the death of Samuel Garland at South Mountain.

McRae was born in 1820 and grew up in Fayetteville, North Carolina. He briefly attended the University of North Carolina before transferring to William and Mary College in Virginia. Following his graduation, McRae opened a law office in his hometown. While widely acknowledged as an exceptional orator and criminal defense attorney, he became best known over the following years as a figure of controversy in North Carolina politics. Despite harboring strong Whig sympathies, McRae won election to the House of Commons in 1842 as a Democrat. After a single term, he returned to the practice of law, first in Raleigh and later in Wilmington and New Bern. In 1853, he ran as an independent candidate for the congressional seat representing the Cape Fear District.

The Franklin Pierce administration quickly intervened by appointing McRae consul general at Paris in return for his withdrawal from the congressional race. After resigning his post in 1857, McRae made the bizarre

Colonel Duncan K. McRae of the 5th North Carolina entered the war with a reputation for controversy in North Carolina politics.

North Carolina Regiments

claim that he had been drugged into accepting the deal. Less than a year later, he launched an independent campaign for governor against the regular Democratic nominee, Judge John W. Ellis. By advocating the distribution of funds to the states from the sale of Federal public lands, McRae attracted support from an unlikely mix of disaffected Democrats and followers of the Whig-American Party, which had declined to put up a candidate.[1]

Despite that promising start, McRae faced some major difficulties in his run for governor. Throughout the campaign, he drew criticism for changing his position depending on which part of the state he was speaking in at the time. By abandoning the Democratic Party, McRae also alienated several members of his family, including his uncle who served as the chief justice of the North Carolina Supreme Court. The worst blow came when the powerful newspaper in his hometown of Fayetteville decided not to support his election because of an "honest difference" over some of McRae's proposals.[2]

Although he eventually lost by a wide margin, McRae refused to give up his stance as a political maverick. He briefly reemerged as a Douglas Democrat before reversing course again in 1861 by supporting secession. His shifting

---

1   Powell, *Dictionary of NC Biography*, 3:189; John McRae to Thomas Ruffin Sr., Feb. 13, 1838, Thomas Ruffin Papers, SHC.

2   Duncan K. McRae to John McRae, May 3, 1858, McRae Papers; Peter M. Hale to Duncan K. McRae, June 29, 1858, Edward Jones Hale Papers, NCOAH.

positions made him a target for opposition editors across the state. "Mr. McRae was a Democrat, then a Distributionist, then a Consul, then a Douglas Democrat and is now a disunionist, having marked all the phases through which he has passed by a candidacy for something, without a solitary election we recollect of," was how one major newspaper in Raleigh described him in early 1861.[3]

McRae's last-minute conversion to support for secession, however, earned the backing of Governor Ellis, who selected McRae as the commander of one of the new regiments being raised by the state. The governor even requested assistance from President Davis in securing McRae's commission. "Mr. McRae is competent, in every way, to this position and would make you a good officer if you choose to give him a commission in the Regular service, instead of the volunteer service to which I propose to appoint him, and his character and position here would materially aid in an Enlistment of recruits," Ellis informed Davis.[4]

The governor eventually appointed McRae as colonel of the 5th North Carolina State Troops. The regiment included two companies from Gates County and two others from Rowan County. The other companies came from Caswell, Cumberland, Johnston, Craven, Bertie, and Wilson counties. The troops received their initial training at the camp of instruction in Halifax, North Carolina. During early July of 1861, the men from the 5th North Carolina moved on to the vicinity of Richmond, Virginia, where they joined the brigade commanded by Gen. James Longstreet.

Soon afterward, Col. McRae's troops moved north and were briefly engaged at the Battle of First Manassas on July 21. The men helped lead the way in pursuing the Federal troops toward the capital. While avoiding the worst fighting, the 5th North Carolina sustained a few casualties during the action there. The regiment transferred to Jubal Early's command in the winter of 1861. During that time, the men engaged in picket duty outside Washington. In the early spring, the brigade was reassigned to the main Confederate army assembled to protect the capital at Richmond.[5]

---

3 *North Carolina Standard*, April 3, 1861.

4 John W. Ellis to Jefferson Davis, April 24, 1861, in Tolbert, *The Papers of John Willis Ellis*, 2:679.

5 James C. McRae and C. M. Busbee, "Fifth Regiment," included in Clark, *NC Regiments*, 2:281-282; "5th Regiment North Carolina Volunteers," *Richmond Dispatch*, July 17, 1861.

In its first major action, McRae's regiment suffered more than 250 casualties, including 87 men killed and mortally wounded, during the afternoon fighting at Williamsburg, Virginia, on May 5, 1862. The 5th North Carolina initially joined the rest of the brigade in an attack against some Federal troops under Brig. Gen. Winfield Scott Hancock, who had reoccupied an abandoned redoubt on the left of the North Carolinians. Several of the regiments, however, "failed to come up" due to the obstructions caused by the thick woods along their front. This left only McRae's regiment and the 24th Virginia to carry out the assault against the Federals amid a driving rainstorm that had engulfed the area.[6]

The Tar Heel troops quickly moved forward through a section of heavy undergrowth before emerging into an open field. "We came out of the woods in full view of their redoubt about 3/4 of a mile distant," Capt. Jacob Brookfield remarked in his diary. "As soon as we made our appearance the battery, which was several hundred yds nearer us, opened upon us. We wheeled and started straight for it—seeking no cover and asking nothing but a fair fight." He noted that "shot and shell tore through our line but we kept on as the Yankees express it, 'just as if there was no firing going on.'"[7]

After forcing the battery to pull back, the men pushed on toward the main enemy entrenchments. An officer from the regiment noted in a letter home that the artillery soon took up a new position alongside the redoubt and opened fire on their line with a barrage of shells, canister, and spherical case. At the same time, the Federal infantry was "dealing death at every volley" from behind the earthworks. He reported, however, that the men continued to march "straight forward over 800 yards right 'through the valley of death'—our line as perfect and unbroken as if on parade."[8]

The regiment eventually advanced within 50 yards of the Federal troops, who had taken cover in the fort. "Victory was in its grasp, the enemy had been driven to his entrenchment," another soldier recalled. "One fresh regiment was all that was needed to go over the works, but none ever came; instead thereof an order to retreat." The survivors were "too few in numbers" to continue the attack without support and soon withdrew to the protection of the woods on

---

6 Mast, *Photographic Record*, 289; D. K. McRae, "Battle of Williamsburg, May 1862," *The William and Mary Quarterly*, Second Series, 2 (1922), 195-197.

7 Brookfield Diary, Entry for May 26, 1862, NA.

8 Peter J. Sinclair to My Dear Alexander, May 12, 1862, Peter J. Sinclair Papers, SHC.

their left, leaving "a large majority of the officers and men dead and wounded on the field."[9]

Less than one month later, the 5th North Carolina again suffered "a serious loss in officers and men" during the heavy fighting under Garland on the peninsula at Seven Pines. Stung by widespread criticism from his political opponents over the severe casualties his troops had sustained at Williamsburg and Seven Pines, McRae railed against his numerous foes, blaming them for the multitude of his troubles. "Although my pride has been cruelly mortified—my duty now forbids me to leave the command," he informed his father at one point.[10]

McRae bristled even more when his Tar Heel regiment was retained in the brigade commanded by Garland of Virginia rather than transferred to one of the new brigades, which were formed soon after the fighting at Seven Pines and headed by North Carolina generals. McRae's failure to gain a promotion to brigadier general made matters even worse. Despite these setbacks, McRae reluctantly swallowed his sizeable pride and remained on duty with his regiment outside the capital. "I refrained from resigning then, because of the impending conflicts around Richmond, yielding to the earnest solicitations of both Generals Hill and Garland," was how he described it in a letter to the governor of North Carolina.[11]

McRae continued at the head of the 5th North Carolina in the Seven Days' Battles at Gaines' Mill but was absent with his regiment on detached duty during the fighting at Malvern Hill. The low point for the colonel personally, however, came in the Maryland Campaign, when the brigade broke and fled from the field twice while under his temporary command—first at South Mountain and again at Sharpsburg. Many in the army placed the blame for this disastrous performance on his inability to manage the troops after Garland was

---

9 McRae and Busbee, "Fifth Regiment," in Clark, *NC Regiments*, 2:285. For an overview of the action at Williamsburg, see Steve French, "Williamsburg Shreds Rebels," *Washington Times*, March 12, 2009.

10 "5th N.C. Regiment, Casualties on May 31, Battle of Seven Pines," *North Carolina Standard*, June 18, 1862; McRae and Busbee, "Fifth Regiment," in Clark, *NC Regiments*, 2:286; Duncan K. McRae to John McRae, Aug. 1, 1862, McRae Papers. For McRae's defense of his actions at Williamsburg, see Duncan K. McRae, "The Battle of Williamsburg—Reply to Colonel Bratton," *SHSP*, 7 (1880), 360-372.

11 Duncan K. McRae to Zebulon B. Vance, Nov. 14, 1862, in Frontis W. Johnston, ed., *The Papers of Zebulon Baird Vance*, Vol. 1 (Raleigh: North Carolina Division of Archives and History, 1963), 356-357.

mortally wounded. One of McRae's most vehement critics was Col. Alfred Iverson of the 20th North Carolina.[12]

As the concerns about his capabilities grew, McRae threatened to resign due to "the injustices I have recd at the hands of the govt." More than anything else, he blamed his many political enemies for blocking his promotion to brigadier general. He aimed his harshest comments at George Davis, one of the Confederate senators from North Carolina. "It is now ascertained that the Prest. did confer the promotion on me and I was defeated by No. Ca. politicians of whom Geo. Davis was conspicuous," McRae explained in one of his letters home.[13]

The controversy was further fueled by some of his allies in the 5th North Carolina. One of them openly complained in a letter to a major Raleigh newspaper about the repeated lack of justice for McRae. The soldier noted that the primary cause for concern was "the total neglect of his claim to promotion, while others, in no particular his superior in merit, have been made Brigadier Generals." He pointed to former Congressmen Thomas L. Clingman and Lawrence O'Bryan Branch as men who had been unjustly promoted ahead of McRae. He insisted that any reasonable person could "well understand how his sensitive spirit must feel goaded and chafed."[14]

Despite those words of support, McRae was not universally liked even within his own regiment. His prickly personality and repeated attempts to gain a promotion for himself left at least some of his subordinates openly dissatisfied with his leadership. Worst of all was his frequent favoritism toward certain officers with regard to promotions. For many of his opponents, their opinions of him came closer to hatred than admiration. The regiment's senior captain, Jacob Brookfield, described him as "a man whose passions and prejudices are paramount to his regard for truth or sense of justice."[15]

McRae's relations proved just as difficult with some of the men from the other regiments in the brigade. "Colonel MacRae was a man of commanding

---

12 Hill, "Battle of South Mountain," in Johnson and Buel, *Battles and Leaders*, 2:563-564; Iverson Jr. to D. H. Hill, Aug. 23, 1885, Hill Papers.

13 Duncan K. McRae to Zebulon B. Vance, Sept. 9, 1862, in Johnston, *Papers of Vance, Vol. 1*, 171; Duncan K. McRae to John McRae, Aug. 1, 1862, McRae Papers.

14 "Col. Duncan K. McRae," *North Carolina Standard*, June 18, 1862.

15 Jacob Brookfield to Zebulon B. Vance, Feb. 19, 1863, Zebulon Baird Vance, Governor's Papers, NCOAH.

gifts, but of very strong prejudices, and the whole brigade knew of his prejudices against the Twelfth Regiment," one veteran from the 12th North Carolina recalled. He noted that "the severity of discipline over his own regiment was universally known, and because the Twelfth was not willing to submit to such discipline in camp as he enforced on his own men, he always spoke of the Twelfth as a lot of 'undisciplined gentlemen who thought themselves better than others.'"[16]

McRae's actions also ruined the friendship with one of his own relatives in the brigade. Following South Mountain, his first cousin, Lt. Col. Thomas Ruffin Jr. from the 13th North Carolina, branded him a "bad, bad man" and as much a coward as the men who broke and ran during the battle. "My intercourse with him is purely official, much to my gratification, as I thought he was disposed to take me into his confidence & I feared would involve me in some [of] the miserable feuds which his presence seems every where to breed," Ruffin wrote in a letter to his father.

The conflict between the two cousins finally reached the breaking point when McRae failed to acknowledge in his official report the gallant stand made by Ruffin's regiment at South Mountain. Despite being surrounded, his men had escaped certain capture that day by charging directly into the enemy. According to Ruffin, "this is well known in the army, and fully admitted by all generous men; and yet because Col. McRae's regiment, led by himself, ran before the shock came on them, he fails to make it known officially."

The fallout from this dispute left Ruffin with no recourse other than open opposition to his cousin's promotion to general. Ruffin made his feelings perfectly clear in a long letter home about a month after the battle. "We split after my having the courage to tell him, when asked by him, that I did not desire him to be our Brig General," he reported to his father. "But, I need not tell you about him, as you know him far better than I do & have had a better opportunity to judge him." By that point, any chance for reconciliation between the two relatives had completely vanished.

The cruelest blow for McRae occurred soon afterwards when Iverson was selected over him as the new brigadier general. That decision came as especially good news for Ruffin, who had twice failed to have his regiment transferred out of the brigade because of his strained relations with McRae. Ruffin could barely disguise his glee when he heard the first reports that his cousin would not be

---

16 Montgomery, "Twelfth Regiment," in Clark, *NC Regiments*, 1:627.

promoted. "I had the satisfaction of learning from Genl Lee, a few days before, that Col McRae would not continue in the command of us many more days," Ruffin declared in a letter home.[17]

The news of Iverson's elevation stunned and angered McRae, who defiantly stepped down from his command on November 13. "I have been obliged on two occasions to suffer the mortification of seeing the brigade pass from my command by the appointment and assignment of newly appointed officers to the command," he complained in a letter to Confederate Adjt. Gen. Samuel Cooper. "In the last case that of Col. Iverson, the appointee is my junior in rank and from a state in no way connected with the regiments constituting the brigade." McRae further declared that "it cannot fail to meet the expectations of all soldiers that this is a blow to my individual and state pride."[18]

Addressing the troops of the 5th North Carolina a day later, McRae called upon them to uphold their reputation for valor and fidelity. "It is the pride of my life to have formed and trained the fifth regt. of North Carolina troops," he proclaimed in his typical flamboyant style. McRae followed by outlining all they had accomplished up to that point in the fight for Southern independence. "When I am dead and my memory shall be forgotten, my children and their children will live in the light of history which your patriotism has enkindled," he proudly remarked.[19]

McRae's fired off his next round in a message to Governor Vance that explained his reasons for resigning. "But, severe as is the trespass upon the individual pride of North Carolina officers who have lately been obliged to submit to the promotion, in several instances, of citizens of other States, to the command of brigades exclusively North Carolinian," penned the colonel, "the slur upon the State is broader, and demands the resentment of her sons in the only mode they can manifest it." For the aggrieved colonel, there was but one proper response. "In the spirit of an earnest protest against this injustice, individually and to my state, I resign my commission," he declared.[20]

---

17 Thomas Ruffin Jr. to Thomas Ruffin Sr., Oct. 14, 1862, Thomas Ruffin Papers.

18 Duncan K. McRae to Samuel Cooper, Nov. 13, 1862, Compiled Service Record of Duncan K. McRae, M 270, R 152, NA.

19 Duncan K. McRae to My Brother Officers and Fellow Soldiers of 5th NC, Nov. 14, 1862, *ibid.*

20 McRae to Vance, Nov. 14, 1862, in Johnston, *Papers of Vance*, Vol. 1, 357.

The letter arrived just as the 32-year-old Vance, who had assumed office on September 8, was struggling to find a workable balance between protecting state rights and the need for continued support of the broader war effort. His immense personal popularity among the major political segments in the state had propelled him to a stunning 33,000-vote victory over his opponent, William Johnston. As a former Whig congressman who came late to support for secession, the new governor was especially sympathetic to McRae's claims that he had been badly mistreated by Confederate authorities in Richmond because of his moderate political views.

Within days of receiving the letter, Vance raised the issue of promotions in his first major speech before the General Assembly. He especially criticized the Richmond government for appointing several outsiders to high positions in North Carolina brigades. "It is mortifying to find entire brigades of North Carolina soldiers in the field commanded by strangers," Vance openly complained to the lawmakers. The governor noted that "in many cases our own brave and war-worn colonels are made to give place to colonels from distant States, who are promoted to the command of North Carolina troops over their heads to vacant brigadierships."

According to Vance, the situation had become so intolerable that many officers "have reported to me their intention to resign, alleging that the road to honorable promotion is almost closed to our citizens." He further chastised Confederate officials for failing to recognize North Carolina's contributions to the war effort. "We are willing that our soldiers should follow any general capable of leading them," he added. "But we contend that as a matter of sheer justice our soldiers are entitled to their fair proportion of the honors won by their gallantry and endurance." [21]

The governor turned over McRae's letter of resignation for publication in the Fayetteville *Observer*, which was edited by one of Vance's closest confidantes. Although the newspaper had opposed McRae politically, its editorial page supported his decision to resign. "It is not often that we have had such a sinking of the heart at any public event as that caused by the letter of Col. Duncan K. McRae, which we publish today," editor William J. Hale declared. "Not that his loss or that of any other officer is fatal to our cause . . . but that his

---

21 OR 2, Series 4, 189. For an overview of Vance's career, see Gordon B. McKinney, *Zeb Vance: North Carolina's Civil War Governor and Gilded Age Political Leader* (Chapel Hill: University of North Carolina Press, 2004).

treatment exhibits a case of injustice to himself and to the state that is heart-sickening."

Hale charged that the Richmond officials had repeatedly discriminated against former secession moderates when making their decisions about promotions. Describing him as a faithful and capable officer, the newspaper contrasted McRae's treatment by Confederate authorities with that of former Congressman Lawrence Branch, who had been promoted to brigadier general early in the war. Hale argued that McRae had been punished for "the unpardonable sin" of being a Douglas Democrat, unlike Branch who had been pampered as "a Breckinridge man" and a secessionist.

The editorial laid most of the blame on President Davis' vindictive nature. "There lies the secret of the different treatment of the two officers," the editorial proclaimed. "Branch promoted before he ever smelt gunpowder—McRae always after the fight recommended for promotion by the great generals who commanded him and knew his worth and his services, and always rejected." Hale described it as "another exhibition of that great defect in the President's character which has marked his course since the beginning of the war—where old political differences exist, like the Bourbons, he 'forgets nothing and learns nothing.'"[22]

Another newspaper in the town of Greensboro echoed similar concerns about the lack of recognition for the state's contributions to the war effort. The editor took pains to note that "the treatment of our officers . . . in regard to appointments and promotions, has been positively shameful." He argued that the promotion of Alfred Iverson over Duncan McRae resulted from a much wider problem that needed to be addressed by the governor and the state legislature. "The idea of appointing officers from other States to command North Carolinians, when we have men among ourselves capable and worthy, is outrageous, and the practice is becoming intolerable," he declared.[23]

Following the governor's lead, Senators William T. Dortch and George Davis, both of whom McRae had once blamed for blocking his promotion to general, also took up his cause in the Confederate capital. "I have for a long time been very indignant at the appointment of persons from other states to command Nor Ca Troops," Senator Davis informed Vance. "But all our efforts so far have been unable to correct the evil." He noted that the problem

---

22 "Resignation of Col. McRae," *Fayetteville Observer*, Nov. 27, 1862.

23 "Resignation of Col. D. K. McRae," *Greensborough Patriot*, Nov. 27, 1862.

occurred because "our recommendations for high military appointments are ignored altogether, and attention is given to nothing but the recommendations of the Generals."

The first step taken by the pair of senators was to stop Iverson's nomination before it was submitted for confirmation in the Senate. "Mr. Dortch and myself some time ago addressed to the Secy of War a strong protest against Gen Iverson's appointment being made as a *North Carolina*, appointment, inasmuch as he has never been a citizen of our state," Davis remarked in a letter to the governor. "I regret to say that the Secy's reply has been highly unsatisfactory, persisting in continuing the nomination as made." Secretary of War James A. Seddon even argued in his reply that Iverson should be "regarded as an adopted citizen of North Carolina, who will do her certainly no dishonor."[24]

Behind the scenes, Dortch attempted to gather information that would help block the appointment once it reached the Senate floor. As part of this effort, he approached several of the top officers in the brigade. "A message was recd. yesterday by the officers of this Brigade from our Senator Mr. Dortch requesting that we state the grounds of our dissatisfaction with Brig. Genl. Iverson that he might use them in endeavoring to prevent his confirmation by the Senate," the 23rd North Carolina's Col. Daniel Christie reported in a letter to Governor Vance in late March.[25]

Obtaining Christie's support remained critical because he was so highly regarded in the brigade. Christie was born in 1833 and grew up in Virginia. Following a business failure in 1857, he moved to North Carolina and opened a military training institute in the town of Henderson. At the outbreak of the war, he was elected as major in what would become the 23rd North Carolina. The regiment included three companies from Granville County and two companies from Lincoln County. The other five companies entered military service from Anson, Montgomery, Richmond, Catawba, and Gaston counties.[26]

---

24 George Davis to Zebulon B. Vance, April 16, 1863, in Joe A. Mobley, ed., *The Papers of Zebulon Baird Vance*, Vol. 2 (Raleigh: North Carolina Division of Archives and History, 1995), 117; James A. Seddon to George Davis and William T. Dortch, April 7, 1863, Letters Sent, Confederate Secretary of War, Record Group 109, NA.

25 Christie to Vance, March 31, 1863, Vance Governor's Papers.

26 Turner and Wall, "Twenty-Third Regiment," in Clark, *NC Regiments*, 2:188; Krick, *Lee's Colonels*, 91.

Private Solomon McLean, who served in the 23rd North Carolina with the Pee Dee Guards from Richmond County, was buoyed by the ease of the Confederate victory at First Manassas.

R. Carol McLean

The Pee Dee Guards of Richmond County received a typical send-off when they departed for war. The troops assembled in the town square at Rockingham, where they were treated to some "stirring remarks" by the local dignitaries. Following that ceremony, the men attended worship in a nearby church. "After the services were concluded came the farewells and such scenes I never witnessed before," one officer recorded in his diary. He noted that "sisters, wives, all were weeping around departing dear ones, and my own heart almost overcome by the scene while I wept bitter tears."27

On July 17, following the completion of their training at the camp of instruction in Garysburg, the men from seven of the companies departed by railroad for Richmond. The other three companies remained behind because of a widespread outbreak of measles. The troops from the main part of the regiment soon moved on to the vicinity of Manassas but arrived too late to take part in the fighting there. The men were assigned initially to Jubal Early's Brigade, which also included McRae's 5th North Carolina. The other companies from the regiment joined them there on August 3.

Despite arriving too late to participate in the July 21 Manassas fight, the green troops were buoyed by the ease of the victory. "I have nothing that is funn to write you only we have broke the Yankees from cursing," Pvt. Solomon McLean joked in a letter to his cousin during the early fall. "When they mean to

---

27 Louis H. Webb Diary, Entry for June 17, 1861, Lewis Henry Webb Collection, SHC.

say to go to hell they say go to bull runn as they think it is the niest that place that they ever ware." Following several months of relative inactivity around Manassas, Early's entire brigade was finally sent to the Richmond area during April of the following year.[28]

In early May, the men from the 23rd North Carolina experienced their first combat during the fighting at Williamsburg on the retreat up the Virginia peninsula. Christie reported that their assault against a Federal battery was greatly "impeded" by the presence of "a fence, two ravines, and woods of thick undergrowth" along their front. According to Christie, they advanced only about 600 yards before losing contact with the left of the brigade and coming to a halt. "Here we were fired upon by the enemy's pickets in the woods on our left," reported Christie, "covering a considerable force, which we returned with a loss to the enemy of 4 killed and severely wounded, involving little injury to us."[29]

The 23rd North Carolina's failure to provide support for the 5th North Carolina during the attack soon drew widespread criticism both in and out of the army. Many of the complaints were directed at the poor performance by Col. John F. Hoke. The 42-year-old Hoke was a graduate of the University of North Carolina and a veteran of the Mexican War. He became a prominent lawyer in Lincoln County and served in the state legislature. At the outbreak of hostilities with the North, he took the position as adjutant general of the state for the troops raised as volunteer regiments. In July of 1861, he won election as colonel of what would become the 23rd North Carolina and resigned his state position.[30]

Some of the harshest criticism about the event came from Gen. D. H. Hill, who charged in his official report that Hoke "had so neglected drill and training that the simplest movements were attended with trouble and delay." During the reorganization that took place only a few days after the battle, Christie easily defeated Hoke for election as colonel of the regiment. Other officers were removed in the voting, including Lt. Col. John W. Leak. Men throughout the regiment greeted the selection of Christie as their new commander with open

---

[28] Turner and Wall, "Twenty-Third Regiment," in Clark, *NC Regiments,* 2:190-194; Solomon McLean to Dear Cousin, Oct. 13, 1861, Civil War Miscellaneous Collection.

[29] OR 11, pt. 1, 612.

[30] Turner and Wall, "Twenty-Third Regiment," in Clark, *NC Regiments,* 2:202; Krick, *Lee's Colonels*, 195.

enthusiasm. One officer proclaimed in a letter to his brother soon after the balloting that Christie was "as good a colonel as there is in N.C."[31]

Christie's first opportunity in the field as the regiment's new commander came at Seven Pines on May 31, with the brigade under the command of Gen. Garland. During the early afternoon, Christie received orders to advance directly through an open area toward a fortified Federal position in the middle of the woods. "After crossing the field, the 23rd found in its front, a swamp thick with undergrowth and tangled vines, and about waist deep in water," Sgt. Henry C. Wall recalled. "At this point was met the fire from the opposing batteries supported by musketry, and many of our boys fell in the water." He concluded that "some, doubtless, were drowned, whose wounds were not necessarily fatal."[32]

As they pushed forward, the men experienced problems just keeping the attack on course. "The balls were falling around us as thick as hale all the time," Pvt. Leonidas Torrence of the 23rd regiment explained in a letter to his mother soon after the battle. "It did not look like there was any chance for a man to go through them without being hit." Torrence noted that he "saw several trees nearly as thick round as my Body cut down with Cannon balls." He readily acknowledged that it "was a verry distresing place" for everyone in the line of battle.[33]

Despite the heavy fire, the North Carolinians eventually carried the Federal position late that afternoon. The cost, however, was steep. The regiment sustained more than 180 casualties, including a large number of men killed and mortally wounded. The toll ran especially high among the field officers. Lieutenant Colonel Robert D. Johnston was shot in the arm, face, and neck and had his horse killed from under him. Major Edmond J. Christian received three

---

[31] *OR* 11, pt. 1, 605; Henry C. Wall Diary, Entry for May 11, 1862, Leak and Wall Family Papers, SHC; Alexander S. Webb to My Own Dear Brother, May 24, 1862, Webb Collection, NCOAH. For Colonel Hoke's defense of his performance at Williamsburg, see John F. Hoke to Dear Editors State Journal, March 10, 1863, *Charlotte Daily Bulletin,* March 20, 1863. The wholesale changes from the elections were widely expected even before the battle. For details, see James F. Gibson to Dear Sister, April 30, 1862, Gibson Papers, Library and Archives, Catawba County Museum of History, Newton, North Carolina.

[32] Henry C. Wall, "The 23rd North Carolina Infantry, Organized in 1861 as the 13th Regiment of Volunteers, Historical Sketch," *SHSP,* 25 (1897), 158. For another version of the same article, see H. C. Wall, "In Their Own Words, 23rd Regiment Infantry (13th Regiment N.C. State Troops), Bits of War History," *Raleigh News and Observer,* April 11, 1897.

[33] Leonidas Torrence to Dear Mother, June 8, 1862, in Monroe, "Road to Gettysburg," 495.

severe wounds in the attack, the last of which proved fatal. Colonel Christie was also among the wounded, hit late in the fighting that afternoon. Luckily, the injury was not life-threatening.[34]

Over the following months, Christie continued to prove his merit as both an effective leader and a brave fighter at Gaines' Mill, South Mountain, and Sharpsburg. "He is a soldier by education and has shown his superiority in drilling and organizing his regiment, and making it one of the best regiments in the Army of Northern Virginia," one private declared in a letter to a Raleigh newspaper. He went on to note that "his gallantry has been proven on many a hard-fought field, and his superior capacity as an officer is acknowledged by all officers in our division."[35]

When Senator Dortch approached Christie for his assistance in blocking Iverson's appointment, the colonel weighed the merits of his offer against his own need to protect his reputation within the brigade. Christie agreed to respond to the request only if his personal views about Iverson were kept confidential. Once Dortch agreed, Christie offered a scathing assessment of his new commanding general. "Brig. Genl. Iverson does not give satisfaction," he wrote to the governor. "By neither Officers nor men is he respected as an officer. This feeling has scarcely an exception. The cause is too plain to be misunderstood." Christie insisted that Iverson "has not the military qualifications & is devoid of that energy & vim essentially prerequisite to a commanding Officer."

Christie implored Vance, who had served as colonel of the 26th North Carolina before being elected governor, to find a way to remove Iverson without forcing him to speak out in public. "Your military experience enables you to appreciate this state of things, & I know you will do all in your power to relieve us of an officer who is an incumbent & supply his place with one who can and will infuse and maintain an *esprit de corps* & efficiency in a Brigade," Christie pleaded, "which will if properly commanded do much more noble service in the cause for which she has already spilled so much blood."[36]

---

34 Wall, "The 23rd North Carolina Infantry," 158.

35 A Private to William W. Holden, May 26, 1863, *North Carolina Standard*, June 2, 1863. For similar comments about Christie's capabilities, see T. B. M. to Mr. Editor, *Spirit of the Age*, March 23, 1863.

36 Christie to Vance, March 31, 1863, Vance Governor's Papers.

When the other officers in the brigade also declined to go public with their complaints, the senators were left with little or no hope of blocking Iverson's promotion to brigadier general. More than innuendo and confidential letters were needed for them to have any hope against someone with direct connections into the highest reaches of the Confederate government. "We have heard of a good deal of dissatisfaction with Gen. I. but, so far as I am aware, it all rests on rumor," Senator Davis admitted to Governor Vance on April 16. "Your own letter is the only exception, and that, you are aware, can hardly be of much use to us."[37]

Despite whatever pressure the North Carolina politicians were able to bring, President Davis refused throughout the dispute to reconsider his support for the son of his longtime political ally. "It was not I who placed this gallant son of Georgia in command of North Carolina troops, but that a regiment of your State adopted him, elected him for its colonel and was commanded by him on many bloody fields," he later explained to Vance. President Davis further declared that he "did not consider myself at liberty to set aside this North Carolina colonel because of his nativity in a sister state, when I had every reason to believe that he was recognized with pride by North Carolina generals and soldiers who had witnessed his bearing in battle."[38]

Long before Governor Vance and his allies abandoned their efforts to block Iverson's confirmation to brigadier general, the question of who would succeed McRae as colonel of the 5th North Carolina became a subject of intense controversy within the ranks of the regiment. Under normal circumstances, the next highest-ranking officer would fill the vacancy. In that case, the honor would fall upon Lt. Col. Peter J. Sinclair. A group of officers in the regiment, however, were bitterly opposed to Sinclair's elevation. The feud that erupted when they attempted to thwart his promotion to lead the 5th North Carolina further undermined Iverson's authority and plunged the entire regiment into chaos.

The 25-year-old Sinclair was born in Scotland and emigrated to Pennsylvania with his Presbyterian minister father. Educated as a lawyer, Sinclair moved to Fayetteville, North Carolina, in 1858 and began publishing a state-rights Democratic newspaper that strongly advocated secession. As the crisis with the North deepened, he suspended his newspaper and enlisted as a

---

37 Davis to Vance, April 16, 1863, in Mobley, *Papers of Vance*, Vol. 2, 117.

38 *OR* 51, pt. 2, 844.

Lieutenant Colonel Peter J. Sinclair of the 5th North Carolina was a leading secessionist and editor of a state-rights Democratic newspaper prior to joining the army in 1861.

North Carolina Regiments

private in the local militia. Sinclair noted that his friend Governor Ellis "soon after appointed me to raise a Company of soldiers for the war, which I accomplished before my state seceded & it was the first company in the state raised for the war."

In May of 1861, his company was assigned to the 5th North Carolina. Sinclair fought that July at First Manassas as captain of that company. After winning promotion to major, he was injured by a falling horse at Williamsburg during the withdrawal toward Richmond. Soon afterward, the Confederate War Department selected Sinclair to replace Lt. Col. John C. Badham, who had been mortally wounded in the same battle. Sinclair continued to serve as the regiment's lieutenant colonel during the Seven Days' fighting, where he suffered a severe wound at Gaines' Mill. His promotion would soon pit him in a power struggle with Capt. Thomas Miles Garrett and a group of his allies in the regiment.[39]

Unlike Sinclair, Garrett remained a moderate on secession until just prior to the outbreak of hostilities. He was born in 1830 and grew up in Bertie County, North Carolina. Following his graduation from the University of North Carolina, Garrett opened a law practice and became active in local Whig politics. Despite his initial opposition to leaving the Union, he entered the war as captain of a volunteer company that soon became part of the 5th North Carolina. After being wounded and captured during the battle of Williamsburg,

---

39 Krick, *Lee's Colonels*, 345-346, 40; Peter J. Sinclair to Jefferson Davis, Aug. 22, 1863, Compiled Service Record of Peter J. Sinclair, M 270, R 154, NA.

Garrett was held as a prisoner of war at Fortress Monroe, Virginia, until his release on August 5.[40]

By then, Henry Toole Clark, the former speaker of the state senate who had taken over as governor after Ellis died in office, was already battling Confederate authorities over the right to appoint field officers. While conceding that the War Department was authorized to select officers in most regiments, the governor claimed several exceptions to that policy. Clark argued that under existing regulations, he alone could appoint officers in the original 10 regiments of state troops, as well as a few others that had been mustered in for the war prior to passage of the Conscription Act.

The governor based his claim on the law that established the first regiments of state troops in May of 1861. Under that legislation, the soldiers in those regiments enlisted for a term of three years or the duration of the war. Both the company and field officers were appointed directly by the governor rather than by election. Unlike those in the former volunteer regiments, the men did not take part in the reorganization and elections mandated by the passage of the Conscription Act. Instead, the incumbent officers remained in place based on their earlier appointments by the governor.[41]

During a visit to Richmond in July of 1862, North Carolina Assistant Attorney General William B. Gullick met with Secretary of War George W. Randolph to discuss the issue of appointing officers in the regiments raised for the war. To his surprise, Randolph replied that the decision on promotions rested with his department alone. "I understood him to say that the President claimed the right to commission all the officers in the Confederate service," Gullick explained to Governor Clark. He further noted that one of the commissions that he had seen at the War Department was the promotion of Peter Sinclair to lieutenant colonel of the 5th North Carolina—which had not been authorized by the governor.[42]

---

40 Powell, *NC Biography*, 2:278-279; Krick, *Lee's Colonels*, 152; John Bowen Hamilton, ed., "Diary of Thomas Miles Garrett at The University of North Carolina, 1849," *North Carolina Historical Review*, 38 (1961), 63-64.

41 "Volunteers for the War," *Hillsborough Recorder*, July 10, 1861; Mast, *Photographic Record*, 25.

42 William B. Gullick to Henry T. Clark, July 23, 1862, Henry Toole Clark, Governor's Letter Book, NCOAH. Gullick reiterated that claim in another letter to the secretary of war during late August. For details, see William B. Gullick to George W. Randolph, Aug. 27, 1862, Letters Received, Confederate Secretary of War.

Despite that stance by the War Department, Governor Clark refused to back down from his position. In mid-August, North Carolina Adjt. Gen. James G. Martin notified Col. McRae that the governor was the only one who could make appointments and issue commissions in his regiment. "He is exercising this power in all the Regiments raised for the war, and he is not advised that any appointments or promotions in them have been made except through his office," Martin admonished. One effect, of course, would be to nullify the appointment of Sinclair as lieutenant colonel of the 5th North Carolina.[43]

After Vance succeeded Clark in early September, McRae urged him to fill the position of lieutenant colonel with his own choice as quickly as possible so there would be no room for confusion if he [McRae] resigned his commission. Vance responded with strong assurances that he intended to carry out his duties in selecting the new officers regardless of the opinion from the secretary of war. "I have the right to fill vacancies in regiments raised in this State (as was yours) originally for the war & I will take pleasure in commissioning such officers as you may recommend as qualified for positions now vacant in your regiment," he informed McRae less than two weeks after taking office.[44]

The governor received full backing for his position from Confederate Congressman William Nathan Harrell Smith, a prominent former Whig. According to Smith, the appointment of Sinclair by Confederate authorities clearly violated the precedent set early in the war when Governor Ellis selected William Dorsey Pender as colonel of the 6th North Carolina. "In my judgment the right of making these appointments of which that case is a precedent fully in point, belongs to the state of N. Carolina and is regulated by our laws," he declared in a letter to Vance.[45]

Even so, the issue of who could authorize promotions in those regiments remained unresolved. In October of 1862, the governor met privately with President Davis to discuss the matter. Davis agreed to turn the dispute over to the Confederate attorney general for a legal opinion. During the following month, Governor Vance openly complained to the General Assembly that he had "not yet had the pleasure of seeing that opinion, and now lay the matter

---

[43] James G. Martin to Duncan K. McRae, Aug. 20, 1862, Henry Toole Clark, Governor's Papers, NCOAH.

[44] McRae to Vance, Sept. 9, 1862, in Johnston, *Papers of Vance*, Vol. 1, 171; Zebulon B. Vance to Duncan K. McRae, Sept. 18, 1862, in *ibid.*, 196.

[45] William N. H. Smith to Zebulon B. Vance, Sept. 5, 1862, in *ibid.*, 168-170.

Captain Thomas M. Garrett led a major faction in the 5th North Carolina that aimed to undermine Alfred Iverson's position as brigadier general.

North Carolina Regiments

before you and recommend you take such steps as will preserve the rights and honor of the state."[46]

Sinclair, meanwhile, continued to serve with his regiment as the lieutenant colonel. Vance responded by repeating the claim that he alone could make such appointments. As late as January of 1863, Vance was still protesting to Secretary of War Seddon that his authority to fill vacancies in regiments originally raised for the war was being ignored. "Latterly commissions have issued from your office to several of these regiments, producing some confusion, and rendering many dissatisfied because the order prescribed by our law was not observed," Vance complained.[47]

With the legality of Peter Sinclair's commission wrapped in so much doubt and controversy, Capt. Garrett began pleading his case for promotion even before Governor Vance took office. Garrett showed no hesitation in using whatever connections he had with the new governor. After reminding the governor-elect that they had been college classmates, he reported that McRae and most of the other officers in the regiment strongly supported his promotion. "This endorsement was prompted I understand by the conviction among the officers of Maj. Sinclair's entire unfitness for the place of Col. of the Regt.," he informed Vance.

---

46 *OR* 2, series 4, 189.

47 Zebulon B. Vance to James A. Seddon, Jan. 22, 1863, in Mobley, *Papers of Vance*, Vol. 2, 22. For further details on the dispute, see James A. Seddon to Zebulon B. Vance, Jan. 30, 1863, in *ibid.*, 35 and Zebulon B. Vance to James A. Seddon, Feb. 4, 1863, in *ibid.*, 45.

Garrett further claimed that Governor Clark, who was a Democrat and an early proponent of secession, had deliberately blocked his promotion to major. "I think Gov. Clark has had his attention directed to me as a whig politician of decided opinions & feelings, and the withholding of this tribute to me, which my companions in arms were willing to see accorded to me, has been actuated by the same spirit of proscription which has governed his whole administration," Garrett informed the incoming governor. He pleaded most of all for Vance to "do justice to one who has labored zealously for the old whig cause and one whose friends in Bertie Co. in the late election were your friends."

Garrett blatantly pointed out that McRae's departure would throw open the position of colonel. "I understand that Col. McRae has again tendered his resignation, and that the officers of the regt. in a body will recommend me for promotion over Sinclair," Garrett continued. "Should this happen and their wishes are disregarded, they express a determination to resign and refuse to serve under him." Perhaps thinking he had crossed the line, he added that Vance should "not regard what I have written as immodest—I preferred to state the facts in regard to this matter myself, and with the spirit of frankness in which I know this will be received."[48]

On September 9, Garrett and 14 other officers from the 5th North Carolina moved directly against Sinclair by sending a scathing letter to the Confederate Senate protesting against his confirmation as lieutenant colonel. "He has on more than one occasion been guilty of conduct wholly unbecoming an officer and a gentleman," they claimed. The officers further charged that Sinclair was "greatly wanting in that knowledge of military matters, strength of judgment, self confidence and coolness which a man occupying that high and responsible position should possess."[49]

Garrett further strengthened his position by persuading Governor Vance's personal secretary, David A. Barnes, to support his selection as colonel of the 5th North Carolina. "Colonel McRae and the state have been treated with great

---

[48] Thomas M. Garrett to Zebulon B. Vance, Sept. 1, 1862, in Johnston, *Papers of Vance*, Vol. 1, 163.

[49] Thomas M. Garrett to Confederate Senate, Sept. 9, 1862, Sinclair Service Record. Just prior to the opening of the general assembly session in late October, Garrett removed a major obstacle to his promotion by resigning from the state senate seat he had won in a disputed election held while he was a prisoner of war. For details, see Thomas M. Garrett to the People of Bertie County, Oct. 20, 1862, *North Carolina Standard*, Nov. 7, 1862.

injustice in the matter of promotions," Barnes told him in late November. "Whenever the authorities here are notified officially of Col. McRae's resignation, I believe Governor Vance will give you the position." Barnes pledged to provide any help that he could in gaining the promotion for Garrett. "At all events, I shall not fail to use my influence to procure that result," he promised.[50]

Colonel Hamilton C. Jones Jr., who was a Whig politician and former officer in the 5th North Carolina, also threw his support behind Garrett by writing directly to Governor Vance. He openly predicted a disaster if Sinclair was selected as the regiment's new colonel. Noting that his former regiment was "fast being demoralized & ruined by faction among its officers," Jones argued that the outcome would "decide the question whether the regiment is to continue as it has heretofore been, one of the best in the service, or whether it is to become an unmanageable mob." He emphasized that Garrett "alone can restore the regiment to what it was six or eight months ago."[51]

As Garrett's allies maneuvered behind the scenes, tensions within the regiment erupted into open conflict in early December. While on picket duty, Garrett and several other officers took quarters in an unoccupied house. Sinclair ordered them to turn the rooms over to him. According to Sinclair, Garrett replied, "'I'll be damned if I do' or words to that effect." Sinclair responded by calling in "a guard of 50 men" to remove the rebellious officers from the house by force. Once that was accomplished, he placed them all under arrest and filed formal charges against Garrett and eight other officers.

The battle between the two factions placed Alfred Iverson in a difficult situation. He initially sent the charges and specifications forward with a note that he "was not disposed to interfere with discipline and arrests enforced by officers commanding regiments." At the same time, Iverson remained wary that he would be accused of favoring Sinclair. With Governor Vance so deeply invested in supporting Garrett, the general had little to gain from a direct confrontation with the officers in the regiment over the issue of who would ultimately succeed McRae.

---

50 David A. Barnes to Thomas M. Garrett, Nov. 22, 1862, Compiled Service Record of Thomas M. Garrett, M 270 R148, NA. Barnes reiterated his full support for Garrett in another letter written only two weeks later. For details, see David A. Barnes to Thomas M. Garrett, Dec. 9, 1862, *ibid.*

51 Hamilton C. Jones Jr. to Zebulon B. Vance, Dec. 18, 1862, in Johnston, *Papers of Vance*, Vol. 1, 440-441.

The arrested officers filed a letter of protest against being held in confinement while awaiting trial. Their move provided Iverson with the perfect opportunity to signal his neutrality. When Sinclair refused to forward the letter because of its "insulting tenor," Iverson brusquely informed him that "it is not the custom of service to confine officers to strict limits when causes are to come before a court martial." Iverson's unwillingness to take sides allowed the infighting to continue unabated throughout the rest of the month. While not under arrest himself, Capt. Isaac E. Pearce of the 5th North Carolina acknowledged to his sister that Christmas in their camp passed that year with "no demonstration of hilarity at all."

Although Sinclair described the incident with Garrett and the other officers as "an open example of rebellion and insubordination," higher command had no inclination to back him, in part because the events that precipitated the original showdown hardly seemed worthy of formal charges. At the least, they should have been dismissed. D. H. Hill, in particular, expressed frustration with both sides in the dispute. "[T]he chief cause of complaint," wrote the division leader, "arises from the occupancy of houses which neither the officer bringing charges nor the accused should have occupied."

Worst still for Iverson was the growing realization among the top generals in the army that he had lost control of the situation. Through his lack of leadership, a minor dispute had escalated into a feud that now threatened to tear the regiment apart. Hill's final comments before sending the matter up the chain of command could hardly have come as good news for Iverson or anyone else involved. "The enclosed papers show a deplorable state of discipline in the regt. to which the attention of Gen. Jackson is particularly called," was how Hill's terse endorsement to the complaint was phrased. Hill was right. The regiment was tearing itself apart.[52]

The case was finally resolved on January 6, when Hill dismissed all the charges and recommended Capt. Garrett to fill the vacancy for colonel in McRae's stead. Sinclair immediately resigned and called for a court of inquiry to clear his name. "After all the service I have rendered my country, I have been subjected to the highest indignity that could possibly be offered a soldier and a gentleman," he wrote to Adjt. Gen. Cooper. Sinclair complained most of all that

---

52 Peter J. Sinclair to Alfred Iverson Jr., Dec. 9, 1862, Garrett Service Record; Thomas M. Garrett to Alfred Iverson Jr., Dec. 9, 1862, *ibid.*; Isaac Pearce to Dear Sister, Dec. 29, 1862, Pearce Papers.

"a junior captain has been recommended over me to fill the position of Col. of the regt." He insisted that "every feeling of self respect, every consideration of honor demands that I tender my resignation."[53]

Little more than a month later, Sinclair sent a strong letter of protest to Governor Vance, in which he claimed that "injustice at the hands of my own state" had forced his resignation. He specifically charged that Garrett had used his influence with Vance and D. H. Hill to spread lies about his political views and military capabilities. "Before McRae's resignation had been accepted, Capt Garrett wrote to Gov Vance reminding him of the fact that they were classmates in college, personal and political friends in after life, that I was northern man and a bitter political opponent of the gov., that he (Garrett) therefore deserved more at Gov. V's hand than did Sinclair," wrote Sinclair.

Sinclair took great pains to deny the allegations that had been leveled against him. "As to the truth of what Garrett wrote, it is a lie that I am or ever was a northern man," he declared. "As to being a political opponent of Gov. V., I must say that if to have been a Democrat and an original secessionist is a shame, then indeed do I glory in my shame!" Sinclair further claimed that he took no part in working against Vance's election within the regiment. "As to have opposed Gov. Vance in the past election," continued Sinclair, "permit me to say, that at the time my regiment passed such an overwhelming vote for Johnston I was at home wounded, and Col. McRae was with the Regt."[54]

Despite Sinclair's vehement complaints, Garrett received his promotion to colonel of the 5th North Carolina on January 16. By then, senior Capt. Brookfield and four other officers in the regiment had already attempted to resign in open sympathy with Sinclair. "Their resignations were not accepted but the regiment will never be at peace while they are compelled to service in it," Sinclair insisted in his letter to Vance. He further pointed out to the governor that all those officers had "expressed their preference to go in the ranks with me rather than remain under Garrett."[55]

All five officers argued in their letters of resignation that Garrett's promotion violated the regulations established by the state and had plunged the regiment into disarray. "Our Regt has been in a state of disorganization for

---

53 Peter J. Sinclair to Samuel Cooper, Dec. 18, 1862, Sinclair Service Record.

54 Peter J. Sinclair to Zebulon B. Vance, Feb. 3, 1863, Vance Governor's Papers.

55 *Ibid.*

some time by reason of a clique of officers combining for the purpose of effecting the promotion of junior over senior," Capt. Brookfield complained to Cooper in Richmond. "That combination is about to accomplish its objective." In another letter, Capt. Elijah C. Cuthbert insisted that it was "the duty of every officer who has opposed the promotion of Captain Garrett as bitterly, as earnestly, and as conscientiously as I have to resign their positions."[56]

Soon afterward, Brookfield was again passed over to fill the newly created vacancy for lieutenant colonel in favor of Capt. John W. Lea. The 24-year-old Lea was a former cadet at West Point, where he became a close friend of George Armstrong Custer's. While being held as a prisoner at Williamsburg, Lea married one of the women who had helped tend the wounds he received during the fighting there in early May of 1862. The guests at his wedding included his old friend Custer, who stood in as best man. Captain William J. Hill, who also outranked Lea, readily agreed to waive his right of promotion to lieutenant colonel and accepted an appointment as the new major in the regiment.[57]

Brookfield placed the blame for that insult directly on the influence of Garrett and his supporters in the regiment. "My rank has been ignored and two Capts., my Jr., have been promoted to fill them," Brookfield complained in a letter of protest to Governor Vance. "Such a proceeding, entirely at variance with established rule, astonishes me and I confess has chafed harshly upon my feelings." Brookfield insisted that "nearly half of our officers are dissatisfied" as a result of the feud and that "the knowledge of those facts make me feel more keenly the gross outrage done me."[58]

---

56 Jacob Brookfield to Samuel Cooper, Dec. 18, 1862, Letters Received, Confederate Adjutant and Inspector General's Office, NA; Elijah C. Cuthbert to Samuel Cooper, Dec. 18, 1862, *ibid.*; Benjamin Robinson to Samuel Cooper, Dec. 18, 1862, *ibid.*; William T. Anderson to Samuel Cooper, Dec. 18, 1862, *ibid.*; David H. Ray to Samuel Cooper, Dec. 18, 1862, *ibid.*

57 Krick, *Lee's Colonels*, 232, 193; Morris Schaff, *The Spirit of Old West Point, 1858-1862* (Boston: Houghton Mifflin, 1907), 179-182; Carol Kettenburg Dubbs, *Defend This Old Town: Williamsburg During the Civil War* (Baton Rouge: Louisiana State University Press, 2002), 234; John Peter Beckendorf, "The Mystery of Wallace's Horse and Saddle," *North South Trader's Civil War*, 31 (2005), 53-55. Hill was a close ally of McRae and Garrett. For details on his appointment, see "Magnanimous Conduct," *Greensborough Patriot*, Feb. 12, 1863.

58 Brookfield to Vance, Feb. 19, 1863, Vance Governor's Papers. Citing failing health and his "unpleasant position" in the regiment, Brookfield was eventually reduced to negotiating a deal with Garrett that would have allowed him to transfer to another unit in exchange for supporting Col. McRae's brother as his successor. For details, see Jacob Brookfield to John C. McRae, March 26, 1863, McRae Papers and Haywood to McRae, March 31, 1863, *ibid.*

None of this deterred Garrett and his allies from establishing virtually complete control of the regiment. One of Garrett's supporters made it perfectly clear in a letter to a statewide religious newspaper during the late spring of 1863 that their new colonel was someone to be reckoned with. "As he jumped many seniors in this leap, his appointment was very unsatisfactory to many of the regiment," the supporter declared. He noted, however, that Garrett soon "won upon the hearts of his bitterest enemies by his impartial management; and all vie with each other now to do him honor."

The letter also gave every indication that Garrett's ambitions extended far beyond his own regiment. With Governor Vance on his side, he appeared to have his gaze firmly focused on attaining a promotion to brigadier general. In what amounted to a veiled threat, his supporter took direct aim at Iverson by expressing his astonishment that "so many North Carolina Brigades are commanded by men from other States, while we have such men as Col. Garrett among our own officers—men who would honor the country and do credit to the State in such position."[59]

The public campaign aimed at undermining Iverson's position in the brigade continued well into the summer of 1863. One soldier openly complained to a major newspaper in Raleigh about the large number of officers from other states serving in high positions. After heaping praise on Garrett and several other Tar Heel officers from the brigade, he turned his attention to Iverson: "I think it would, perhaps, be better for Georgia Brigadiers to command Georgia troops, and for North Carolina troops to be commanded by a North Carolinian, when one can be found who is competent, and I think I have shown that we have them in plenty in the brigade."[60]

---

[59] Centurion to Mr. Editor, May 27, 1863, *North Carolina Presbyterian*, June 13, 1863.

[60] A Private to W. W. Holden, May 26, 1863, *North Carolina Standard*, June 2, 1863.

CHAPTER FOUR

There is Quite a Stir in Our Regiment

For Alfred Iverson, the fight raging in the 20th North Carolina over who would succeed him as colonel was even more upsetting than the troubles with Duncan McRae.

The problems began soon after Iverson's promotion. The situation escalated into an open feud in early December when he nominated Lt. Col. William S. Devane from the 61st North Carolina to fill the vacancy in the 20th regiment. A friend of Iverson's from early in the war, Devane accepted the chance to join the Army of Northern Virginia rather than remain on boring garrison duty with his regiment as part of the defense forces around Wilmington.

The 34-year-old William Devane had served as an attorney in Sampson County, North Carolina, before enlisting in the army as a private. His company was assigned initially to the 20th North Carolina at Fort Johnston. Following the selection of Capt. Franklin Faison as its lieutenant colonel in July of 1861, Devane ran as a candidate for the vacant position of captain against Lt. James C. Holmes. The divisive election led quickly to a significant rift within the ranks of the company. "There were strong feelings on both sides in the company," one veteran recalled. "The Devane men, of who I was one, said we would not serve under Holmes." The regimental command dispute grew to such contentious proportions that Governor Ellis was forced to split the factions into two companies.¹

Following his election as captain, Devane and the men from his newly formed company were transferred out of the regiment and sent to nearby Fort Caswell. In August of 1862, the company became part of the 61st North Carolina. Devane continued to serve as captain until he was promoted to lieutenant colonel on September 5, 1862. From the time of its formation, the regiment remained on duty in North Carolina, first around Goldsboro and later around Wilmington. The men experienced their only fighting during a minor battle at Kinston, North Carolina, on December 13, 1862.²

The selection of Devane to succeed Iverson became a subject of controversy from the moment it was announced. Although his brother, Capt. Duncan J. Devane, commanded a company in the 20th North Carolina, the officers of the regiment were nearly unanimous in opposing his appointment. Major Nelson Slough instead emerged as their choice for colonel after Lt. Col. W. H. Toon declined to seek the position and resigned due to a "congestive chill." According to

Lieutenant Colonel Nelson Slough of the 20th North Carolina served as an officer in the Mexican War and was acknowledged as one of the bravest men in the regiment.

North Carolina Museum of History

---

1 Sprunt, *Chronicles of Cape Fear*, 355. Captain James Holmes' portion of the company remained for a time as part of the 20th North Carolina and was assigned to duty at Fort Caswell. Soon afterward, the company transferred permanently to the 30th North Carolina. For more details, see "The Sampson Rangers, Company A. 30th N.C.R," *Fayetteville Observer*, April 4, 1864.

2 N. A. Ramsey, "Sixty-First Regiment," included in Clark, *NC Regiments*, 3:509; Krick, *Lee's Colonels*, 119.

Capt. John S. Brooks, the major obstacle to his promotion was that "Genl Iverson now and all ways did hate Major Slough."[3]

Slough was 40 years old at the time. He served as a lieutenant in Company C of the 1st North Carolina Regiment of Foot Soldiers during the Mexican War. The men spent most of their time in Mexico serving under Maj. Gen. Zachery Taylor in the area south of the Rio Grande, near the villages of Camargo and Saltillo. Slough became involved in a major controversy when he joined several other officers in calling for the resignation of their commander, Lt. Col. Robert T. Paine. The regiment took no part in any fighting but suffered the death of 38 men from fever after they drank tainted water. Many others died or were rendered unfit for duty from various other diseases.[4]

Following the Mexican War, Slough held the position as Clerk of the Courts in Cabarrus County. While serving an arrest warrant, he was severely wounded in his leg, the effects of which remained "evident in his halting step." When his home state left the Union, Slough joined the 20th North Carolina as a captain of a company from that county and was promoted to the rank of major a little more than one year later. He commanded temporarily the 20th North Carolina during the fierce fighting at Malvern Hill in early July of 1862. "A braver man never lived," one soldier from the regiment remarked in a letter to a Wilmington newspaper. "This has been demonstrated, and is acknowledged by all."[5]

---

3   Krick, *Lee's Colonels*, 374; Toon, "Twentieth Regiment," in Clark, *NC Regiments*, 2:126; John S. Brooks to Dear Brother, Jan. 4, 1863, Brooks letters.

4   William Hugh Roberts, *Mexican War Veterans: A Complete Roster of the Regular and Volunteer Troops in the War Between the United States and Mexico, from 1846 to 1848* (Washington: Brentano's, 1887), 66; Helen Arthur-Cornett, "Cabarrus Troops in the Mexican War," *Charlotte Observer*, Aug. 21, 2005; James K. Polk, "Message of the President of the United States (July 12, 1848), in answer to a resolution of the Senate, calling for the proceedings of the court of inquiry convened at Saltillo, Mexico, January 12, 1848, for the purpose of obtaining full information relative to an alleged mutiny at Buena Vista, about the 15th August, 1847," 192-193, Americas Collection, Woodson Research Center, Fondren Library, Rice University, Houston, Texas. For additional details on their service in Mexico, see "Our Regiment Complete," *Raleigh Register and North Carolina Gazette*, Jan. 19, 1847; "Our Army Correspondence," *Raleigh Register and North Carolina Gazette*, June 4, 1847; "Our Army Correspondence," *Raleigh Semi-Weekly Register*, June 18, 1847; and "Death of Capt. Martin Shive," *Charlotte Journal*, Sept. 30, 1847.

5   Krick, *Lee's Colonels*, 348; "XX" to the Editors, March 24, 1863, *Wilmington Journal*, April 2, 1863. Slough received the wound to his leg in January of 1855. For a brief account of the incident, see Carolyn Gibbons, "Abstracts from Fayetteville Observer 1855," online at www.ncgenweb.us/richmond/1855newsabstracts.html. At least one soldier from his regiment mistakenly assumed that his limp resulted from a wound in the Mexican War.

Despite the strong opposition from the company officers, Iverson displayed his usual stubbornness by moving ahead with his plans for Devane to take over command of the regiment. "The major of the Regiment is a brave man but I do not think him qualified to fill and discharge the important duties of a colonel," he wrote to Adj. Gen. Cooper during mid-December. "Nor do I know of an officer in the Regiment who can properly discharge those duties." Iverson further argued that "some of them may in time become able and competent I do not doubt but consulting solely the good of the service, I am constrained to object to the appointment of any one of them to the position of Col."

He insisted that the appointment of Devane by President Davis represented the only possible solution to the problems in the regiment. "I know this gentlemen to be a man of ability, a good officer and unobjectionable in every respect," Iverson remarked. "He is from the state of North Carolina and was at one time in the 20th Regt as Captain." He emphasized that "the service will not suffer in his hands, and I believe that he will pass any board of examination that may be called." Iverson called on the adjutant general to endorse the appointment "by forwarding this letter with your own remarks."[6]

Once word spread that Iverson had submitted Devane's nomination to the War Department in Richmond, his opponents in the regiment immediately moved to thwart the plan. Captain Brooks reported to his brother that Iverson had improperly recommended Devane to the president for appointment as the new commander of the 20th North Carolina. He explained that, when the officers of the regiment found out about it, they submitted a protest to Cooper "against Genl Iverson's recommendation and he refused to forward it."

Rather than passing their list of complaints up the chain of command, Iverson returned it with his own comments. He brusquely informed Maj. Slough and the other officers that such a protest "was not admissible" under any circumstances. He refused to budge from his position unless they toned down their language considerably. Iverson added, however, that "when the officers shall send a respectful communication through these Headqrtrs it will be forwarded with great pleasure." Brooks noted that the officers responded by sending the letter "over hiss head."[7]

---

6 Alfred Iverson Jr. to Samuel Cooper, Dec. 18, 1862, Letters Received, Confederate Adjutant and Inspector General's Office.

7 Brooks to Brother, Jan. 4, 1863, Brooks Letters.

The officers from the regiment declared in the letter that they were "not willing to submit to a <u>one man power</u>." Most of all, they steadfastly objected to Iverson's assertion that, because Lt. Col. Toon had declined promotion, no officer of lower rank in the regiment could be promoted. "Sir this Reg't has been through a number of hard fought battles and through some of them without the assistance of Col now Gen Iverson, and we cannot tamely submit to the reflections, the <u>insult</u> cast upon the officers of this Regiment," they argued. "We say we <u>cannot</u>. Nay, we <u>will not</u>."

They forcefully spelled out their case for reversing Iverson's decision. The officers insisted that the only fair way to select a new colonel was through a board of examination. "Sir, give us justice," they pleaded. "It is all we ask. If the officers at the head of the list are incompetent go through the whole line and if all are found to be incompetent their will be time enough to make an appointment outside of the regiment." The extent of their disapproval was obvious from the fact that the document had been signed by all but four of the 30 officers present in the regiment.[8]

The reaction from Iverson was not long in coming. On December 27, he retaliated by arresting all those whose names appeared on the protest. "At this time, there is quite a stir in our Regt," Lt. Oliver Mercer told his father. "26 officers under arrest and I am one of the No." Brooks reported to his brother that Asst. Adj. Gen. Don Halsey came "over to the regiment and arrested all the officers that sign the protest which was 26 of us." He added that "we protested against having a Col appointed over us who was not in our Regiment and upon this he arrested us."

Brooks expressed outrage that "officers of this Regt who have fought through a number of hard fought Battles and took scars upon there bodys that Yankee musket balls have placed upon them" were passed over for promotion in favor of an outsider. Most of all, Brooks argued that it was a shame "for Genl Iverson to tell the President of the Confederate States that there was no officer in the Regt fit to be promoted to the position of Col when there is the brave old Nelson Slough who fought through the Mexican war as an officer and has commanded this Regt in the hard fight at Malvern Hill."

---

8 Officers of the 20th North Carolina to Samuel Cooper, Dec. 18, 1862, Letters Received, Confederate Adjutant and Inspector General's Office, underlined as in original; Brooks to Brother, Jan. 4, 1863, Brooks Letters.

The officers based their protest on the specific grounds that Iverson had violated their rights by nominating Devane. "The vacancy caused by Ivenson's promotion, he (Ivenson) wanted to fill by appointment, which is contrary to law," Lt. Mercer explained. "And we all protested against it, feeling that our self and Regt'l pride had not all vanished, so Gen. I-n has arrested us all and preferred charges against us and will court martial us. Everybody looks upon us as doing right and honorable." He pointed out that "there were only a few officers who did not sign the document."

Captain Brooks remained just as adamant about his opposition to their brigade commander. Brooks stated defiantly that he was "unwilling to have the rights that congress had gave us taken away to please Genl. Alfred Iverson." In a letter to his parents, the captain pledged that "if the same thing was to be done tomorrow morning we would do it with grate pleasure." Although confined to quarters, the officers of the 20th North Carolina continued defying Iverson. "Quite a jolly crowd," was how Mercer described the mood in a letter home. "We have a big time. Nothing to do. Ivenson is very unpopular with the Brigade already."[9]

In a further complication for Iverson, the officers persuaded two of the most prominent lawyers in the state—Col. William P. Bynum from the 2nd North Carolina and Col. Alfred M. Scales from the 13th North Carolina—to join Capt. William J. Stanley from their own regiment as defense counsels. Bynum had graduated from Davidson College in 1842 and built a thriving law practice in Lincoln County. Scales was a graduate of the University of North Carolina and spent several years as the state solicitor in Rockingham County. He later turned to politics, serving in the North Carolina General Assembly and in the U.S. Congress from 1857 to 1859.[10]

With their assistance, the officers grew even more confident that they could successfully resist Iverson's appointment of an outsider as the new commander of the regiment. Almost to a man, they remained defiant and ready to take on their former regimental commander. "Don't be uneasy about us," Lt. Mercer declared in a letter to his family. "We have good counsel and will come out right." Brooks told his father that "you and mother may be well assured that our

---

9 Oliver E. Mercer to Dear Father, Dec. 30, 1862, in Wyatt, *The Reeves, Mercer, Newkirk Families*, 265; Brooks to Brother, Jan. 4, 1863; John S. Brooks to Dear Parents, January 4, 1863, Brooks Letters.

10 Powell, *NC Biography*, 1:295; Krick, *Lee's Colonels*, 78; Warner, *Generals in Gray*, 268-269.

cases are in good hands for Scals and Biham is as smart as [the] Gen or J. Davis."[11]

On December 30, Iverson notified Cooper in Richmond that he had decided to withdraw Devane's nomination. "Lieut Col Devane will have too much delicacy to accept a position when there is so much opposition to him," he admitted. Nevertheless, he continued to blame his subordinates for all the problems. "The officers of the Regiment seem to have entirely misapprehended my motives in making the recommendation and to believe that instead of trying to do the Regiment a service, I have endeavored to do it injury," he insisted. Iverson noted that he had "arrested all the officers concerned in the protest for a grave military offence that of combination to pass censure upon my official actions."[12]

Although Devane's appointment was no longer an issue, Iverson demonstrated his poor judgment by waiting almost one month before releasing the officers from arrest. "We are free from them again and got out 'honorably,'" Mercer informed his sister on January 29. Major Slough gleefully told a friend on the same day that "General Iverson has withdrawn the charges against the officers of this regiment, including myself." Slough and Brooks then agreed to a compromise in which they waived their rights of seniority in favor of Capt. Thomas F. Toon, the half brother of their former lieutenant colonel.[13]

In an apparent act of petty retaliation, however, Confederate authorities soon afterward turned down Col. Bynum's application to leave his regiment so that he could take the post of solicitor in his home judicial district. The dispute remained unresolved until Governor Vance complained directly to Secretary of War Seddon in late February. "I beg leave to protest against this disrespect towards the civil government of N.C.," he declared. The governor went on to note that "common courtesy, it seems to me, requires that his resignation should be accepted, and I am confident that upon a consideration of the whole

---

11 Mercer to Father, Dec. 30, 1862, in Wyatt, *The Reeves, Mercer, Newkirk Families*, 265; Brooks to Parrents, January 4, 1863, Brooks Letters.

12 Alfred Iverson Jr. to Samuel Cooper, Dec. 30, 1862, Letters Received, Confederate Adjutant and Inspector General's Office.

13 Oliver E. Mercer to Dear Sister, Jan. 29, 1863, in Wyatt, *The Reeves, Mercer, Newkirk Families*, 267; Nelson Slough to S. J. Alexander, Jan. 29, 1863, Compiled Service Record of Nelson Slough, M 270, R 276, NA.

Captain Thomas F. Toon was barely into his 20s when he won promotion as colonel of the 20th North Carolina.

North Carolina Office of Archives and History

matter it will be done at once." Even then, the government did not formally approve Bynum's resignation until the 21st of March.[14]

Implementation of the deal went much more smoothly for Toon who was promoted to colonel on February 26 after passing the board of examination. Although barely into his 20s, he had already proven to be an outstanding officer. Toon was born and raised in Columbus County, North Carolina. He entered the army from Wake Forest College, where he was finishing his senior year. After helping to raise a volunteer company that became part of the 20th North Carolina, he returned to the school just long enough to earn his degree. Toon served with distinction as captain of the company in several major battles, including Gaines' Mill and the Maryland Campaign.[15]

The men from the ranks of the 20th North Carolina greeted his appointment as colonel with open enthusiasm. "He is quite young, being only 22 years, but entire satisfaction with him prevails," one man in the regiment commented to the major newspaper in Wilmington at the time of his promotion. "We entertain the best hopes that he will give a good account of himself." Another private in the brigade reported to a Raleigh newspaper that

---

14 Zebulon B. Vance to James A. Seddon, Feb. 27, 1863, in Mobley, *Papers of Vance*, Vol. 2, 69-70; Powell, *NC Biography*, 1:295.

15 Warner, *Generals in Gray*, 89.

he "is a gallant young officer, and impresses every one with the conviction that he is destined to become one of our best officers."[16]

In another major turn of events, Slough and Brooks also appeared before the board to be examined for the ranks of lieutenant colonel and major, respectively. Although Slough passed the examination, Capt. Brooks continued to complain about the process. "I was examined with Col Toon," he told his sister. "I miss one or two more questions than he did." Despite those results, the outcome was far from what he had hoped. "As for major he knows more than the rascal on the board does and they only pass him for Lt Col which is a disgrace to the confederacy," he grumbled.

Captain Brooks grew even angrier when "the diabolical Board" decided that he was unfit for promotion to major. Threatening to resign, he blamed the outcome directly on the influence of their commanding general. Brooks openly charged that "no one officer passes that... Genl. Iverson dont want to pass." In a calmer moment, the 22-year-old captain admitted that "sometimes I think it was on the account of my age & then think Genl Iverson was the cause." When he submitted his resignation in early March, the request was immediately turned down. Colonel Robert H. Chilton, inspector general on Lee's staff, stated in his endorsement on the letter that it had been rejected because there was "no reason for resignation appended or surgeon's certificate of disability."[17]

After one last attempt to convince the board of his qualifications, Brooks finally received his coveted promotion to major on May 16. "Capt. now Maj. Brooks went before the board yesterday and passed and I expect promotion now, but I will let you know when it takes place," Lt. Mercer told his sister. "It may be now, the Col. told me to add another bar to my coat and take the company as Capt. but you need not address as such yet." Little more than a week later, he reported to his father that his promotion to captain also had been confirmed. "My qualifications have not been disputed, therefore I don't go before the board for examination," Mercer said.[18]

---

16 Iverson's Brigade, Special Order No. 47, Feb. 26, 1863, Thomas F. Toon Papers, NCOAH; "XX" to the Editors, March 24, 1863, *Wilmington Journal*, April 2, 1863; A Private to William W. Holden, May 26, 1863, *North Carolina Standard*, June 2, 1863.

17 John S. Brooks to Dear Sister, March 1, 1863, Brooks Letters; John S. Brooks to Dear Parrents & Sister M, March 8, 1863, *ibid.*; John S. Brooks, Letter of Resignation, March 10, 1863, *ibid.*

18 Oliver E. Mercer to Dear Sister, May 17, 1863, in Wyatt, *The Reeves, Mercer, Newkirk Families*, 270; Oliver E. Mercer to Dear Father, May 26, 1863, in *ibid.*, 271.

Most embarrassing of all for Iverson was another incident that involved Pvt. Nathan Sneed from the 20th North Carolina. Following Sharpsburg, Sneed's name was advertised as a deserter in a Raleigh newspaper. Such ads had become commonplace as desertion continued to escalate in the North Carolina regiments during the fall of 1862. The ads often branded the men as cowards and offered a reward for their capture. In some cases, however, the soldiers were incorrectly identified as deserters, leading to some embarrassing moments for their friends and families back home.

At the age of 21, Pvt. Sneed left the state university to enlist in the 20th North Carolina. Family friends described him as a "young man of irreproachable character" and "refined" morals. Despite his university education, he decided to enter military service as an enlisted man. "Although his education, native intellect, sterling integrity of purpose, and highly respectable family connections justly entitled him to a position in the Regiment, and I have no doubt he could have obtained a position had he sought it, but he preferred to go as a private," one family friend remarked.

The problem in this instance was that Pvt. Sneed had not deserted. He had, in fact, been killed in action during the fierce fighting at Sharpsburg in September of 1862. His family reacted almost immediately by launching a major campaign to clear his name from any wrongdoing. "And now for his name to be published as a deserter, is not only the grossest injustice to the gallant dead, but must be humiliating, in the highest degree, to his family connections, especially to his brothers and sisters," the friend complained to the newspaper that had published the advertisement.[19]

Some of the students at the University of North Carolina responded to the incident by drafting a resolution of protest. Private Sneed's brother also wrote a long letter of complaint to Iverson, who had commanded the regiment at Sharpsburg. In it, he laid out the facts of the matter as he knew them. "It is very painful and humiliating to the family to see his name advertised as a deserter, knowing that he was killed," he explained. "His comrades reported to me that he was mortally wounded and left on the field." He noted that his brother "has never been heard from since."[20]

---

[19] L. Eldridge to the Editor, Feb. 10, 1863, *North Carolina Weekly Standard*, Feb. 18, 1863; University of North Carolina Alumni Association, *Alumni History of the University of North Carolina* (Durham, NC: Christian and King, 1924), 579.

[20] E. D. Sneed to Alfred Iverson Jr., Jan. 16, 1863, *North Carolina Standard*, Feb. 20, 1863.

Iverson immediately directed Maj. Slough to conduct a full investigation of the matter. The lieutenant commanding Sneed's former company quickly confirmed that the young man had indeed died during the fighting at Sharpsburg. In a letter to Sneed's brother, Iverson explained that, after Sharpsburg, the captain of each company in the regiment had been required to forward a list of all men who were absent without leave. A consolidated list from the brigade was then sent to the governor and the sheriff of each county to alert them about potential deserters who might be hiding in the state.

He pointed out that all such reports were prepared for use by the civil authorities only. "The lists were not intended for publication, nor have I ever seen them in print or known of their being printed," Iverson claimed in his response that was published in the newspaper. "The names amounted to considerably over a thousand from the brigade." Most important, Iverson denied any direct role in the mistake and the resulting false report printed in the newspaper. He insisted that "errors made by Captains could not, of course, be discovered at this office."

Iverson once again showed that his stubbornness could sometimes extend beyond all reason. While conceding that Pvt. Sneed had been incorrectly listed as a deserter, Iverson placed all the blame for the error on his subordinates. "It is very much to be regretted that, through the carelessness of his company commander, his name should have been sent forward on the list of absentees," he told Sneed's brother. Although refusing to take any responsibility, Iverson was left little choice other than to admit that a major injustice had been done. "And, you are at liberty to use this letter in any way you think proper to refute the charge of his having deserted," he declared.[21]

As the controversies in the 20th North Carolina continued to simmer into the late spring, Iverson was having no better luck dealing with another conflict over promotions in the 12th North Carolina. The problems began in late 1862 when both Col. Benjamin O. Wade and Lt. Col. Thomas L. Jones resigned their positions, leaving the regiment desperately short on experienced officers. The only remaining field officer was Maj. David P. Rowe, who was often absent from duty due to the lingering effects of a wound he received at Gaines' Mill and was not considered qualified for promotion.

Although Lt. Col. Jones departed for apparent medical reasons, Col. Wade had resigned over a threat by Iverson to court martial him on the petty matter of

21 Alfred Iverson Jr. to E. D. Sneed, April 9, 1863, *North Carolina Standard*, May 26, 1863.

allowing two substitutes to join the regiment during a single month, which was contrary to regulations. "Maj. Gen. D. H. Hill suggested to me to require that Col Wade should resign on account of incompetency," Iverson explained. "I sent his note to Col Wade upon which many promises of amendment were made." He claimed that "shortly after however so gross a violation of law was committed that I was compelled to offer Col Wade the alternative of resignation or having charges preferred against him."[22]

One of Wade's friends reported that his resignation on December 18 came only after he was "put under arrest and informed that he would be called before a court martial" on those charges. "Indignant and mortified under what he considered unjust censure, he resigned his commission in a moment of vexation to the regret of his regiment and his countrymen at home," his friend complained to Cooper. He further argued that Wade's action resulted directly from "the impulse of a sensitive and honorable heart smarting under the (supposed) wrongful imputation of misconduct and threatened with what he believed to be unwarranted punishment."[23]

The resulting turmoil from Wade's departure only worsened the decline in discipline that had been going on in the regiment for several months. "We have beheld for some time the rapidly increasing demoralization of the Reg. and the growing lack of confidence in us of our general," one of the enlisted men wrote to Iverson soon after Wade resigned. "At one time holding the proud place of 'the finest and best disciplined Reg. from our state' we have become a byword for disorder and lack of discipline." He insisted that "we cannot but attribute it, in a great measure, to the character of many of the officers of the Regt."[24]

Even Col. Duncan McRae from the 5th North Carolina had attempted to influence the situation. At one point, he urged D. H. Hill to consider replacing Wade with Capt. John W. Lea from the 5th North Carolina. "He is both gallant and brave—and his conduct in the march and on the battle field has been most exemplary," McRae declared in his letter of recommendation. "The interest of the Regt. could not be better served than by his selection." This plan initially

---

22 Krick, *Lee's Colonels*, 217, 327, 382; Richard S. F. Peete to Robert E. Lee, Oct. 11, 1862, Compiled Service Record of Thomas L. Jones, M 270, R 204, NA; Benjamin O. Wade to Samuel Cooper, Dec. 18, 1862, Compiled Service Record of Benjamin O. Wade, M 270 R 209, NA; Alfred Iverson Jr. to Henry E. Coleman, Aug. 26, 1863, Letters Received, Confederate Adjutant and General's Office.

23 R. C. Pritchard to James A. Seddon, April 7, 1863, Wade Service Record.

24 A. Tew to Alfred Iverson Jr., Jan. 1, 1863, John T. Gregory Papers, NCOAH.

won approval from Hill, who described Col. Wade in his endorsement as "remarkably inefficient."²⁵

The company officers, however, staked out their own position by recommending to Iverson that Lt. Col. Thomas Ruffin Jr. from the 13th North Carolina be appointed as their colonel. The regiment's senior captains, Robert W. Alston and William S. Davis, agreed to waive their rank in Ruffin's favor during a hastily called meeting in mid-December. As part of the deal for Ruffin's promotion, the majority of the officers at the meeting reluctantly consented to accept Iverson's favorite, Capt. Henry Eaton Coleman, as the regiment's new lieutenant colonel. Although both of the men nominated for promotion were already well known in the regiment, their reputations could hardly have differed more.²⁶

Ruffin was the son of the former chief justice of the State Supreme Court and a first cousin of Col. McRae. A graduate of the University of North Carolina, he practiced law and served in the state legislature prior to the war. Although he was a Democrat and a Breckinridge supporter, he held moderate views on secession. He entered the army as a captain, first in the 13th North Carolina and later in the 6th North Carolina. In the spring of 1862, he returned to his old regiment as the lieutenant colonel. He earned widespread respect for his fighting abilities during the time that the 13th North Carolina served in Garland's Brigade. Ruffin's open contempt for his cousin remained another point in his favor as far as many of the men in the 12th North Carolina were concerned.²⁷

The officers also remembered Coleman as a former company commander in the 12th North Carolina. Coleman was born in 1837 and grew up on a large estate in Halifax County, Virginia. He briefly attended Virginia Military Institute before being dismissed in 1852 for exceeding the allowable number of demerits. After graduating from William and Mary College, he worked as a civil engineer and supervised his family's properties in Virginia and North Carolina. In 1858, Coleman purchased a plantation near the Virginia border in Granville County, North Carolina. He entered military service from that county as captain of a

---

25 Duncan K. McRae to D. H. Hill, Nov. 15, 1862, Letters Received, Confederate Adjutant and Inspector General's Office.

26 Iverson Jr. to Coleman, Aug. 26, 1863, *ibid.*

27 Krick, *Lee's Colonels*, 328.

volunteer Tar Heel company that had been largely raised and equipped by his uncle.[28]

Coleman soon became widely disliked by the men under his command. One soldier from the regiment recalled that Capt. Coleman proved to be "a too strict disciplinarian." Sergeant Adolphus Pitcher noted that there was also "bitter hatred existing against him amongst the men of the regiment in consequence of his bad treatment of them while on guard." Another sergeant, Archibald Henderson, reported in a letter to his brother during early 1862 that Coleman's reputation had sunk so low by that point that he "could not get two men in the company to go under him in action."[29]

As the time approached for their one-year term of service to expire, the men showed little inclination to continue serving under him. Coleman acknowledged to his wife in March of 1862 that the men "are not enlisting rapidly." He also noted that one of his lieutenants was "endeavoring to raise a company and so is my O[rdnance] Sergt." Coleman pointed out that "they have split and are on their own hook." The dissatisfaction with Coleman ran so deep that he was handily defeated for reelection during the reorganization in May and returned to civilian life at his family's plantation in Virginia.[30]

The harsh feelings toward Coleman surfaced again during the December meeting to select Col. Wade's replacement. Captain Davis noted that the final decision by the officers to recommend Coleman's promotion to lieutenant colonel had been far from unanimous. "While there were none who were unwilling to see Col Ruffin promoted over them, there was a considerable minority present and others absent <u>entitled to promotion</u> who did not favor the appointment of Col Coleman," he later explained. The final vote among the officers present at the impromptu meeting was 13 in favor of the agreement for Coleman's promotion and nine against it.

---

28 "Sketch of Colonel Henry Eaton Coleman," Henry Eaton Coleman Papers, Mariner's Museum, Library, Newport News, Virginia; Summary Sheet of Henry Eaton Coleman, Alumni Files, Virginia Military Institute, Lexington, Virginia; Handwritten Sketch of Henry Eaton Coleman, *ibid.*

29 Montgomery, "Twelfth Regiment," in Clark, *NC Regiments*, 1:642, Adolphus R. Pitcher Diary, Entry for Aug. 6, 1861, NCOAH; Archibald Henderson to Dear Brother, Feb. 26, 1862, Archibald Erskine Henderson Papers, William R. Perkins Library, Duke University, Durham, North Carolina (hereafter cited as Duke).

30 Henry Eaton Coleman to My Own Darling Wife, March 10, 1862, Coleman Papers.

A motion was then proposed to certify the vote for Coleman as being unanimous. "In this meeting I voted for neither motion and when afterwards the paper of recommendation was presented to me, I positively refused to sign it stating that I was willing to waive my claims to promotion in favor of Col Ruffin but not in the other case," Davis declared in a letter to Adjt. Gen. Samuel Cooper. According to Davis, he informed Iverson immediately after the meeting that he was unwilling to step aside in favor of Coleman. Despite his vehement protests, Iverson "forwarded and approved however the paper representing it to be the unanimous wish of the officers to have the appointment of Lt. Col. given to . . . Coleman."[31]

Iverson remained unwavering in his support for Coleman. He described the meeting as an "informal election" in which the officers were free to recommend whomever they wanted to take over command of the regiment. He further claimed that Davis had failed to make his objections to Coleman's appointment known prior to the original vote, thereby nullifying any complaints he might have about the results. "I had been informed that he was President of the meeting and I asked him if he had made an objection before the officers," Iverson remarked. "He replied that he had not."[32]

The outcome, however, proved far different from what Iverson had anticipated. Even with Iverson's strong backing, Coleman's nomination for lieutenant colonel failed to win support from division headquarters. "In a few days it was known that D. H. Hill then commanding the division disapproved the appointment of Col Coleman on the grounds that he was not in the service and as it was thought both at Brigade Hd Qtrs and in the regiment that the appointment had proved a failure I gave the matter no further consideration," Davis later commented.[33]

Despite that setback, Iverson refused to give up his plans for reshaping the top command in the 12th North Carolina. Rather than accepting the deal without Coleman, he instead attempted to have Col. Solomon Williams transferred to command of the regiment from the 2nd North Carolina Cavalry. Williams was 27 years old and had graduated from the U.S. Military Academy in the class of 1858. He served for nearly three years as a lieutenant in the 2nd U.S.

---

31 William S. Davis to Samuel Cooper, Aug. 21, 1863, Letters Received, Confederate Adjutant and Inspector General's Office, underlined as in original.

32 Iverson Jr. to Coleman, Aug. 26, 1863, *ibid.*

33 Davis to Cooper, Aug. 21, 1863, *ibid.*

Colonel Solomon Williams of the 12th North Carolina was a former West Point cadet with strong political connections in North Carolina. *Edward Porter Alexander Papers, University of North Carolina at Chapel Hill*

Dragoons and saw action alongside Iverson's regiment in the campaign against the Kiowa Indians. At the outbreak of the war, Williams resigned his commission and returned to his home state of North Carolina.[34]

34 Krick, *Lee's Colonels*, 400; Heitman, *Historical Register*, 1:1042.

On May 16, 1861, he was elected colonel of what would become the 12th North Carolina State Troops. The regiment included two companies from Warren County and two more from Granville County. The other six companies came from Catawba, Cleveland, Duplin, Halifax, Nash, and Robeson Counties. After leaving the camp of instruction at Garysburg, the troops were assigned to the defense forces around Norfolk, Virginia. This garrison duty soon had a major effect on the discipline within the regiment. Little more than a month after their arrival, Pvt. William H. Burwell reported to his father that "there is no duty to be performed in camp except 'dress parade.'"[35]

Further attempts by the officers to resume regular training during their stay were greeted with derision. Sergeant Pitcher described one drill session carried out by their lieutenant colonel as "one of the greatest farces I ever saw, he not being sufficiently versed in military tactics to command a regiment." Another soldier noted in the early spring of 1862 that the men did "scarsely any drilling" at all by that point. Even the few training exercises that took place most often lasted no more than five or 10 minutes. "The men made fun of such drilling," he declared in a letter home.[36]

Sergeant Walter A. Montgomery noted that many of the problems occurred because the regiment "embraced in considerable proportion a class of men of education, of social refinement and wealth, who mingled freely on terms of social equality with field and staff and company officers, and military discipline was thereby rendered impossible." The task of maintaining order was further complicated by their close proximity to town. "The camp was the constant scene of gayety, and the City of Norfolk was daily thronged with members of the regiment on social visits to the citizens," he explained.[37]

The townspeople treated the soldiers from the 12th North Carolina as heroes from the moment of their arrival. A group of citizens staged a concert for the troops in the opera house, and several young girls held a fair for their benefit. Some of the local women even mended the men's clothes and darned

---

35 Montgomery, "Twelfth Regiment," in Clark, *NC Regiments*, 1:606-607; "Letter from the Army Camp, 2nd Regiment, N.C. Volunteers," *North Carolina Standard*, June 5, 1861; William H. Burwell to My Dear Father, July 1, 1861, Burwell Family Papers, SHC.

36 Pitcher Diary, Entry for Aug. 12, 1861, NCOAH; Charles C. Durham to Dear Son, March 30, 1862, in Ann J. Thompson, ed., *North Carolina Confederate Letters, 1861-1865*, 2 Vols. (Shelby, NC: Broad River Genealogical Society, 2002-2004), 1:42.

37 Montgomery, "Twelfth Regiment," in Clark, *NC Regiments*, 1:607.

their socks. Many others regularly visited the nearby army camp with gifts of fruit and other delicacies. A delegation of young ladies from the town also presented them with a new battle flag as a "testimonial of their appreciation and esteem." Pitcher noted happily in his diary that the ceremony was attended by "the majority of Norfolks fair daughters."[38]

The atmosphere during the off-hours often resembled that of a huge party rather than a military camp. "Our service at Norfolk was that of holiday soldiers," Sgt. Montgomery admitted. "We visited the city whenever we wished, were in almost daily communication with our homes, and had frequent visits from our friends and members of our families." He noted that the men "formed friendships and social relationships with the people of the city, and kept our trunks filled with citizen's wearing apparel, including dress-suits and thin longlegged boots, then the fashionable footwear."[39]

The situation spun so out of control that guards were posted around the main camp to keep the men from going into town without the passes. At least one soldier acknowledged that some restrictions were needed to maintain order in the ranks. "Of course no sensible man can complain," he admitted in a letter to his cousin during the early fall of 1861. "For you know as near the city as we are if there was not some restraint put upon the men going to the city that more of them would go up there and get drunk & play thunder generally."[40]

The growing lack of discipline eventually spread all the way to some of the top officers in the 12th North Carolina. In one major incident, Col. Williams dismissed the regiment's commissary officer, who was his cousin, after he "spoke very insultingly" to him in public. Behind the scenes, the problems between the two relatives extended far beyond this single confrontation. "It is also reported that he spoke very insultingly of the Col's family behind his back," Cpl. Harry Williams, another one of the colonel's cousins, explained in a letter to his parents.

Many others in the regiment blamed the trouble on the colonel himself. Corporal Williams informed his parents that "it is thought by some that the Col

---

38 Thomas J. Wertenbaker, *Norfolk: Historic Southern Port* (Durham, NC: Duke University Press, 1931), 230; "Letter from Camp, 2nd Regiment, N. C. Volunteers, Near Norfolk, Va.," *North Carolina Standard*, June 19, 1861; "The Twelfth North Carolina Troops," May 28, 1863, *Raleigh Daily Progress*, June 8, 1863; Pitcher Diary, Entry for May 29, 1861, NCOAH.

39 Walter A. Montgomery, "Memoirs," 23, Elizabeth M. Montgomery Collection, NCOAH.

40 Robert A. Bullock to Dear Cousin, Sept. 17, 1861, Henderson Papers.

was somewhat under the influence of whiskey" during the confrontation between the two officers. While not sure whether to believe the story, Cpl. Williams admitted that he would "hate to fight under a drinking Col, even if he is my first cousin." Colonel Williams reported in a letter to his uncle only that he "regretted very much that he acted as he did toward me and the family and only did what I was forced to do in my defence."[41]

During early winter, the bulk of the men moved into camp a few miles from town in "a thick grove of pine trees" near Sewell's Point opposite the Federal naval base at Hampton Roads, Virginia. From there, the men were in a perfect position to keep a close watch on the enemy's activities. "By walking one-half a mile we had a good view of Fortress Monroe and the Ripraps, and we could very often hear the United States Marine Band playing at dress parade, and could see the ships and other vessels moving to and fro," one soldier recalled.[42]

As spring approached, they also had frequent opportunities to observe the ironclad warship *Merrimac* in action. One of the men informed his brother that he "expected certainly to see the huge old sea monster to day 'walking the water like a thing of life.'" Another soldier reported in a letter home that "the beach was for a mile and half covered with men" when the *Merrimac* finally engaged the blockading Federal fleet outside Norfolk, setting one frigate on fire and sinking another. "You never heard such cheers as went through the air when it went to the bottom," he declared. Corporal Williams noted that "it was a sight that will never be forgotten by me."[43]

The men also witnessed the climactic battle between the *Monitor* and *Merrimac* from their vantage point along the beach. "They fought all day," Pvt. George W. Rabb recalled. "They would shoot and ram each other and shoot and ram. Neither one could gain an advantage." He continued to watch until late in the evening when both ships finally withdrew. "I have often been asked who won the fight," Rabb commented. "I say it was draw, a dog fall. It seemed

---

41 Harry Williams to My Dear Parents, Aug. 8, 1861, Williams-Dameron Family Papers, NCOAH; Solomon Williams to Dear Uncle, Oct. 24, 1861, Archibald Hunter Arrington Papers, SHC.

42 Robert Alexander Jenkins, "From Harper's Ferry to the Surrender," 16, Gertrude Jenkins Collection, Duke.

43 Francis R. Gregory to My Dear Brother, March 29, 1862, Ferebee, Gregory, and McPherson Family Papers, SHC; Joseph B. Jones to Dear Bettie, March 10, 1862, Joseph B. Jones Letter, NCOAH; Harry Williams to My Dear Brother, March 10, 1862, Williams-Dameron Papers.

that both ships agreed to stop." Captain Coleman described this famous encounter in a letter to his wife as "the grandest sight I ever saw."[44]

By the beginning of May, the men turned their attention to the upcoming elections of their new officers. The discontent ran so high that the outcome of the voting for the three field officers was far from certain. Colonel Williams remained popular enough that he retained his position in the balloting by the company officers. The results that day proved less positive for Lt. Col. Edward P. Cantwell and Maj. Augustus W. Burton, who were both defeated for reelection. They were succeeded by Captains Wade and Jones, who assumed the ranks of lieutenant colonel and major, respectively.[45]

Less than a week later, the regiment finally withdrew from Norfolk. While temporarily attached to Branch's Brigade, the soldiers experienced their first combat at Hanover Court House on May 27, where they lost seven men killed and about 20 wounded. Within days of that battle, the regiment was sent to the Richmond area, where it was immediately assigned to Garland's Brigade. "We have been marching and on picket duty every day for the last month," Pvt. Seaton Gayles Durham remarked in a letter to his brother soon after their arrival outside the capital. "We have learned Something more of what it takes to make a Soldier than we knew at Norfolk."[46]

Just prior to the beginning of the Seven Days' Battles, Williams accepted a commission as colonel of the 2nd North Carolina Cavalry and transferred from the regiment along with Adjt. John C. Pegram. The vacant position was filled by the promotion of Lt. Col. Wade, the remaining senior field officer in the 12th North Carolina. After serving in the Tar Heel state for several months, Williams' new regiment was finally dispatched to the Virginia theater, where it joined Brig. Gen. W. H. F. "Rooney" Lee's Brigade in Gen. Jeb Stuart's Cavalry.[47]

---

44 Rebecca Ikerd Alghrary, ed., *A Confederate Remembers Northern Virginia: George Rabb, Catawba County Soldier* (Newton, NC: Catawba County Historical Society, 1994); Coleman to Wife, March 10, 1862, Coleman Papers. For additional descriptions of the naval activities during their stay, see John H. Fain to My Dear Mother, March 10, 1862, Henderson Papers; and William R. Cheek to Aunt Bettie, April 12, 1862, William R. Cheek Letter, Mariner's Museum, Library.

45 Henderson to Brother, Feb. 26, 1862, Henderson Papers; Krick, *Lee's Colonels*, 77, 82.

46 Montgomery, "Twelfth Regiment," in Clark, *NC Regiments*, 1:606-609; "General Branch's Brigade: The Fight Near Hanover Court House," *Spirit of the Age*, June 9, 1862; Seaton Gayles Durham to Dear Brother, June 22, 1862; quoted in Mast, *Photographic Record*, 316.

47 Krick, *Lee's Colonels*, 400.

Throughout his career, Col. Williams had not hesitated to use the considerable political influence of his uncle, Confederate Congressman Archibald Hunter Arrington, to gain further advancement. In almost every case, the congressman proved more than willing to assist his relative. As early as the spring of 1862, Arrington wrote to Secretary of War Judah Benjamin asking that Williams' appointment be changed to the regular Confederate army from the volunteers. The Congressman emphasized that he would "esteem it as a great personal favor" if his request were granted.[48]

Despite those political connections, the Adjutant Generals Office revoked Williams' transfer to the cavalry on January 17, 1863, and ordered him to return to the 12th regiment. This action drew an immediate protest from Stuart. "Unless it is the intention of this order to prepare the way for Col William's promotion, I hope it will be revoked," he wrote in his endorsement. "He is now Col of a fine cav regt to which he is very much attached, and there is no field officer competent to take his place." Stuart noted that he "would be glad to have him promoted but if he is to remain Col let him remain where he is."

Although the order was effectively dead once Gen. Lee recommended that Williams "be retained in the command" of his cavalry regiment, the transfer was not officially revoked until March 21. During that time, Williams once again turned to Congressman Arrington for help. At his uncle's urging, the entire North Carolina congressional delegation requested in mid-February that President Davis consider Williams for promotion to brigadier general. "He is the senior Colonel of the state & is a man of good habits and good abilities," they wrote in the letter of recommendation.[49]

After hearing nothing further about Williams' transfer, Iverson reluctantly agreed to support Lt. Col. Ruffin for promotion to colonel. He expressed his growing frustrations in a letter to Cooper at the end of January. "Col Williams has not reported here and I respectfully request information in regard to him," Iverson declared. If the order for his return would not be enforced, he called for the appointment of Ruffin to head the 12th North Carolina. Iverson pointed

---

48 Archibald H. Arrington to Judah P. Benjamin, March 5, 1862, Letters Received, Confederate Secretary of War.

49 Special Order No. 14, Confederate Adjutant and Inspector General's Office, Jan. 17, 1863, Compiled Service Records of Solomon Williams, M 230, R 18, NA; Special Order No. 70, Confederate Adjutant and Inspector General's Office, March 21, 1863, *ibid.*; North Carolina Congressional Delegation to Jefferson Davis, Feb. 21, 1863, Letters Received, Confederate Secretary of War.

out that all the other ranking officers in the regiment had already declined "promotion in his favor."[50]

Even that concession failed to resolve the problems. The arrangement that would have brought Ruffin into the regiment began to unravel almost immediately. Because of his slow recovery from the hip wound that he suffered while standing next to Gen. Samuel Garland at South Mountain, Ruffin decided against remaining on field duty. Instead, he accepted an appointment as judge of the military court in the Trans-Mississippi Department and took himself out of consideration for promotion to colonel of the 12th North Carolina.[51]

Despite the opposition he faced, Iverson refused to give up on obtaining a promotion for Coleman. When D. H. Hill transferred from the division in late January, Iverson surprised everyone by moving ahead with the earlier nomination of his friend for lieutenant colonel. The move drew an angry response from Capt. Alston, who wrote a letter of protest directly to Adjt. Gen. Cooper. While conceding that the commission could not be issued until confirmed by the Senate, one of Cooper's assistants reported to Iverson soon afterward that "it is now too late for the company officers to reconsider their actions in this matter."[52]

At the same time, formal approval of the promotion ran into a major delay when the paperwork for Coleman's appointment was misplaced in the Adjutant General's Office at Richmond. In mid-April, Iverson informed Robert Rodes, who had temporarily replaced D. H. Hill as division commander, that Coleman had been nominated as lieutenant colonel and would rise by seniority to colonel and that the board of examination would determine the other field officers. He noted that Capt. Davis "will I think be able to pass a board for Lt. Col. but I do not know any officer in the regt whom I can recommend for major and will leave it to the test of a board of examiners."

Rodes quickly made it clear that he was dissatisfied with the arrangement to bring Coleman back into the regiment. "Attention called to Lt. Col. Coleman's failure to come through the reorganization of these regiments," the division commander stated in an endorsement before passing Iverson's letter up the

---

50 Alfred Iverson Jr. to Samuel Cooper, Jan. 31, 1863, Letters Received, Confederate Adjutant and Inspector General's Office.

51 Krick, *Lee's Colonels*, 328; "North Carolina Troops," *Charlotte Daily Bulletin*, March 6, 1863.

52 Samuel W. Melton to Alfred Iverson Jr., April 15, 1863, Compiled Service Record of Henry Eaton Coleman, M 270, R 202, NA.

chain of command. At the same time, he remained anxious to deal with the major vacancies at the top of the regiment. "As other field officers have been strangely delayed somehow, most strenuous efforts have been made to promote field officers," Rodes remarked.

Lieutenant Colonel Walter H. Taylor, Lee's adjutant, noted in a final endorsement that "the recommended promotion within the 12th reg. must necessarily be delayed until some official notice is received of the appointment of Lt. Col. Coleman." He also wrote that senior regimental captains should be "ordered before a Board of Exam with a view of determining their qualifications for the several vacancies." By the time the board convened, another opening had been created by the death of Maj. Rowe in the fighting at Chancellorsville.[53]

On the board's recommendation, Captain Davis was approved for promotion to colonel on May 22 and Captain Alston for lieutenant colonel two days later. Despite losing at every turn, Iverson found that decision impossible to endorse. "Genl Iverson however refused to assign me to duty as Colonel stating that he must hear from the war-department first," recalled Davis. "I looked upon Col Coleman at this time as sustaining the relation of a citizen to the regiment and could not see how he could interpose with promotions in the regiment....[In] a few days I was ordered on duty as Lt Col and Capt Alston as Major."[54]

Because Coleman was still absent and had not received a formal commission, Davis immediately assumed command of the regiment as the senior officer. Although he was only 23 years old at the time of his appointment, Davis had earned a reputation as one of the finest officers in the brigade. He attended Randolph-Macon College and the University of Virginia prior to the war and had already built an exceptional record as a company commander through several major battles. Coleman's paperwork, meanwhile, remained lost in the Richmond bureaucracy. "Nothing was further heard of this matter in camp, and everyone thought it was dropped," one veteran of the regiment remembered.[55]

---

53 Alfred Iverson Jr. to Green Peyton, April 13, 1863, Coleman Service Record.

54 Davis to Cooper, Aug. 21, 1863, Letters Received, Confederate Adjutant and Inspector General's Office.

55 Krick, *Lee's Colonels*, 114; Evans, *Confederate Military History*, 5:464; Montgomery, "Twelfth Regiment," in Clark, *NC Regiments*, 1:643.

CHAPTER FIVE

I Did Not Think to Look in the Rear

Although he had not given up his efforts to have Henry Coleman appointed colonel of the regiment, Alfred Iverson focused most of his attention throughout the spring of 1863 on the impending military action along the Rappahannock River. His anticipation ran especially high because he still had not faced major combat as a brigadier general. Following the fighting at Sharpsburg, the troops from Garland's former brigade briefly went into camp near Bunker Hill, Virginia. Soon afterward, they moved farther into the upper Shenandoah Valley, where they were assigned to guard the passes through the mountains.

During their stay in the Shenandoah Valley, the men endured nearly constant marching over the steep mountain roads. After heading south to New Market, their route took them over the Massanutten mountains and into the neighboring Luray Valley. From there, the North Carolinians "twisted and turned" their way over the "great Blue Ridge" before reaching the area around Gordonsville. The repeated forced marches proved so "hard and tough" that many of the men longed to return to eastern Virginia. "We are now in the Valley of Virginia, where I had been wanting to visit for some time before our raid in Maryland," Capt. Isaac Pearce from the 5th North Carolina explained in a letter to his sister. "But I assure you I never was as anxious to visit the Valley of Virginia as I am now to leave it."[1]

In early December, the men from the brigade finally received orders to rejoin the main part of the army at its winter quarters along the Rappahannock River near Port Royal, Virginia. This soon turned into a trip that none of them would ever forget. Private J. L. Wallace from the 23rd North Carolina noted that they were "almost naked and barefooted" as they started their long journey through the mountains. Private James Ireland from the 20th North Carolina recalled that a line of "bloody footprints" in the snow marked the route by the time they reached their destination three days later.[2]

Conditions proved almost as difficult following their arrival in the area of their new camp. One soldier from the 23rd North Carolina reported in a letter to his hometown newspaper that they initially "suffered from exposure from a snow, not having any tents." The men in the brigade quickly moved to alleviate the situation. "We did not long remain idle, but went to work and built winter quarters, which were constructed after the collier huts," he explained. Within days, the men settled into their improvised shelters where they enjoyed themselves as "best we can."[3]

When a major engagement broke out at nearby Fredericksburg on December 13, the newly arrived troops shifted from their camp into the area just outside of Hamilton's Crossing as a reserve force. "During the fight our Regiment was posted on the right, some five miles below Fredericksburg where the fighting was extremely severe & where the enemy lost thousands in killed and wounded & our loss was very small," Maj. Charles C. Blacknall from the 23rd North Carolina commented in a letter to his mother. "We lost but few in our Regiment & that from cannon shot."[4]

Even from his position behind the front lines, Blacknall found the sights on the battlefield to be "horrible beyond description." He noted that "the enemy

---

1 "History of the Montgomery Volunteers, Company C., 23rd N.C. Regiment (March 8, 1862 to March 4, 1863)," *Fayetteville Observer*, March 16, 1863; Oliver E. Mercer to Dear Sister, Dec. 2, 1862, in Wyatt, *The Reeves, Mercer, Newkirk Families*, 264; Isaac E. Pearce to Dear Sister, Oct. 7, 1862, Pearce Papers.

2 J. L. Wallace, "Reminiscences," 3, Military Collections, NCOAH; Ireland, "Memoirs."

3 "History of the Montgomery Volunteers, Company C., 23rd N.C. Regiment (March 8, 1862 to March 4, 1863)," *Fayetteville Observer*, March 16, 1863.

4 Charles C. Blacknall to Dear Ma, Dec. 29, 1862, Oscar W. Blacknall Papers, NCOAH.

advanced through an open smooth plain upon our lines, when the columns were mown down by the hundreds by our artillery & infantry." Many of the wounded were left lying on the ground all night in the cold winter weather. "The suffering on their part was immense," he said. "We took many prisoners, and much in the way of arms, blankets &c. Our men went to work robbing the dead without ceremony and many were stripped of all their clothing, presenting a strange appearance lying on the field."[5]

Following the battle, Iverson's men set up new quarters a few miles south of Hamilton's Crossing. They spent most of their time there keeping a close eye on the Federal troops, who remained in force just across the river. The only major problems resulted from the severe weather that they endured throughout much of the winter. "Our regiment did a great deal of shivering picket duty on the Rappahannock below Fredericksburg," recalled Capt. Vines Turner from the 23rd North Carolina. "The winter was one of great rigor." He noted that "the men, though pretty well hardened, suffered severely from want of proper clothing and food and from exposure."[6]

As the weather continued to deteriorate over the months that followed, the situation on the Rappahannock River lapsed into an uneasy stalemate. The routine of constant patrols along the winding waterway was interrupted only by a brief foray during early February to counter a Federal probe in the area of Mine Run. The harsh conditions during the advance led to open grumbling from the men in the brigade. "The boys suffered extremely from cold weather in this move, being held in line of battle several days and nights, in sight of the enemy, and without fire or blankets," a soldier from the 23rd North Carolina recalled.[7]

The huge snowstorms that hit the area during January and February added to their problems. "Well sister, you ought to just see this country now," Lt. Oliver Mercer from the 20th North Carolina wrote at the end of January. "It is nothing but a white mass of snow ½ leg deep; its beautiful but Oh! How cold. It commenced night before last and snowed until last night in the night. It would have been 2 ft. deep if it had not rained before hand." He found the weather

---

5 Charles C. Blacknall to Dear Jinny, Dec. 18, 1862, *ibid.*

6 Turner and Wall, "Twenty-Third Regiment," in Clark, *NC Regiments*, 2:227.

7 H. C. Wall, *Historical Sketch of the Pee Dee Guards, From 1861 to 1865* (Raleigh, NC: Edward Broughton and Company, 1876), 49.

much worse than what he had ever experienced at home. "I don't suppose you have any such thing with you," he commented to his sister.[8]

Following one storm in mid-January, a gigantic snowball fight broke out between Iverson's Brigade and some Georgian troops from their division. "The battle, though brief, was sharp," Capt. Turner recalled. "Many of us were knocked down and several quite seriously hurt, but the snow fort was stormed, our opponents routed and chased back through their camp. Many prisoners were taken." The captain went on to note that "the horse play was ended by rolling in the snow a supercilious general officer participating in the fun." Whether this was Iverson or not remains impossible to know.[9]

Other major snowball fights within the brigade took place as the days of January passed. In some cases, they turned into pitched battles between the various regiments involved. "The snow hear was very deep and the twelfth Regt came up into our Regt in a line of battle," Pvt. John Coghill from the 23rd North Carolina remarked in a letter to his family. "We formed our Regt and went to fighting with snow balls." He noted that they soon "made a charge on them and wee ran them to thare camp and thare they ware reinforced by the 20th Regt and finely we whiped the hole Brigade."[10]

By mid-February, the storms became so severe that all outside activities virtually ceased. "The weather is absolutely intolerable, the worst I have seen or felt," Major Blacknall declared in a letter to his brother-in-law. "We were just visited by a tremendous snow full 'two feet deep' which tapered off into a rain, which all together makes such a mixture as I have never before experienced." He pointed out that "the ground is now wetter, muddier & more ungetaboutable than at any former time this winter and the roads are actually impassable, being in many places from three to six feet deep in mud."[11]

With the men largely confined to camp because of the heavy snow, their daily work details quickly turned into mind-numbing routines. The situation soon proved more than some of them could take. "It is Just Drill [and] Drill and carry wood and cook," Pvt. Charles D. Sides from the 5th North Carolina

---

8   Mercer to Sister, Jan. 29, 1863, in Wyatt, *The Reeves, Mercer, Newkirk Families*, 267.

9   Turner and Wall, "Twenty-Third Regiment," in Clark, *NC Regiments*, 2:227.

10 John F. Coghill to Dear Pappy and Mit, Feb. 6, 1863, James O. Coghill Papers, Duke. For another description of the snowball fights in Iverson's Brigade, see Oliver E. Mercer to Dear Sister, Jan. 29, 1863, in Wyatt, *The Reeves, Mercer, Newkirk Families*, 267.

11 Charles C. Blacknall to Dear Bro. George, Feb. 19, 1863, Blacknall Papers.

griped in a letter to his wife. "This embraces the whol day. We have to carry our wood about one quarter of a mile." He complained most of all that their meager daily rations of flour and rancid beef were not "fit for dog to eat and a dog at home would not nigh eat it."[12]

One of the few distractions from the grueling routine and weather came from the Federal observation balloons that could be clearly seen floating in the sky along the opposite side of the Rappahannock. The balloons were the brainchild of a self-styled professor named Thaddeus S. C. Lowe. He first used them to good effect during the spring of 1862 in the Peninsula Campaign, where the balloons became a common sight above the Federal lines. They were regularly deployed throughout early 1863 as a means of keeping watch for unusual movements by the Confederate army in the region just west of Fredericksburg.[13]

Although the Iverson's men became quickly accustomed to the balloons, one soldier who arrived with a group of conscripts in mid-March still found their presence startling. "He says he never saw anything of the kind before," Adjt. Fabius Haywood from the 5th North Carolina informed a friend. "He halted his detachment near Col Garrett's quarters in order to get a fair view of it." He noted that "the old men of the Regt. collected around his detachment, making all kinds of remarks about the conscripts, and when they found out what Fred had halted for, they thought him the most verdant man they had seen in many days."[14]

Despite the difficult conditions, Iverson maintained his policy of strict discipline within the brigade. In mid-March, Pvt. Daniel Moose from the 5th North Carolina described in a letter home how three deserters from his regiment were forced to run shirtless between the men of his company assembled in ranks on both sides. "Each man had a hickory and as they came along gave them a lick," wrote the private. "Their backs looked tolerably red until they got through and the colonel said the next man that would desert had to run the lines of the regiment and the next then had to be shot."[15]

---

12 Charles D. Sides to Dear Wife, Feb. 10, 1863, Civil War Miscellaneous Collection.

13 Earnest B. Ferguson, *Chancellorsville,1863: The Souls of the Brave* (New York: Vantage Books, 1992), 6-8.

14 Haywood to McRae, March 31, 1863, McRae Papers.

15 Daniel M. Moose to Dear Father-in-law, March 15, 1863, in Troxler and Barrier Auciello, *Dear Father*, 132.

The 23rd North Carolina's Pvt. John T. Thompson also witnessed this public display of "gauntlet" discipline, and what he saw sickened him. He noted that each of the unfortunates making the run received numerous hard blows as they maneuvered between the two long lines of soldiers. "I tell you they made the Blood fly," he declared in a letter home. "It looked horrid." Private Leonidas Torrence from the same regiment was struck most of all by the severity of the injuries inflicted by their comrades. "One of them died the 8th day after he was whipped," he told his mother in a letter home. "The Dr. said it was the whipping killed him."[16]

Earlier in the year, another deserter from the brigade had even been scheduled for execution. Private Sides from the 5th North Carolina found the incident especially upsetting. "We were all ordered out last Saturday to the field, our whole Brigade to see a man Shot, one of our own men in the 12th Regt," he penned his wife. "But as good luck would have it, he was Reprieved, so he was not shot." Sides noted that he "was very glad for I did not want to see such work as that for there is no fun in seeing men shot and I think men die fast enough in this Confederacy."[17]

The bad weather that kept the men confined to camp persisted throughout early spring, with heavy snow falling as late as the first week in April. "We are now having terrible weather," Maj. Blacknall wrote his brother-in-law at the beginning of the month. "Moved our camp yesterday about two miles, and before the men could get well settled in the woods, a severe snow storm commenced. It fell all night & is now 6 inches deep, so the troops are having quite a rough time, as they have not erected huts or sheds as usual." Blacknall went on to note that "we have no indication of spring, not a bud or flower."[18]

By the end of the month, however, the conditions had finally improved enough for the Federal Army of the Potomac under Maj. Gen. Joseph Hooker to open the campaign season along the Rappahannock. On April 29, Hooker sent a large portion of his army across the river upstream from Fredericksburg. General Lee countered the move on May 1 by marching Stonewall Jackson's Second Corps along the Orange Plank Road in the direction of Chancellorsville.

---

16 John T. Thompson to My Dear Wife, March 15, 1863, in Thompson, *North Carolina Confederate Letters*, 2:185; Leonidas Torrence to Dear Mother, March 28, 1863, in Monroe, "The Road to Gettysburg," 504.

17 Sides to Wife, Feb. 10, 1863, Civil War Miscellaneous Collection.

18 Charles C. Blacknall to Dear Bro. George, April 5, 1863, Blacknall Papers.

Following a flurry of fighting, the Federal troops pulled back into a defensive position amid the tangled wilderness just west of Fredericksburg.

The chance for Iverson to prove his leadership abilities in combat finally arrived on May 2, when the men from Rodes' Division responded to the presence of the enemy troops on their front by moving "higher up the river" along the Furnace Road southwest of Chancellorsville. "We knew not where we were going, but a great many of us rightly conjectured that we were making for the enemy's rear," Capt. Claudius B. Monk from the 20th North Carolina remarked in a letter to his brother. "The march was very rapid and pretty long. Any quantity of blankets, old clothes, etc. were thrown away." He pointed out that "the road was strewn with them." What none of the men realized was that they were taking part in one of the greatest flanking operations in military history.[19]

Captain Turner of the 23rd North Carolina remembered that "strict silence" was enforced throughout the long journey, with only a whisper allowed and only then when it was necessary to issue an order. "Occasionally a courier would spur his tired horse past us as we twisted through the brush," he later wrote. "For hours at the time we neither saw nor heard anything. Great was the curiosity to know where we were going and what 'Old Jack' was about. But we agreed that he did know and that the novel march meant much." Captain John Brooks from the 20th North Carolina finally realized what was transpiring once the long Southern column turned north and headed toward the Orange Turnpike. Only then did he know for certain that "old Jack was going to the rear of old Joe."[20]

Their target was the right flank of Joe Hooker's army, held by Maj. Gen. Oliver O. Howard's XI Corps. Southern cavalry reported that Howard's flank was not anchored to any strong point and completely vulnerable to an attack. By late in the afternoon, Iverson's men were directed to a point north of the turnpike on the edge of the tangled wilderness that stretched along their front. Iverson noted that the brigade "came up with General Rodes about 4 p.m., and was posted on the extreme left, in the front line." The 5th North Carolina held

---

19 Claudius B. Monk to Dear Brother, May 7, 1863, *Wilmington Daily Journal*, May 27, 1863. Although unsigned, details in the letter point to Capt. Claudius B. Monk of the 20th North Carolina as the most likely author.

20 Turner and Wall, "Twenty-Third Regiment," in Clark, *NC Regiments*, 2:228; John S. Brooks to Dear Father, May 8, 1863, Brooks Papers.

the right flank, with the 12th North Carolina directly on its left. The 20th North Carolina moved into place on the left center of the line, while the 23rd North Carolina took up position on the far left.[21]

Jackson quickly assembled the men from Rodes', Raleigh Colston's, and Ambrose Powell Hill's divisions for the assault against the enemy troops in the nearby woods. Iverson's Brigade occupied the left-front in the first rank of the attack. The rest of Rodes' Division formed along a line extending south from there to just below the turnpike. The brigades commanded by Edward O'Neal, George Doles, and Alfred Colquitt, from left to right, moved into place at the front of the attack. Stephen Dodson Ramseur's Brigade set up slightly to the rear on the far right. Another heavy line of battle took up position directly behind them, while a third began taking form farther to the rear.

Iverson's men soon found that the heavy undergrowth along their front obscured their line of sight. "I think I never did see chinquapin bushes so thick," Capt. Monk later remembered. "We were ordered to throw off knapsacks, &c. The General told us, just a little hard fighting and all will be over." Captain Brooks estimated that they completed preparations for the attack about five o'clock in the afternoon. According to Brooks, the Confederate pickets soon thereafter "commenced firing on the enemy." He reported that it was less than five minutes later when the Southern line of battle unleashed "a volley that will last them until peace is made."[22]

In the wake of the volley, Iverson's troops rushed headlong through the woods directly into the rear of Howard's XI Corps. It would be a day that none of them would ever forget. "Immediately after getting into position, the line moved forward to the battle of the 'Wilderness,'" was how Iverson described the action that day. He reported that the soldiers advanced directly "through the dense and tangled undergrowth." According to his account, the skirmishers from his brigade were "soon engaged, and the whole pressed hotly and quickly to the attack."[23]

Lieutenant Mercer was just as ecstatic about what they accomplished in the opening phase of the attack. "Very soon our whole sight was engaged," he reported to his sister. "The noise was terrific. In a few minutes we also were at

---

21 OR 25, pt. 1, 984.

22 Monk to Brother, May 7, 1863, *Wilmington Daily Journal*, May 27, 1863 Brooks to Father, May 8, 1863, Brooks Papers.

23 OR 25, pt. 1, 984.

them and here it commenced. We poured it into them and they to us for a short while." Mercer and his comrades soon "charged them and they fled like dogs leaving everything behind—knapsacks, trunks, arms, about 25 fat beeves already skinned and cannon and horses and everything valuable." According to the young lieutenant, they "pursued them hotly until after dark."[24]

The 23rd North Carolina's Captain Turner recalled that the men in his regiment were "ordered to yell our loudest" as they moved at the "double quick" into the woods. "We struck their very rear, chasing over their beef slaughtering and cooking detail," he wrote. "The enemy began jumping up before us and holding up their hands to surrender. But little resistance was met with, the surprised enemy surrendering or breaking before us in the wildest rout and disorder. Chasing them like hares, our boys surged forward." The captain noted that the field along their front soon became a place of utter confusion through which "rushed helter-skelter cannon, wagons, loose horses, dogs, men, everything."[25]

Iverson gloated in his report of the campaign that Howard's Federals "made no organized resistance" and "the whole affair from the moment of attack was a wild scene of triumph on our part." He declared that "hungry men seized provisions as they passed the camps of the enemy, and rushed forward, eating, shouting, and firing." At least one wounded soldier from the brigade, however, clearly recalled seeing the brigade commander well to the rear while his men were pursuing the fleeing Federal troops. "I went first to the field hospital station to have my wound dressed," recalled Pvt. George Rabb of the 12th North Carolina. "As I was going to the hospital, I passed by Brigadier Gen. Iverson, and told him the Yankees were running like turkeys."[26]

Iverson's apparent absence from the front lines notwithstanding, the initial attack proved to be a remarkable success. Private Ruffin Richardson from the 5th North Carolina proclaimed in a letter home that "we whiped the yankees like dogs." Another private, John C. Ussery of the 23rd North Carolina, reported colorfully in a letter to his father that the enemy troops "commenced the second edition of the Bull Run races" as they fled in terror from the field. "I tell you we carried them two miles and a half at 2.40 speed and would believe

---

24 Oliver E. Mercer to Dear Sister, May 9, 1863, in Wyatt, *The Reeves, Mercer, Newkirk Families*, 269.

25 Turner and Wall, "Twenty-Third Regiment," in Clark, *NC Regiments*, 2:229-230.

26 *OR* 25, pt. 1, 985; Alghrary, *A Confederate Remembers*.

have routed the whole army if we made the attack three hours earlier," Ussery explained.²⁷

The area along their front line quickly swarmed with untold hundreds of Federal soldiers fleeing for their lives. As Captain Monk described the scene in a vividly worded letter to his brother, the chase took place amid the sounds of "musketry, artillery and cheers of the men" coming from the middle of the woods. "The surprised Yankees ran in dismay before us–the brave men of our army rushed on them while the cowards, plunderers, &c. got behind trees," explained the officer. "We drove them through woods and fields, right by splendid breastworks, for about 2½ miles." The captain added that they continued the pursuit until "it was dark, and our troops were almost exhausted."²⁸

Captain Turner remembered being startled amid the "frenzied flight" of the Federal troops along their front by the bizarre sight of a large cannon hanging precariously from a tree limb. The scene was unlike anything he had experienced during the war. "In the panic it had been driven over a small tree which bent under its weight, but finally broke it loose from the caisson in front," Turner explained. "Then the upspring of the tree raised the entangled gun from the ground. There it hung as eloquent an attest of mad flight as perchance war has ever seen."²⁹

Despite the rout of the Federal forces, the fighting in the woods remained disorganized and chaotic. Iverson's regiments, in particular, became widely scattered during the headlong advance through the dense woods. The problem grew much worse when the brigade behind Iverson advanced too quickly, throwing the two commands together into a mixed-up jumble of often indistinguishable infantrymen. "The second line, commanded by Brigadier-General Colston, closed in with us at that point, and caused great confusion, the two lines rushing forward pell-mell upon the enemy, and becoming mingled in almost inextricable confusion, no officer being able to tell what men he commanded," Iverson reported.³⁰

---

27 Ruffin P. Richardson to Leslie M. Richardson, May 15, 1863, Richardson Family Papers, NCOAH; John C. Ussery to Dear Father, May 8, 1863, Fredericksburg and Spotsylvania National Military Park Collection, Fredericksburg, Virginia.

28 Monk to Brother, May 7, 1863, *Wilmington Daily Journal*, May 27, 1863.

29 Turner and Wall, "Twenty-Third Regiment," in Clark, *NC Regiments*, 2:229.

30 *OR* 25, pt. 1, 985.

The men soon had no recourse other than to push blindly forward. Lieutenant Mercer admitted in a letter home that "our Brigade was all mixed up and no one knew where his company or regiment was; everything going on their own hook." He added that "some parts of the lines were engaged off and on all night; not knowing how things were arranged, our men fired into each other." By the time darkness was falling, recalled Pvt. Benjamin B. Carr of the 20th North Carolina, the brigade had turned into "a disorganized rabble, every one his own commander doing as pleased him but going forward all the time."[31]

Stonewall Jackson was already planning his next move. Although his surprise attack had smashed Howard's command, it did not destroy it or even cripple the Army of the Potomac. The effort came too late in the day to deliver all that it could have. While the Federal XI Corps was shoved back about two miles, Jackson's men were also in a chaotic state and remained separated from the troops operating under General Lee. Even so, the aggressive Jackson wanted to reorganize for a night attack. The pitch darkness, the confusion in the ranks, the mixed up commands, the low ammunition, the heavy casualties, and the sheer exhaustion from the long march, along with the powerful Federal artillery positions at Fairview and Hazel Grove, all determined otherwise.

Any chance for an attack that evening ended when troops from Brig. Gen. James H. Lane's North Carolina Brigade accidentally wounded Jackson and several of his staff as they were performing a reconnaissance along the Plank Road. Other firing in the darkness subsequently wounded Gen. A. P. Hill. "Our wonderful success made us greedy of more and we rushed in until Oh! an awful calamity befell us," Lt. Col. John W. Lea of the 5th North Carolina lamented in his diary. "Jackson's left arm was broken and A. P. Hill wounded in the leg (left) by the firing of our own troops. Lane's Brigade had marched almost into the enemy and halted when they were fired on with shell." He noted that "this created an alarm and they fired on nothing–for several minutes our troops cut each other to pieces."[32]

After a fitful night of rest, Iverson's men immediately ran into trouble when they returned to action north of the Orange Turnpike the next day. The undergrowth proved so heavy that the 5th North Carolina quickly became separated from the rest of the brigade, its flank exposed to attack. Colonel

---

31 Mercer to Sister, May 9, 1863, in Wyatt, *The Reeves, Mercer, Newkirk Families*, 269; B. B. Carr, "Sketch of the Battle of Chancellorsville," 11, Military Collections, NCOAH.

32 Diary and Account Book of Col. John Lea, Entry for May 2, 1863, Record Group 109, NA.

Daniel Harvey Christie from the 23rd North Carolina complained in his official report that "alas, our left had not been taken care of," which was a thinly veiled reference to Iverson's failure to supervise the attack. According to the 20th North Carolina's Captain Monk, "by some mistake some of the regiments of our brigade got detached, and the enemy came very near flanking us." He added that his regiment soon "got into the hottest sort of fight."

The fragmented nature of Iverson's front battle line exposed his brigade to the real danger of being defeated in detail, one regiment at a time. Major Nelson Slough from the 20th North Carolina reported that "the enemy out-flanked us on our left, and poured destructive volleys into our left flank, which compelled us to fall back." As Colonel Christie described it, the regiments "on my left came doubling back upon my line, pressed with overwhelming numbers." Calling it "the hardest fight of the war," Private Ussery from the 23rd North Carolina told his father that "the enemy flanked this regiment completely and cut us up terribly."[33]

Captain Monk explained that the pressure from the Federal troops "compelled" them to fall back toward some breastworks that the enemy had abandoned in the heavy woods. "We reformed and went up again," he reported. "The Yankees were vastly superior to us in numbers, and had good breastworks, but we held them in check and had them running when our other troops came to our assistance." According to Pvt. William H. Brotherton from the 23rd North Carolina, his regiment maneuvered around the rear of the abandoned breastworks and "then we charge[d] on them and drove them back." The North Carolinians soon pressed forward and captured several of the enemy's guns.[34]

Although the Confederate attack on May 3 eventually swept the enemy troops from that part of the field, Lieutenant Colonel Lea still blamed Iverson for ordering the charge that nearly led to disaster. For him, the general's decision to launch the attack into the middle of the thick undergrowth proved impossible to forgive. "This order was given strange to say when a dense pine thicket and forest was immediately in our front," Lea openly complained in his

---

33 *OR* 25, pt. 1, 991, 993; Monk to Brother, May 7, 1863, *Wilmington Daily Journal,* May 27, 1863; Ussery to Father, May 8, 1863, Fredericksburg and Spotsylvania National Military Park Collection.

34 Monk to Brother, May 7, 1863, *Wilmington Daily Journal,* May 27, 1863; William H. Brotherton to Dear Father, May 9, 1863, William H. Brotherton Papers, Duke.

diary. "As was to be expected, the Brigade became very much separated, and the 5th N.C. was entirely lost from the rest of the Brigade."

By maneuvering the 5th North Carolina "under a terrible fire of artillery," Lea located the other regiments in the midst of the woods. To his surprise, Iverson "was no where to be found in my front or on either flank (I did not think to look in [the] rear)." After getting lost again, the lieutenant colonel finally managed to rejoin the rest of the brigade. "When I reached their position I learned they had been driven back in disorder," he said. Iverson's failure to lead his men into the action drew similar criticism from another veteran in the 23rd North Carolina. He noted, in fact, that it "has never been explained" exactly where Iverson was when the attack went forward.[35]

The concerns voiced about Iverson's performance on May 3 appear justified. Rather than lead his men into the fight, he again directed the action from well behind the lines. He claimed to have consulted with Rodes and Jeb Stuart, the acting commander of the Second Corps, while he was there. Iverson reported that he later assisted Brig. Gen. Edward L. Thomas in rallying some Louisiana and Alabama troops to meet the enemy attack from the left. Toward the end of the day, he "received a contusion in the groin from a spent ball, which made walking very painful, and, as the battle ceased shortly after, I requested Colonel Christie to take command of the till I could procure my horse."[36]

The stories about Iverson's alleged cowardice at Chancellorsville soon spread beyond his own brigade and reached General Ramseur, who commanded the other Tar Heel brigade in Rodes' Division. "Brig. Gen'l Iverson comd'g. a N.C. Brig I learned behaved badly himself, his brigade doing well," Ramseur wrote to his best friend about three weeks after the battle. The rumors apparently involved more than just the widespread complaints about Iverson's misconduct from the men in his brigade. Although there is nothing official to back up his claim, Ramseur heard that "charges will be preferred against him."[37]

---

35 Lea Diary, Entry for May 3, 1863, NA; V. E. Turner and H. C. Wall, "Twenty-Third Regiment," in Clark, *NC Regiments*, 2:240.

36 OR 25, pt. 2, 986-987.

37 Stephen Dodson Ramseur to My Dear Brother, May 22, 1863, in George G. Kundahl, ed., *The Bravest of the Brave: The Correspondence of Stephen Dodson Ramseur* (Chapel Hill: University of

The appalling losses suffered by the brigade that day made the situation even worse. Lea described the scene as "awful" all along their front lines once the fighting ended on May 3. "Everything looked like devastation, caissons exploded, horses in every conceivable position dying and dead, men groaning with the most horrible wounds," Lea declared in his diary. "Many a gallant pale face boy could be seen who had breathed his last. Oh! the horrid sights! Heads shot off, limbs shattered, and blood streaming every where."[38]

The aftermath was just as upsetting for the 23rd North Carolina's Private Brotherton, who lamented to his family that it was a "terrible thing to see the wounded men suffering with their legs and arms shot off and shot to pieces, it is awffell." Private E. Faison Hicks of the 20th North Carolina recalled the distressing sights at the makeshift field hospital, where he was receiving treatment for his wounds. "At the back door of every tent piles of amputated limbs lay waist deep," he wrote. "The sight was a sickening one, and I shuddered for my future."[39]

The intensity of the action scarred the Wilderness for years to come. According to a private in the 23rd North Carolina, the artillery and musket fire was so intense that it caused "the destruction, not only of humans but everything else" in the woods on their flanks. "On the one side, you will see a large body of woods completely torn to pieces, by artillery," he explained in a letter to his sister. "Trees two & three feet in diameter, shot through or boughs broken off. On the other where the growth is smaller, trees are worn to a complete frazzle, by the incessant passing of the minie balls."[40]

The most horrific events occurred near the end of the battle, when the shelling ignited the thick underbrush along their front. One eyewitness reported that the raging inferno trapped several hundred soldiers from both sides. "Such was the exigency of the hour, the battle being at its fiercest, that none could be spared from the ranks to save the poor wounded wretches from the most horrible of deaths—being roasted alive," he declared in a letter to a newspaper. The soldier went on to note, "as the flames approached them and they became

---

North Carolina Press, 2010), 136. Ramseur repeatedly addressed his best friend, David Schenck, as "Brother" in his letters.

38 Lea Diary, Entry for May 3, 1863, NA.

39 William H. Brotherton to Dear Grandmother and Aunts, May 10, 1863, Brotherton Papers; Hicks, "Reminiscences," Brake Collection.

40 Allie Clack to Carrie Clack, May 23, 1863, Carrie H. Clack Papers, SHC.

aware of their situation, their frantic screams were distinctly heard above the roar of battle that raged around them."[41]

The fire spread through the dry leaves and piles of debris littering the battlefield, leaving most of the bodies incinerated beyond recognition. "I can't give you any idea what a sight it was to walk over the Battle Field and see men lying with their cloth[e]s burnt off, their hair burnt close to their Head, their Arms and legs all drawed up with the fire," Private Torrence of the 23rd North Carolina wrote his mother. "I never saw such a distressing sight before and hope I may never see such another." One of the Tar Heels who burned to death in the woods was Lt. Washington F. Overton, a member of Torrence's regiment.[42]

After the Confederate attack on May 3 that had reunited the wings of Lee's divided army, another Federal column from Hooker's army under Maj. Gen. John Sedgwick moved against Lee's rear from Fredericksburg. Sedgwick's thrust was rebuffed in heavy fighting at Salem's Church on May 4. The tactical masterpiece that was Chancellorsville, which many regard today as one of Lee's greatest battlefield achievements, ended on May 6 when Hooker withdrew his Army of the Potomac across the Rappahannock.

The honor of spearheading Stonewall Jackson's surprise attack was balanced by the heavy damage inflicted upon the five brigades in Rodes' Division. During the two days of vicious fighting that involved Iverson's men, his four regiments sustained nearly 500 casualties. The losses proved especially heavy among the top regimental officers. Of the nine field officers present during the battle, six were killed, wounded, or captured. In the 5th North Carolina alone, Colonel Garrett, Lieutenant Colonel Lea, and Major Hill were all wounded. Major Rowe from the 12th North Carolina was mortally wounded on May 2, while Colonel Toon from the 20th North Carolina suffered a severe wound the following day. The 23rd North Carolina's Major Blacknall was captured late in the fighting on May 3.[43]

---

41 "The Battle of Chancellorsville," *North Carolina Presbyterian*, May 23, 1863.

42 Leonidas Torrence to Dear Mother, May 8, 1863, in Monroe, "Road to Gettysburg," 507; Turner and Wall, "Twenty-Third Regiment," in Clark, *NC Regiments*, 2:231. For additional accounts of the aftermath from the fire, see Mercer to Sister, May 9, 1863, in Wyatt, *The Reeves, Mercer, Newkirk Families*, 269, and John T. Thompson to My Dear Mary, May 10, 1863, in Thompson, *North Carolina Confederate Letters*, 2:186.

43 Toon, "Twentieth Regiment," in Clark, *NC Regiments*, 2:118; Krick, *Lee's Colonels*, 152, 193, 232, 327.

The other four brigades also suffered heavy losses. Brigadier General Stephen Dodson Ramseur's North Carolina brigade sustained more than 700 casualties during the two days of combat. Rodes' former brigade, temporarily headed by Col. Edward A. O'Neal from the 26th Alabama, lost almost 900 men in the battle to all causes. The last two brigades, both all-Georgia commands under Brig. Gen. George P. Doles and Brig. Gen. Alfred H. Colquitt, each suffered more than 400 killed, wounded, and missing.[44]

The widespread devastation had a profound effect upon the men in Iverson's Brigade. The 23rd North Carolina's Pvt. Allie Clack openly acknowledged in a letter to his sister that he was "quite low spirited just after the battle." If anything, the outlook appeared even worse for Pvt. Thompson of the same regiment. Most of all, the private was dumbstruck by the large number of men killed or mortally wounded during the campaign. "I fear if peace is not soon made we will all be killed," he declared in a letter to his wife in the days following their hard-fought victory. "I am so anxious for this distressing war to stop."[45]

Many of the soldiers in the brigade realized that the victory had done nothing to alter the strategic situation around Fredericksburg. "I fear the grand results of this fight are very few," Pvt. John H. Fain from the 12th North Carolina concluded in letter to his mother less than a week after the end of the battle. Fain placed most of the blame on the substantial difference in the size of the two armies. As Fain saw it, "the smallness of our force kept us from pursuing the enemy," and when all was said and done, "both armies have taken up their old positions."[46]

Adding to their sense of gloom was the death of Second Corps commander Stonewall Jackson, who finally succumbed on May 10 to the wounds he had suffered eight days earlier at Chancellorsville. "Sincerely do we all mourn the loss of our Jackson from the lowest private up," Private Clack lamented to his sister. "It is not the confidence we lack in the military skill of our other commanders who I haven't a doubt, some are his superior in planning, but it is his peculiar mode of fighting, always flanking, instead of risking a forward movement on a fortified enemy, thereby saving the lives of thousand[s] of his

---

44 OR 25, pt. 1, 947.

45 Allie Clack to Carrie Clack, May 23, 1863, Clack Papers; Thompson to Mary, May 10, 1863, Thompson, *North Carolina Confederate Letters*, 2:186-187.

46 John H. Fain to My Dear Mother, May 8, 1863, Henderson Papers.

men." Clack insisted "there is no man's death, just at this time, which has caused such universal sorrow."[47]

A week after Jackson's death, Iverson's soldiers gathered for prayer services to honor their fallen hero. Surgeon William Marston from the 12th North Carolina noted in his diary that he heard "an eloquent discourse" on Jackson's career during a memorial held that day at the nearby Round Oak Baptist Church. Lieutenant Mercer from the 20th North Carolina reported to his sister after the service that "the death of Genl. Jackson provides a sadness throughout the whole army." He added that "it was a great loss, but hope his place can be supplied soon."[48]

The fighting at Chancellorsville had been so exhausting and brutal that many men in the North Carolina regiments succumbed to the temptation of returning home. The upsurge in desertions following the battle escalated into a major point of friction between Governor Zeb Vance and the Confederate authorities in Richmond. "I do not believe that one case in a hundred is caused by disloyalty—have no apprehensions on that score," the governor insisted to President Davis. "Home sickness, fatigue, hard fare &c have of course much to do with it."[49]

Vance complained repeatedly that North Carolina was being unfairly criticized by other states. Most of all, he blamed those attacks on "a too ready disposition to believe evil of the state, when it is known that No. Ca. is the only State in the Confederacy which employs her militia in the arrest of Conscripts and deserters; that she has better executed the conscript law, has fuller regiments in the field than any other and that at the two last battles on the Rappahannock in Dec, and in May, she furnished more than half of the killed and wounded."[50]

These statements did little to dispel the widespread belief that Chief Justice Richard M. Pearson of the State Supreme Court had undermined the morale of the Tar Heel troops when he released several deserters on writs of *habeas corpus* and declared that the state militia had no right to enforce the Conscription Act.

---

47 Allie Clack to Carrie Clack, May 23, 1863, Clack Papers.

48 Marston Diary, Entry for May 17, 1863, Emory; Mercer to Sister, May 17, 1863, in Wyatt, *The Reeves, Mercer, Newkirk Families*, 270.

49 Zebulon B. Vance to Jefferson Davis, May 13, 1863, in Mobley, *Papers of Vance*, Vol. 2, 151-152.

50 Zebulon B. Vance to James A. Seddon, May 25, 1863, in *ibid.*, 173-174.

"News of Judge Pearson's decision went abroad to the Army in a very exaggerated and ridiculous form," the governor explained. He noted that "soldiers were induced to believe the conscription law unconstitutional and that they were entitled if they came home to the protection of the civil authorities."[51]

Many in the Army of Northern Virginia blamed the increase in desertion on the movement for a separate peace, which was being pushed by populist editor William W. Holden in his Raleigh newspaper. Although his rhetoric was just beginning to heat up, it already had raised major concerns among the Tar Heel commanders. "Our N.C. soldiers are deserting very rapidly," Gen. Dorsey Pender told his wife in late April. "I have had about 30 in the last 20 days, and all due to those arch traitors Holden and Pearson. Poor old N.C., she will disgrace herself just when the worst is over, and after two years faithful service."[52]

Whatever the cause, desertion among the Tar Heel regiments in Rodes' Division escalated dramatically in the weeks following the Chancellorsville victory. Where once only one or two men would leave from a regiment at a time, the simultaneous desertions now numbered in the dozens. Private Coghill of the 23rd North Carolina reported in a letter to his sister that "our soldiers are running away most every night by squads." Private Brotherton of the same regiment observed that in "some regiments 35 and forty leaves at a time."[53]

Following his promotion to company commander in late May, the 20th North Carolina's Captain Mercer was shocked to find that seven of his men had "tried to get away but were apprehended in their mean design and arrested." What troubled Mercer the most was that the would-be deserters were not skulkers or cowards but instead some of the best soldiers in his company. "They were men of whom I had no idea of ever thinking of such a thing as that," complained the surprised captain. "They said they intended to come back. They only wanted to see their people. That may be true, but by no means it excuses the matter."[54]

---

51 Vance to Davis, May 13, 1863, in *ibid.*, 151-152.

52 William Dorsey Pender to Fanny Pender, April 21, 1863, in William B. Hassler, ed., *One of Lee's Best Men: The Civil War Letters of General William Dorsey Pender* (Chapel Hill: University of North Carolina Press, 1999), 227.

53 John F. Coghill to Dear Mit, May 24, 1863, James O. Coghill Letters; William H. Brotherton to Dear Grandmother and All The Rest, June 3, 1863, Brotherton Papers.

54 Oliver E. Mercer to Dear Brother, May 26, 1863, Wyatt, *The Reeves, Mercer, Newkirk Families*, 271.

The problem soon became so widespread that normal provost details proved inadequate. During the last days of May, Rodes assigned men from the 23rd North Carolina to round up the large groups of soldiers who were running away from their commands. "There is a great deal of desertion going on in our army, at this time," Private Clack from that regiment remarked to his sister. "We have to send a large guard from our regt every day to the principal roads, forks, & crossings to take up all deserters."[55]

Similar efforts to stem the flood of desertions were implemented in the 5th North Carolina. "We must stand guard around the camp all the time and after dark let no man pass and then have another guard about two miles off for catching runaways," Private Moose wrote in a letter home. During their first night on duty, the guards captured 13 Tar Heel soldiers from another brigade endeavoring to make their way home. His own regiment was not exempt from the problem. According to Moose, his unit "lost more runaways since the fight than they lost in the killed and wounded."[56]

Another major concern circulating through Iverson's Brigade was the reduction in rations in the weeks following the battle. Although a few soldiers complained bitterly about the shortage of supplies, others found it more of an annoyance than a major problem. "We get enough to eat," Pvt. Adam Seagle of the 23rd North Carolina insisted in a letter to one of his female friends. "We get a mess of fish every day or so. Some folks write home that we are starving. We get little enough to eat, it is a fact." At the same time, he assured her that the men in his regiment were "nary <u>Starving</u> yet."[57]

The men might not have been starving, but the reduction in rations still proved to be a significant hardship. For some of Iverson's men, the only alternative was to return home without leave. "There runaway fourteen men out of our Redgment since the fight and four runaway from our Company," Private Richardson from the 5th North Carolina informed his sister. "They all ran off the same knight." Richardson insisted that he would "stay as long as there is a pea in the dish and when they all leave then I will come home if life last[s]."[58]

---

55 Allie Clack to Carrie Clack, May 23, 1863, Clack Papers.

56 Daniel M. Moose to Dear Father-in-law, May 28, 1863, in Troxler and Barrier Auciello, *Dear Father*, 134.

57 Adam Seagle to Miss E. W., May 12, 1863, John R. Peacock Collection, SHC.

58 Richardson to Sister, May 15, 1863, Richardson Papers.

Reverend Charles Force Deems, whose son served in Iverson's Brigade, held several prayer meetings in Rodes' Division during early June 1863.

Brock Historical Museum, Greensboro College

Rather than deserting, many other soldiers responded to their hardships by joining in the religious fervor that was sweeping through large swaths of the Army of Northern Virginia in the wake of the terrible slaughter at Chancellorsville and the death of the beloved Stonewall Jackson. "Jackson though dead, yet speaketh by his Christian example, and officers in high command, are doing all they can to encourage this glorious work," Reverend Need B. Cobb declared to the *Wilmington Journal* newspaper. He insisted that "thousands are enquiring what they shall do to be saved, and scores and hundreds are being added to the different Christian denominations daily." Cobb went on to note that "there has been a special out-pouring of the spirit" in both Ramseur's and Iverson's brigades.[59]

The revival attracted the attention of several well-known clergymen from outside the Virginia army. Reverend William J. Hoge, the brother of the famed minister Moses Drury Hoge, conducted a series of prayer meetings for the soldiers in the division during May. "He seems to be preaching to the different brigades about here, expects to visit us again in a week or so," Private Clack wrote home after one of the services that so impressed him. Clack pointed out that "the singing was very good, one of our bands was in attendance, which combined with vocal music, made the old pine grove reverberate with joyous

---

59 "Great Religious Revival in the Army of Northern Virginia," *Wilmington Journal*, May 29, 1863.

anthems, which reminded one of by gone days, big meetings & such like, minus the women."[60]

For some of Iverson's men, the religious services conducted by Reverend Hoge drew more mixed reviews. Private Coghill from the 23rd North Carolina found nothing to fault about the huge gathering that he attended in the middle of the month. "Yesterday, the hole Brigade went to preaching and a better sermont I thought I had never herd," he informed his sister in a letter home. The same could not be said for one of Coghill's best friends in the regiment, who "did not like such a big meeting" because there was "nothing to eat nor any young girls to be seen."[61]

In early June, the division received a welcomed visit from the prominent North Carolina clergyman Reverend Charles Force Deems, whose son was serving with the 5th North Carolina in Iverson's command. Deems was a native of Maryland and attended Dickinson College in Carlisle, Pennsylvania. Following his graduation in 1839, he won early fame in his adopted state of North Carolina as a "boy preacher" for the American Bible Society, and later served as professor of logic and rhetoric at the University of North Carolina and as president of the Greensboro Female College. In 1859, Deems established the St. Austin's Institute in the town of Wilson, where his son trained as a military cadet.[62]

Reverend Deems held a series of worship services for the troops from the Tar Heel state. One of the first gatherings took place in the brigade commanded by Iverson. "At Gen. Iverson's request, I preached for his Brigade, officers uniting with men as heretofore," Deems explained to a fellow clergyman. According to the popular clergyman, he "did not see a single careless look at divine service, nor did I hear a word of disrespect towards religion or its ministers, but I did see more devoutness than usual in congregation and a great

---

60 Allie Clack to Carrie Clack, May 23, 1863, Clack Papers. For a firsthand account of the services in the other brigades from the division, see William J. Hoge to Dear Wife, May 22, 1863, in Peyton Harrison Hoge, *Moses Drury Hoge: Life and Letters* (Richmond: Whittet and Shefferson, 1899), 212-214. The famed Presbyterian minister Moses Drury Hoge from Richmond was absent on a trip to Europe at the time. For details, see Moses Drury Hoge to Dear Sir, May 19, 1863, in *ibid.*, 183.

61 John F. Coghill to Dear Mit, May 24, 1863, James O. Coghill Papers.

62 Charles Force Deems Journal, June 4, 1863, in Edward M. Deems and Francis M. Deems, eds., *Autobiography of Charles Force Deems* (New York: Fleming H. Revell Company, 1897), 184; Powell, *Dictionary of North Carolina Biography*, 2:49-50; Charles Lee Raper, *The Church and Private Schools of North Carolina: A Historical Study* (Greensboro, NC: Joseph Stone, 1898), 130, 206-207.

desire to hear preaching." During his nearly week-long stay, Deems continued preaching to North Carolina soldiers throughout the division.[63]

One of the brigades Deems held services for was led by Brig. Gen. Junius B. Daniel. His more than 2,200 fresh troops had only recently joined the division in exchange for Alfred Colquitt's Georgia brigade, which was transferred to North Carolina after Chancellorsville. The change came about because of Gen. Lee's clear dissatisfaction with Colquitt's performance during the attack at Chancellorsville on May 2, coupled with the depleted condition of his brigade.[64]

The 38-year-old Junius Daniel hailed from a prominent North Carolina family. His father was a successful lawyer who had served as a U.S. congressman and the state's attorney general. Rather than enter politics, Junius pursued a career in the military. He graduated from West Point in the class of 1851 and spent nearly seven years on the western frontier as an officer in the 3rd U.S. Infantry. Daniel resigned his commission in 1858 so that he could take charge of one of his family's plantations near Shreveport, Louisiana.

At the outbreak of war, Daniel was elected as colonel of the 14th North Carolina. Soon afterward, he accepted a commission at the same rank in the 45th North Carolina. His regiment served briefly under Lee at the end of the Seven Days' Campaign without seeing any significant action. Daniel's lone brush with combat was at Malvern Hill on July 1, where his troops suffered a handful of casualties from Federal artillery fire. His brigade remained on garrison duty near Drewry's Bluff in Virginia, and in North Carolina before finally joining Rodes' Division. Daniel's much deserved promotion to brigadier general would arrive on September 1, 1862.[65]

Despite the desperate need for reinforcements that Daniel's arrival helped alleviate, the unexpected transfer of Colquitt's Brigade to North Carolina produced widespread dissension among the Tar Heel veterans in the division. As soon as word of the exchange leaked, reports circulated that Ramseur had

---

63 "An Interesting Letter," *Spirit of the Age*, June 22, 1863.

64 John W. Busey and David G. Martin, *Regimental Strengths and Losses at Gettysburg* (Highstown, NJ: Longstreet House, 1986), 164. For details on the arrival of Daniel's Brigade in camp, see Jeff Robinson to Dear Brother and Sister, May [29], 1863, Hugh Harrison Mills Collection, Joyner Library, East Carolina University, Greenville, North Carolina (hereafter cited as ECU) and Thomas C. Land to Brother Hufham, May 31, 1863, *Biblical Recorder*, June 10, 1863.

65 Warner, *Generals in Gray*, 67.

declined a direct request from D. H. Hill to return with his brigade to their home state in exchange for Daniel's because Ramseur was opposed to leaving the Virginia army. For most of the men in Ramseur's command, the decision to remain behind instead of going home was a major disappointment.[66]

The reaction was worse in Iverson's Brigade, where rumors spread among the troops that their commander had turned down the chance for them to return home because of his fears about their loyalty. "Our brigade, the other day, I learn had the refusal of going to N.C. but, Genl. Iverson, who is a Georgian, wouldn't avail himself of the opportunity; said that all his men would desert," the 23rd's Private Clack complained. "So Genl Colquitt had to go, with his brigade of Georgians. Most of the men grumbled very much, but couldn't help themselves." Nearly all of them "seem anxious to get nearer home."[67]

Private Brotherton from the same regiment informed his parents that "we had the chance of going to old N. Carolina but our General refuse[d] gowing but their is strong talk of us gowing their yet." Unable to give up his dream of transferring to his home state, Brotherton placed his faith in his regimental commander, Colonel Christie. Describing him as "one of the best connel[s] in the world," Brotherton reported to his family that Christie "is trying his best to get us back to old N.C." At the same time, he admitted that "if we get back their I don't think we will have much to do."[68]

---

[66] William E. Ardrey Diary, Entry for May 20, 1863, in "Civil War Account of the Great-Grandfather of Alliance Resident," *The Pamlico News*, Sept. 2, 1992; Francis M. Parker to Sarah Parker, May 21, 1863, in Michael W. Taylor, ed., *To Drive the Enemy From Southern Soil: The Letters of Col. Francis Marion Parker and the History of the 30th Regiment North Carolina Troops* (Dayton, Ohio: Morningside House, 1998), 277-278; Stephen Dodson Ramseur to Ellen Richmond, May 25, 1863, in Letter Extracts, Stephen Dodson Ramseur Papers, SHC.

[67] Allie Clack to Carrie Clack, May 23, 1863, Clack Papers.

[68] William H. Brotherton to Dear Father and Mother, May 28, 1863, Brotherton Papers.

Chapter Six

We Have No Doubt Succeeded in Deceiving Hooker

Rather than returning home, the men from Iverson's Brigade remained in camp just south of Fredericksburg through the end of May. By then, Robert Rodes had received a well-deserved promotion to permanent command of the division. More than six feet tall and sporting an imposing sandy mustache, the 34-year-old major general exemplified the image of the emerging breed of Confederate warriors. Unlike every other general of the same rank in Lee's army, Rodes did not attend West Point. A native of Lynchburg, Virginia, he instead graduated from VMI in 1848. After a brief stint teaching at his *alma mater*, he moved to Alabama and built a thriving career as a civil engineer in the railroad industry.

Just prior to the outbreak of war, Rodes accepted an appointment as a professor of applied mechanics at VMI but never served in that position. Rather than returning to his former school, Rodes stayed in Tuscaloosa, Alabama, and organized a volunteer company known as the "Warrior Guards." Soon after arriving in camp at Montgomery, he was elected colonel of the newly formed 5th Alabama. His regiment reached Virginia just in time for the Battle of First Manassas but had only a minor part in the fighting. Rodes was promoted to brigadier general in October of 1861.

Rodes' first major combat at the head of his new brigade took place in late May of 1862 at Seven Pines in the Peninsula Campaign, where he was wounded and cited for bravery. Despite his injury, Rodes returned to duty in time to lead his men in the bloody fighting at Gaines' Mill. Rodes further enhanced his reputation at South Mountain in the Maryland Campaign, when his brigade single-handedly held off an entire Federal division threatening Lee's supply lines. He again performed gallantly and was slightly wounded during the fierce action along Bloody Lane at Sharpsburg three days later.

Despite his enviable record, Rodes failed to earn further advancement during the ensuing months. The most disappointing moment came when it appeared that he would be passed over as head of the division in which he was serving. Following the transfer of D. H. Hill from the Virginia army in early 1863, Rodes assumed temporary leadership of the division. Even so, Stonewall Jackson favored the selection of Brig. Gen. Edward "Allegheny" Johnson rather than Rodes as the division's permanent commander. The final decision remained on hold until Johnson could heal from a severe ankle wound he suffered while serving alongside Jackson in northwestern Virginia during the previous year.[1]

Although Johnson's recovery extended well into the spring of 1863, Rodes held out little hope that he would gain the promotion. Jackson certainly gave no indication that he had any intention of changing his preference for Johnson. Rodes was further convinced that the first opportunity that existed to fill any other vacancy for division commander would go to Brig. Gen. Cadmus M. Wilcox. "As he is a West Point man he will beat me almost to a certainty," Rodes commented during early spring. "I would prefer being beaten by a baboon but will submit to it quietly, unless they place [him] in command of this Div."[2]

The scales tipped dramatically in Rodes' favor when his brilliant tactical leadership helped rout Howard's XI Corps at Chancellorsville on May 2. "Gen.

---

[1] Warner, *Generals in Gray*, 263; Larry Tagg, *The Generals of Gettysburg: The Leaders of America's Greatest Battle* (Campbell, CA: Savas Publishing Company, 1998), 284. For specific details on Rodes' career, see Robert K. Krick, "We Have Never Suffered a Greater Loss Save in the Great Jackson: Was Robert E. Rodes the Army's Best Division Commander," included in Robert K. Krick, ed., *The Smoothbore Volley That Doomed the Confederacy* (Baton Rouge: Louisiana State University Press, 2002), 117-143 and Darrell L. Collins, *Major General Robert E. Rodes of the Army of Northern Virginia: A Biography* (New York: Savas Beatie, 2008).

[2] Robert Rodes to Richard S. Ewell, March 22, 1863, Polk, Brown and Ewell Papers, SHC.

Rodes distinguished himself much and won a proud name for himself and his division," Maj. Gen. A. P. Hill declared in his official report. Lee indicated that one of Jackson's "dying messages to me was to the effect that General Rodes should be promoted major general and his promotion should date from May 2." Rodes was elevated to his new rank within days after the battle, and Johnson was assigned to command Jackson's former division.[3]

Rodes quickly confronted the problem of who would succeed him as permanent commander of his former brigade. Colonel Edward O'Neal of the 26th Alabama had held that position from early January. O'Neal was 44 years old and the senior officer in the brigade. Prior to the war, he had been a prominent lawyer in Alabama and unsuccessfully ran for Congress in 1848. He joined the 9th Alabama as a major at the beginning of the war and was promoted to lieutenant colonel. O'Neal transferred to the 26th Alabama on his appointment as colonel and suffered wounds at Seven Pines, South Mountain, and Chancellorsville.[4]

As a leading advocate of secession, O'Neal had cultivated strong ties with politicians throughout the state. Although he used his connections to vigorously lobby the Confederate government for promotion, Rodes failed to include him among his top choices for permanent command of the brigade. The new division leader preferred to have Brig. Gen. John B. Gordon transferred from his position as temporary commander of a Georgia brigade in Jubal Early's Division. If that proved unsuccessful, he requested the promotion of Col. John Tyler Morgan who had formerly served with him as a field officer in the 5th Alabama.[5]

As was always the case, the final selection of a new brigade commander remained with Lee. When difficulties arose with securing the services of both Gordon and Morgan, he decided to give the position to O'Neal. Lee noted that the selection of O'Neal was based on his seniority and the fact that he "has been identified with his regiment and the brigade by long service as Lieut. Col. and Colonel." On Lee's recommendation, the War Department in Richmond

---

3 *OR* 25, pt. 1, 886; *OR* 33, 1134.

4 Warner, *Generals in Gray*, 226.

5 Robert E. Rodes to A. P. Hill, May 13, 1863, Compiled Service Record of Edward A. O'Neal Sr., M 311, R 315, NA; Robert E. Rodes to R. H. Chilton, May 13, 1863, *ibid.* For details on O'Neal's attempts to use his political influence, see George S. Houston to James A. Seddon, Jan. 12, 1863, *ibid.*; James Phelan to Jefferson Davis, Feb.19, 1863, *ibid.*

formally issued a commission for O'Neal's promotion to brigadier general on June 6.⁶

In a break with normal procedure, news of the appointment was not immediately passed on to the colonel and his family, who had long expected a much different outcome. "If any man has ever done his duty or won his promotion, you have," O'Neal's wife wrote to him on the day before the commission was issued. "And yet I think it very doubtful whether you will have justice done you." The failure to inform O'Neal of the commission resulted from a last-minute protest by Rodes that caused Lee to put the promotion on hold. The final decision on O'Neal's future with the Army of Northern Virginia would have to await his performance in the upcoming summer campaign.⁷

The problems with O'Neal did nothing to diminish Rodes' growing reputation in the army. The first official recognition of his new status came on May 29 when the men from Iverson's Brigade joined the rest of the division near Hamilton's Crossing for a grand review by the army's top commanders. Private John Coghill of the 23rd North Carolina reported to his family that the troops enjoyed "a nice and pretty review of our brave and noble General R. E. Lee." Private Allie Clack from the same regiment remembered that the event "was attended by a good many of our Genls & their wives." He pointed out that the officers and their staffs "made quite an imposing cavalcade of horsemen."⁸

Despite the festive surroundings, some of the men who had emerged unscathed from the bloody fighting at Chancellorsville still found it difficult to shake their somber mood. Ramseur, in particular, took little pleasure in watching his own troops as they marched by that day. Almost a month after the battle, the effects on the brigade remained plainly evident. "We made a splendid appearance, but it was very sad to see the thinned ranks of our Veterans," he lamented in a letter to his fianceé. "So many now lie in their graves and so many more lie on beds of pain."⁹

---

6   Robert E. Lee to Jefferson Davis, May 26, 1863, in Douglas S. Freeman, ed., *Lee's Dispatches: Unpublished Letters of General Robert E. Lee* (New York: G. P. Putnam's Sons, 1957), 95.

7   Olivia O'Neal to Edward A. O'Neal Sr., June 5, 1863, Edward Asbury O'Neal Papers, SHC; Collins, *Major General Robert E. Rodes*, 305-306.

8   John F. Coghill to Dear Mit, May 29, 1863, James O. Coghill Papers; Allie Clack to Carrie Clack, May 31, 1863, Clack Papers.

9   Stephen Dodson Ramseur to Ellen Richmond, May 29, 1863, in Christopher M. Watford, ed., *The Civil War in North Carolina: Soldiers and Civilian Letters and Diaries, 1861-1865, Vol. 1, The*

More uplifting for Iverson's war-weary soldiers was the sight of Daniel's troops forming on the parade grounds for the first time since arriving in camp. "A new brigade of ours attracted marked attention on account of the number of men each regiment contained," Private Clack remarked in a letter to his sister. "Daniel's Brigade took the place of Colquitts which has gone south." Most impressive of all was its size compared to the other brigades in the division. According to Clack, Daniel's fresh command was "as large as any two of our brigades & never been in much of a fight."[10]

The highlight of the ceremony came when the color bearer from each regiment dipped his flag as Lee passed in front of the troops. The commanding general responded by taking off his hat as the men in turn marched by in columns to the stirring sounds of martial music provided by the division's regimental bands. "Brass one in Iversons [played] very good music," Pvt. Samuel D. Pickens from the 5th Alabama in O'Neal's Brigade scribbled in his diary. "Rodes carried us thro it all as rehearsal before Lee came, so it was a most fatiguing day."[11]

Besides serving as a major showcase for Rodes and the men in his division, the review marked the return to the army of Lt. Gen. Richard S. Ewell, who had just been selected to succeed Stonewall Jackson as commander of the newly reorganized Second Corps. His arrival came earlier that day on the train from Richmond. At the age of 46, Ewell was now third in command of the Army of Northern Virginia. In addition to Rodes' troops, the corps he would take over on June 1 included Johnson's new division and the division headed by Gen. Jubal Early.[12]

Ewell's background gave every indication that he was well qualified for his new command. He graduated from West Point in 1840, where he ranked 13th

---

Piedmont (Jefferson, NC: McFarland and Company, 2003), 111. The quote is reported as "so many now in their graves—& many languishing upon beds of pain" in Ramseur to Richmond, May 29, 1863, in Letter Extracts, Stephen Dodson Ramseur Papers.

10 Allie Clack to Carrie Clack, May 31, 1863, Clack Papers.

11 Samuel D. Pickens Diary, Entry for May 29, 1863, in G. Ward Hubbs, ed., *Voices from Company D: Diaries by the Greensboro Guards, Fifth Alabama Infantry, Army of Northern Virginia* (Athens: University of Georgia Press, 2003), 172.

12 Ardrey Diary, Entry for May [2]9, 1863, in *The Pamlico News*, Sept. 2, 1992; Jedediah Hotchkiss Journal, Entry for May 29, 1863, in Archie P. McDonald, ed., *Make Me a Map of the Valley: The Civil War Journal of Stonewall Jackson's Topographer* (Dallas: Southern Methodist University Press, 1973), 149.

in his class. Ewell fought in the Mexican War under Maj. Gen. Winfield Scott and was cited for gallantry during the fighting at Contreras and Churubusco. He continued to serve in the U.S. Army after the war as an officer in the dragoons on the western frontier, eventually rising to the rank of captain. Bald-headed with bulging eyes and a distinct lisp to his speech, Ewell was still a bachelor when he joined the Confederate service in early 1861.

As an experienced military man, Ewell rose quickly to command of a division under Stonewall Jackson. During the Shenandoah Valley Campaign in the spring of 1862, Ewell emerged as one of Jackson's most trusted subordinates. His service with Jackson, however, was cut short when he was severely wounded in the leg at Groveton during the Second Manassas Campaign. While recovering from the amputation of his leg, Ewell courted and married Lizinka Campbell Brown, his cousin and the widow of a wealthy plantation owner from Mississippi. By the time of Stonewall Jackson's death in mid-May, Ewell had recovered from his wounds and was ready to rejoin the army.[13]

Because of his long association with Jackson, Ewell's appointment as head of the Second Corps was greeted warmly by nearly all the officers who had been closest to the fallen general. "We have our wishes gratified here in having Gen. Ewell to command the old army of Gen. Jackson," Jed Hotchkiss, who had served on Jackson's staff as the chief topographer, confided to his wife. "As much of the ardor as could possibly be transferred to any man has been transferred by this corps to Gen. Ewell." Jackson's former assistant adjutant general, Maj. Alexander S. "Sandie" Pendleton, felt the same way. Sandie described Ewell in a letter to his fiancé as "the old hero, friend and fellow soldier & sufferer, comrade in battle and on the march and a fellow mourner with each one of us."[14]

What grumbling there was about his promotion came largely from those who had close ties to A. P. Hill, who was selected as the commander of the newly created Third Corps in the Virginia army's major post-Chancellorsville reorganization. Yet, even for some of his friends in Jackson's former corps, a major cause for concern was not about his prior experience or injury, but that

---

13 Warner, *Generals in Gray*, 84. For a detailed account of Ewell's career, see Donald C. Pfanz, *Richard S. Ewell: A Soldier's Life* (Chapel Hill: University of North Carolina Press, 1998).

14 Jedediah Hotchkiss to Sara Hotchkiss, May 31, 1863, Hotchkiss Papers; Alexander S. Pendleton to Kate Corbin, June 4, 1863, William Nelson Pendleton Papers, SHC.

Richard Ewell decided to have his new wife accompany him on his return to the army. "General Ewell arrived in camp with his wife—a new acquisition—and with one leg less than when I saw him last," wrote one officer who had served with him throughout much of the war. "From a military point of view the addition of the wife did not compensate for the loss of the leg." He went on to observe that "we were of the opinion that Ewell was not the same soldier he had been when he was a whole man—and a single one."[15]

Despite these misgivings, the selection of Ewell as their new corps commander was generally well received by the men in Iverson's Brigade. For many of them, the most telling point in his favor was the widespread rumor that Jackson had requested on his deathbed that Ewell be appointed as his successor. "I have also seen it, in print, that it was Jackson's wish that it should fall on Gen Ewell, speaking of him in the highest terms, but as yet, I have heard nothing definite as to his successor," Private Clack commented just prior to Ewell's appointment.[16]

The promotion of someone so close to Jackson signaled to many veterans that the time had finally arrived to break the stalemate along the Rappahannock that had existed since the previous December following the defensive victory at Fredericksburg. Many in the army believed that Lee, rather than Joe Hooker, would be the first one to make a move. "If there is any forward movement it will no doubt be initiated by Genl. Lee, as our army is now in fine condition & everything looks favorable for an aggressive campaign," Maj. Charles Blacknall from the 23rd North Carolina declared to his brother-in-law at the beginning of June.[17]

The first clear sign that a new summer campaign was imminent arrived late on the afternoon on June 3. Brigade commissary officers began to procure extra rations—a sure indication something was about to take place. When company commanders received orders to requisition a four-month's supply of clothing, all doubt was removed. Despite the activity, there remained no indication of exactly what their destination might be. "We have just recd orders to prepare for the march & I expect will be off tonight," General Ramseur explained in a

---

15 William Dorsey Pender to Fanny Pender, May 14, 1863, in Hassler, *One of Lee's Best Men*, 237; Randolph H. McKim, *A Soldier's Recollections: Leaves from the Diary of a Young Confederate* (New York: Longman, Green, and Co., 1910), 134.

16 Allie Clack to Carrie Clack, May 23, 1863, Clack Papers.

17 Charles C. Blacknall to Dear Bro. George, June 1, 1863, Blacknall Papers.

letter to his fianceé that same day. "Where or why we go, none but Genl Lee & his Lieuts know."[18]

Even the top generals in the army had been informed of the final plan only two days earlier. After slipping away from the Fredericksburg area, Lee intended to seize the initiative by pushing his army through the Shenandoah Valley, across the Potomac River, and directly into the heart of Maryland and Pennsylvania. As the army moved forward, Lee hoped to gather huge quantities of badly needed supplies and, at the same time, provide Virginia with weeks and perhaps months of relief from rampaging armies. Lee expected that the advance would draw Hooker's force away from his own supply base at Falmouth and thus transfer the "the scene of hostilities north of the Potomac." It also offered "a fair opportunity to strike a blow at the army then commanded by General Hooker."[19]

About one-thirty in the morning on June 4, the men from Ramseur's Brigade finally received the command to make their way "as speedily and noiselessly as possible" from their camp about two miles south of Hamilton's Crossing. Within half an hour, O'Neal's Brigade began moving out along the same route. Surgeon William Marston from the 12th North Carolina noted in his diary that Iverson's troops were also soon "on the march." Even then, their final destination was still "not known." Just after dawn, all five of the brigades comprising Rodes' Division were assembled on the road a few miles south of Fredericksburg near the railway depot at Guiney's Station.[20]

The decision to begin their advance "quietly and with dispatch" well before dawn was because of the need to keep out of sight from the Federal balloons operating along the far side of the river. Adding to the deception was the initial line of march, which took Rodes' men south past Guiney's Station before turning to the northwest toward Spotsylvania Court House. That move was part of the plan that called for Rodes to make his way west and north along the back roads to Culpeper Court House, where Lee intended to concentrate his forces before moving westward through the mountain gaps into the

---

18 Ardrey Diary, Entry for June 3, 1863, in *The Pamlico News*, Sept. 2, 1992; Stephen Dodson Ramseur to Ellen Richmond, June 3, 1863, Stephen Dodson Ramseur Papers.

19 OR 27, pt. 2, 305.

20 "From the Fourth North Carolina," June 7, 1863, *Carolina Watchman*, June 22, 1863; Thomas S. Taylor to My Dear Wife, July 17, 1863, Thomas S. Taylor Papers, Alabama Department of Archives and History, Montgomery, Alabama (hereafter cited as ADAH); Marston Diary, Entry for June 4, 1863, Emory.

Shenandoah Valley. The initial part of the trip was expected to take three days and cover more than 40 miles.[21]

Ewell's other two divisions joined the advance early the following day. Jubal Early's brigades departed under cover of darkness at one o'clock in the morning, while Johnson's command began moving out from camp about one hour later. Major General Lafayette McLaw's Division, the only part of James Longstreet's First Corps in the immediate vicinity of Fredericksburg, had already slipped away from the area on the morning of June 3. A. P. Hill's new Third Corps remained behind along the Rappahannock River to screen the departure from prying Federal eyes.[22]

Despite the proximity of the enemy, the massive troop movement went off without a hitch. By all indications, Hooker was unaware that more than half of Lee's men had made their way out of the Fredericksburg area. Because of the darkness, even the balloons failed to provide any warning of unusual enemy activity. Major Blacknall of the 23rd North Carolina insisted in a letter to his wife that the entire force had departed in such complete secrecy that they "have no doubt succeeded in deceiving Hooker & will fall on him suddenly in a place where he is least expecting it."[23]

Whatever high spirits Iverson's men departed with plummeted when they found the conditions on the road nearly unbearable. Worst of all were the high temperatures and the severe shortage of rain during the past month. "It is very dry up here, and the dust rises from the roads in clouds," Pvt. George Davis from the 12th North Carolina, who was detailed as a teamster, explained in a letter to his mother. "The troops look like old men. Their hair and eye brows white with dust." The trip proved just as difficult for the 23rd North Carolina's Private Clack, who admitted to his sister that he came "about as near giving out

---

21 James I. Harris to Burton Williford, Aug. 24, 1863, in Michael W. Taylor, "Ramseur's Brigade in the Gettysburg Campaign: A newly Discovered Account by Capt. James I. Harris," *Gettysburg Magazine*, 17 (July 1997), 28. The balloons were especially prominent during the recent review by General Lee. For details, see Irvin Boyles to Mary Ann Boyles, June 2, 1863, Mary Ann Boyles Papers, Duke, and Nathan R. Frazier to Beloved Wife, May 30, 1863, Nathan R. Frazier Papers, ECU.

22 Clement A. Evans to Allie Evans, June 5, 1863, in Robert G. Stephens Jr., ed., *Intrepid Warrior: Clement Ansley Evans* (Dayton, OH: Morningside Books, 1992), 185-186; McKim, *Soldier's Recollections*, 138. For details on the routes for the various divisions, see Charles B. "Bud" Hall, "The Army Is Moving: Lee's March to the Potomac, Rodes Spearheads the Way," *Blue and Gray Magazine*, 21, Issue 3 (Spring 2004), 14-15.

23 Charles C. Blacknall to Dear Jinny, June 8, 1863, Blacknall Papers.

as any one could" as they pushed forward from Fredericksburg on the first day of the trip.[24]

After a hard day of marching, the weary Tar Heel troops went into camp for the night just beyond Spotsylvania Court House along the Po River. They resumed the advance about five o'clock in the morning on June 5. Their route initially took them west along the Catharpin Road past the nearby Shady Grove Church. The men continued to follow this secondary road as it curved northwest for several miles to the area of Mine Run. From there, they marched west along Mine Run Road as far as the tiny hamlet of Old Verdiersville.

According to Surgeon Marston, Iverson and his men began their trip that day just before dawn in order to avoid the worst of the heat. Even so, the intense temperatures and long hours on the road continued to plague the troops as they proceeded north along the back roads toward Culpeper Court House. The conditions became so bad that many of the soldiers found it impossible to keep up. Blacknall described it as "a most disagreeable march, the heat & dust insuportable." He reported seeing "many of our men falling and some dieing in the road."[25]

By late afternoon, dozens of men who had passed out from the excessive heat and lack of water littered the division's entire line of march. "I saw one poor fellow lying on the side of the road sucking his thumb & foaming at the mouth," wrote an officer from Daniel's Brigade in a letter to his wife. "He perished to death for water. The men are not allowed to stop to get water when they are Suffering for it. I understand some three or four more died the same way this man did." He added that "when men have to march until they fall dead it looks hard."[26]

At least one soldier from O'Neal's Brigade blamed these problems on the officers leading the advance to Culpeper Court House. "Gens. Early and Rodes seemed to be ambitious to see who could reach the Court House first, and the consequence was a foot race, which resulted in laming about one third of the men and dropping a good many by the roadside who otherwise would have

---

24 George Davis to Ma, June 5, 1863, in Lafayette Claud Eaton Jr., ed., *Rebecca's Letters: A Saga of a Confederate Family* (Vallejo, CA: n.p., 2000), 58; Allie Clack to Carrie Clack, June 6, 1863, Clack Papers.

25 Charles C. Blacknall to Dear Bro. George, June 6, 1863, Blacknall Papers.

26 Ruffin Barnes to Dear Wife, June 8, 1863, in Hugh Buckner Johnston Jr., ed., "The Confederate Letters of Ruffin Barnes of Wilson County," *North Carolina Historical Review*, 31 (1954), 81.

been able to keep up," he declared in a letter to his hometown newspaper. He insisted that "such conduct on the part of general officers is not only cruel, but detrimental to the service."[27]

The rigors of the march were somewhat alleviated by the scenes that greeted the men as they trudged along on the afternoon of June 5. Private Clack reported to his sister that their trip carried them "through a country that doesn't show much sign of an armys depredation." All along the way, the local populace received them with open enthusiasm. Best of all was the sight of the young women who made up most of the crowd that lined the road. "At every farm house & crossing ladies were out waving their handkchs &c," recalled the private.

After tramping nearly 20 miles, the exhausted troops finally halted for the night just north of Old Verdiersville along a branch of Black Walnut Run. To their relief, the pace slowed considerably the following day. One private calculated that he and his comrades marched only "two or three miles this morning" before coming to a stop and setting up camp just south of the Rapidan River. "We left camp day before yesterday with three days rations and after two days march & a few hours over, we are resting here this morning in a cool delightful woods."[28]

The orders to halt the advance came in response to a Federal incursion that day across the Rappahannock River south of Fredericksburg. Just after daylight, a single division from Maj. Gen. John Sedgwick's VI Corps pushed over a hastily laid pontoon bridge directly opposite A. P. Hill's position. The objective of this reconnaissance in force was to ascertain the reason for the Confederate troop movements Federals had observed along the river. Sedgwick's thrust was easily repelled after it advanced but a short distance. More important, the attempt failed to uncover the fact that much of Lee's army had already left the area and was well on its way toward Culpeper Court House.[29]

With the situation along the Rappahannock under control, Rodes received orders to resume the advance early on the morning on June 7. After a short march, the troops reached the Somerville Ford on the Rapidan River only a few

---

27 "Letter From the Army of Virginia," June 16, 1863, *Mobile Daily Advertiser and Register*, June 30, 1863.

28 Allie Clack to Carrie Clack, June 6, 1863, Clack Papers; John T. Nichols Diary, Entry for June 6, 1863, John Thomas Nichols Papers, Duke.

29 *OR* 27, pt. 2, 293, 546.

miles upstream from the better-known Raccoon Ford. Private William Brotherton reported in a letter to his parents that Iverson's men "had a good deal of fun wading the river." Some of the men even "hired two Negroes [to] carry them across" at a cost of only five dollars apiece.[30]

The soldiers from Rodes' Division had just finished scrambling up the opposite bank of the river when Richard Ewell and his staff arrived at the front of the column. It was the first time during the march they had assumed that position. "We found Rodes well on the road and across the Ford," Jed Hotchkiss from Ewell's staff recorded in his diary. He noted with satisfaction that "the troops soon recognized General Ewell and began to cheer him as had been their habit with General Jackson, thus transferring to him the ardor they felt for their old commander." In response, Ewell "took off his cap and rode rapidly along the line."[31]

From the Rapidan River, the men proceeded north through the area of Cedar Mountain where some of Jackson's men had fought a battle less than a year earlier. They continued to push forward from there until about noon, when they reached Culpeper Court House. This hotbed of Southern support was strategically located between the Rapidan and Rappahannock rivers, with ready access to the fertile Shenandoah Valley just beyond the Blue Ridge Mountains a handful of miles to the west. Culpeper also served as an important terminus on the railroad line with a direct connection to the Confederate capital at Richmond.[32]

Iverson's troops halted along the Rixeyville Road that afternoon about three miles north of town. By the end of the day, all of the Second Corps and most of Longstreet's First Corps had moved into the surrounding area. Jubal Early's and Edward Johnson's divisions trailed closely behind Rodes' infantry. Major General Lafayette McLaw's Division from First Corps had arrived the previous day, and Maj. Gen. John B. Hood's Division, also part of First Corps, had been near Culpeper Court House since June 4. The only First Corps division missing was that of Maj. Gen. George E. Pickett, which remained on

---

30 "From the Fourth North Carolina," June 7, 1863, *Carolina Watchman*, June 22, 1863; William H. Brotherton to Dear Father and Mother, June 8, 1863, Brotherton Papers.

31 Hotchkiss Journal, Entry for June 7, 1863, in McDonald, *Make Me a Map*, 149.

32 Wilbur Sturtevant Nye, *Here Come the Rebels!* (Dayton, OH: Morningside Press, 1988), 45. For details on the town during the Civil War, see Daniel E. Sutherland, *Seasons of War: The Ordeal of a Confederate Community* (New York: The Free Press, 1995).

detached duty near Hanover, Virginia. The all-Virginia command would not reach the vicinity of Culpeper until June 10.[33]

Iverson's weary men settled into their camp and began cooking additional rations for the impending campaign. "We are now on the march, leaving Fredericksburg on last Thursday & arriving near Culpeper C.H. last night where we remain today, making preparations for an extensive operation into the enemy's country," Maj. Blacknall reported in a letter to his wife. The major added that he could not "say exactly what will be our programme, but it is supposed that we are to have another great battle & all look for a more important victory than we have heretofore gained."[34]

Major Pendleton, an assistant adjutant general on Ewell's staff, was well satisfied with the conduct of the new corps commander during the advance. "The more I see of Gen Ewell the more I am pleased with him," he confided to his fianceé. "He resembles Gen. Jackson very much in some points of his character, particularly his utter disregard of his own personal comfort & his inflexibility of purpose." Pendleton reported to his mother that he expected "great things from him and am glad to say that our troops have for him a great deal of the same feeling that they had towards Gen. Jackson."[35]

The men were in camp during the early hours of June 9 when reports of a major cavalry engagement underway at nearby Brandy Station arrived. The fighting had started just after dawn when Maj. Gen. Alfred Pleasonton led a large force of Federal cavalry supported by two infantry brigades across two different fords on the Rappahannock. The move caught the cavalry pickets along the river completely by surprise. As they fell back in disarray, Jeb Stuart's cavalry division, which had been camped outside Culpeper Court House since May 20, engaged in a fluid and fierce combat along a broad front in the area of Brandy Station.[36]

---

33 Thomas Ware Diary, Entry for June 7, 1863, in Mark Nesbitt, ed., *35 Days to Gettysburg: The Campaign Diary of Two American Armies* (Mechanicsburg, PA: Stackpole Books, 2002), 41; Hall, "The Army is Moving," 16.

34 Blacknall to Jinny, June 8, 1863, Blacknall Papers.

35 Alexander S. Pendleton to Kate Corbin, June 8, 1863, William Nelson Pendleton Papers; Alexander S. Pendleton to Dear Mother, June 9, 1863, *ibid.*

36 For detailed accounts of the fighting at Brandy Station, see Thomas, *Bold Dragoon*, 219-231 and Edward G. Longacre, *The Cavalry at Gettysburg* (Lincoln: University of Nebraska Press, 1983), 65-86.

We Have No Doubt Succeeded in Deceiving Hooker 137

The route taken by Iverson's Brigade during the fighting at Brandy Station on June 9, 1863 carried the men directly through the farm owned by former Congressman John Minor Botts. *Library of Congress*

By mid-morning, the sounds of battle were clearly heard several miles away. Displaying his initiative, Rodes began filing his men out of camp along the main road heading south. "Anticipating an order to do so, I moved the division toward Brandy Station, to the support of General Stuart's cavalry," he explained in his official report. After proceeding only a short distance along the Rixeyville Road, his troops veered off to the east on a narrow country lane. From there, they continued pushing ahead in the general direction of Brandy Station.[37]

Their route carried them across a large farm owned by former U.S. Congressman John Minor Botts, who had been vilified throughout the Confederacy because of his ardent support for the Union. An officer in George Doles' Brigade reported that the troops "marched in line of battle through fields of clover, timothy & h[ay] grass for two miles or more." It was, he added, a "beautiful farm indeed and too good for such a traitor to live upon." Private

---

37 David R. E. Winn to My Darling Son, June 9, 1863, David Read Evans Winn Papers, Emory; OR 27, pt. 2, 546.

Pickens from O'Neal's Brigade was also impressed by the sight of Botts' large home known as "Auburn," which he described as "a very nice residence."[38]

The sudden and noisy activity of an army on the march across his property quickly drew the attention of the retired politician. Campbell Brown, one of Ewell's staff officers, watched in disbelief as Botts "came out in great rage, inquiring for the commanding officer of the force." The landowner began berating Rodes with "copious oaths," demanding that he move his men off his land because he was neutral and did not want his family and property endangered. Rodes responded to all the commotion by ordering "some of his Staff to make that d[amned] old fool go back to his house & behave himself—which cooled him down."[39]

With that problem solved, Rodes rejoined his marching troops as they tramped steadily toward the scene of the cavalry fight. One of the men reported that they "advanced to half mile of our Cavalry line of Battle where they were engaging the enemy's cavalry—found line of battle just on the left of Hon. Mr. Barbour's house." The referenced property belonged to Maj. James Barbour, who had once served as an assistant adjutant general on Ewell's division staff. His large two-story home, known as "Beauregard," stood only a short distance away from their position on the western spur of Fleetwood Ridge.[40]

While Rodes and Ewell rode ahead to the Barbour house, Junius Daniel at the front of the column began deploying his troops in support of Stuart's beleaguered troopers, who were heavily engaged along the nearby ridge. Ewell's orders called for Daniel to take up a position directly behind the front lines while the rest of Rodes' Division remained hidden behind Congressman Botts' farm. One soldier wrote in his diary that Daniel's men formed immediately "in line of battle with two lines of skirmishers in front."[41]

---

38 John H. Harris Diary, Entry for June 9, 1863, in Raynor Hubbell, *Confederate Stamps, Old Letters and History* (Griffin, GA: n.p., 1959), Appendix, 10; Pickens Diary, Entry for June 9, 1863, in Hubbs, *Voices from Company D*, 175.

39 G. Campbell Brown Journal, in Terry L. Jones, *Campbell Brown's Civil War: With Ewell and the Army of Northern Virginia* (Baton Rouge: Louisiana State, 2001), 190.

40 William H. Hodnett Diary, Entry for June 9, 1863, in Georgia Division, United Daughters of the Confederacy, *Confederate Reminiscences and Letters, 1861-1865*, 18 Vols. (Atlanta: United Daughters of the Confederacy, 1995-2000), 4:255 (hereafter cited as *Confederate Reminiscences and Letters*); OR 27, pt. 2, 564.

41 Louis Leon Diary, Entry for June 9, 1863, in Louis Leon, *Diary of a Tar Heel Confederate Soldier* (Wilmington, NC: Broadfoot Publishing Company, 1992), 29-30.

The first formal skirmish detachments were established throughout Rodes' Division in January of 1863. New orders required each regiment to select one-twelfth of the men present for duty as members of the sharpshooters. Although armed with long-range rifles, these men were most often used as skirmishers. The regimental detachments were organized into a single unit at the brigade level under the command of a major or captain. The men were exempt from most other duties, but remained with their individual regiments except "in the immediate presence of the enemy." The arrangement proved so successful that a second sharpshooter corps of the same size was formed in each regiment at the end of May.[42]

Captain Benjamin Robinson from the 5th North Carolina commanded the sharpshooter detachment in Iverson's Brigade. Nineteen-year-old Robinson came from a prominent family in Fayetteville, North Carolina. His father was a successful physician and commanded a local militia company in the years prior to the war. Like so many others, the younger Robinson seemed transformed by the realities of military life. A teenage girl, who was also a family friend, observed during one of his furloughs that he "has changed a great deal, has a moustache and has a stern look."

Despite his youth, Robinson proved to be a gallant leader. He experienced his first major combat during the fighting at Williamsburg in early May of 1862. After three color-bearers were shot down in the attack, Robinson grabbed the regiment's battle flag from the ground and carried it forward "until the staff of the flag was shivered to pieces in his hand." In January of 1863, he was selected to head the newly formed sharpshooter detachment in the brigade. Robinson continued to serve with distinction at that post during the fighting at Chancellorsville.[43]

The 23rd North Carolina's Private Brotherton, who joined Iverson's sharpshooters in late May, explained in a letter to his parents that the men in these units were "excuse[d] from standing guard and gowing on pickett" while

---

[42] James Z. Branscomb to Dear Sister, Jan. 11, 1863, in Frank Anderson Chappell, ed., *Dear Sister: Civil War Letters to a Sister in Alabama* (Huntsville, AL: Branch Springs Publishing Company, 2002), 128; Iverson's Brigade, General Order No. 6, Jan. 28, 1863, General and Special Orders, 23rd North Carolina, RG 109; Iverson's Brigade, General Order No. 10, May 25, 1863, *ibid*.

[43] Roy Parker Jr., "Heroes Flag Back in NC," *Fayetteville Observer*, Dec. 26, 2002; McRae, "Battle of Williamsburg, May 1862," *The William and Mary Quarterly*, Second Series, 2, No. 3 (July 1922), 196; Melinda Ray Diary, Entry for Nov. 18, 1861, North Carolina Room, New Hanover County Public Library.

in camp. "All the Sharp Shootters has to go in front tell they find the Yankees picket and then they commence firing," he explained. "We will have a better chance of showing battel." Brotherton also noted that "when the Yanks get two hard for us we have to fall back in the pair and then the main boddy gows on."[44]

Similar sharpshooter units were organized in Daniel's Brigade soon after his troops joined Rodes' Division in mid-May. "When we got to the Army of Northern Virginia we were told that each company must furnish one skirmisher out of every six men, and there was a call for volunteers for that service," Pvt. Louis Leon of the 53rd North Carolina penned in his diary. "So I left the colors and went as a skirmisher." He noted that their duty in time of battle was "to go in front of the line and reconnoiter and engage the enemy until a general engagement, then we fall in line with balance of the army."[45]

Although the men from Daniel's newly formed detachment were spoiling for a fight at Brandy Station, their instructions called for them to proceed cautiously. "I received orders from the major-general commanding the division to throw out skirmishers to the front, and move my line some half mile to the rear," Daniel explained in his campaign report. "After remaining in this position a short time, the enemy began to retire, and I received orders to advance my skirmishers and retire my line still farther to the rear, keeping my troops concealed behind the hills during the movement." He noted that "the enemy retired before my line of skirmishers."[46]

While prepared for action, Iverson's troops remained hidden from view with the rest of the division behind the lines on the Botts farm throughout the Brandy Station fight. Private Leonidas Torrence reported to his mother that most of Rodes' command "formed a line of battle . . . near Brandy Station but the Cavalry forced the Enemy [to] runn across the River before we got in to it." Major Blacknall from the same regiment noted in a letter to his brother-in-law that "when we advanced on the Yankee cavalry they immediately fell back across the river."[47]

---

44 William H. Brotherton to Dear Mother and Father, May 28, 1863, Brotherton Papers. For a detailed study of sharpshooter units, see Fred L. Ray, *Shock Troops of the Confederacy: The Sharpshooter Battalions of the Army of Northern Virginia* (Asheville, NC: CSF Press, 2006), 45-61.

45 Leon Diary, Entry for June 9, 1863, in Leon, *Diary of a Tar Heel Confederate*, 30.

46 OR 27, pt. 2, 564.

47 Leonidas Torrence to Dear Mother, June 17, 1863, in Monroe, "The Road to Gettysburg," 508; Charles C. Blacknall to Dear Bro. George, June 18, 1863, Blacknall Papers.

Rodes and Ewell, together with General Lee, spent their time observing the swirling battle around Brandy Station from just behind the front lines at the Barbour house. At one point the action came so close to their position that it seemed likely all three officers might be captured. Jed Hotchkiss recalled that Ewell responded to the danger by calling for them to "gather into the house and defend it to the last." The crisis quickly passed, however, as Stuart's troopers rallied along the nearby ridge and forced the Union cavalry to withdraw from the field.[48]

With the enemy in retreat, Rodes received orders in the early evening to stand down. The troops set up their camp a short distance away "in a nice piece of woods on the farm of John Minor Botts." As they settled in for a much-needed rest, they began to see clear indications that their stay in the vicinity of Culpeper Court House would be short-lived. Surgeon Marston noted in his diary that the troops halted "not far from Brandy Station with orders to cook rations and be prepared to march."[49]

Although the infantry had not been engaged, Stuart's cavalry suffered almost 500 casualties in the Brandy Station fight. Among those killed was Col. Solomon Williams from the 2nd North Carolina Cavalry, who six months earlier had been Iverson's pick to command the 12th North Carolina. According to one eyewitness, Williams "was shouting to the men to fall in when he was shot through the head and died immediately, his body being carried from the field by his adjutant, John C. Pegram." The same officer lamented that Williams was "indulgent to his men in camp almost to a fault, yet, when duty called and occasion required, he proved himself a leader worthy of their admiration."[50]

In a strange twist of fate, Williams had married Pegram's sister only two weeks prior to the battle. "A day or two before the battle of Brandy Station he had returned from a furlough to Petersburg, where he had gone to marry a lovely woman, a friend of mine," wrote one of the dead officer's female friends. Following his return to duty, Williams paid her a visit. She recalled that "the day

---

48 Hotchkiss Journal, Entry for June 9, 1863, in McDonald, *Make Me a Map*, 150.

49 Leon Diary, Entry for June 9, 1863, in Leon, *Diary of a Tar Heel*, 29; Pickens Diary, Entry for June 9, 1863, in Hubbs, *Voices from Company D*, 175; John T. Gay to Dear Pussie, June 10, 1863, Nix-Price Collection, Troup County Archives, LaGrange, Georgia; Marston Diary, Entry for June 9, 1863, Emory.

50 W. A. Graham, "Nineteenth Regiment," included in Clark, *NC Regiments*, 2:92-93.

before he was killed he sat at table with me, chatting pleasantly of mutual friends at home from whom he had brought messages, brimful of happiness, and of the charming wife he had won."[51]

For Dorsey Pender, who so desperately missed his own young wife, Colonel Williams' death came as especially sad news. "Poor Sol Williams and just married," he wrote his wife. "I pity his desolate young widow. A strong argument against marrying while the war last[s]. It would be much better if she were Miss Pagonne [Pegram] instead of Mrs. Williams." Like many in the army, Pender found fault with Jeb Stuart for allowing himself to be surprised along the river. "I suppose it is all right that Stuart should get all the blame, for when anything handsome is done he gets all the credit," wrote Pender. "A bad rule either way. He however retrieved the surprise by whipping them in the end."[52]

At least one soldier from O'Neal's Brigade found Stuart's conduct in hosting a series of lavish celebrations during the period leading up to the cavalry fight at Brandy Station as a cause for even greater blame. He noted with disgust in a letter to his hometown newspaper that Stuart "has been frolicking and dancing with the ladies of Culpeper" for several weeks prior to being surprised by the Federal cavalry. "No officer, whatever his ability may be, can devote himself to the ladies and do justice to himself or command," he argued. "This surprise and disaster has cost Stuart much of his reputation, and lost the confidence of his men in him. I hope it may be a lesson to him."[53]

The Federal cavalrymen made a strong statement at Brandy Station that they were now a credible force that was finally coming of age. At the same time, Stuart clearly suffered a major embarrassment at the hands of the enemy. "The cavalry fight at Brandy Station can hardly be called a victory," the brother of one of Stuart's staff officers admitted in a letter home. More important for the Confederate side, Hooker still failed to realize even after the end of the day that nearly two-thirds of Lee's Army of Northern Virginia was already on the move more than 40 miles from its prior camps outside Fredericksburg.[54]

---

51 Myrta Lockett Avary, ed., *A Virginia Girl in the Civil War 1861-1865: Being a Record of the Actual Experiences of a Wife of a Confederate Officer* (New York: D. Appleton and Co., 1903), 245.

52 William Dorsey Pender to Fannie Pender, June 12, 1863, Hassler, *One of Lee's Best Men*, 246.

53 "Letter From the Army of Virginia," June 16, 1863, *Mobile Daily Advertiser and Register*, June 30, 1863.

54 Letter of June 12, 1863, quoted in Susan Leigh Blackford, ed., *Letters From Lee's Army* (New York: Charles Scribner's Sons, 1947), 175; Thomas, *Bold Dragoon*, 225-231.

CHAPTER SEVEN

A Perfect Triumphal March

Despite the threat of additional fighting around Culpeper Court House, the troops from Rodes' Division resumed their advance about two o'clock in the afternoon on June 10.

Along with the other two infantry divisions in Richard Ewell's Second Corps, Rodes' men were assigned the tasks of sweeping whatever Federals they found there out of the nearby Shenandoah Valley and seizing the various crossings over the Potomac River. Once that was mission was accomplished, James Longstreet's First Corps would push forward and secure the major gaps cutting through the Blue Ridge Mountains. Thereafter, A. P. Hill's new Third Corps would withdraw as quietly as possible from the Fredericksburg area and march rapidly into the Valley behind Ewell's column.

From their camp on the Botts farm, Rodes' men initially headed west past Rixeyville Road before turning north to move along the Richmond Turnpike. The troops covered about 10 miles before stopping to rest along the Hazel River near the Gourd Vine Church. They resumed their advance on the following day at about five o'clock in the morning. After a short march, the division arrived at the small village of Newby's Cross Roads. Because of the poor conditions on the assigned route that ran west through the town of Little

Washington, Rodes decided to continue marching his brigades north toward Gaines' Cross Roads.[1]

The conditions on the alternative road proved much easier for the weary soldiers. Following a trip of almost 15 miles, the troops went into camp just north of Flint Hill at the threshold of the Shenandoah Valley. Although his men were supposed to lead the advance, Jubal Early experienced significant problems with road conditions along his assigned route. The marching proved so difficult that he only made it as far as Gaines' Cross Roads before darkness fell. Edward Johnson's Division lagged even farther behind and halted a short distance to the west.[2]

After conferring with Early and Johnson that evening, Ewell hurried forward in his carriage on the morning of June 12 to catch up with Rodes. The journey took longer than expected because Rodes' men had resumed their advance at the first sign of daylight. Ewell finally overtook the division leader "on the road between Flint Hill and Sandy Hook." Once Rodes joined Ewell in his carriage, the officers rolled "on in advance of the army." During the ride, Ewell spelled out his plans now that Rodes' troops would be at the front of the advance as the army pushed forward into the Shenandoah Valley.[3]

By then, the troops from Iverson's Brigade had begun the steep climb toward the main pass through the nearby Blue Ridge Mountains. The severity of the trip from Flint Hill broke down soldiers throughout the division. Their weariness was offset somewhat by the sheer beauty of the surrounding countryside. "We then took up the line of march for the valley, making forced marches and greatly fatiguing the men," Maj. Charles Blacknall wrote in a letter to his brother-in-law. "We passed over the mountains & through the finest country I ever saw."[4]

After crossing through Chester's Gap, the troops reached Front Royal, near the point where the north and south branches join to form the winding and scenic Shenandoah River. Their arrival provoked an outpouring of relief from the town's many Southern sympathizers, who had chafed for months under the threat of frequent raids by Maj. Gen. Robert H. Milroy from the main Federal

---

1 OR 27, pt. 2, 547; William Alexander Smith, *The Anson Guards: Company C, Fourteenth Regiment North Carolina Volunteers 1861-1865* (Charlotte, NC: Stone Publishing Co., 1914), 198.

2 For details on Early's march, see Hall, "The Army Is Moving," 44.

3 Hotchkiss Journal, Entry for June 12, 1863, in McDonald, *Make Me A Map*, 150-151.

4 Blacknall to George, June 18, 1863, Blacknall Papers.

headquarters at nearby Winchester. Surgeon William Marston from the 12th North Carolina noted happily in his diary that he and his comrades were "received with great enthusiasm."[5]

Local resident Lucy Buck was quickly caught up in the stirring emotion that erupted when the Confederate troops marched by her home about 11 o'clock in the morning. "Oh how the gallant boys cheered and shouted—Ma and I went up on the house and when they saw us they waved and hurrahed to us," the Valley resident wrote in her diary. "Oh! It was glorious!" She watched in near ecstasy as "column after column filed past with glistening bayonets, flying colors and rolling artillery, while the strain of martial music and their soul burning shouts mingled in one unbroken, soul thrilling volume of sound." The scene proved so stirring that she was "almost frantic with excitement and delight."[6]

Thomas Ashby, who was a young boy at the time, recalled later in life that the troops from Rodes' Division "presented a most interesting and impressive sight." The soldiers, he continued, appeared to be "in splendid condition and in high spirits" when they tramped into town. "As they passed through the village the men closed up their ranks and the bands played as if on parade," he said. Ashby took special notice of the long column of artillery and wagons, which "added to the impressiveness of the occasion and gave a good idea of the details and appurtenances of war."[7]

Amid cheering crowds, Rodes' Division marched its way about two miles north of Front Royal to the south bank of the Shenandoah River. "The passing of a pontoon train the day before had made the people anticipate our coming and they came out everywhere to welcome us," Jed Hotchkiss of Ewell's staff scribbled into his journal. After a short trip, the Southern troops reached the main fords along Winchester Road and began feeling their way into and across the river. "Our pontoons were on the shore there but Gen. Ewell said it would

---

5   Marston Diary, Entry for June 12, 1863, Emory.

6   Lucy Rebecca Buck Diary, Entry for June 12, 1863, in Elizabeth R. Baer, ed., *Shadows on My Heart: The Civil War Diary of Lucy Rebecca Buck of Virginia* (Athens: University of Georgia Press, 1997), 212.

7   Thomas A. Ashby, *The Valley Campaigns: Being the Reminiscences of a Non-Combatant While Between the Lines in the Shenandoah Valley During the War of the States* (New York: Neale Publishing Co., 1914), 240. For another description from a local citizen of their arrival, see Charles Eckhardt Diary, Entry for June 12, 1863, Warren County Heritage Society, Front Royal, Virginia.

take too long to put them down, so our advance waded the rivers," Hotchkiss remarked.[8]

As the troops from the other two divisions lined up to cross the Shenandoah, Rodes halted the front of the column just north of Front Royal so he could attend a meeting with Ewell and Early in the nearby town of Cedarville. During this gathering on the afternoon of June 12, Ewell "fully unfolded" his intentions for the campaign in the Shenandoah Valley. "The main features of the plan were the simultaneous attack of Winchester and Berryville, the subsequent attack of Martinsburg, and the immediate entrance into Maryland, via Williamsport or any other point near there which events indicated as best," Rodes noted in his official report.

Early's and Johnson's divisions would carry out the primary attack against the Union stronghold at Winchester under the direct supervision of Ewell. For his part, Rodes was ordered to seize the town of Berryville with his division and "then to advance without delay on Martinsburg." From there, he was to proceed into Maryland and await further orders that would follow once the other two divisions in the corps had captured Winchester. To enable Rodes "to carry out this plan the better," a cavalry brigade under Brig. Gen. Albert Gallatin Jenkins was assigned to Rodes' command.

Following the meeting, Rodes' troops resumed the march along "an unfrequented road" that angled northeast from Cedarville. They proceeded only a few miles before halting for the night near the small settlement at Stone Bridge. By then, the bulk of the Jenkins' troopers had already joined the division under orders from Ewell. The portion of the brigade assigned to Rodes' command included three regiments and two battalions of cavalry, all of which had been raised in the western mountains of Virginia. The mounted force consisted of some 1,600 roughneck troopers, most of whom had no experience operating in coordination with a large infantry force.[9]

General Albert Jenkins cut a rather dashing figure with his long flowing beard that reached almost to his waist. He was born in 1830 and grew up on a large estate in the western part of Virginia, along the Ohio River. Jenkins attended Jefferson College and Harvard Law School and served in the U.S. Congress from 1857 to 1861. Following the outbreak of war, he took a seat in

---

8   Hotchkiss Journal, Entry for June 12, 1863, in McDonald, *Make Me a Map*, 152.

9   OR 27, pt. 2, 546-547; Thomas D. Gold, *History of Clarke County Virginia and Its Connections With the War Between the States* (Berryville, VA: Chesapeake Book Co., 1962), 226.

the first Confederate Congress before resigning and accepting a commission as brigadier general. Jenkins carried out several major raids in the mountains of western Virginia and even into Ohio. Despite its accomplishments in the guerilla-style fighting along the border, Jenkins' command was widely regarded as poorly disciplined and ill suited for regular cavalry service.[10]

For anyone paying close attention, it took but a short time for signs of problems to appear. On the morning after their arrival, Rodes learned that his advance on Berryville had been detected by an enemy cavalry patrol because of Jenkins' failure to occupy the nearby town of Millwood during the night. Rodes responded to the news by pushing his troops forward from their camp about six o'clock in the morning. "Finding our movements discovered, the division was marched with the utmost celerity through Millwood upon Berryville," Rodes stated in his official report.[11]

Iverson's men were struck by the sights along the road leading to the north. "The valley far surpasses anything that I ever conceived of in beauty & fertility," Maj. Blacknall remarked in a letter to his brother-in-law. He reported that "the whole country as far as the eye could reach on every side is an extensive meadow & clover field, with inexhaustible supplies of forage for the thousands of animals with our army, and in all respects is the most splendid country I ever saw." The 12th North Carolina's Marston described the Shenandoah Valley as "the most beautiful country in the sun."[12]

Typical of the greetings they received in that region was the reaction of Matella Page Harrison from Millwood, who recorded in her diary that it was "one of the brightest days of my life" when the troops marched by her house on the way to Berryville. Most impressive of all was the huge size of the invading force. "They soon came thick and fast," she remarked. "I ran down through the woods to feast my eyes and oh what a joyful array. Rhodes' gallant men were marching. Johnston they said was on the left. Early in the center. There was no escape for Milroy."[13]

---

10 Warner, *Generals in Gray*, 154; Tagg, *The Generals of Gettysburg*, 367.

11 OR 27, pt. 2, 547.

12 Blacknall to George, June 18, 1863, Blacknall Papers; Marston Diary, Entry for June 13, 1863, Emory.

13 Matella Page Harrison Diary, Entry for June 13, 1863, in Richard C. Plater Jr., ed., "Civil War Diary of Miss Matella Page Harrison of Clarke County, Virginia, 1835-1898," *Proceedings of the Clarke County Historical Association*, 22 (1982-1983), 64.

From Millwood, Rodes pushed his men north toward Berryville, which served as the seat of government for Clarke County. The town was originally laid out on land owned by Benjamin Berry near the site of a former crossroads tavern. Samuel Scollay Moore, who was a young boy at the time the war began, recalled that Berryville "was then a town of 500 people—most of them professional people, merchants, mechanics, and laborers." The most notable landmark in the town was the nearly 100-foot-high spire of the Grace Episcopal Church.[14]

On arriving there during mid-morning on June 13, Rodes discovered that Jenkins had inexplicably halted his troopers in front of the town, where they were being "held at bay by the Federal artillery." The troops defending Berryville comprised about 1,800 men under the command of Col. Andrew T. McReynolds from the 1st New York Cavalry. The force, which formed part of Milroy's division of the Federal VIII Corps, included the 6th Maryland, 67th Pennsylvania, 1st New York Cavalry, and a battery of Maryland artillery under the command of Lt. Frederick W. Alexander.[15]

The sudden appearance of Rodes' Division prompted McReynolds to adopt a different tactical plan. Rather than take a determined stand against overwhelming odds, he decided on a holding action that would allow his troops to withdraw safely to the Union stronghold at Winchester. While the bulk of the men prepared to make their escape, he deployed four companies from the Maryland regiment, about 150 men from the New York cavalry, and one section of artillery on the south end of town. From there, they kept up an active skirmish and artillery fire against the approaching Confederates.[16]

After conferring with Jenkins, Rodes observed that the mixed force of infantry, cavalry, and artillery appeared to be preparing for evacuation. He decided to take action before the enemy troops could make good with their escape. "I immediately determined to surround them, if possible, and ordered General Jenkins to march to the left of the town, to cut off the enemy toward Winchester," Rodes explained. "The infantry, save one brigade, without being halted, were ordered to move to the right and left of the place, to unite in the rear."

---

14 Samuel Scollay Moore, "Through the Shadows: A Boy's Memories of the Civil War in Clarke County," *Proceedings of the Clarke County Historical Association*, 24 (1989-1990), 2.

15 *OR* 27, pt. 2, 54, 108-109.

16 *Ibid.*, 54, 108-109.

Within minutes, the brigades began taking up position for an attack. Just as the flanking movement got under way, noted Rodes, "it became apparent to me that the enemy was retreating, and I ordered the Alabama brigade, Colonel O'Neal commanding, to advance rapidly upon the town, which was done." The Alabama troops pushed forward from their position directly in front of the town. According to O'Neal, once his brigade began its advance, the enemy "precipitately retired, leaving their tents, camps, and a great many valuables in our hands."[17]

While George Doles' Brigade remained in the rear, Iverson's troops joined the other two Tar Heel brigades as they encircled Berryville. Iverson's men expected a fight and were shocked when the enemy put up virtually no resistance when the Southern troops moved forward against them. Marston recorded in his diary that "we arrive at or near Berryville about 12 pm, form our line of battle, make our advance, but the Yankees have left." Private John Coghill from the 23rd North Carolina reported something similar in a letter to his family. His regiment, he explained, "flanked their breastworks but when we marched up to fight they ware gone and so wee did not get them."[18]

Despite the escape of the main enemy force, Rodes' fast and decisive thrust against Berryville was a solid success. Inside the town the men found huge quantities of food and other goods that had been abandoned by the retreating Federals. "We capture the hospital with about 90 prisoners—also many supplies of various kinds," Surgeon Marston declared in his diary. Best of all was the warm reception that Iverson's troops received from the local residents. Marston happily noted that the many ladies he encountered there were "very Southern siscesh."[19]

The arrival of the soldiers from Rodes' Division came as a major relief for the majority of the citizens in Berryville. Despite changing hands several times during the war, the town remained a stronghold of Confederate support. Among the most ardent Southern sympathizers was Treadwell Smith, who had suffered numerous indignities during the repeated Federal occupations of the town during the past year. "The Yankees left Berryville in a hurry," he

---

17 *Ibid.*, 547, 592.

18 Marston Diary, Entry for June 13, 1863, Emory; John F. Coghill to Dear Pappy, Ma and Mit, June 25, 1863, John Fuller Coghill Letters.

19 Marston Diary, Entry for June 13, 1863, Emory.

proclaimed with joy in his diary. He noted with even more delight that "the Confederates came soon after they left."[20]

While the troops gathered up the spoils, Rodes assessed the situation in and around the captured town. It did not take him long before he realized his victory was not as fruitful as it might otherwise have been. The general was "mortified to learn that the enemy, abandoning his tents, a few stores, &c., had left his cavalry and artillery to keep our cavalry in check, and had some time before retreated with his infantry toward Charlestown, without being discovered." Captain John C. Gorman of the 2nd North Carolina, part of Ramseur's Brigade, reported that, "after a short rest, the bugle sounded us to our places, and we followed our cavalry who had gone in pursuit—But neither we nor the cavalry came up with them that night."[21]

The closest Jenkins came to capturing the retreating Federal force was at the town of Bunker Hill. During the late afternoon, his main body of gray troopers closed in on 42 Federal wagons and several sutler vehicles escorted by a cavalry company from McReynold's command on the road to Martinsburg. At Bunker Hill, Jenkins encountered four companies of enemy infantry on detached duty from Milroy's Winchester garrison. The cavalry commander called off the chase following a brisk skirmish in which the enemy soldiers took refuge in two fortified churches. The Federal troops sustained about 95 casualties before making their escape later that night under the cover of darkness.[22]

While Jenkins was pursuing the enemy and fighting at Bunker Hill, the 36th Virginia Cavalry Battalion under Maj. James W. Sweeney continued after McReynolds' main force westward along the road to Winchester. A portion of

---

20 Treadwell Smith Diary, Entry for June 13, 1863, Civil War Centennial Committee, *Treadwell Smith's Diary of the Civil War, October 17, 1859-April 20, 1865* (Berryville, VA: Berryville and Clarke County Chamber of Commerce, 1965), 9.

21 *OR* 27, pt. 2, 547-548; John C. Gorman to Dear Friend Holden, June 22, 1863, *North Carolina Standard*, July 3, 1863.

22 Nye, *Here Come the Rebels!*, 87-88; Addison Austin Smith, "A Story of the Life and Trials of a Confederate Soldier and the Great Loop He Made in Three Years," 15, 17, Jackson County Public Library, Ripley, West Virginia; W. K. to Messrs. Editors, June 19, 1863, *Richmond Enquirer*, June 30, 1863; *OR* 27, pt. 2, 67; Isaac Hamilton Brisco to Dear Father and Mother, Brothers and Sisters, Sept. 30, 1863, in Brian Stuart Kesterson, *Campaigning With the 17th Virginia Cavalry* (Washington, WV: Night Hawk Press, 2005), 235; James Harrison Hodam, "The Hodam Manuscript: Reminiscences of a Confederate Soldier," included in Kesterson, *Campaigning With the 17th Virginia*, 285; For a detailed account of the fight at Bunker Hill, see Steve French, "Federals on 'Safe' Road to Trouble," *Washington Times*, Dec. 3, 2005.

the 1st New York Cavalry, supported by a single artillery piece, set up a strong skirmish line at Locke's Ford on the Opequon Creek near Brucetown, in order to protect the rear of the retreating column. A flurry of fighting took place along the creek before Sweeney's command was forced to withdraw after sustaining about 20 casualties including Maj. Sweeney, who was severely wounded in the arm. The stout rearguard defensive action allowed the bulk of McReynolds' command to reach Winchester.[23]

Despite the failure to capture the retreating Federal troops, one officer from Ramseur's North Carolina brigade described the offensive against Berryville as "quite a brilliant little affair." He readily admitted, however, that the enemy had "about one hour start on us" before the cavalry and the sharpshooters began their pursuit. Rodes blamed the enemy's escape primarily on the failure of Jenkins' cavalry to cut off their retreat. "In the absence of any official report from General Jenkins, I cannot explain why he did not intercept at least a portion of the enemy's force," he declared with some obvious exasperation.[24]

After a brief rest in the town, Rodes' men were once again on the move by late in the afternoon on June 13. Their line of march carried them northward along the same route the Federal troops had used for their escape from Berryville. According to Surgeon Marston, the soldiers spent most of the trip wet and miserable, traveling through "a very heavy thunderstorm." After marching only a few miles, Iverson's rain-soaked troops established a soggy camp along the Winchester and Potomac Railroad line near the small hamlet of Summit Point.[25]

As his victorious troops settled in for the night, Rodes faced a decision about whether to continue the advance toward Martinsburg. His main concern was that he had still not received word about Ewell's attack against Milroy's main Federal force at Winchester. "Not having heard anything from Winchester, though I had dispatched several couriers to the lieutenant-general

---

23 OR 27, pt. 2, 83; Nye, *Here Come the Rebels!*, 128; William H. Beach, *The First New York (Lincoln) Cavalry* (New York: Lincoln Cavalry Association, 1902), 232-234; "Letter from Captain Woodruff's Company," July 24, 1863, New York Civil War Newspaper Clipping Files, 1st New York Cavalry, New York State Military Museum, Albany, New York. The Federal losses amounted to two men killed and nine or 10 men wounded.

24 OR 27, pt. 2, 548; William E. Calder to Dear Mother, June 20, 1863, Calder Family Papers, SHC.

25 Marston Diary, Entry for June 13, 1863, Emory.

commanding, I hesitated for a few moments between proceeding toward Martinsburg, in accordance with my general instructions, and turning toward Winchester," was how Rodes explained his dilemma in his official campaign report.[26]

Putting aside those concerns, he decided to press ahead to Martinsburg early in the morning on June 14. Along the way, crowds of women lined the route in open celebration of their arrival in the Shenandoah Valley. The mood among the local populace began to change once the division reached Berkeley County. The county seat was located at the town of Martinsburg, which served as the site of an important repair facility for the Baltimore and Ohio Railroad. Although the older families in the town were overwhelmingly pro-Southern, most of those associated with the railroad industry held strong Unionist views.[27]

As a major rail center, Martinsburg proved to be of strategic importance for both sides during the Civil War. In June of 1861, Thomas Jackson destroyed most of the locomotives and all the railroad cars at the repair facility. The destruction caused by Jackson's men remained clearly visible as late as the following spring. "Forty-four locomotives stand on the tracks here—all a perfect wreck," a Federal soldier serving there observed in a letter home. He also noted that "the workshops have been stripped of all their tools and machinery, and the wonder is that they, too, were not destroyed—even the turntables are all gone."[28]

By the time Rodes' Division arrived in the area, the county had already joined the "Restored Government of Virginia" under Governor Francis Pierpont and would soon become part of the new state of West Virginia. "We were now in Berkeley County which voted itself into the Pierpont government, and our reception was not so joyous as before and we passed many houses with doors and windows closed against us," Lt. William E. Calder of the 2nd North

---

26 *OR* 27, pt. 2, 548.

27 J. E. Norris, *History of the Lower Shenandoah Valley* (Chicago: A. Warner and Co., 1890), 242; Sylvester Myers, *Myers' History of West Virginia*, 2 Vols. (Wheeling, WV: Wheeling News Lithography Co., 1915), 2:139; Fred B. Voegle, "Chronology of the Civil War in Berkeley County," *The Berkeley Journal*, 26 (2000), 3-4.

28 James I. Robertson Jr., *Stonewall Jackson: The Man, The Soldier, The Legend* (New York: McMillan Publishing, 1997), 245-246; Prock to Friend Greene, March 10, 1862, in William Landon, "The 14th Indiana Regiment in the Valley of Virginia: Letters to the Vincennes Western Sun," *Indiana Magazine of History*, 30 (1934), 286.

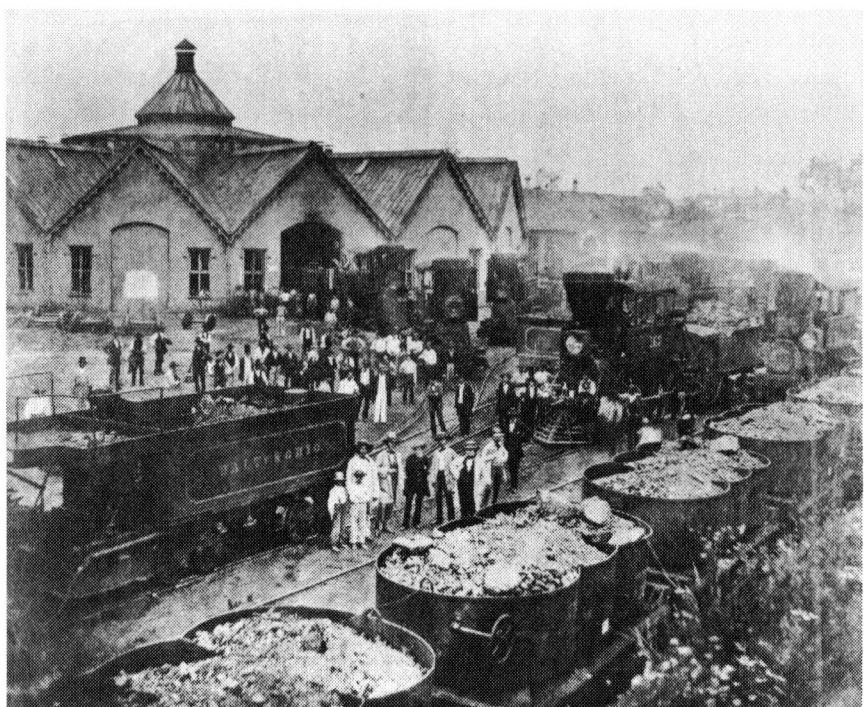

The Baltimore and Ohio Railroad repair facility, which opened in 1848, made Martinsburg, Virginia, a major target for both sides during the war. *Baltimore and Ohio Railroad Museum*

Carolina, part of Stephen Ramseur's Brigade, wrote in a letter home to his mother. Another officer from one of the artillery batteries described it a bit differently when he declared that "all that part of Virginia, I fear, with very few exceptions, is unsound to the core."[29]

After marching northwest along a difficult secondary road, the Confederate troops finally linked up with the Winchester Turnpike at Bunker Hill. Evidence of Jenkins' sharp cavalry skirmish on the previous day remained visible as the foot soldiers tramped through the center of town. "There was a brick house where Yanks had made port-holes & filled up part of windows with rocks & made a stubborn resistance," Pvt. Samuel Pickens from O'Neal's Brigade scribbled into his daily journal. "The house was marked & scaled up in great

---

29 Calder to Mother, June 20, 1863, Calder Papers; "From Williamsport, Maryland," June 17, 1863, *Macon Daily Telegraph*, July 1, 1863.

many places by Grape shot." The private went on to observe that even "the telegraph wires were cut down."[30]

By then, Jenkins' cavalrymen had already reached the outskirts of Martinsburg, which was defended by approximately 1,200 Federals under the command of Col. Benjamin F. Smith. That force included the 126th Ohio, 106th New York, a company of Maryland home guard cavalry, and a six-gun West Virginia battery commanded by Capt. Thomas A. Maulsby. Colonel Smith initially deployed his men about one mile south of town along the Winchester Turnpike. These arrangements were carried out under the supervision of Brig. Gen. Dan Tyler, who had arrived earlier that day to ensure that proper defenses were in place. Tyler was also tasked with providing support for Milroy's command at Winchester.

As the skirmishing escalated into the early afternoon, Colonel Smith was finally forced to withdraw his men toward town. The bulk of the troops moved into position in the area around Shower's Hill on the southeastern outskirts of Martinsburg. He placed four guns from the battery facing south along a ridge about 150 yards in front of the main battle line. Another section of two guns moved into position on the right of the hill to cover the approaches from the west. Most of the infantry remained in the rear, where they began loading up their wagons in preparation for evacuation.[31]

While all that was going on, Rodes was making his way to Martinsburg. When he arrived, the division commander found that Jenkins had halted his brigade along the turnpike, where it continued to receive sporadic fire from the Federal artillery. "The enemy's forces were drawn up in line of battle on the right of the town, exhibiting infantry, cavalry, and artillery," Rodes observed in his official report. "General Jenkins, through Captain Harris, of my staff, had summoned the Federal commander to surrender, which he had declined doing."

Rather than attacking immediately, Rodes decided to wait until all his infantry brigades had moved into position. In the meantime, he ordered Jenkins "to move most of his force to the left of town, to dismount it, and send it

---

30 Coghill to Pappy, Ma and Mit, June 25, 1863, John Fuller Coghill Letters; Pickens Diary, Entry for June 14, 1863, in Hubbs, *Voices From Company D*, 178.

31 *OR* 27, pt. 2, 16-17, 38-39. For detailed accounts from the Union perspective, see James R. Droegemeyer, "The Battle of Martinsburg, June 14, 1863," *The Berkeley Journal*, 27 (2001), 53-77 and Steve French, "The Battle of Martinsburg," *Gettysburg Magazine*, 34 (January 2006), 7-25.

forward as skirmishers to endeavor to get possession of the town, thus cutting off the enemy's retreat toward Hedgesville and Williamsport, and to report to me what force he discovered in and to the left of the town." One of Jenkins' troopers reported, however, that "the enemy, supposing we had no artillery, formed their lines on our left wing, under cover, so as to command a cross fire of musketry and front our men with their shell, which placed our column in a most perilous position."[32]

The harassing fire from the Federal battery continued as the rest of Rodes' troops filed into the area during the hours just before sunset. Colonel O'Neal reported that the enemy guns fired on his brigade "furiously for a few moments." According to Pvt. Coghill, "the Yankees shelled a little" as Iverson's troops moved into place for the attack on the town. The artillery fire eventually became so annoying that Rodes directed Lt. Col. Thomas H. Carter to position the guns from the division's artillery battalion so as to "silence the opposing battery."[33]

Carter, who had just turned 32 years old the previous day, came from a prominent family in King William County, Virginia, and was one of General Lee's cousins. A graduate of VMI, Carter attended medical school at the University of Virginia and during the following years devoted most of his time managing his family's vast estates. He entered military service as captain of the King William (Virginia) Artillery, which was soon attached to Rodes' Brigade. His friendship with Robert Rodes dated back to their days together at VMI, where they served as cadets.[34]

After displaying his abilities during several major battles, Carter was promoted to command the artillery battalion in D. H. Hill's Division in December 1862. Carter continued in that position when Rodes took over the division about a month later. The battalion consisted of the Orange (Virginia) Artillery under Capt. Charles W. Fry; the Morris (Virginia) Artillery under Capt. Richard Channing Moore Page; the Jeff Davis (Alabama) Artillery under Capt.

---

32 *OR* 27, pt. 2, 548-549; W. K. to Messrs. Editors, June 19, 1863, *Richmond Enquirer*, June 30, 1863.

33 *OR* 27, pt. 2, 548, 592; Coghill to Pappy, Ma and Mit, June 25, 1863, John Fuller Coghill Letters.

34 Krick, *Lee's Colonels*, 86; Everard Kidder Meade, "Col. Thomas A. Carter, C.S.A.—A Sketch," *Proceedings of the Clarke County Historical Association*, 3 (1943), 41-42; Thomas H. Carter to Daniel Harvey Hill, July 1, 1885, Lee Family Papers, VHS.

William J. Reese; and Carter's former battery, which was headed by his half-brother Capt. William P. Carter.[35]

Within minutes of receiving Rodes' orders, Lieutenant Colonel Carter opened fire with his 16 guns on the two sections of enemy artillery posted in front of the main Federal lines at Martinsburg. Additional rounds poured into the other artillery section and the supporting troops located around the hill, sending them scurrying for cover. An officer from one of the Confederate batteries bragged to his hometown newspaper that "in the brief time of 20 minutes—before our infantry could get into position—we had the enemy flying in great haste from the 'ragged rebels.'"[36]

By then, Rodes had nearly finished deploying four of his brigades south of town in battle formation along both sides of Winchester Turnpike. Most of Daniel's Brigade remained in the rear guarding the wagon train. As a result, only one regiment from that brigade was available for the attack on Martinsburg. "Before these preparations had been completed, however, the enemy's battery had been nearly silenced, and, fearing he would retreat, I ordered Ramseur's brigade and each of the others in turn to advance with speed upon the enemy's position," Rodes explained.[37]

Stephen Ramseur's infantry on the far left of the line responded by pushing forward directly toward the Federal troops in front of the high ground. "With a cheer we ascended the hill, and after a few random shots the enemy broke and fled through town," Captain Gorman wrote to a Raleigh newspaper. Lieutenant Calder declared that the enemy "had no idea that we had any artillery within ten miles of them until they suddenly found themselves in a perfect hornet's nest, and before they knew that they were about the blamed rebels were within fifteen feet of their battery and they were all prisoners."[38]

Colonel Bryan Grimes of the 4th North Carolina, part of Ramseur's command, reported that the men from his brigade were "in advance on the left and charged the enemy driving them pell mell through town—being a mile or

---

35 Gregory J. Macaluso, *Morris, Orange, and King William Artillery* (Lynchburg, VA: H. E. Howard, 1991), 19.

36 John Purifoy, "With Jackson in the Valley," *CV*, 30 (1922), 383; "From Williamsport, Maryland," June 17, 1863, *Macon Daily Telegraph*, July 1, 1863.

37 OR 27, pt. 2, 549.

38 Gorman to Holden, June 22, 1863, *North Carolina Standard*, July 3, 1863; Calder to Mother, June 20, 1863, Calder Papers.

more in advance of all other troops." Despite the approaching darkness, the Tar Heel troops continued their pursuit directly into the center of Martinsburg. "We captured the town about dark, and pressed the flying Yankees through the streets when there was barely enough daylight to distinguish friend from foe," Calder informed his mother in a letter home.[39]

By then, Jenkins' troopers had joined the attack with a wild charge from the opposite side of town that was intended to cut off the enemy's lines of retreat to the north and west. "The musketry fire was fierce for about five minutes," one of Jenkins' cavalrymen remembered. "Then rose high in the air the signal yell of Jenkins' Brigade for a charge the musketry was hushed into silence, and the race frantic; our artillery, in the meantime, entertaining that of the enemy." He continued: "very soon all was silent, save the mighty sounds of the dashing steeds and shouts of those in pursuit."[40]

As the men at the front of the attack made their way into town, Capt. James I. Harris from the 30th North Carolina, Ramseur's Brigade, could see "black rows" of Federal troops along the heights above Martinsburg. "It was their backs however which we saw, for they were getting away as fast as their legs could carry them," he observed. "Our cavalry now charged through town like a streak of lightening and on after the flying wretches. A huge column of smoke now was high in the air & I thought that the rascals had fired the town." To his relief, Captain Harris quickly determined that the fires in the town were limited to "the long platform at the station on which was piled long rows of corn & hay."[41]

The Confederate troops continued in hot pursuit as the main part of the enemy artillery battery attempted to escape toward the north along the road to Williamsport. "Ramseur's brigade, being in the lead, pursued the enemy at almost a run for 2 miles beyond the town, but, quick as it was, the dismounted cavalry and a squadron or two on horseback, under General Jenkins, were ahead of them, and, after a few shots, compelled the enemy to abandon all his guns, with perhaps one exception," Rodes stated in his report. He noted that

---

39 Bryan Grimes to My Dearest Little Darling, June 16, 1863, Bryan Grimes Papers, NCOAH; Calder to Mother, June 20, 1863, Calder Papers.

40 W. K. to Messrs. Editors, June 19, 1863, *Richmond Enquirer*, June 30, 1863; Robert P. Hodam, ed., *The Journal of James Hoddam* (Eugene, OR: Western Printing, 1995), 60.

41 Harris to Williford, Aug. 24, 1863, in Taylor, "A Newly Discovered Account," 28.

"five of his pieces, with their caissons and most of their horses, were thus captured."[42]

The men from Iverson's Brigade joined the rest of the troops from the division in the assault on the town. According to Pvt. Coghill, the troops from his regiment "rushed in thare and run them out." He added that they captured the enemy's artillery and "a good deal of provisions but they run so that wee did not get them." Major Blacknall also reported that they "dashed into town, capturing all their artillery and stores, and many prisoners, the rest escaping as best they could." Another private pointed out that they "had no Fight except a few Artillery and skirmish shots."

Despite the lack of resistance, the situation quickly turned chaotic as the troops from the brigade moved into the town. "Such a terrible yell as was raised simultaneously by all the brigade & such a noise as was caused by charging over the numerous stone fences surrounding the town was never heard before on earth," Maj. Blacknall remarked. "There was such confusion & terror & running to & fro by the Yankees & Citizens as I never before witnessed." He further reported that "the Yankees immediately set fire to the army stores & commenced running in every direction."[43]

Although the maneuvering that day had been relatively simple, Iverson's soldiers had lagged far behind Ramseur's troops throughout the attack. At least one North Carolina officer from the latter brigade openly bragged about the advance and implicitly criticized Iverson's lack of military skills in directing his command. "It was said that Iverson's brigade had about fifteen minutes the start of ours, but so rapid was our movement that we got in town full fifteen minutes before he did," a captain from the 30th North Carolina boasted to a fellow officer who was absent due to wounds he had received at Chancellorsville.[44]

Any problems festering between the two Tar Heel brigades evaporated when the troops were greeted from every side with ecstatic cheers from their supporters in the town. For at least one Southern sympathizer, the arrival of Confederate troops was an event almost beyond belief. "The first gray coat road

---

42 OR 27, pt. 2, 549.

43 Blacknall to George, June 18, 1863, Blacknall Papers; Coghill to Pappy, Ma and Mit, June 25, 1863, John Fuller Coghill Letters; Leonidas Torrence to Dear Mother, June 17, 1863, in Monroe, "Road to Gettysburg," 508.

44 Harris to Williford, Aug. 24, 1863, in Taylor, "A Newly Discovered Account," 28.

down the hill," Susan Nourse Riddle wrote in her journal. "Oh! the joy at seeing it once more—another & another & soon the town is full. Rhodes Division enters the town." To her astonishment, the cavalrymen continued to pursue "the flying Yankees," capturing all of their artillery pieces except one. "Such a happy comfortable night we have not spent for six long months," she proclaimed.[45]

Unlike the greeting they received in most of the towns in the upper Valley, their reception in Martinsburg was far from completely friendly. Surgeon Marston estimated the town was "about one half Yankees, though we have many strong Southern friends here." Union sentiment proved so strong that a large part of the populace reacted to the presence of Rodes' troops with open hostility. Despite their mixed welcome, Major Blacknall wrote that the men from Iverson's Brigade enjoyed "a gay time" as they swept through the streets. "The whole thing was confusion, night had arrived, our troops filled the town & everything was in an uproar," he recalled.

When he entered the town, Blacknall moved to gather up as many goods as he could lay his hands on. "I immediately took possession of the Qr. Master & Commissary stores & Provost Marshall office, & found everything that could be desired in abundance," he explained to his brother-in-law. Blacknall admitted that among the articles he located were several boxes marked as containing 12 dozen Colt repeaters. "But I found on opening them that they contained each 12 doz. bottles [of] fine French brandy, which I proceeded to capture," he joked.[46]

Once the area was secure, the division pioneers began tearing up the railroad tracks and other facilities for the Baltimore and Ohio line. During that time, "the appropriate officers" also set to work taking inventory of the supplies captured in Martinsburg. According to General Rodes, the wide stock of goods abandoned by the enemy included "some 6,000 bushels of fine grain, some commissary stores, about 400 rounds of rifled artillery ammunition, and small-arms and ammunition in small quantity." The division leader further reported that his victorious soldiers "captured two excellent ambulances." Captain

---

45 Susan Nourse Riddle Diary, Entry for June 14, 1863, in Mabel Henshaw Gardiner and Ann Henshaw Gardiner, *Chronicles of Old Berkeley: A Narrative History of a Virginia County from Its Beginning to 1926* (Durham, NC: The Seeman Press, 1938), 160.

46 Marston Diary, Entry for June 14, 1863, Emory; Blacknall to George, June 18, 1863, Blacknall Papers.

Harris from Ramseur's Brigade was also pleased. According to the captain, "some of the finest artillery horses I ever saw also were brought in amid the shouts of our men."[47]

The most valuable items were the five artillery pieces seized from Maulsby's battery, which turned out to be nearly new three-inch rifles. Four of those guns, along with the horses and other equipment, were immediately transferred to the Alabama battery commanded by Captain Reese. "The old guns of the company, two Rome, Ga. rifles, one bronze Napoleon, and a twelve-pounder howitzer, and the greatly worn equipment, which had been in constant use for about two years, were turned in to the Confederate Ordinance Department," one of the men from the battery recalled.[48]

All those spoils came at the cost of only a handful of casualties, most of which occurred early in the fight among the troopers from the cavalry brigade. "Our loss, according to the best information, is less than ten, in killed, wounded, and captured, embracing the afternoon skirmishing," one of Jenkins' men wrote in a letter to a Richmond newspaper. "Our men captured about two hundred prisoners." The only other known casualties were suffered in Capt. Fry's Battery, which had one gunner killed and another man wounded during the artillery duel prior to the attack on the town. The losses on the Federal side amounted to "four or five killed, about a dozen wounded and some 150 taken prisoner."[49]

Although the assault on the town had been remarkably swift, the main body of Federal troops once more eluded capture at the last minute. Rodes conceded in his report that "nothing was seen of the Federal infantry after the attack began, nor was it known for some hours after their retreat that it escaped by the Shepherdstown road, while the cavalry and artillery fled by way of Williamsport." Their escape left left him far from pleased. Just as at Berryville, Rodes placed much of the blame on the failure of Jenkins' troopers to cut off the enemy's lines of retreat.[50]

---

[47] *OR* 27, pt. 2, 549; Harris to Williford, Aug. 24, 1863, in Taylor, "A Newly Discovered Account," 28.

[48] Purifoy, "With Jackson in the Valley," 384.

[49] W. K. to Messrs. Editors, June 19, 1863, *Richmond Enquirer*, June 30, 1863; Macaluso, *Morris, Orange, and King William Artillery*, 44; *OR* 27, pt. 2, 456.

[50] *Ibid.*, 549.

The troops remained in camp just outside Martinsburg until the following morning, when Rodes finally received word that Ewell's other two divisions had captured the bulk of the Federal forces at Winchester. Although Milroy had escaped to the north toward Harpers Ferry, Ewell's sharp attack had been a stunning success. The assault on the town netted almost 4,000 prisoners, 23 pieces of artillery, and some 300 loaded supply wagons. The victory was accomplished at the cost of only 47 men killed, 219 men wounded, and three men missing.[51]

Rodes responded to the news by ordering his troops forward toward the Potomac River crossing at Williamsport. The temperatures soon proved nearly as intolerable as those they had encountered at the beginning of the advance from Fredericksburg. "It being the latter part of June, and the hottest spell of weather that I have almost ever seen, the troops suffered intensely on the march, fainting in numbers by the roadside," an officer from Daniel's staff recalled. Rodes agreed, describing this part of the journey as "the most trying march we had yet had; most trying because of the intense heat, the character of the road, and the increased number of barefooted men in the command."[52]

Their grueling trek finally came to an end in the late afternoon on June 15 when they reached the south shore of the wide Potomac. Despite all their successes, renewed friction between Iverson's and Ramseur's troops surfaced when the three leading brigades in Rodes' Division began pushing across the river in the hours just before dark. The main problem revolved around who would lead the way into Maryland, an honor given to the Ramseur's troops. Captain Harris openly admitted that "this created some jealousy in other brigades and it was not uncommon to hear the sneering remark 'be bound if there is any advantage given, Ramseur's Brigade will get it.'"[53]

The intense rivalry between the Tar Heel brigades was nothing compared to the troubles that erupted when Iverson once again tried to force the 12th North Carolina to accept former Capt. Henry Eaton Coleman as its new colonel. The latest move in this ongoing dispute came in early June when

---

51 *Ibid.*, 442.

52 Wharton Jackson Green, *Recollections and Reflections: An Auto of Half a Century and More* (Raleigh: Edwards and Broughton Printing Co., 1906), 171-172; OR 27, pt. 2, 550. For additional details from an officer in Daniel's Brigade on the difficulty of the march, see William Gaston Lewis to Mittie Pender, June 18, 1863, William Gaston Lewis Papers, SHC.

53 Harris to Williford, Aug. 24, 1863, in Taylor, "A Newly Discovered Account," 28.

Iverson ordered Coleman to report for duty with the regiment. Although his appointment had still not been confirmed by the War Department in Richmond, Coleman arrived in the brigade camp opposite Williamsport with the intention of assuming full command of the regiment.

Iverson summoned Lt. Col. William Davis to inform him of the change in command. The meeting soon turned into an open confrontation between Davis and his brigade commander. "I felt outraged and indignant," Davis recalled. "I said to him that I would never surrender the command of the regiment to Coleman unless I saw the commission in his hands. He did not then have the commission." Coleman reported simply that "the senior captain who had been passed to the Lt. Colonelcy objected in Genl. Iverson's presence to my taking command of the regt."[54]

The result of the command impasse was that Iverson had to leave Davis in charge of the 12th North Carolina and refer the case to Rodes for a full review. Davis also kept Ramseur, his "very warm friend," fully informed of the troubles brewing in the regiment. Despite the embarrassing setback, Iverson refused to withdraw Coleman's nomination. While awaiting the final decision from Rodes, he appointed Coleman as a volunteer aide on his staff. The two men soon became so close that Coleman later recalled "reposing on a sheepskin" with Iverson during one of their bivouacs on the march to Gettysburg.[55]

For most of the men in Iverson's Brigade, however, the problems in the 12th North Carolina were largely overshadowed by their stunning success in sweeping the enemy forces out of the verdant Shenandoah Valley. Major Blacknall described the Second Corps' powerful advance as nothing less than "a perfect triumphal march." He noted with pride that Ewell's soldiers "swept the enemy before us & captured everything they had, the result of the campaign being 6000 prisoners, half a dozen towns & cities, villages without number, government stores in great abundance, & all without any loss of consequence."[56]

---

54 Henry E. Coleman to James A. Seddon, Aug. 8, 1863, Coleman Service Record; Davis to Cooper, Aug. 21, 1863, Letters Received, Confederate Adjutant and Inspector General's Office, NA.

55 Montgomery, "Twelfth Regiment," in Clark, *NC Regiments*, 1:643; Letter From Henry Eaton Coleman, June 8, 1886, Reid Family Papers, Manuscripts Division, Alderman Library, University of Virginia, Charlottesville, Virginia (hereafter cited as UVA).

56 Charles C. Blacknall to Dear Jinny, June 22, 1863, Blacknall Papers; Charles C. Blacknall to Dear Bro. George, June 23, 1863, *ibid*.

Spirits in Rodes' Division continued to soar as the brigades of Iverson, Ramseur, and Doles moved into place along the Maryland shore of the Potomac River at Williamsport. "Our Brigade is about two miles from town, our advance Cavalry now in Penn.," Blacknall informed his brother-in-law. "We are expecting every day to advance, but cannot say what is the programme at this time." O'Neal's and Daniel's brigades also waited eagerly on the Virginia side of the river, where they were assigned to guard Martinsburg and the major approaches to the Potomac River.[57]

The scenic town of Williamsport was located on the upper part of the Chesapeake and Ohio Canal near the point where Conococheague Creek flows into the Potomac River. It did not take the Confederates long to find out that public sentiment in the area along the canal tilted strongly toward the Union cause. According to a Southern officer from one of the artillery batteries, "not a soul, save a few boys and scattering Confederate cavalry graced the scene" as they entered town. "All the stores and every house was closed; and every window, and even curtain was down, as if the sight of a rebel could not be tolerated," he explained.[58]

Despite their less-than-friendly greeting, Rodes reported that a halt at Williamsport was absolutely necessary. One reason was the obvious fatigue among the troops. Another important factor was because a large number of men in the division simply had no shoes. "Very many of these gallant fellows were still marching in ranks with feet bruised, bleeding, and swollen, and withal so cheerfully as to entitle them to be called the heroes of the Pennsylvania campaign," the general commented in his official report. He went on to observe that "none but the best of soldiers could have made such a march under such circumstances."[59]

The men marching in the ranks of Iverson's Brigade echoed those sentiments about the difficulty of the journey. For nearly two full weeks the

---

57 Blacknall to George, June 18, 1863, *ibid.* For details on their arrival, see Lucius T. C. Lovelace to Dear Father, June 17, 1863, in Chattahoochee Valley Historical Society, *War Was the Place: A Centennial Collection of Confederate Soldier Letters* (Chambers County, AL: Chattahoochee Valley Historical Society, 1961), 88 and "Our Northern Campaign: Notes from the Diary of Capt. J. B. R.—No. 1," *The Countryman*, Sept. 22, 1863.

58 "The Confederates in Maryland," June 17, 1863, *Richmond Daily Dispatch*, June 27, 1863. For a detailed history of the canal, see Walter S. Sanderlin, *The Great National Project: A History of the Chesapeake and Ohio Canal* (Baltimore: Johns Hopkins University Press, 1946).

59 OR 27, pt. 2, 550.

An 1860 view across the Potomac River to Williamsport, Maryland, with the aqueduct over Conococheague Creek in the distance on the left. *Steve French*

soldiers had averaged about 20 to 30 miles a day under some of the hottest weather any of them had ever experienced. As a result, almost all of them were broken down from the long march. A private in the 23rd North Carolina reported to his mother that they had "been marching nearly study" since they left the area around Fredericksburg on June 4. He openly admitted that "we all have verry sore feet."[60]

For many of the men, their safe arrival in Maryland called for thanks to God. After setting up camp in a "beautiful grove" just outside of town, Iverson's troops assembled for a prayer service conducted by James M. Sprunt, the Presbyterian chaplain from the 20th North Carolina. "Nothing is better calculated to bring to one's mind scenes of bygone happy hours than the musical strains being sent up this morning by our soldiers' cheerful desire to

---

60 Torrence to Mother, June 17, 1863, in Monroe, "Road to Gettysburg," 508. For similar comments from members of O'Neal's and Daniel's Brigades, see Henry B. Wood to Dear Parents and Sarah, June 22, 1863, in Wayne Wood, ed., "From Montgomery to Gettysburg: War Letters from Alabama Soldier Henry B. Wood," *Alabama Heritage Magazine*, 15 (1990), 44 and John T. Wells to Dear Mother, June 18, 1863, Louis Redmon Wells Papers, Duke.

praise every word of its man of God," the 12th regiment's Surgeon Marston commented in his diary.⁶¹

Meanwhile, Major Blacknall assumed the duties as provost marshal in Williamsport. "When I took charge of the town there was a mob breaking open stores & committing every possible deprecation," he explained in a letter to his brother-in-law. "The streets were crowded with hundreds of drunken men as there are any number of bar rooms & distillieries in town." Blacknall noted that "the citizens were shut up in their homes & frightened nearly to death, but in less than an hour I had order & quiet restored, the stores & houses guarded & the citizens protected."

With the streets under control, Blacknall set about stripping the town bare of usable supplies. "I immediately took possession of all stores, Hotels, Bar rooms, the Bank & all other species of property, put them under guard & selected through the Qr. Master such articles as were needed by the Government," the major explained. "The stocks are very large & goods of all descriptions cheap." Another officer reported that "the merchants had concealed their goods in every conceivable place, but a rigid search soon brought them to light." He noted that "the people say nothing to all this, but you can see that they sell with a very bad grace."

Their work proved so successful that Blacknall remained busy for several days "engaged in gathering up our immense stores and sending back to the rear." The huge haul of supplies they obtained there also attracted the attention of Rodes. He noted in his official report that they confiscated more than 5,000 pounds of leather and 35 kegs of gunpowder during their stay. In addition, Jenkins' troopers rounded up several hundred head of cattle and horses from the surrounding countryside. The troopers also secured large quantities of foodstuffs and other commissary stores in the town.

---

61 Alexander D. Betts, "The Chaplain Service," included in Clark, *NC Regiments*, 4:608-609; Marston Diary, Entry for June 18, 1863, Emory. Sprunt was born in Scotland in 1818. After immigrating to the United States in 1840, he worked as a teacher at several schools in Duplin County, North Carolina. In 1849, he became a Presbyterian minister and later served as the pastor of the Grove Church in Kenansville. He served as Chaplain for the 20th North Carolina from early in the war. Sprunt resigned from the regiment just prior to reaching Gettysburg, due to a severe case of dysentery. For additional details on his career, see Powell, *Dictionary of North Carolina Biography*, 5:417-418; and Faison Wells McGowen and Pearl Canady McGowen, eds., *Flashes of Duplin's History and Government* (Raleigh: Edwards and Broughton Co., 1971), 73-74, 90.

Included in the list of loot ready for shipment south to Virginia were some of the "many hundred slaves" the division had captured up to that point of the march. Jenkins' troopers, in particular, had indiscriminately rounded up any runaway slaves and free blacks unfortunate enough to have come within their reach during the campaign down the Shenandoah Valley. "I have several negroes, free & slave, in my hands but negroes are worth nothing at all," Major Blacknall wrote in a letter home. "No kind of negroes will sell for one hundred dollars. I expect to make some purchases in that line for southern exportation."[62]

As the division pioneers began destroying the aqueduct over Conococheague Creek and the locks on the canal, Blacknall issued passes for the remaining men in the division to purchase scarce goods for themselves and their relatives back home. Rather than go shopping, Surgeon Marston used that opportunity to meet with some of the pro-Southern families in the town. Although they were certainly in the minority, Marston insisted after his round of visits that "we have a few strong friends to our cause in the town & neighborhood."[63]

While the main part of the division rested in town, the troopers from Jenkins' Brigade were off on a cavalry raid deep into Maryland and Pennsylvania. Following their departure from Martinsburg in the hours just before dawn on June 15, the Southern horsemen crossed over the Potomac River into Maryland and rode for the town of Greencastle, Pennsylvania, which they reached early that same afternoon. By midnight, Jenkins and his men had advanced all the way to Chambersburg in the central part of the scenic Cumberland Valley. The main body went into camp just north of town, while Jenkins set up headquarters at the Montgomery House Hotel near the central square.[64]

The following day, the Confederate cavalrymen rounded up blacks, both runaway and free, and requisitioned a lengthy list of badly needed supplies from

---

62 Marston Diary, Entry for June 16, 1863, Emory; Blacknall to George, June 18, 1863, Blacknall Papers; "The Confederates in Maryland," June 17, 1863, *Richmond Daily Dispatch*, June 27, 1863; OR 27, pt. 2, 550.

63 Marston Diary, Entry for June 16, 1863, Emory.

64 "Jenkins' Raid into Pennsylvania," in Frank E. Moore, ed., *The Rebellion Record: A Diary of American Events*, 12 Vols. (New York: D. Van Norstrand, 1863), 7:195; "The Rebel Invasion," *Valley Spirit*, July 8, 1863; Jacob Hoke, *Reminiscences of the War in and about Chambersburg* (Chambersburg, PA: M. A. Foltz, 1884), 37.

local merchants. According to the newspaper in Lancaster, Jenkins' troopers "went to the part of the town occupied by the colored population, and kidnapped all they could find, from the child in the cradle up to men and women of fifty years of age." Local resident Jemima Cree claimed the gray cavalry grabbed up "even little children whom they had to carry on horseback before them." One of the town's merchants described the affair to his wife as "a sorrowful sight to see the poor creatures taken away; free and slave alike were taken."[65]

General Jenkins also demanded that the citizens hand over all the guns in town within two hours. If they did not, Jenkins continued, he would burn down the house of anyone found concealing a weapon. Late in the morning on June 17, however, Jenkins' attention was distracted by a false report of a large body of the enemy approaching rapidly from the north. "About eleven o'clock news reached headquarters of the advance of a strong Yankee force, and consequently we evacuated the city and fell back upon Hagerstown, Md," Lt. Hermann Schuricht of the 14th Virginia Cavalry recalled for posterity in his diary.[66]

Despite widespread rumors that a large Federal army had assembled at Harrisburg, there was no enemy activity around Chambersburg at the time that would have justified Jenkins' hasty withdrawal from the city. According to one account, the enemy force that prompted Jenkins' retreat amounted to nothing more than a group of citizens from a nearby village that had come to witness the occupying army firsthand. Other reports suggest this enemy force consisted of

---

65 "Correspondence of the Express," June 17, 1863, *Lancaster Daily Express*, June 20, 1863; Jemima K. Cree to My Dear Husband, June 18, 1863, in Jemima K. Cree, "Jenkins Raid," *Kittochtinny Historical Society Papers*, 5 (1905-1908), 95; Letter from Mr. Wallace to his Wife, June 17, 1863, *Lancaster Daily Express*, June 20, 1863. For further details on the slave hunting activities in Chambersburg, see Ted Alexander, "A Regular Slave Hunt," *North & South Magazine*, 4, No. 7 (September, 2001), 82-89; Henry Reeves to My Dear Sister Lizzie, July 4, 1863, Excerpts, Gregory A. Coco Collection, Gettysburg National Military Park Library. Gettysburg, Pennsylvania (hereafter cited as GNMPC); Jacob Hoke, *The Great Invasion of 1863* (Dayton, OH: W. J. Suey, 1887), 101; and Rachel Cormany Diary, Entry for June 16, 1863, in James C. Mohr, ed., *The Cormany Diaries: A Northern Family in the Civil War* (Pittsburgh: University of Pittsburgh Press, 1982), 329-330.

66 Hermann Schuricht Diary, Entry for June 17, 1863, in Hermann Schuricht, "Jenkins' Brigade in the Gettysburg Campaign: Extracts from the Diary of Lieutenant Hermann Schuricht, of the Fourteenth Virginia Cavalry," *SHSP*, 24 (1896), 339; Amos Stouffer Diary, Entry for June 19, 1863, in William Garrett Piston, ed., "The Rebs Are Yet Thick About Us: The Civil War Diary of Amos Stouffer of Chambersburg," *Civil War History*, 38 (1992), 215.

about 40 Federal cavalrymen conducting a patrol just north of Scotland village. Whether citizens or a few dozen enemy troopers, their presence posed no threat to Jenkins' Brigade.[67]

Whatever the cause, this unexpected retreat directly contradicted Jenkins' orders, which called for him to remain in Chambersburg until Rodes' Division arrived. "The result was that most of the property in that place which would have been of service to the troops, such as boots, hats, leather, &c., was removed or concealed before it was reoccupied," Rodes complained in his official report. Jenkins' performance was deemed so unreliable that he was forced to operate "directly under [Ewell's] orders" during the rest of the campaign.[68]

While Jenkins was off on his raid, Daniel's and O'Neal's brigades finally made their way across the Potomac River into Maryland. Daniel's men were the first to reach the far shore, crossing the river on June 17. After scrambling up the north bank, they went into camp just "out of Williamsport down the river." They were joined there during the early hours on June 19 by O'Neal's troops, who waded across the main ford directly opposite the town. The men reacted to their arrival on the northern shore with open celebrations.[69]

With all five brigades safely in Maryland, Rodes issued orders for the men to take up the march northward. Following a short halt, the newly arrived troops from O'Neal's Brigade headed straight through town and joined the rest of the division on the road to Hagerstown, which had already been secured by Jenkins' troopers. After traveling about six miles, Rodes turned his command onto the main thoroughfare leading into the town. Although loyalties there were about evenly split between the Union and the Confederacy, huge numbers of people crowded onto the streets to greet the troops as they made their way into Hagerstown.[70]

---

67 Nye, *Here Come the Rebels!*, 146; Hoke, *Reminiscences of the War*, 39.

68 *OR* 27, pt. 2, 551; part 3, 914.

69 For details on the arrival of Daniel's and O'Neal's Brigades, see Charles F. Bahnson to My Dear Father, June 19, 1863, Sarah Chapman, ed., *Bright and Gloomy Days: The Civil War Correspondence of Charles Frederic Bahnson* (Knoxville: University of Tennessee Press, 2003), 65; Pinckney Hatrick to Dear Bro and Sister, June 18, 1863, Hatrick Family Papers, SHC; Pickens Diary, Entry for June 19, 1863, in Hubbs, *Voices from Company D*, 178; and Eugene Blackford Memoirs, 225, Civil War Miscellaneous Collection.

70 J. Thomas Scharf, *History of Western Maryland*, 2 Vols. (Philadelphia: Louis H. Everts, 1882), 2:1059-1061; John F. Shaffner to My Dearest Friend, June 23, 1863, John F. Shaffner Diary and

The outpouring of Southern sentiment in Hagerstown shocked most of the soldiers who had passed through the area during the thrust into Maryland the previous year. During that campaign, the local residents offered but little sympathy for their cause. This time no one in the ranks failed to notice the dramatic transformation among the people living there. According to Capt. Oliver Mercer of the 20th North Carolina, the citizens appeared "much more loyal to us now than when we were here before." Best of all was the open enthusiasm displayed by the throngs of women who lined their route. Mercer reported to his sister that "there are many good Southerners here."[71]

Amid the cheering crowds, the men from Rodes' men came to a halt along one of the main streets in the middle of town. Surgeon Marston reported in his diary that the 20th North Carolina's band used that opportunity to entertain the crowds of people who greeted them with "some elegant music." The Hagerstown residents responded to this impromptu concert with open enthusiasm. The break lasted for almost two hours, giving Marston enough time to visit "some old friends" who lived nearby.[72]

When the march resumed, the troops turned south in the direction of Boonsboro, so that the remaining Federals at nearby Harpers Ferry would think they were moving in for an attack. With that deception out of the way, the men halted along the road about two miles from Hagerstown directly opposite the village of Funkstown. Marston noted in his diary that the camp for Iverson's troops was "situated immediately on Antietam River—the site thickly set with majestic oaks, its ground is undulating & thickly interspersed by the most huge rocks imaginable."[73]

The only damper on their enthusiasm was the series of torrential downpours that began inundating the region that afternoon. The rain came down so hard that Antietam Creek threatened to overrun its banks. The thunderstorms continued almost uninterrupted through most of the night and

---

Papers, NCOAH; "Forty-Fourth Georgia Regiment, The Advance into Pennsylvania," June 23, 1863, *Augusta Weekly Chronicle and Sentinel,* July 7, 1863.

[71] William Stanley Hoole, ed., *History of the Third Alabama Regiment by Col. Charles Forsyth* (University, AL: Confederate Publishing Co., 1991), 40; "Extract from a private letter from one of the 3rd Ala. to a Mobile friend," June 21, 1863, *Macon Daily Telegraph,* July 3, 1863; Oliver E. Mercer to Dear Sister, June 18, 1863, in Wyatt, *The Reeves, Mercer, Newkirk Families,* 272.

[72] Marston Diary, Entry for June 19, 1863, Emory.

[73] OR 27, pt. 2, 550; Marston Diary, Entry for June 19, 1863, Emory.

well into the following morning. By then, everyone was frustrated with the storms. "We had a hard rain last night & everything is wet & disagreeable this morning," admitted one North Carolina doctor.[74]

Despite the terrible weather, large numbers of troops walked into town the following Sunday to attend the local churches. One of the biggest gatherings took place at the Roman Catholic Church. "Hundreds of soldiers went to church in Hagerstown to-day," Pvt. Pickens from O'Neal's Brigade wrote in his journal. "Those from our Co. went to the Catholic where Gens. Ewell & Rodes were. Heard a very good sermon on the importance of prayer—St. Matt. 15th Chap. 21 to 29th verse. After service a good many ladies & men went to the carriage & shook hands & conversed with the Gens." He noted with pride that "most of the Catholics are secessionists"[75]

The presence of Ewell, who was in town for a strategy meeting with Rodes, also attracted a good deal of attention from the crowds of people waiting outside the church along the nearby street corner. Even a fleeting look at the commanding general as he hobbled away from the service and left the scene in his carriage was enough to make local Southern sympathizer Mary Louisa "Lutie" Kealhofer gush with excitement. "Gen. Ewell has just passed from the R. C. Church in a carriage," she happily exclaimed in her diary. "But has driven so rapidly that we had only a glimpse of him."[76]

The religious services at Hagerstown were not limited to the churches. Reverend J. A. Stradley, who was serving as a missionary with Ramseur's Brigade, also reported that "a vast crowd was in attendance" during a series of baptisms that took place along the banks of nearby Antietam Creek. He found that location to be an especially ironic choice for such a sacred ceremony. "Over this creek about a year ago the battle of Sharpsburg was fought," he recalled in a letter to a statewide religious newspaper in North Carolina. "How different the scene!"[77]

Iverson's men were among those who held prayer meetings in their camp that day. Marston noted that he was "forcibly struck" by the natural beauty of

---

74 *Ibid.*, Entry for June 20, 1863, Emory.

75 Pickens Diary, Entry for June 21, 1863, in Hubbs, *Voices From Company D*, 179.

76 Mary Louisa Kealhofer Diary, Entry for June 22, 1863, in Fletcher M. Green, ed., "A People at War: Hagerstown, Maryland, June 15-August 31, 1863," *Maryland Historical Magazine*, 40 (1940), 255.

77 J. A. Stradley to Brother Hufham, June 29, 1863, *Biblical Recorder*, July 22, 1863.

the area along the creek where they had assembled while their chaplain preached to the large crowd of veterans. "We occupied a position under a huge oak," he wrote, noting that the ground was littered with a large number of boulders. The men, he continued, "arranged those rocks as seats for the soldiers."[78]

Throughout that time, Richard Ewell focused his attention on planning the future course of the campaign. On June 19, he traveled to Leetown, Virginia, for a meeting with James Longstreet, whose troops had moved into place along the major mountain gaps on the eastern side of the Shenandoah Valley. By then, A. P. Hill's Third Corps had left the Fredericksburg area for the Valley and was closing fast on the rest of the Army of Northern Virginia. Ewell also made frequent visits to the headquarters of his three divisions, including a trip to Hagerstown on June 20 for a war council session with Rodes.[79]

The advance farther north remained on hold until all three of Ewell's divisions crossed from Virginia into Maryland. The first move to consolidate his divided command came on the afternoon on June 18, when the troops from Edward Johnson's Division forded the Potomac River about 10 miles downstream from Williamsport at Shepherdstown. By the time Early's troops arrived there on the following day, the heavy rainstorms had rendered the ford impassable. The water along that stretch of the river remained so high that Early's Division was unable to make it over the river until early in the morning on June 22.[80]

Ewell, meanwhile, maintained direct contact with the commanding general on what his orders would be once all the divisions from his three corps had moved north of the Potomac River. "If you are ready to move, you can do so," Lee finally informed the new leader of the Second Corps on the afternoon of June 21. Lee went on to note that he was "much gratified at the success which has attended your movements, and feel assured, if they are conducted with the same energy and circumspection, it will continue." The army commander also told Ewell that "your progress and direction will, of course, depend upon the

---

78 Marston Diary, Entry for June 21, 1863, Emory.

79 OR 27, pt. 2, 442; Hotchkiss Journal, Entry for June 19, 1863, in McDonald, *Make Me a Map*, 153.

80 OR 27, pt. 2, 440; McKim, *Soldier's Recollections*, 155; Clement A. Evans to Allie Evans, June 23, 1863, in Stephens, *Intrepid Warrior*, 210.

development of circumstances." Most emphatic of all were Lee's directions that "if Harrisburg comes within your means, capture it."[81]

The plan called for Rodes to lead the way along the main turnpike through the center of Pennsylvania toward the state capital at Harrisburg, with Johnson's division marching closely behind him. During the advance, a single brigade would be detached from the column and sent west to seize additional provisions at the town of McConnellsburg. Early, meanwhile, was instructed to move his division ahead through Cashtown Gap and proceed along the east side of South Mountain toward the Susquehanna River. The troopers from Jenkins' Brigade would once again screen the front of the advance and gather up as many supplies as possible from the surrounding countryside.[82]

With his orders firmly in hand, Ewell issued the command for Rodes to resume the advance on the morning of June 22. After passing through Hagerstown, Rodes led his division north to the village of Middleburg, which straddled the border between Maryland and Pennsylvania. With the 20th North Carolina in the lead, the soldiers from Iverson's Brigade took the place of honor at the front of the column and marched across the state line about ten o'clock that morning. "Our Brigade led the division this morning & was first of rebel infantry that ever entered the state of Penn.," boasted Surgeon Marston.[83]

---

81 OR 27, part 3, 914. For speculation in the division about their destination, see David Ballenger to Nancy Ballenger, June 21, 1863, David Ballenger Letters, Schoff Civil War Collection, William L. Clements Library, University of Michigan, Ann Arbor, Michigan.

82 OR 27, pt. 2, 550.

83 Marston Diary, Entry for June 22, 1863, Emory.

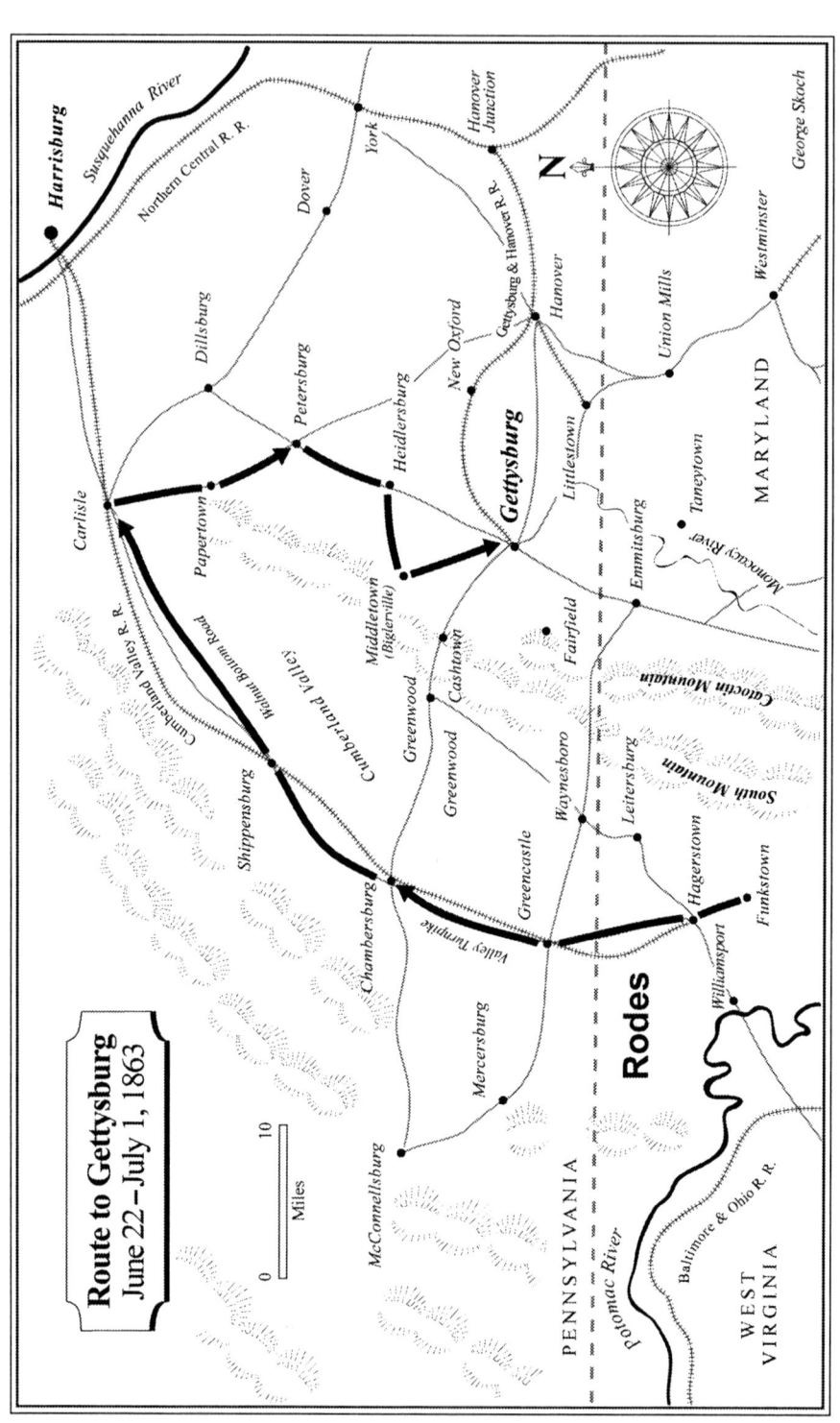

CHAPTER EIGHT

He That Soweth of the Flesh

After lightly skirmishing with a squad of Federal cavalry, the troops from Rodes' Division settled in for a brief stay at Greencastle, located a few miles north of the Pennsylvania border in the lower part of the fertile Cumberland Valley. While the soldiers set up camp just outside of town, Rodes mounted his horse and rode to nearby Boonsboro for another meeting with Ewell. The final arrangements decided upon called for Rodes to pause at Greencastle and await the arrival of Johnson's Division before pushing on to the north. He was further instructed to secure an extensive list of supplies from the town.[1]

While Rodes met with his corps commander, Iverson's men took in the local sights. What they found disgusted them. Surgeon William Marston noted in his diary that "the sorriest set of Yankees you ever saw inhabit this place and the largest collection of ugly dirty looking women I ever saw." Major Charles Blacknall was also unimpressed, describing the residents as "trembling culprits." He pointed out that they "are all hostile to us, but we are quite docile

---

1   OR 27, pt. 2, 551; George W. Wilson, "First Fighting in Pennsylvania," *CV*, 31 (1913), 70; Hotchkiss Journal, Entry for June 23, 1863, in McDonald, *Make Me a Map*, 154.

as they are frightened out of their lives, & offer us everything we wish to save them from utter destruction."[2]

Civilians and soldiers continued sizing up one another as Col. Edward Willis from the 12th Georgia, part of George Doles' Brigade, assumed duties as the provost marshal in Greencastle. Under his directions, commissary details throughout the division began gathering up needed goods from all over town. Willis demanded that city officials hand over large quantities of leather, tin, lead, and food of all kinds. The call for supplies extended to items of almost every description. The requisitions even included 200 currycombs and brushes and 100 saddles and bridles.[3]

The list of requested goods shocked town officials. "These demands were so heavy that the Council felt it impossible to fill them," the local newspaper declared. Cooperation in carrying out the seizures was eventually guaranteed by detaining the town council under an armed guard. "Heavy demands were made upon us for salt, meat, onions, and such," Councilman Charles Hartman recorded in his diary. "Also bridles and saddles, harness. The town council was held till their demands were complied with." He described it as "the hardest day in all my life."

The details assigned to the search uncovered a large number of useful items hidden away by various merchants throughout Greencastle. "The Rebels got a few saddles and bridles, and some vegetables, about town," the editor of the local newspaper reported. He further noted that Rodes' men "seized and carried away about $2000 worth of leather from Mr. Stiffel." Especially notable among the supplies impressed from all over the town was the huge quantity of onions that the residents handed over to commissary details on the courthouse square.

While the infantry plundered, Jenkins's troopers embarked on a hunt for runaway slaves in the region surrounding the town. The plight of the local black residents did not go unnoticed by Councilman Hartman. "One of the exciting features of the day was the scouring of the fields about town and searching of houses for negroes," he remarked. "These poor creatures, those of them who had not fled upon the approach of the foe, [were] concealed in wheat fields around the town." He went on to note that the "cavalrymen rode in search of

---

2   Marston Diary, Entry for June 22, 1863, Emory; Blacknall to George, June 23, 1863, Blacknall Papers.

3   Samuel R. Bates, *History of Franklin County* (Chicago: Warner, Beers, and Co., 1876), 542-543.

them and many of them were caught after a desperate chase and being fired at." Some of Doles' Georgians, and probably others from the division, joined in rounding up the "contrabands" whenever the opportunity presented itself.[4]

None of those slave-hunting activities triggered any major concern within the ranks of Iverson's command, where the men remained firmly focused on all they had accomplished in marching nearly unopposed deep into the enemy's territory. Describing the achievements up to then as "brilliant & imposing," Maj. Blacknall reported during their stop in Greencastle that "our army is in splendid condition, & the spirits of the men better than I have ever seen them. I think that we can continue our advance with slight resistance."[5]

Accompanied by Ewell, the troops from Rodes' Division once again resumed their march northward on the morning of June 24. Their route during the next week carried them directly into the heart of Pennsylvania's Cumberland Valley, which had long served as a major breadbasket for the North. After more than two years of bitter fighting, it still remained largely untouched by the ravages of war. Blacknall declared to his wife that he "never saw such a country before" in all his travels. "They have not suffered at all & everything is in the highest state of prosperity," he said. "The country looks like one extensive City, & one garden of vegetables & grain & clover."[6]

The widespread opportunity for plundering was something Lee had anticipated, so the soldiers in the Army of Northern Virginia operated under strict orders to guard their conduct while in enemy territory. "No private property shall be injured or destroyed by any person belonging to or connected with the army, or taken, excepting by the officers hereinafter designated," read the orders. Lee further emphasized in his General Order No. 72 that the rules

---

4 "Rebel Invasion of Pennsylvania," *Greencastle Pilot*, July 28, 1863; Hoke, *The Great Invasion*, 133; Charles Hartman Diary Typescript, Entry for June 22, 1863, Allison-Antrim Museum, Greencastle, Pennsylvania. For details on the slave-hunting activities in Doles' Brigade, see Lucius T. C. Lovelace to Dear Father, June 23, 1863, in *War Was The Place*, 89-90; Thomas M. Hightower to Dear Lou, June 22, 1863, Thomas M. Hightower Letters, Georgia Archives, Morrow, Georgia (hereafter cited as *GA*); and John T. Gay to Dear Pussie, June 23, 1863, Mary Barnard Nix Collection, Special Collections Division, Hargrett Library, University of Georgia, Athens, Georgia.

5 Blacknall to George, June 23, 1863, Blacknall Papers. For similar comments from other soldiers in the division, see Berry Kinney to W. H. Badgett, July 18, 1863, Badgett Collection, Davidson County Historical Museum, Lexington, North Carolina, and Asbury Hull Jackson to Dear Sister, June 23, 1863, Edward Harden Papers, Duke.

6 Blacknall to Jinny, June 22, 1863, Blacknall Papers.

were to be "strictly observed, and any violations of them promptly and vigorously punished."[7]

Although minor violations proved impossible to stop, only a few cases of outright violence against the local citizens and their property were reported while Rodes' troops operated in Pennsylvania. Aside from the murder of one local farmer by a handful of drunken stragglers from Jenkins' Brigade, the exceptions to Lee's policies usually involved some form of extenuating circumstances. "Not a house was burned and I knew of but two that were plundered, one of these by orders on account of the owner's firing upon our men," recalled Lt. Joseph B. Oliver from the 20th North Carolina. "The other was deserted and plundered by stragglers, who were caught and severely punished."[8]

Their behavior even drew praise from Rodes, who noted in his official report that "the conduct of the troops of this division was entirely in accordance with those orders, and challenged the admiration of their commanding officers, while it astonished the people along the line of march." Rodes emphasized that only "a few instances of forced purchases were reported, but never established." Ewell was equally pleased with the conduct of the men in his corps. He reported to his niece that "it is wonderful how well our hungry, foot sore, ragged men behave in this land of plenty, better than at home."[9]

While forced seizures by individual soldiers were banned, commissary and quartermaster officers were allowed to pay for confiscated items with nearly worthless Confederate money and scrip. "During our march through Maryland and Pennsylvania, a regular system of impressment at market prices was organized and executed by authorized agents only," one Tar Heel soldier explained in a letter home. "Wagons, horses, hats, shoes, clothing, saltpetre, stationery, &c, were thus seized and sent to the rear, except such as were needed

---

7 OR 27, pt. 3, 912-913.

8 Oliver, "Recollections," 1. The most notable exception was the murder of farmer Isaac Strite, just north of Greencastle on June 20 by three drunken stragglers from Jenkins's Brigade. For details, see Henry B. Hege, "The Civil War Unvarnished—Henry B. Hege to Henry G. Hege, July 12, 1863," *Mennonite Research Journal*, 5, No. 2 (April 1964), 19 and Steve French, "Gettysburg Fatal to Unheralded Civilians," *Washington Times*, Jan. 12, 2008.

9 OR 27, pt. 2, 550-551; Richard S. Ewell to Dear Lizzie, June 24, 1863, Richard Stoddert Ewell Papers, LOC.

for immediate use." He noted that "subsistence was procured in the same way."[10]

The amount of supplies confiscated under this system far exceeded even the most optimistic expectations. "We have captured hundreds of the finest horses and cattle I ever saw—everything we need we have," Capt. Oliver Mercer of the 20th North Carolina boasted in a letter to his brother. Rodes was also impressed by the rich haul of goods, noting that "some 2,000 or 3,000 head of cattle were taken, and either appropriated for the command or sent to the rear for other divisions." According to Ewell, his troops secured more than 5,000 barrels of flour during the advance.[11]

The soldiers from the division remained well aware of the devastating impact that forced seizures had on the local population—and were pleased. "We have given the people of Pennsylvania to understand that war is in the land, by capturing thousands of their cattle and horses," Lt. Medicus M. Ward from the 12th North Carolina in Iverson's Brigade declared in a letter to his parents. If anything, those sentiments were even more widespread among the Jenkins' cavalrymen. One of the troopers openly bragged in a letter to his wife that "the dutch never knew any-thing of the war until we invaded them and fought all round them and stoled their horses and cattle."[12]

For Iverson's men, the bounty offered up from the rolling farms and prosperous hamlets of lower Pennsylvania proved almost beyond belief. "Here we found literally a land of plenty, and for the few days we remained in Pa., we feasted on the fat of the land," Lieutenant Oliver recalled. "Along the road-sides, on every lane, and on every farm were the finest cherries just ripening." He further noted that "every spring-house was filled with crocks of rich milk and golden butter, the barn-yards with poultry, and the pastures with fat cattle."[13]

---

10 A North Carolinian to Mr. Editor, July 10, 1863, *Wilmington Daily Journal*, July 17, 1863. For complaints about the leniency of Lee's policy, see Seaton Gales to Dear Wife, July 8, 1863, Gales Papers, NCOAH and John F. Christian to Dear Mother, June 24, 1863, *The Alabama Beacon*, July 10, 1863.

11 Mercer to Brother, June 26, 1863, in Wyatt, *The Reeves, Mercer, Newkirk Families*, 273; OR 27, pt. 2, 550, 443.

12 Medicus M. Ward to Dear Ma and Pa, July 7, 1863, *Raleigh Weekly State Journal*, July 22, 1863; Isaac V. Reynolds to Dear Wife, July 20, 1863, Isaac V. Reynolds Papers, Duke.

13 Oliver, "Recollections," 1.

Supplies became so plentiful that the campsite for the brigade overflowed with every kind of food a hungry soldier could desire. "We are now in the most splendid country I ever saw, everything in the way of subsistence being in the most profuse abundance," wrote Maj. Blacknall. He went on to report that "our army being amply and abundantly supplied from this country, we cannot consume one tenth of the supplies before us, wheat, corn, oats, clover, beef, bacon, butter, &c. being in waste on all sides." Captain Mercer noted that details from the brigade were "sent out daily to get butter, chickens, eggs, and such things as we must have." According to the captain, "some take our money very readily while others are forced to do it."[14]

As Rodes' Division pushed deeper into Pennsylvania, the enthusiasm of the soldiers at the front of the invasion contrasted sharply with the increasingly gloomy mood of the local residents. Despite Lee's orders, most of the citizens remained convinced that the Southern soldiers intended to plunder the countryside all along their line of march. "The people here are all hostile to us & in a terrible state of alarm for fear we are going to burn and destroy everything in the country," Blacknall wrote to his wife. Private John Coghill reported to his family that "the people was very near skerd to death."[15]

The concern among the local populace continued to grow as the cavalrymen from Jenkins's Brigade again pushed forward to Chambersburg on the afternoon of June 23. By then, the gray troopers had advanced nearly 20 miles into the heart of the Cumberland Valley. Local resident Rachel Cormany noted in her diary that the troopers "rode in as leisurely as you please, each one having his hand on the trigger though, to fire any minute." While one detachment tore up railroad tracks and destroyed a nearby railroad bridge, the rest of Jenkins's men moved to secure the town and gather up essential supplies from the local merchants.[16]

The main portion of Rodes' command arrived at Chambersburg the following morning after an 11-mile march from Greencastle. Blacknall described Chambersburg as "a city of 6 or 7000 inhabitants, situated in a highly

---

14 Blacknall to George, June 23, 1863, Blacknall Papers; Mercer to Brother, June 26, 1863, in Wyatt, *The Reeves, Mercer, Newkirk Families*, 273.

15 Blacknall to Jinny, June 22, 1863, Blacknall Papers; John F. Coghill to Dear Pappy, Ma and Mit, June 25, 1863, John Fuller Coghill Letters.

16 Bates, *History of Franklin County*, 45; Rachel Cormany Diary, Entry for June 23, 1863, in Mohr, *The Cormany Diaries*, 333-334.

beautiful & fertile country." The citizens, he reported, were "almost entirely of Dutch origin & seem to be peaceable, quiet, & prosperous people." The faces of the local residents displayed their concern as the troopers moved into the population center. Captain Mercer joked to his brother that the people there "expected to find us a rude, unprincipled horned set of animals but they were agreeably surprised to find us on the human order."[17]

About 10 o'clock that morning, Ewell entered the main square with an escort of horsemen. The corps commander's carriage stopped in front of the Franklin Hotel, where Ewell climbed out of the wagon. "When he emerged from the carriage, which he did only by the assistance of others, it was discovered that he had an artificial limb and used a crutch," recalled a surprised local merchant named Jacob Hoke. "After making his way into the hotel, he at once took possession of a large front parlor, and, surrounded by six or eight gentlemenly-looking men, he was prepared for business." Hoke, a careful scribe of contemporaneous events, went on to note that "a flag was run out of a window, and head-quarters was established."[18]

After shifting his headquarters to a Mennonite church just outside town, Ewell issued orders for the store owners in Chambersburg to turn over a long list of requisitioned goods. When the appointed hour arrived and a meeting was called, all but one of the merchants refused to comply with Ewell's demands. "After this refusal, guards were sent to all the stores, the military authorities took pos[s]ession of such groceries, hardware, flour, drugs, soaps &c. as they wanted," reported the local newspaper. "And then the merchants were directed to keep their stores open and sell to those who wish to buy for confederate scrip, on pain of having their doors burst open and their goods taken without any remuneration."[19]

In the middle of the afternoon, commissary and quartermaster details started rounding up the required goods from the shops. "About two, the pillage of our stores began," business owner William Heyser complained in his journal. "Not a place escaped, never in the history of our boro was there such a scene. The merchants were compelled to pack up the wagons with their goods, which

---

17 Charles C. Blacknall to Dear Bro. George, June 25, 1863, Blacknall Papers; Marston Diary, Entry for June 24, 1863, Emory; Mercer to Brother, June 26, 1863, in Wyatt, *The Reeves, Mercer, Newkirk Families*, 273.

18 Hoke, *The Great Invasion*, 136.

19 "The Rebel Invasion," *Valley Spirit*, July 8, 1863.

is being sent to Richmond." According to Heyser, the streets of Chambersburg were "crowded with Rebels who try to interrogate our lesser citizens as to where things are hidden or sent to, and also as to the movements of the Federal troops that had left."[20]

Jacob Hoke reported that the stores in town were soon "relieved of a considerable part of their contents." One of the local newspapers noted that the business owned by S. S. Shryock was forced to sell "books and stationary to the amount of $8000" in Confederate scrip. "The Messrs. Eyster sold dry goods and groceries to the amount of $5000, and a number of others to the amount of $2000 and $3000," the newspaper declared. "There was not a store of any prominence that did not suffer heavily. Those who did not open at the first demand were compelled to see their doors broken in."[21]

While all that was going on, commissary officers also gathered up food and other supplies from individual residents at the town square. A steady stream of people with their goods in hand extended along the main streets in the middle of town. The items they were required to surrender included their personal riding tackle. "It was one of the most amasing sights I ever saw to see the broad-clothed gentry coming in and bringing saddles, bridles, etc., and making a pile of them in the square for the use of the Rebels," Jed Hotchkiss of Ewell's staff observed in a letter to his wife.

Although many goods had been hidden away, Hotchkiss still expressed amazement at the huge quantity of supplies that they confiscated in the area around Chambersburg. "Our success is wonderful," he declared. "We shall get nearly a million dollars worth of horses, supplies of all kinds &c. from this county (Franklin). We have invaded Fulton and Adams Cos also and shall levy on them in like manner—supporting our army entirely on the enemy. They say they never felt the war before but the first taste is enough for them." He pointed out that the local residents "do not care for more."[22]

For Junius Daniel's troops, their stay among the citizens of Chambersburg proved relatively brief. By early morning on June 25, the brigade was once more

---

20 William Heyser Diary, Entry for June 25, 1863, in William S. Bowers, ed., "William Heyser's Diary," *Kittochtinny Historical Society Papers*, 16 (1970-1978), 77-78; "The Invasion," *Franklin Repository*, July 15, 1863. For another civilian account of the occupation of Chambersburg, see Reeves to Lizzie, July 4, 1863, Excerpts, Coco Collection.

21 Hoke, *Reminiscences of the War*, 49; "The Rebel Invasion," *Valley Spirit*, July 8, 1863.

22 Jedediah Hotchkiss to Dear Sara, June 24, 1863, Hotchkiss Papers.

on the move to nearby Shippensburg, which had been occupied the day before by Jenkins's troopers. The remainder of the division joined them there on the next day, despite having to travel through a heavy rainstorm. Just as at their other stops, the commissary officers began gathering up supplies from all over town. One local resident reported to his son that "as near as can be sumbd up about 20 or 25 thousand dollars worth" of goods were seized by Rodes' men during their stay.[23]

The rich haul of supplies impressed Iverson's soldiers, but the region's populace certainly did not. "The town has about 3000 inhabitants & a hard looking set I can tell you—mostly Dutch," Surgeon Marston remarked in his diary. By that point in the campaign, however, not even the hostile stares from the local residents could dampen the spirits of the men. "This is the richest part of Pa. and it is the most beautiful country I ever saw," Mercer declared. He noted that they were "faring sumptuously—no army ever fared better in the world than we do—plenty to eat, light marches and a squad of Pennsylvania Militia before us too badly frightened to make a stand."[24]

From Shippensburg, Jenkins's cavalry pushed forward on the morning of June 27 toward the town of Carlisle. As they approached the outskirts of town, a group of local officials emerged under a flag of truce to inform Jenkins that the Federal troops had left. Based on those assurances, the brigade's lead troopers made their way into the west end of town along High Street without having to fire a shot. Lieutenant Herman Schuricht from the 14th Virginia Cavalry noted in his diary that they quickly "passed the obstructions and fortifications, and occupied the city at 10 o'clock." From there, it was only 18 more miles to the state capital at Harrisburg.[25]

The troopers were joined in Carlisle late that afternoon by the main part of the division. "At five o'clock in the afternoon the sound of music announced the entrance of Ewell's corps," reported one of the local papers. "It came by way of the Walnut Bottom road, down South Pitt to Main street, thence to Bedford street. The band at the head of the column played 'Dixie' as it passed

---

23 Lawrence Strumbaugh to Dear Son, July 9, 1863, Harrisburg Civil War Roundtable Collection, USAHEC. For additional details on the occupation of Shippensburg, see "Excerpts from the Diary of J. C. Atticks, Shippensburg, Penna.; during June and July 1863," Entries for June 24-27, *Civil War Times Illustrated* Collection, USAHEC.

24 Marston Diary, Entry for June 26, 1863, Emory, Mercer to Brother, June 26, 1863, in Wyatt, *The Reeves, Mercer, Newkirk Families*, 273.

25 Schuricht Diary, Entry for June 27, 1863, in Schuricht, "Jenkins' Brigade," 345.

through the streets." Another eyewitness noted that the Confederate troops made their way through town "to martial music, banners flaunting and posted their guards at each corner."[26]

One of those who watched the soldiers from the Army of Northern Virginia tramp through Carlisle was 15-year-old James Sullivan. To the teenager's surprise, Rodes' veterans appeared to be outfitted well and disciplined. "Knapsacks and the whole personal kit was in order," he remarked. "Arms were at every man's command. A significant touch to neatness was a toothbrush at hat band or buttonhole." Sullivan recalled that "further opportunity for inspection of the cavalry, infantry, artillery, and transportation service confirmed my first impression of a fit, well-fed, well-conditioned army."[27]

Edward O'Neal's men, marching at the front of the long infantry column, moved east through the main square and halted outside of town near "a large orchard." George Doles' Georgians followed O'Neal, turning off on the west side of town into the "ample yard" of Dickinson College. John Dickinson and Benjamin Rush—the latter a signer of the Declaration of Independence—founded the school in 1783. Lieutenant Thomas M. Hightower of the 21st Georgia, part of Doles' Brigade, informed his wife that it was "one of the oldest institutions in the once United States." The college was especially renowned because its first permanent building, known as Old West, had been designed by Benjamin Latrobe, the major architect for the Capitol building in Washington, D.C.[28]

As they made their fitful way onto the college grounds, the Georgia troops assumed control of the major campus buildings. The son of one of the professors recalled that the Southern infantry took over East College for use as

---

26 The Invasion," *Carlisle Volunteer American*, July 9, 1863; R. K. Hitner to My Dear Friend, July 6, 1863, Carlisle Barracks Collection, USAHEC.

27 James W. Sullivan, *Boyhood Memories of the Civil War, 1861-'65* (Carlisle, PA: Hamilton Library Association, 1933), 14.

28 Pickens Diary, Entry for June 27, 1863, in Hubbs, *Voices From Company D*, 181; Jedediah Hotchkiss to Sara Hotchkiss, June 28, 1863, Hotchkiss Papers; Conway P. Wing, *History of Cumberland County Pennsylvania* (Philadelphia: James D. Scott, 1879), 103-106; Thomas M. Hightower to Dear Lou, June 28, 1863, Hightower Letters; John T. Gay to Dear Pussie, June 27, 1863, Nix Collection. The Students finished their final exams just as the Rebels were entering the state. The 13 graduating seniors received their diplomas during a brief ceremony in the chapel at Old West on June 24. "Commencement at Dickinson College," *Baltimore Sun*, June 27, 1863.

He That Soweth of the Flesh 185

A view of the courthouse square at Carlisle, Pennsylvania, during the winter of 1865. Note the sheds for the local market house in the foreground. Alfred Iverson's North Carolinians marched through this square on their way to the U.S. Army Barracks, which were located just north of Carlisle along the turnpike leading to the capital at Harrisburg. *Cumberland County Historical Society*

---

a hospital. While Doles established his headquarters at Old West, the bulk of his command set up camp in the middle of the scenic college grounds and promptly began cooking fresh sides of beef they had procured during the long journey to Carlisle. "One barbecue frame was made at a point in the front campus about where the northeast corner of Bosler Hall is now," the professor's son remembered. "Another was directly north of the center of Old West about halfway to Louther Street."[29]

By this time, the North Carolina brigades commanded by Ramseur, Daniel, and Iverson had also arrived in town and were marching along the main street. Accompanied by Generals Ewell and Rodes, the soldiers from the three brigades turned north and crossed the courthouse square. From there, they proceeded along the Harrisburg Turnpike to the U.S. Army Barracks on the northern outskirts of town. The gunners from the division's four artillery batteries followed closely behind the infantry along the same route. The troops set up quarters in the barracks buildings, while the horses from the batteries were housed in the nearby stables.[30]

Edward Johnson's Division, meanwhile, was on the march toward Carlisle along the Valley Turnpike. His long and winding column included the corps' supply train. Just before reaching town, Johnson's troops halted in a large grove about three miles to the west along Cedar Spring Run. The area provided ample pasture land for the hungry animals in the wagon train and easy access to a good and plentiful source of water. Jubal Early's command, the last of Ewell's three divisions, continued its advance east of South Mountain along a route that carried them through a town called Gettysburg to the bustling commercial center at York.[31]

Not long after he and Rodes entered Carlisle, Ewell dispatched an officer from his staff into the town "with a demand on the authorities for supplies, medicines, amputation instruments, &c." When the merchants failed to comply with Ewell's request, he dispatched quartermaster details the following morning to begin scouring the area for food and military goods of every kind. One of those who "went in town with a party" to carry out the seizures was John S. Tucker, a quartermaster sergeant from the 5th Alabama, part of Ed O'Neal's command. A disappointed Tucker soon realized there was little of real value left on the shelves of the local merchants. "Opened nearly all the stores but found

---

29 Conway Hillman to Dear Morgan, Sept. 9, 1930, James Henry Morgan Presidential Papers, Archives and Special Collections, Waidner-Spahr Library, Dickinson College, Carlisle, Pennsylvania (hereafter cited as Dickinson).

30 OR 27, pt. 2, 551; Leonidas L. Polk to Dear Wife, June 28, 1863, Leonidas L. Polk Papers, SHC; John Purifoy, "With Ewell and Rodes in Pennsylvania," CV, 30 (1922), 464.

31 OR 27, pt. 2, 443.

them empty," he commented in his diary. "Everything having been hid or removed."[32]

Ewell, however, reported that "many valuable stores" were found once all the shops in Carlisle were searched. Rodes was equally pleased with the final results. He pointed out in his official report that "large supplies of cattle, horses, and flour" were found throughout the town, as well as "a large quantity of grain" in the barracks stables. He added that "most of the Government property, excepting the grain, had been removed by the enemy, but musketoons, holsters, tents, and a small quantity of subsistence stores were found in the barracks."[33]

In the end, nearly every merchant had something of value confiscated. Local resident Thomas Miller Griffith noted that "those who had warehouses & groceries suffered most." Although the quantity of supplied fell short of Confederate demands, those assigned to gather up the hospital supplies secured "all the drugs and medicines they wanted, also surgical instruments." Jed Hotchkiss of Ewell's staff estimated in a letter to his wife that they "obtained some $50000 of medicines & large supplies of provisions &c."[34]

The men from the three Tar Heel brigades, meanwhile, settled into their quarters at the barracks. One of Ramseur's soldiers described the main officers' headquarters as "a big two-story building with wide verandahs around the house, up-stairs and down." An officer from the same brigade noted that the rest of the complex comprised "seven or eight buildings, each about one hundred yards long and each containing about fifty or sixty rooms, besides numerous other smaller buildings." This place, he declared with a note of nostalgia, "reminds me very much of Chapel Hill."[35]

For Alfred Iverson, the barracks must have stirred memories much more poignant than those of Chapel Hill. He already knew the town well from the time he served there as a lieutenant with the 1st U.S. Cavalry. Many of the locals

---

32 John S. Tucker Diary, Entry for June 28, 1863, ADAH. Excerpts from the same diary have been published in Gary Wilson, ed., "The Diary of John S. Tucker: Confederate Soldier from Alabama," *Alabama Historical Quarterly*, 43 (1981), 5-33.

33 *OR* 27, pt. 2, 443, 551.

34 Thomas Miller Griffith to Dear Bro. and Sister, July 3, 1863, Thomas Miller Griffith Papers, Dickinson; Hotchkiss to Sara, June 28, 1863, Hotchkiss Papers.

35 J. D. Hufham Jr., "Gettysburg: Being an Account of the Experiences of a Veteran, Told By Himself," *Wake Forest Student*, 16 (April 1897), 451; Weldon Davis to Dear Ma, June 28, 1863, in Eaton, *Rebecca's Letters*, 63.

Officers' quarters at Carlisle Barracks in 1860, similar to the one that Brig. Gen. Alfred Iverson occupied while serving at Carlisle. *Cumberland County Historical Society*

recognized Iverson on the street from his happier days as a young U.S. Army officer. The Pennsylvanians cheerily greeted him as "Mr. Iverson"—the term "mister" being the common form of respect for officers serving at the barracks. More bittersweet was the fact that Carlisle was where Iverson had lived with his now-deceased wife, and where they had conceived his oldest child.[36]

Captain John Gorman from Ramseur's Brigade reported that Iverson "took quarters in the identical rooms" he occupied during his earlier tour of duty there. The general, Gorman observed in a letter home, "doubtless met many of his well known friends, whom he had business with, while in the Quartermaster's Department, in times of peace, and who [were] now so eager to crucify him, at the breaking out of the war, when they found that he took a South-side view of things." Unfounded rumors, which the captain repeated in his letter, claimed that Iverson had been forced to flee the town because of his

---

36 Kross, "That One Error," 48; V. E. Turner and H. C. Wall, "Twenty-Third Regiment," in Clark, *NC Regiments*, 2:233; "Memoirs of Charles C. Blacknall by His Son Oscar W. Blacknall," Blacknall Papers.

support for secession. "It is said, he had to give 'leg-bail' when he left the place last," he explained.37

On the surface at least, Iverson appeared completely unfazed by this unexpected homecoming. "Gen. Iverson (on whose staff Don Halsey serves) is occupying the same quarters he did while stationed here as Lt. of Cavalry some years ago," Maj. Eugene Blackford from the 5th Alabama in O'Neal's Brigade informed his father. "I called upon him and found him about to go out on a visiting tour among his old friends. I am curious to know how he was received and shall inquire tomorrow on the march." Blackford also pointed out that Captain Halsey remained "in high glee at the prospect of making the town with him."38

Richard Ewell had also served at Carlisle during his time in the U.S. Army. After his graduation from the U.S. Military Academy in 1840, he received his initial training there before joining the 2nd U.S. Dragoons. Ewell was again assigned to recruiting duty at the barracks during 1848 following his service in the Mexican War. Although he still had many acquaintances in the town, a severe headache kept him from making the social rounds in the days following his arrival. In his stead, Ewell asked several of his staff officers to check on the welfare of his many old friends in town.39

While a handful of the locals offered a warm welcome to the former U.S Army officers, the majority of the townspeople responded to the occupying force with barely concealed contempt. Some of the Confederate officers from Rodes' Division held out higher expectations for the professors and students at Dickinson College. Over the years, the distinguished institution had included a large number of young men from the South among its students. "Many soldiers who were in our corps met with those with whom they had spent pleasant days while at this place," one officer from Doles' Brigade wrote his hometown newspaper. "This is the *Alma Mater* of many a Southern gentlemen." He pointed out that "many a noble Confederate soldier received his tuition at old Dickerson."40

---

37 John C. Gorman to Dear Mother and Wife, July 8, 1863, *Raleigh Daily Progress*, July 22, 1863.

38 Eugene Blackford to Dear Father, June 28, 1863, Lewis Leigh Collection. Both Halsey and Blackford lived in Lynchburg, Virginia, prior to the war.

39 Pfanz, *A Soldier's Life*, 28-30, 60-61; Campbell Brown Journal, in Jones, *Campbell Brown's Civil War*, 202.

40 J. W. B. to Mr. Editor, Aug. 12, 1863, *Augusta Weekly Chronicle and Sentinel*, Sept. 5, 1863.

One of the school's better-known alumni was Reverend Charles Force Deems, whose son was serving with the 5th North Carolina in Iverson's Brigade. Rumors long persisted among the Dickinson professors that Deems had played a major role in protecting the college from harm during its occupation by Rodes' troops. While saying "Goodby and good luck" to a colonel from one of the Tar Heel brigades just prior to their departure for the North, Reverend Deems supposedly "told him to take good care of his old college home in Carlisle, if he ever got there." The colonel turned out to be one of the senior officers who bivouacked in the town and reportedly went to great efforts to fulfill his promise.[41]

The chance to visit the college proved enjoyable for at least some of the men from the division. Surgeon Marston of Iverson's Brigade reported that he "was much pleased" with his reception there. "Professor Nelson was kind enough to show me around," Marston penned in his diary. Chaplain Alexander D. Betts from the 30th North Carolina in Ramseur's Brigade, who had close ties to Reverend Deems, arranged a brief meeting with the president of the college, Herman Merrills Johnson. Betts also met with the president's daughter and engaged her in lively debate about the merits of the war.[42]

Even so, the faculty provided a less than friendly welcome during another tour by several officers from General Ewell's staff. This group included Maj. Alexander "Sandie" Pendleton and Dr. Hunter H. McGuire, Stonewall Jackson's former surgeon and the medical director for the Second Corps. Initially, the conversation with some of the professors, including several who were strong Northern Democrats, was amiable. The mood changed quickly when the school's chemistry professor openly defended the recent destruction of Darien, Georgia, by Federal troops and the burning of William and Mary College in Virginia during the previous year. The declaration shocked both staff officers. The comment so enraged Sandie Pendleton that he threatened to take vengeance on the professor. "I'll pay him for that sentiment," Pendleton declared in a letter to his fianceé. "McGuire & I are going this afternoon to confiscate his chemicals, etc. in reprisal for William & Mary College." Hospital

---

41 James Henry Morgan, *Dickinson College: The History of One Hundred and Fifty Years 1783-1933* (Carlisle, PA: Mount Pleasant Press, 1933), 316.

42 Marston Diary, Entry for June 29, 1863, Emory; Alexander D. Betts Diary, Entry for June 29, 1863, in A. D. Betts, *Experience of a Confederate Chaplain: 1861-1864* (Greenville, SC: n.p., 1907), 38-39.

Steward John S. Apperson from the Second Corps Medical Department later wrote that he paid a visit to the chemistry department the following day "for the purpose of taking the Chemical Apparatus from the College but for some reason it was forbidden."[43]

The stay in Carlisle was also filled with frustrations for Ewell, who had to deal with the unexpected appearance of Maj. Gen. Isaac Ridgeway Trimble at his headquarters on the morning of June 28. A former successful brigade commander under Stonewall Jackson, the 61-year-old Trimble fell with a severe wound during the Second Manassas Campaign and was promoted to major general while recovering from his injuries. Trimble returned to active duty in mid-June as commander of the Valley District. Once that area was cleared of Federals, he made his way to Chambersburg and visited General Lee at his headquarters.

After briefly conferring with Lee, Trimble rode to Carlisle in the hope of obtaining a new combat assignment. The presence of a capable major general hovering about without a command soon became a distraction for Ewell and his staff. Trimble began pestering them with unwanted advice about how Ewell should conduct the campaign. At one point, the old general even called for a quick strike to seize the state capital at Harrisburg. "Told General Ewell it could be easily taken, and I thought General Lee expected it," recalled the unemployed major general. "I volunteered to capture the place with one brigade."[44]

While Trimble offered his advice, the men in the ranks found that Carlisle was filled with many nearly forgotten pleasures. Even so, most of Iverson's veterans remained content to enjoy their brief rest in the barracks. "It was a nice place," Private Coghill explained in a letter home. "Good houses to stay in. Good water and ice a plenty as long as we staid." After settling in his quarters,

---

43 Alexander S. Pendleton to Kate Corbin, June 28, 1863, William Nelson Pendleton Papers, SHC; John S. Apperson Diary, Entry for June 29, 1863, in John Herbert Roper, ed., *Repairing the March of Mars: The Civil War Diaries of John Samuel Apperson, Hospital Steward in the Stonewall Brigade, 1861-1865* (Macon, GA: Mercer University Press, 2001), 481. For details on another visit to the College from a soldier in O'Neal's Brigade, see Elihu Wesley Watson to My Dear Brothers, July 10, 1863, Watson Family Papers, SC.

44 Campbell Brown Journal, in Jones, *Campbell Brown's Civil War*, 201; Tagg, *The Generals of Gettysburg*, 238; Isaac Ridgeway Trimble Diary, Entry for June 28, 1863, in William Starr Myers, ed., "The Civil War Diary of Isaac Ridgeway Trimble," *Maryland Historical Magazine*, 17 (1922), 10; Isaac Trimble, "The Battle and Campaign of Gettysburg," SHSP, 26 (1898), 122.

Surgeon Marston declared in his diary that "everything is comfortable," adding, "we have plenty supplies of every description."[45]

For those who were so inclined, the comforts of religion were also readily available. Reverend Beverly Tucker Lacy, who had been Stonewall Jackson's favorite chaplain, held two worship services at the barracks on the day after their arrival. Chaplains Betts and E. S. Brooks from the 2nd North Carolina Battalion in Daniel's Brigade were also on hand to minister to the troops that Sunday. "Bro. Lacy preaches to three North Carolina Brigades in the forenoon," Chaplain Betts wrote in his diary. "I preach in the afternoon and baptize five by pouring." Afterwards, the two preachers moved outside where they baptized four more soldiers in a nearby pool.[46]

Many of the officers in the division chose to attend Sunday worship at one of the local churches. "The Gen. sent word to the clergy to have their services as usual, as no one would disturb them," Jed Hotchkiss informed his wife. Although the response from the ministers in town was far from overwhelming, both the Presbyterian and Lutheran churches conducted services that morning. According to Hotchkiss, "the preachers, though nervous, prayed for their country in peril and their friends in danger—they also prayed for the strangers that were among them; some of them prayed for peace."[47]

Rather than searching for a local church to attend, Marston remained behind at the barracks, where a large crowd gathered to hear Reverend Lacy deliver an oration on the career of Stonewall Jackson and a fiery sermon from Paul's letter to the Galatians. According to the doctor, the text of the sermon that day was "Be not deceived." Marston continued: "God is not mocked. Whatsoever a man soweth, that he shall reap. He that soweth of the flesh shall of the flesh reap corruption; he that soweth of the spirit shall of the spirit reap life everlasting."[48]

---

45 Coghill to Pappy, Ma and Mit, July 17, 1863, John Fuller Coghill Letters; Marston Diary, Entry for June 28, 1863, Emory. For additional comments on the amenities at the barracks, see Alexander Murdock to My Dear Nephew, July 19, 1863, Alexander Murdock Papers, Pearce Civil War Collection, Navarro College, Corsicana, Texas, and Polk to Wife, June 28, 1863, Polk Papers.

46 Betts Diary, Entry for June 28, 1863, in Betts, *Confederate Chaplain*, 38; Stradley to Hufham, June 29, 1863, *Biblical Recorder*, July 22, 1863.

47 Hotchkiss to Sara, June 28, 1863, Hotchkiss Papers.

48 R. T. Bennett, "Fourteenth Regiment," included in Clark, *NC Regiments*, 1:719; Marston Diary, Entry for June 28, 1863, Emory.

Despite those words of admonition, many of Iverson's men turned to alcohol rather than religion as their primary source of solace during their sojourn in Carlisle. To their delight, large supplies of whiskey and other liquors were readily available. At one point, a group of foraging soldiers from the 23rd North Carolina located a "great deal of brandy" hidden away inside one of the rooms at the barracks. Their plunder was distributed generously throughout the brigade. "Many men of the 23rd and I presume of other regiments drank pretty fully of the Yankee treat," one veteran soldier recalled as the final payoff from their startling find.[49]

With so much alcohol available to the troops, the task of maintaining order in the town sometimes required extreme measures. One troubling incident occurred soon after the Confederates arrived. "Four of our men broke into and pillaged a house near the barracks," one of Daniel's officers reported in a letter to his hometown paper. "[A]s soon as it was made known to Gen. Ewell, he adopted means for their detection—placarded them with the words 'Thief and Rogue' in large letters, and marched them through our Division to the 'Rogue's March.'"[50]

Despite that show of force, the men from the 21st Georgia in Doles' Brigade, who were serving as provost guards for the town, continued to encounter problems with large groups of drunken soldiers. Among the worst offenders were some of the troops from the 23rd North Carolina. "Many of our jaded, weary boys, drank too much United States Government whiskey and a battle with a Georgia regiment, for the time likewise drowning their weariness, was narrowly averted," one of Iverson's officers openly admitted years later.[51]

Most of the ranking officers from the division also took part in the excessive drinking at Carlisle. While preparing for a Sunday ceremony at the barracks, someone from Rodes' staff found a keg of lager beer. Within minutes,

---

49 Blacknall Memoirs, Blacknall Papers. For details on the drinking at Carlisle in the other brigades, see William Beavans Diary, Undated Entry, William Beavans Diary and Letters, SHC and William W. Sillers to Dear Sister, Aug. 7, 1863, Sillers-Holmes Family Correspondence, Rare Books and Special Collections, University of Notre Dame, Notre Dame, Indiana.

50 "From the Forty-Third Reg't N. C. T.," July 20, 1863, *North Carolina Argus*, July 30, 1863. The scene was also witnessed by 15-year-old John Cabell Early, who had arrived at the town in the hope of joining the staff of his uncle, General Early. For details, see John Cabell Early, "A Southern Boy's Experience at Gettysburg," *Journal of the Military Service Institution of the United States*, 48, No. 169 (January-February 1911), 416-417.

51 Turner and Wall, "Twenty-Third Regiment," in Clark, *NC Regiments*, 2:233.

everyone was sharing the contents. Rodes enjoyed beer as well—and became "somewhat affected" by the potent brew. "The beer was the strongest I ever saw, I must add by the way of excuse—probably mixed with whiskey," Maj. Campbell Brown, Ewell's stepson and staff officer, concluded in his journal. Brown went on to note that he "never saw Rodes intoxicated before or since and it was an accident this time."

No one knows for sure if Iverson joined in consumption of alcohol, although events that day, coupled with the consequences of his later actions on July 1, would eventually spark rumors that he was drunk at Gettysburg. Several other officers, however, did take the opportunity to drown their sorrows that afternoon. Isaac Trimble, who was attached temporarily to Ewell's staff, was described as "quite jolly." Some of the heaviest drinkers included officers from Rodes' staff. One of them became so "utterly incoherent" that another officer had to grab his coattails to keep him from falling flat on the ground.[52]

The open drunkenness among some of the corps' top officers drew especially harsh condemnation from Reverend J. A. Stradley, who was serving as a missionary in Ramseur's Brigade. "Many officers, some occupying important positions, have been drunk, and many others have been drinking freely, and at the same time punishing men for doing the same thing," he chastised in a letter to a statewide religious newspaper in North Carolina. Stradley found these actions so intolerable that he called for alcohol to be banned for men of all ranks. "O that this fatal destroyer of all that is good were itself destroyed!" he proclaimed.[53]

The ostensible cause for all the revelry that day was the scheduled raising of the newly authorized Second National Confederate flag. Although that version was not yet in general use, the officers at Carlisle soon came up with a suitable banner by incorporating some white bunting with a battle flag from one of Junius Daniel's regiments. "Finding a number of U.S. garrison flags at the Barracks & the flagstaff standing, we concluded to raise a Confederate flag for the benefit of the ignorant citizens," wrote Campbell Brown, who noted that "the Battle flag of the [32nd] NC was made the ground-work, two or three tailors were procured and in an hour or two we had a handsome flag ready for hoisting."

---

52 Campbell Brown Journal, in Jones, *Campbell Brown's Civil War*, 201.

53 Stradley to Hufham, June 29, 1863, in *Biblical Recorder*, July 22, 1863.

The new Confederate banner was fluttering above the parade ground that afternoon when some of the officers stumbled onto the balcony of the barracks to give short speeches to the throng of men assembled below. "The troops were gathered round, the flag raised," Brown recalled. "A short neat speech [was] made from the balcony of the house by Rodes, another by Junius Daniel, and then old Trimble made a few remarks, not so very neat." General Ewell, suffering from a severe headache, offered only "a few words to the men at first raising of the flag" before returning to his sickbed.[54]

Men throughout the division greeted the ceremony with rampant enthusiasm. Surgeon Marston from the 12th North Carolina noted in his journal that they "raised our new flag today in the barracks—great cheering & speech making." Jed Hotchkiss described the gathering as "quite an animating scene." An enlisted man serving under Ramseur reported that they "hoisted the Confederate flag over this place to be attended or greeted by Dixie from one of our best bands." Another soldier from Junius Daniel's Brigade declared in a letter to his sister that "the Band played Dixie & Bonnie-blue flag, and we heard little talks from Gens. Ewell, Trimble, Rodes, Daniel & felt like going on to N.Y."[55]

At least one man, and probably many others, left the parade grounds that June day more inspired than ever to meet and fight the enemy wherever General Lee took them. "No one has the least idea what we are going to do," Lt. William Calder from Ramseur's Brigade informed his mother in a letter home. "Some say we are to take Harrisburg, others say not and thus it goes." Despite the rampant uncertainty about their ultimate destination, the soldiers remained supremely confident that their leaders had the strategic situation well in hand. "This much is certain," Calder continued. "We are far advanced into Pennsylvania and we did not come here for nothing." The lieutenant concluded

---

54 Campbell Brown Journal, in Jones, *Campbell Brown's Civil War*, 201. There appears to be no basis for the often-repeated story that this "elegant new flag" had been sent by the ladies of Richmond to General Lee "for him to present to the regiment most worthy of receiving and carrying it." For details on the claim of this honor for the 32nd North Carolina in Daniel's Brigade, see Henry A. London, "Thirty-Second Regiment," included in Clark, *NC Regiments*, 3:525.

55 Marston Diary, Entry for June 28, 1863, Emory; Hotchkiss Journal, Entry for June 28, 1863, in McDonald, *Make Me a Map*, 155; Preston H. Turner to My Dear Parents, June 28, 1863, Preston H. Turner Papers, SHC; George W. Wills to Dear Sister, June 28, 1863, George Whitaker Wills Letters, SHC.

that "Gen Lee knows what we are to do and it is our part to obey orders without questioning."[56]

Uncertainties notwithstanding, most of those in attendance remained convinced that their next move would be an attack on Harrisburg. Ewell's orders already called for Rodes to resume his advance toward the city early in the afternoon on June 29. North of Carlisle, Jenkins's cavalry were operating within three miles of the Pennsylvania state capital. Farther east, John Gordon's brigade from Early's Division stood on the banks of the Susquehanna River near Wrightsville. With the city's defenses largely in the hands of militia, Harrisburg appeared ready to fall at the first sight of the invading Rebel army.[57]

Nothing up to that point in the campaign had given Iverson's men any cause for concern about the outcome if a move against the capital indeed took place. "It is thought they will make a stand at Harrisburg," Captain Mercer predicted to his brother. "But if we go there they will fly away is my opinion." Another officer from O'Neal's Alabama brigade was even more emphatic about the likelihood of capturing the city. He openly boasted in a letter to his wife that "the Capital of this State is most certainly gone up the spout."[58]

Just as Rodes' troops were preparing to leave Carlisle on the afternoon of June 29, however, Ewell received a message from Lee that canceled the movement toward Harrisburg and directed Ewell's entire Second Corps to instead concentrate in the area of Chambersburg. Those new orders were the result of intelligence received from a scout the previous day. According to "Harrison," Joe Hooker had been removed from command, Maj. Gen. George Gordon Meade had replaced him, and the Army of the Potomac had crossed

---

56 William E. Calder to Dear Mother, June 29, 1863, Calder Papers.

57 For details on Jenkins's activities outside Harrisburg, see "The Rebel Invasion," *Cumberland Valley Journal*, July 23, 1863; C. B. Niesley to Dear Parents, July 1, 1863, Harrisburg Civil War Roundtable Collection, USAHEC; Micajah J. Woods to My Dear Mother, June 30, 1863, Micajah Woods Papers, UVA; Robert G. Crist, *Confederate Invasion of the West Shore-1863* (Carlisle, PA: Cumberland County Historical Society, 1963); Robert G. Crist, "Highwater 1863: The Confederate Approach to Harrisburg," *Pennsylvania History*, 30 (April 1963), 158-183; and Uzal Ent, "Rebels in Pennsylvania," *Civil War Times Illustrated*, 37, No. 4 (August 1998), 46-52, 64-66.

58 Mercer to Brother, June 26, 1863, in Wyatt, *The Reeves, Mercer, Newkirk Families*, 273; Thomas S. Taylor to My Dear Wife, June 28, 1863, Taylor Letters. For similar comments from other soldiers in the division, see William C. Ousby to Dear Brother, June 28, 1863, William Clark Ousby Papers, NCOAH and Abner E. McGarity to My Own Dear Tinie, June 28, 1863, in Edmund Cody Burnett, ed., "Letters of a Confederate Surgeon: Dr. Abner Embry McGarity, 1862-1865," *Georgia Historical Quarterly*, 24 (1945), 159.

the Potomac River and was moving north along the east side of South Mountain.

In response to his orders, Ewell dispatched Johnson's Division, which was camped about three miles outside of Carlisle, toward Chambersburg along Valley Turnpike on the western side of South Mountain. Rodes was preparing to depart along the same route when a second courier arrived from Lee with updated instructions that called for them to move directly south through the mountains in the direction of Gettysburg. Jubal Early's troops were ordered to proceed toward the same area from their main encampment just outside the town of York.[59]

Rather than depart so late in the day, Ewell decided instead to hold Rodes and his brigades in place at Carlisle until the following morning. The command to stand down for the day caught most of the men from Iverson's Brigade by surprise. "Orders to march to the front at 12 pm today," Marston scribbled into his daily journal. "I hate very much to give up our good quarters here but supposedly will be committed to the flames." The doctor also noted that their orders were unexpectedly "countermanded & we do not leave till it is the morning."[60]

The sudden change in plans proved especially frustrating for Richard Ewell, who had expected and looked forward to the great prize of capturing Harrisburg with little or no enemy opposition. His displeasure was readily apparent to everyone serving under his direct command. "The General was quite testy and hard to please, because disappointed, and had every one flying around," confided Jed Hotchkiss. Ewell's only satisfaction came when Gen. Lee agreed that his Second Corps commander would not need to burn the U.S. Army barracks where he had been stationed during his earlier days as a young officer in the dragoons.[61]

---

59 *OR* 27, pt. 2, 443, 552.

60 Marston Diary, Entry for June 29, 1863, Emory.

61 Hotchkiss Journal, Entry for June 29, 1863, in McDonald, *Make Me a Map*, 155. Despite Ewell's forbearance, the barracks were burned down on the following day by troopers from Brig. Gen. Fitzhugh Lee's Brigade in Stuart's Cavalry Division. For details of the attack on the town, see Eric J. Wittenberg and J. David Petruzzi, *Plenty of Blame to Go Around: Jeb Stuart's Controversial Ride to Gettysburg* (New York: Savas Beatie, 2006), 139-154; Mary P. Moore to Dear Father, July 31, 1863, Moore Family Papers, Pennsylvania State Archives, Harrisburg, Pennsylvania; Hitner to Friend, July 6, 1863, Carlisle Barracks Collection; and Mary Margaret

When Iverson and his Tar Heels finally marched out of Carlisle early on the morning of June 30, their destination was not one of the major cities in the east like Baltimore, or even the state capital at Harrisburg, as most of them expected. Writing to his family a little more than two weeks later, a shocked and exhausted private in Iverson's Brigade reported that he and his comrades "came back through Carlisle and took the road that went to Baltimore but instead of going to Baltimore we went to the horrible place of Gettysburg."[62]

Fleming Murray to Harmar Denny Murray, July 3, 1863, Civil War Collection File, Cumberland County Historical Society, Carlisle, Pennsylvania.

62 Coghill to Pappy, Ma and Mit, July 17, 1863, James O. Coghill Letters.

Chapter Nine

We are Brought in Hearing of Artillery

Rodes' men moved south from Carlisle along the main turnpike toward Baltimore. Their first stop was the village of Papertown, home to one of the largest paper mills in the North. The Kempton and Mullen paper factory stood along the banks of nearby Mountain Creek, which provided a reliable source of power for the machinery. Although the mill was not operating at the time, a large amount of paper was stored at the site.

The chance to secure high-quality paper for the army proved impossible for Ewell to pass up. Jed Hotchkiss noted in his journal that the general and some of his staff officers "stopped awhile to examine the extensive paper mill there." Another officer from O'Neal's Brigade recalled that he also "went in and saw more paper than I ever heard of before." The visitors ordered the quartermaster department to seize more than $5,000 worth of paper. To the owner's dismay, payment was made with nearly worthless Confederate scrip.[1]

Generals Rodes and Ewell continued leading the men from the division south through the mountains at Mount Holly, where they passed by another

---

1 Nye, *Here Come the Rebels!*, 358-359; Hotchkiss Journal, Entry for June 30, 1863, in McDonald, *Make Me a Map*, 156; Blackford, "Memoirs," 236, Civil War Misc. Collection.

paper mill owned by Robert and Samuel Given. Despite intermittent rain, Jed Hotchkiss described the day as "quite pleasant." Most enjoyable of all was the spectacular mountain scenery that greeted them along the way. Captain John Gorman from Ramseur's Brigade noted that he had "never seen, in all my travels, a more lovely spot than Mt. Holly Gap." He declared that "its picturesque beauty and grandeur must be seen to be realized."[2]

Their route carried them to Petersburg, the site of the famed York Sulphur Springs resort. Following a short break, the men were once more on the move along the turnpike toward Baltimore. "We had no idea of our destination," a Georgia veteran recalled. "We knew we were going in a southeasterly direction and on a forced march, and that, too, on a most intensely hot day." To their surprise, they proceeded only about three-quarters of a mile before turning onto the main road running southwest. That highway served as the primary connection between the state capital at Harrisburg and the crossroads town of Gettysburg.[3]

Following an uneventful trip of some 18 miles, Rodes' men finally stopped for the night just northeast of Gettysburg near Heidlersburg. Early's Division arrived soon afterward from York and halted along the banks of Plum Run about three miles east of Rodes. Ed Johnson and his division camped more than 20 miles away on the western side of South Mountain near Scotland village and would not rejoin the rest of the corps until early the next evening. After pulling back from the immediate vicinity of Harrisburg, Jenkins' troopers only made it as far as Petersburg before halting during the early morning hours on July 1.[4]

The rest of Lee's Army of Northern Virginia remained a good distance away from Ewell's Second Corps. The divisions of Richard H. Anderson and Dorsey Pender from A. P. Hill's Third Corps, together with all three divisions from James Longstreet's First Corps, were still on the far side of the Cashtown gap along the road between Chambersburg and Greenwood. Henry Heth's

---

2 Wing, *History of Cumberland County*, 224; Hotchkiss Journal, Entry for June 30, 1863, in McDonald, *Make Me a Map*, 156; Gorman to Mother and Wife, July 8, 1863, *Raleigh Daily Progress*, July 22, 1863.

3 Nye, *Here Come the Rebels!*, 359; C. D. Grace, "Rodes' Division at Gettysburg," *CV*, 5 (1897), 614. Petersburg is known today as York Springs.

4 OR 27, pt. 2, 555; Vincent A. Witcher to John W. Daniel, March 1, 1906, John Warwick Daniel Papers, UVA.

View of the Given Brothers paper mill, which stood along Iverson's route through Mt. Holly, prior to burning down in 1865. *Cumberland County Historical Society*

Division (Hill's Corps) was in camp near Cashtown. Earlier in the day on June 30, one of Heth's brigades carried out a brief reconnaissance eastward in the direction of Gettysburg. Plans were already in the works for Heth to return there the following morning.

Once they reached Heidlersburg, Ewell took the special precaution of dispatching Capt. Frank Bond's cavalry company—which had finally rejoined the main column—to scout the area around Gettysburg for any signs of the enemy activity. "We marched about eight miles, to within full sight of Gettysburg, without encountering opposition," Captain Bond recalled years later. He added that "there was nothing to be seen, but a quiet city with a heavy backing of mountains behind, and a large area of fertile fields in front and on the right." Before making his return, however, the captain posted some pickets about three miles north of Gettysburg under the command of Sgt. Hammond Dorsey.

Bond's foresight paid off later that night when the cavalry patrol captured three enlisted men from a Pennsylvania battery just outside Gettysburg. "It seems they found themselves within a few miles of home for the first time in a year or more, and asked for leave to see their folks," Bond explained. Although their captain refused permission, the men slipped out of camp under cover of darkness and were apprehended up by Bond's Southern troopers. Bond turned in the Federal prisoners and "furnished the first information of the whereabouts of Meade's Army."[5]

Later that same evening on June 30, Rodes and Early joined Ewell for a strategy session. Trimble, who ached for a more active role since his arrival two days earlier and never failed to communicate that fact to Ewell, joined the gathering. The primary topic centered around a discussion of the latest dispatches from Lee and A. P. Hill. As Ewell later reported, "At Heidlersburg, I received orders from the general commanding to proceed to Cashtown or Gettysburg, as circumstances might dictate, and a note from A. P. Hill, saying he was at Cashtown."[6]

Unfortunately, the only surviving account of the conference comes from Trimble, who claimed that Ewell "read over the order of Gen'l Lee several times, commenting on its 'indefinite phraseology,' as he expressed it, in very severe terms, and asking each one what was meant by 'according to circumstances.'" According to Trimble, Rodes and Early had little to say while the unattached major general forcefully argued that Lee wanted them to advance directly to Gettysburg the following day. Trimble noted, however, that "this explanation did not satisfy Gen'l Ewell, who more than once impatiently remarked, 'Why can't a commanding General have some one of his staff who can write an intelligible order?'"[7]

---

5 Frank A. Bond, "Company A, First Maryland Cavalry," *CV*, 6 (1898), 79; Frank Bond, "Memoir," 169, Confederate States Army Bound Volumes, MOC.

6 *OR* 27, pt. 2, 444.

7 Isaac Trimble to John Bachelder, Feb. 8, 1883, in David L. and Aubrey J. Ladd, eds., *The Bachelder Papers: Gettysburg in Their Own Words*, 3 Vols. (Dayton, OH: Morningside House, 1994), 2:927; Trimble, "The Battle and Campaign of Gettysburg," 122. It is important to keep in mind that Trimble's recollections, written many years after the fact, were cobbled together with the hindsight of the Gettysburg defeat and Ewell's controversial role there.

Based on his own interpretation of the orders, Ewell decided to push forward to Cashtown early the following morning with Rodes' Division. Ewell's operational plan called for his corps to proceed west from Heidlersburg through the village of Middletown. From there, they would move to Cashtown, where A. P. Hill had camped the night before with Heth's Division. Early was ordered to follow closely behind and make his way through Hunterstown to the vicinity of Cashtown. With his decision made, Ewell rightly concluded that everything was in place for his Second Corps to link up with the main body of Lee's army.[8]

Rodes' infantry awoke just before dawn on July 1 with orders to make preparations for resuming the advance. The weather on June 30 had been hot and humid, but the first day of July proved nearly perfect for marching. One of Doles' officers informed the folks back home that "the morning was bright and beautiful." Another soldier from the 3rd Alabama in O'Neal's Brigade recalled that it "was a beautiful sun lit morning, the clear mountain atmosphere cooled by the rains of the preceding night were invigorating, one could say almost intoxicating."[9]

Iverson's Tar Heels led the division on the march from Heidlersburg, followed by the brigades of O'Neal, Doles, and Daniel. Next in line rolled the division's four artillery batteries, followed by the heavily laden supply and ordnance wagons. Ramseur's Brigade, remembered one officer, "moved in rear of the division train to protect it against any dash the enemy might make." The position of each brigade in the line of march was determined by a standard rotation from its place during the advance the previous day.[10]

Despite a few initial delays, the troops were soon on their way toward Cashtown along the road running west through the small village of Middletown, about seven miles north of Gettysburg. The direction of the march changed in the middle of the morning with the arrival of a fresh dispatch from A. P. Hill. "Before reaching Middletown," Ewell explained in his official report, "I received notice from General Hill that he was advancing upon Gettysburg, and turned the head of Rodes' column toward that place, by the

---

8 OR 27, pt. 2, 444. Middletown is known today as Biglerville.

9 J. W. B. to Mr. Editor, Aug. 12, 1863, *Augusta Weekly Chronicle and Sentinel*, Sept. 5, 1863; "War Memories by an Old Hornet," 95, 3rd Alabama File, Confederate Regiment Files, GNMPC.

10 William E. Calder to Dear Mother, July 8, 1863, Calder Papers.

Middletown Road, sending word to Early to advance directly on the Heidlersburg road."[11]

Ewell promptly dispatched Col. John Evans Johnson, who served as a volunteer aide on his staff, with a message for Hill informing him of his decision to move toward Gettysburg rather than Cashtown. According to Capt. Bond from the 1st Maryland Cavalry, his full company was sent "to escort Col. Johnson . . . who had despatches for Gen. Hill, who was on our right, about ten miles away." Ewell took the additional step of ordering staffer Campbell Brown to ride "towards Cashtown" and inform Lee in person about their change in direction.[12]

The first indications that something more was going on around Gettysburg than farming and commerce arrived in the form of distant gunfire. As soon as they turned south, Iverson's Tar Heels at the head of the column heard the distinct sound of artillery fire. According to Surgeon Marston, the march from Heidlersburg began about six o'clock in the morning. "Much to surprise after marching about 7 miles we are brought in hearing of artillery in front," he wrote. Private J. L. Wallace of the 23rd North Carolina also recalled that "the sounds of strenuous battle reached our ears" as the men tramped south toward town.[13]

Ewell and Rodes heard it as well and discerned quickly that the gunfire was coming from the vicinity of Gettysburg, a thriving city with a population of about 2,400. The town served as the commercial and governmental center for Adams County. The crossroads community boasted both a college and a Lutheran seminary and enjoyed a direct railroad connection to Hanover, Pennsylvania. A series of steep ridges and several rugged hills dominated the surrounding countryside. The most important military attribute was Gettysburg's location: the city served as the intersection of 10 major roads extending in nearly every direction like the spokes on a giant wheel.

The sounds of gunfire drifting on the light breeze that morning were the result of the growing escalation of a meeting engagement between Heth's Division of Hill's Corps and Federal troops just west of Gettysburg. Heth had moved toward the town in division strength on the mistaken assumption that

---

11 OR 27, pt. 2, 444.

12 Krick, *Lee's Colonels*, 210; Bond, "Company A, First Maryland Cavalry," 79; Campbell Brown Journal, in Jones, *Campbell Brown's Civil War*, 204.

13 Marston Diary, Entry for July 1, 1863, Emory; Wallace, "Reminiscences," 4, Military Collections, NCOAH.

nothing more than militia was in his front. In fact, the rolling ridges outside Gettysburg were held by veteran troopers from Brig. Gen. John Buford's division, part of the Army of the Potomac. Through a skillful use of delaying tactics, Buford's dismounted cavalrymen slowed down Heth's advance long enough for infantry from the Federal I Corps to begin arriving on the field. Within a short time, Heth's command had been sucked into a heavy and disastrous fight along both sides of the turnpike leading into town from Chambersburg.[14]

Spurred on by artillery fire, Rodes' men were about three miles north of Gettysburg around ten o'clock that morning when they met Federal cavalry videttes from Col. Thomas C. Devin's brigade posted along both sides of the road near Keckler's Hill. According to Sgt. Charles Timothy Furlow, a courier on Doles' staff, they "could see no Yankee force when we first arrived except small detachments of cavalry & Yankee sharpshooters (cavalry)."[15]

The troopers were from the 17th Pennsylvania Cavalry, part of a line of videttes from Buford's division running all the way from the Black Horse Tavern on the south to the Harrisburg Road on the north. Each vidette squad comprised four or five men under the command of an officer (or noncommissioned officer) posted in a forward position around the perimeter at intervals of 500 to 600 yards. The rest of the troopers remained in the rear as a reserve. Once contact was made, the troopers were instructed to fire on the enemy and retire. After repeatedly employing these delaying tactics, the cavalrymen had orders to fall back to a pre-determined skirmish line.[16]

Rodes responded to the presence of the Federal cavalrymen arrayed across his front by deploying Iverson's first corps of sharpshooters under Capt. Benjamin Robinson of the 5th North Carolina. The detachment moved quickly into position across the front of the brigade. "The Yankee cavalry threatening our left, we threw out our skirmishers on our left front, and watched them fight

---

14 For detailed accounts of the morning of July 1, see David G. Martin, *Gettysburg July 1* (Conshohocken, PA: Combined Books, 1995), 59-202; Harry W. Pfanz, *Gettysburg: The First Day* (Chapel Hill: University of North Carolina Press, 2001), 51-130; and Richard S. Shue, *Morning at Willoughby Run, July 1, 1863* (Gettysburg, PA: Thomas Publications, 1995).

15 Charles Timothy Furlow, "Record of Current Events from the Time the 4th Ga Regt Left Camp Jackson, Va.," 45, Diaries Miscellaneous Collection (MS 181), Manuscripts and Archives Library, Yale University, New Haven, Connecticut.

16 Gary Kross, "Fight Like the Devil to Hold Your Own: General John Buford's Cavalry at Gettysburg on July 1, 1863," *Blue and Gray Magazine*, 12, Issue 3 (February 1995), 12, 14.

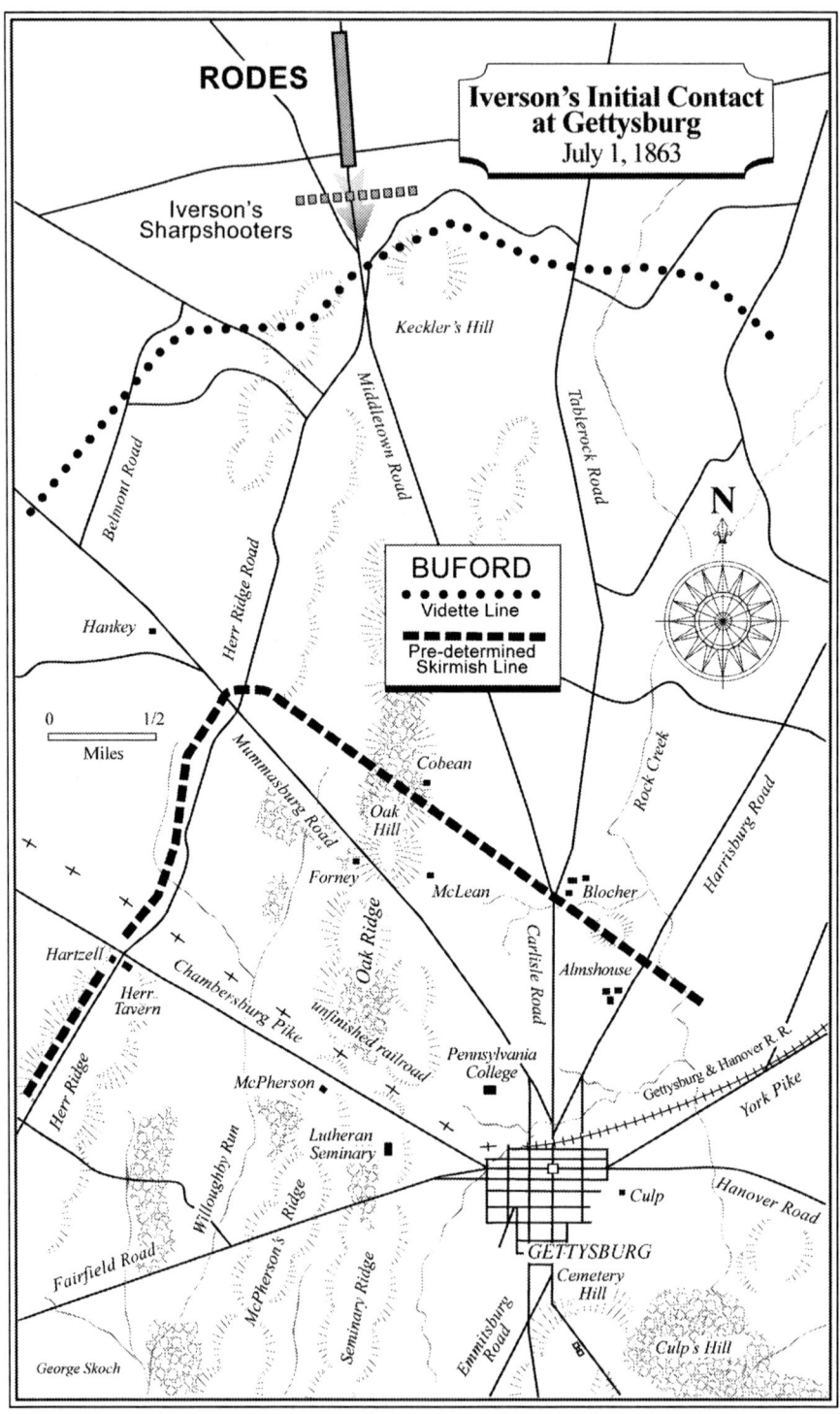

the Yankee cavalry for perhaps an hour," Lt. Joseph Oliver recalled. Private John Coghill reported that the men "formed a line of battle and then the sharp shooters was ordered to the front so I went and very soon wee commenced shooting at the Yankes."[17]

Sharpshooter detachments from O'Neal's and Doles' brigades joined the fight as they approached within two miles of town. "We could distinctly hear the roar of the cannon in front," Capt. William S. Evans from the 4th Georgia in Doles' Brigade wrote his sister. "We had marched very hard and the boys were all very much worn, but the roar of artillery seemed to give them strength. Soon we came in sight of the Yankee pickets, as skirmishers. We made no stop, but soon threw the skirmishers in." The Georgia captain went on to note that "the town of Gettysburg was now in full view about one mile distant."[18]

The swelling Confederate skirmish force of more than 400 men slowly but steadily pushed the Federal troopers back along the west side of the road leading into Gettysburg from nearby Middletown. Major Eugene Blackford, in command of O'Neal's detachment of sharpshooters, reported that his men "moved steadily forward upon the town, driving in the cavalry videttes, posted in the road and on commanding hills" along their front. Blackford observed that the Federal troopers "repeatedly charged, but my men rallying coolly & promptly sent them back every time with more empty saddles."[19]

After more than an hour of fighting, Rodes' sharpshooters finally came up against Devin's main skirmish line at the southern end of the Samuel Cobean farm. As Blackford described it, "About half a mile from the suburbs, a large force of cavalry was observed in line, with a heavy line of men dismounted as skirmishers. The former charged us twice, but were easily repulsed." Captain Robinson from Iverson's Brigade described the location where they encountered the cavalry skirmish line as "a low flat land about one thousand yards from the town."[20]

---

17 Robinson to Vance, July 9, 1863, *Raleigh Daily Progress*, July 24, 1863; Oliver, "Recollections," 2; Coghill to Pappy, Ma and Mit, July 17, 1863, John Fuller Coghill Letters.

18 Taylor to Wife, July 17, 1863, Taylor Papers; William S. Evans to My Dear Sister, Oct. [July] 9, 1863, in *Confederate Reminiscences and Letters*, 10:212.

19 OR 27, pt. 2, 597; Blackford Memoirs, 239, Civil War Miscellaneous Collection. The Gettysburg portion was published in Noah Andre Trudeau, ed., "5th Alabama Sharpshooters: Taking Aim at Cemetery Hill," *America's Civil War*, 14, No. 3 (July 2001), 46-53.

20 OR 27, pt. 2, 597; Robinson to Vance, July 9, 1863, *Raleigh Daily Progress*, July 24, 1863.

Devin realized the importance of holding his position and moved to reinforce his battle line on the west side of the road. According to the Federal cavalry leader, he "immediately placed the Ninth New York in support, and dismounting the rest of my available force, succeeded in holding the rebel line in check." The skirmishing swelled and continued unabated for almost two hours from the time Devin's videttes first encountered Rodes' sharpshooters near Keckler's Hill. Only after Federal infantry began arriving on that part of field did Devin finally pull his cavalry back to the east along the York Turnpike.[21]

While the three sharpshooter detachments engaged Devin's troopers, Rodes led the rest of the division to the right along the main ridge line toward "a prominent hill" overlooking the town from the north and west. "On arriving on the field, I found that by keeping along the wooded ridge, on the left side of which the town of Gettysburg is situated, I could strike the force of the enemy with which General Hill's troops were engaged upon the flank, and that, besides moving under cover, whenever we struck the enemy we could engage him with the advantage in ground," Rodes explained in his report.

As the terrain opened up in front of them, Rodes' set about to deploy his brigades in battle formation rather than in columns. "The division was, therefore, moved along the summit of the ridge," reported the division leader, "with only one brigade deployed at first, and finally, as the enemy's cavalry had discovered us and the ground was of such character as to admit of cover for a large opposing force, with three brigades deployed; Doles on the left, Rodes' (old) brigade, Colonel O'Neal commanding, in the center, and Iverson on the right, the artillery and the other two brigades moved up closely to the line of battle."[22]

Although the temperature on July 1 did not exceed about 75 degrees, the men soon found the combination of heat, exhaustion, and high humidity difficult to endure. The conditions proved especially trying for O'Neal's men, who had to scramble across an area of mixed fields and woods along the eastern slope of the hill. "As it was an excessively hot day & we were going through wheat fields & ploughed ground & over fences, it almost killed us," Pvt. Samuel Pickens wrote in his diary. "I was perfectly exhausted & never suffered so from

---

21 *OR* 27, pt. 1, 939.

22 *Ibid.*, pt. 2, 552.

heat & fatigue in my life." The private also observed that "a good many fell out of ranks being completely broken down & some fainted."[23]

Despite the difficult terrain, the soldiers pushed on for almost a mile across the rough ground before arriving about noon in the area around Oak Hill. From that position, Doles deployed his men on the "open plain" to the left of the high ground. O'Neal moved his brigade into place on the eastern slope of the ridge. With Iverson's troops in the lead, the three North Carolina brigades moved into the woods blanketing much of the hill. Iverson formed his regiments on the southwestern side of the summit, while Junius Daniel took up a position with his brigade behind and slightly to Iverson's right. Ramseur's men, meanwhile, halted near the rear of the hill as a reserve force.

Oak Hill, just northwest of town, rose nearly 60 feet above the farm fields across the Mummasburg Road on the south and about 80 feet above the Moses McLean farm to the east. Much of the hill was covered in woods. The eastern slope formed a steep ridge extending south past the Chambersburg Pike. Although connected to the larger Seminary Ridge, this section of high ground between Oak Hill and the turnpike was commonly known as Oak Ridge. Another smaller ridge with two distinct branches ran directly south from Oak Hill through the area of the Edward McPherson farm about one-half mile to the west of Seminary Ridge.[24]

Lieutenant Colonel Thomas Carter's artillery battalion and the division's wagon train followed closely behind the main column on nearby Herr Ridge Road. A narrow country lane, Herr Ridge Road angled southwest from the Middletown Road along the western flank of Oak Hill before finally linking up with the main road leading into town from Mummasburg. The three sharpshooter detachments that had engaged Devin's troopers formed a thin line of skirmishers across the division's entire front. Their position extended all the way from Carlisle Road on the left to the area of Mummasburg Road at the top of the ridge on their right.[25]

---

23 Pickens Diary, Entry for July 1, 1863, in Hubbs, *Voices From Company D*, 182.

24 Martin, *Gettysburg July 1*, 584. The McLean farm was owned by former congressman and prominent local attorney Moses McLean, who lived in town on Baltimore Street. At the time of the battle, the property was rented by David H. Beams, who was absent serving with the Federal Army in Virginia. His wife and three-year-old child remained behind and fled for safety from the farm as the fighting began.

25 *OR* 27, pt. 2, 553.

With Rodes' troops in place, Ewell sized up the battlefield situation from his vantage point along the southern front of the hill. From there, the entire right flank of John Reynolds' Federal I Corps was visible about one mile away to the south. The enemy troops were deployed in a long line of battle extending along the main section of McPherson's Ridge all the way to the unfinished railroad bed just north of the Chambersburg Pike. The two Southern divisions under Henry Heth and Dorsey Pender, A. P. Hill's Corps, opposed them from Herr Ridge to the west.

Ewell enjoyed a sweeping line of sight, as did many of his men posted on other parts of the hill. One veteran from O'Neal's Brigade recalled that he could quite easily see Hill's troops "moving slowly but steadily on the long blue lines" in the distance. He found the scene to be unlike anything he had encountered during his nearly two years of service in the army. "It was the only time during the war that we were in position to get such a view of contending forces," he recalled years later. "It seemed like some grand panorama with the sounds of conflict added."[26]

By this time Lee had notified Ewell that, "in case we found the enemy's force very large, he did not want a general engagement brought on till the rest of the army came up." However, Lee also encouraged his lieutenants to use aggressive discretion when the circumstances warranted it. Given the circumstances confronting the Second Corps leader, he decided the exposed Federal flank only a short distance away presented an opportunity impossible for him to pass up. "It was too late to avoid an engagement without abandoning the position already taken up," concluded Ewell, "and I determined to push the attack vigorously."[27]

Even before Rodes' infantry brigades were in position, two of Lt. Col. Carter's artillery batteries moved into place on the southern slope of Oak Hill and opened fire on the Federal troops engaged with Hill's Corps. The platform offered the Confederate gunners a clear field of fire against the enemy spread out in the rolling distance. "The batteries of Captain Carter and Captain Fry were ordered to a high point in front of Rodes' lines . . . to enfilade the enemy's lines and batteries, which stretched along the small crest to the railroad cut," was how the battalion commander explained the situation in his report.

---

26 James M. Thompson, *Reminiscences of Autauga Rifles* (Autauga, AL: n.p., 1879), 7.

27 OR 27, pt. 2, 444.

The fire from the four three-inch rifles of Capt. William Carter's King William Artillery and the two Napoleons and two 10-pounder Parrotts of Capt. Charley Fry's Orange Artillery extracted a terrible toll on the Federals along the ridge. "The batteries fired with very decided effect, compelling the infantry to take shelter in the railroad cut, and causing them to change front on their right," Lieutenant Colonel Carter observed in his report. The return fire, however, killed four men in Carter's battery and wounded seven.

While the artillery duel was progressing, Rodes learned of a new threat and ordered the Morris Artillery commanded by Capt. Richard Page, and the Jeff Davis Artillery commanded by Capt. William Reese, to move to the east side of the hill and shell Federals marching north out of Gettysburg. "The artillery of the enemy by this time had taken position in the valley north of Gettysburg, and delivered a very destructive oblique fire on Page's battery," Lieutenant Colonel Carter reported. He insisted, however, that the enemy fire "was borne with unflinching courage by the gallant captain and his officers and men until ordered to retire to another position."[28]

The return fire from Capt. Hubert Dilger's Company I, 1st Ohio Light Artillery, proved especially effective. In less than one hour, Page's battery suffered two men killed, two mortally wounded, 26 wounded, and 17 horses killed and disabled. From his position near a fence about 150 yards behind the battery, Private Pickens of O'Neal's Brigade observed that "5 or 6 dead horses & 1 or 2 broken caissons or gun carriages were left by our battery when it moved off." Capt. Reese's Southern battery of four three-inch rifles sustained far fewer casualties because it was posted farther north along the edge of the woods on the Cobean farm.[29]

The severity of the damage inflicted upon his batteries caught battalion commander Carter by surprise. He was especially upset when he discovered that, without his knowledge, Page's four Napoleons had been unlimbered in a vulnerable position "on a declining slope facing Gettysburg." The faulty deployment exposed the artillerists to a nearly incessant enemy fire. Carter went on to note that the ground in that area was shaped "like seats in an amphitheatre, one tier above another." Because of its poor location, the battery served as the target for "every shell & was almost torn to pieces."

28 *Ibid.*, 602-603; Busey and Martin, *Regimental Strengths*, 186.

29 OR 27, pt. 2, 603; Pickens Diary, Entry for July 1, 1863, in Hubbs, *Voices From Company D*, 182.

Most annoying of all was that Carter had no idea who was to blame for selecting such an unsatisfactory location. When he learned of Page's deadly predicament, Carter turned "mad as a hornet" and confronted the division commander for an answer. "What fool put that battery yonder?" demanded Carter. According to the artillerist, Rodes responded with "an awkward pause" before quietly ordering Carter to move the guns back toward the woods. Within minutes, the battery was safely in place in a more protected area. Only later did Carter learn that Rodes had personally ordered the battery into its initial exposed position.[30]

Despite the cover provided by the trees, the infantry around the hill also attracted repeated volleys from the Federal artillery. O'Neal's Alabama brigade, in particular, was shelled heavily and endured a number of casualties. "The enemy being in heavy force between the division and the town, I was ordered to form to the right of the road and immediately in rear of our batteries, there engaging the enemy," reported O'Neal. "A severe engagement between a portion of Lt. Col. Thomas H. Carter's artillery and the enemy's here took place, which lasted for more than an hour."[31]

At the same time, the troops on the western side of Oak Hill came under fire from the enemy's guns posted near the Chambersburg Pike. Although the volleys were less intense than those from the other side of the hill, the shelling produced some anxious moments for the men in both Iverson's and Daniel's brigades. Lieutenant Oliver reported that the position of the 20th North Carolina of Iverson's Brigade was "just far enough back to get the full benefit of the shells from the Yankee battery." Fortunately for the Tar Heels, the bombardment was noisier than it was injurious. Only one man in the regiment was wounded during the incoming artillery fire from the enemy batteries to the south.[32]

Lieutenant Colonel Wharton J. Green of Daniel's staff recalled that his brigade suffered heavily from the same enemy guns. "The brigade was drawn up in line at a no remote distance from those of the Federals, who at once began to shell us," he said. "The order was given for the command to lie down, and here exploded perhaps the most destructive single shell fired during the war.

---

30 Thomas H. Carter to Daniel Harvey Hill, July 1, 1885, Lee Family Papers.

31 *OR* 27, pt. 2, 592.

32 Oliver, "Recollections," 2.

While General Daniel and I were holding our horses some six or eight paces in front of the line, it fell just to our rear." His best estimate "was that it killed and disabled eleven of my old command."³³

O'Neal's Brigade suffered the most because it was located close to the Confederate guns exchanging fire with the Federal batteries on the east side of Oak Hill. "Captain James T. Davis of Company D was killed near me," Lt. Robert E. Park from the 12th Alabama recorded in his journal. "Another shell exploded in my company and wounded Corporal J. H. Eason and Private Lucius Williams, while we halted in a hilly woods." According to Lt. Thomas S. Taylor of the 6th Alabama, the enemy "soon began to throw shell into our ranks, killing some & wounding many."³⁴

The situation proved especially precarious for the men of the 3rd Alabama, who had moved into place directly behind Page's guns. "Across some beautiful wheat fields on the next range of hills could be seen the enemies batteries stationed at intervals amusing themselves throwing out shells feeling for our position," one veteran recalled. The Federal artillery, he continued, made "it extremely unpleasant for us." Another soldier from that regiment also reported that "it was not a very pleasant place lying behind those guns, at which the Yankees were hurling shell upon shell."³⁵

The enemy fire became "so annoying" that Rodes decided to pull O'Neal's men back under cover of the woods on the southern part of the hill. His orders called for the brigade "to fall back abreast with Iverson, so as to obtain some little shelter for the troops." As the troops maneuvered into position, overcrowding at the foot of the hill forced the 3rd Alabama on the right of the brigade to shift to the rear of the other four regiments on a line parallel with Daniel's Brigade. That small tactical difference separated the regiment from the rest of O'Neal's Brigade for the remainder of the day.

As the artillery exchange continued, Rodes watched with some unease as larger numbers of enemy troops on the east side of Oak Hill spilled out of Gettysburg and moved in his direction. To the south, some of the Federals opposing A. P. Hill's Corps had moved into the woods north of the

---

33 Green, *Recollections and Reflections*, 175.

34 Robert E. Park Diary, Entry for July 1, 1863, in Robert E. Park, "War Diary of Robert Emory Park," *SHSP*, 26 (1898), 13; Taylor to Wife, July 17, 1863, Taylor Papers.

35 "War Memories by an Old Hornet," 99-100; "Letter from the 3rd Ala., from a member of the Gulf City Guards," July 9, 1863, *Mobile Daily Advertiser and Register*, July 24, 1863.

Chambersburg Pike directly opposite his position. Others were later discovered emerging from the woods into the open field south of Oak Hill. By early afternoon, the Federal threat had grown to the point that Rodes needed to take some decisive action.

After conferring with Ewell, Rodes decided to launch an attack. The brigades of O'Neal, Iverson, and Daniel would advance south off the high ground. Doles' Brigade, meanwhile, would contain the threat taking form north of town until Jubal Early's Division, marching in from Heidlersburg along the Harrisburg Road, arrived on the scene. Ramseur's Brigade, posted near the rear of the hill, would serve as the division's reserve, available to be called up to support any of the other brigades during the advance.[36]

About two o'clock, Rodes ordered Iverson forward from the woods for an attack against a line of Federals posted in a nearby farm field that appeared to be threatening the two batteries posted on the southern slope of Oak Hill. "When we reached the edge of the woods, where our guns were stationed, in front of us lay a large field, perhaps a half mile or more in width," recalled Lt. Oliver. "Through this ran a road." From his vantage point, the officer spotted "on the farther side the dark blue line of the enemy was advancing toward us."[37]

Iverson's troops assembled in the open area at the foot of the hill, with the 5th North Carolina taking up a position on the left side of the line of battle. With all three field officers absent due to wounds suffered at Chancellorsville, command of the regiment fell to Capt. Speight B. West, one of the few remaining officers who had supported Lt. Col. Peter Sinclair during the recent power struggle for regimental command. The 20th North Carolina, led by two of Iverson's bitterest enemies, Lt. Col. Nelson Slough and Maj. John Brooks, deployed on on the left of the 5th regiment.

Colonel Daniel Christie, who had lobbied behind the scenes for Iverson's removal, maneuvered his 23rd North Carolina into place next to the 20th, taking up a position on the right center of the brigade line. On the far right of the line was the 12th North Carolina under Lt. Col. William Davis and Maj. Robert Alston. Because of the recent bitter dispute over Iverson's efforts to have Capt. Henry Eaton Coleman appointed to lieutenant colonel, Davis and Alston were barely on speaking terms with their brigade commander.

---

36 *OR* 27, pt. 2, 553.

37 Oliver, "Recollections," 2. For details on the timing of Rodes' attack, see G. Campbell Brown to Henry Jackson Hunt, May 6, 1885, in Jones, *Campbell Brown's Civil War*, 324-325, 328.

Postwar view looking northwest along the Mummasburg Road with the Forney farm buildings in the distance on left. Iverson's men formed for the advance against Baxter's position in the area just west of these buildings. *National Archives*

All told, Iverson's Brigade numbered approximately 96 officers and 1,220 men. The plan called for four officers and about 120 men from the sharpshooter detachment to take up a position near the Moses McLean farmhouse on the east side of Oak Hill, acting as a separate unit guarding Iverson's left flank. Because the line of enemy troops remained clearly visible in the middle of the field, no skirmishers were assigned to screen the front of the brigade.

When the regiments were finally aligned, the brigade's position stretched across the Mummasburg Road at the edge of the 150-acre John S. Forney farm, northwest of Gettysburg on Oak Ridge. "Very close to the road on the south side stands the Forney farm house," Capt. Vines Turner, who served as assistant quartermaster for the 23rd North Carolina, recalled. "This house stands in the northwest corner of the Forney field, which extends about half a mile from the house along the Mummersburg road, and is about a quarter of a mile broad." As Turner described it, "a body of woods extended from the southeastern corner of the field for about two hundred yards along its southern side."[38]

A low stone wall ran along the crest of the ridge bordering the far end of the main Forney farm field. The stone wall extended north from the woods almost all the way to the Mummasburg Road. Forney described it as "a tumble-down stone wall or fence." The area in front of the wall, he continued, was "an open meadow covered with a rank crop of timothy," a type of hay grass grown statewide as forage for horses and other farm animals.[39]

While Iverson's regiments were marching into position, O'Neal's Alabama brigade took position just north of the Mummasburg Road on Iverson's left. O'Neal's battle line extended from the area of the Moses McLean farm on the left to the top of the ridge on the right. The only exception was the 3rd

Postwar view looking northwest along the Mummasburg Road. Note the McLean farm buildings and Oak Hill. Edward O'Neal's initial July 1 attack was delivered toward this road between the McLean barn and the top of the ridge.

National Archives

38 Turner and Wall, "Twenty-Third Regiment," in Clark, *NC Regiments*, 2:235.

39 Bates, *History of Cumberland and Adams Counties*, 355; Statement of John S. Forney, July 1, 1884, in Isaac Hall, *History of the Ninety-Seventh Regiment New York Volunteers: The Conkling Rifles* (Baltimore: Butternut and Blue, 1991), 139.

Alabama, which remained in place directly alongside Daniel's Brigade on nearby Oak Hill. Major Blackford's sharpshooters formed a line at the bottom of the ridge to protect the wide gap between O'Neal's position and Doles' right flank. Because their position was along the eastern side of the hill, the bulk of the Alabama troops were invisible to Iverson's men aligned on the far end of the Forney farm.[40]

Rodes' plan called for O'Neal to attack enemy troops that had moved into place along the south side of the Mummasburg Road. The division leader was so concerned about O'Neal's tactical abilities that he delivered the orders to him personally rather than through a staff officer. "Finding that the enemy was rash enough to come out from the woods to attack me, I determined to meet him when he got to the foot of the hill I occupied," Rodes explained in his official report. "And, as he did so, I caused Iverson's Brigade to advance, and at the same moment gave in person to O'Neal the order to attack, indicating to him precisely the point to which he was to direct the left of the four regiments then under his orders."[41]

Given the lingering doubts about O'Neal's competence, Rodes' selection of him for such an important role is curious. Even Edward A. O'Neal Jr., who served as a volunteer aide on Rodes' staff, was convinced that his father had already lost his chance for a promotion because of Rodes' preference for another officer. "I expect to go home soon," the younger O'Neal wrote in disgust to one of his friends only a few days earlier. "Col John T. Morgan of Ala. has been appointed over this Brigade and of course Pa will resign."[42]

The Federals who had taken up a position along nearby Oak Ridge consisted of six regiments under Brig. Gen. Henry Baxter. His brigade formed part of Brig. Gen. John Robinson's Second Division of Reynolds' I Corps. The troops had been rushed into action just past noon from the area around the Lutheran Seminary. "Arriving near the town of Gettysburg we learned that the 1st and 3rd Divisions were already engaged and that the whole rebel army was advancing," recalled Maj. Benjamin F. Look of the 12th Massachusetts. "After a few minutes rest, awaiting orders, the 2nd Brigade advanced through the suburbs and crossing the field took possession of the right of the line."

---

40 *OR* 27, pt. 2, 552-553.

41 *Ibid.*, 553.

42 Edward A. O'Neal Jr. to George Peek, June 28, 1863, Peek Family Papers, SHC.

After crossing the Chambersburg Pike, the 11th Pennsylvania and the 97th New York moved into position along the edge of the woods directly north of the unfinished railroad bed, where one of Heth's brigades under Joseph Davis had been mauled badly in the early morning fighting. From there, the 97th New York pushed two companies of skirmishers into the open field to their front. The remaining four regiments of Baxter's brigade—the 88th and 90th Pennsylvania, 83rd New York, and 12th Massachusetts—continued marching north and formed a line along the south side of the Mummasburg Road opposite the McLean farmhouse at the foot of Oak Hill.

The only resistance encountered during this portion of Baxter's advance came from a line of Confederate skirmishers operating in the vicinity of Mummasburg Road. Major Look observed that the enemy's position behind a stone wall along the road provided Baxter's men with "an opportunity to annoy us considerable." Baxter responded to the skirmish threat by deploying some of his men to push them back. The Southerners, recalled Maj. Look, were "handsomely dislodged" by a company from the 12th Massachusetts, which "moved forward at double-quick, and drove them at the point of the bayonet."[43]

Once the area was cleared of Confederate troops, the 11th Pennsylvania and 97th New York shifted to the right from their positions along the edge of the railroad woods near the Chambersburg Pike. A short time later, they took up a new position on the crest of Oak Ridge behind the long stone wall, facing west into the Forney farm field. A few scattered oak trees formed a small grove just to their rear on the eastern slope of Oak Ridge. The cluster of trees extended about 80 yards south from the Mummasburg Road. The wooded area had little underbrush and covered only the non-arable land on the steepest part of the ridge.[44]

Within minutes of their arrival, the Federals posted along the south side of the Mummasburg Road watched as O'Neal's Alabama troops stepped off to attack them from the area west of the McLean farmhouse. Lieutenant George W. Grant of the 88th Pennsylvania noted that Baxter's regiments deployed "just in the nick of time" to meet the Alabama brigade, which was advancing to the

---

43 Benjamin F. Look to John B. Bachelder, Feb. 17, 1884, in Ladd, *Bachelder Papers*, 2:1021.

44 Pfanz, *Gettysburg: The First Day*, 166. For a detailed overview of their deployment from the Federal perspective, see Gary G. Lash, "Brigadier General Henry Baxter's Brigade at Gettysburg, July 1," *Gettysburg Magazine*, 10 (January 1994), 6-27.

We are Brought in Hearing of Artillery 219

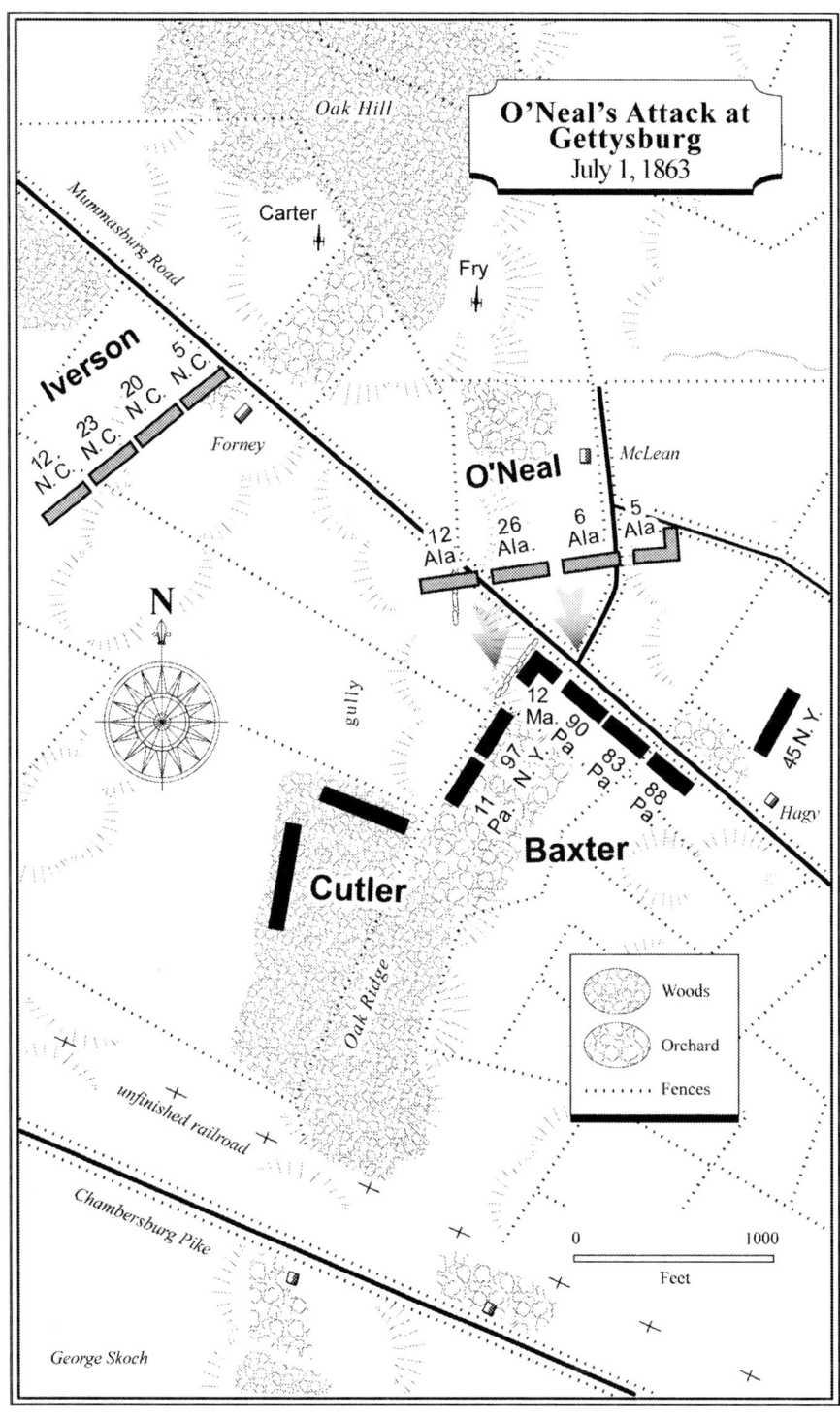

southwest toward their position on the far right of the Federal I Corps. Private John D. Vautier from the same regiment reported that the Southern troops "were coming right along, supported by O'Neal's Alabama brigade in line of battle, cocked and primed for a fight."[45]

O'Neal's attack was plagued with problems before it started. Instead of moving the 3rd Alabama under Col. Cullen A. Battle forward into the crowded area on the southern part of Oak Hill where the rest of O'Neal's regiments were formed, Rodes ordered the regiment to go into action on the right with Daniel's Brigade. According to Battle, "just before the advance was ordered General Rodes said to me, 'keep well up on Daniel's left.'" At the last minute, Rodes also decided to hold the 5th Alabama on the left of O'Neal's Brigade in reserve under his personal command to defend the yawning gap between O'Neal's left and Doles' right.[46]

Because of geographic features and questionable command decisions, Colonel O'Neal had only three regiments—about 880 officers and enlisted men—with which to launch his assault. The 12th Alabama and 26th Alabama, O'Neal's right and center regiments respectively, attacked across the Mummasburg Road on the upper part of Oak Ridge. The 6th Alabama moved forward on the left in the area just west of the McLean farmhouse along the lower slope of the ridge. Although the main thrust was aimed at Baxter's Federals along the road, O'Neal's diminished force also faced a major threat from the leading elements of Maj. Gen. Oliver Howard's Federal XI Corps, which had moved into the area between the Mummasburg and Carlisle roads on Baxter's right flank.[47]

The troops threatening O'Neal's exposed left flank consisted of three regiments from Brig. Gen. Alexander Schimmelfennig's brigade, temporarily under the command of Col. George Von Amsberg. The brigade was part of

---

45 George W. Grant, "The First Army Corps on the First Day at Gettysburg," included in Ken Brady and Florence Freeland, eds., *The Gettysburg Papers* (Dayton, OH: Morningside House, 1988), 255; John D. Vautier, *History of the Eighty-Eighth Pennsylvania*, 105.

46 OR 27, pt. 2, 553; Brandon H. Beck, ed., *Third Alabama!: The Civil War Memoirs of Brigadier General Cullen Andrews Battle, CSA* (Tuscaloosa: University of Alabama Press, 2000), 82. O'Neal implies in his battle report that he was not informed beforehand as to the reason why his brigade was parceled apart right before the attack began. "Why my brigade was thus deprived of two regiments, I have never been informed." *OR*, pt. 2, 592.

47 OR 27, pt. 2, 553; Busey and Martin, *Regimental Strengths*, 166. About three officers and 90 additional enlisted men from those three regiments were on detached service with Blackford's sharpshooter battalion.

Brig. Gen. Carl Schurz's division. The 45th New York on the left of the line deployed four companies as skirmishers under Capt. Francis Irsch. The other six companies from the regiment followed closely behind along the Mummasburg Road. The line of battle that stretched across the Hagy farm on their right also included the 61st Ohio and 74th Pennsylvania. Directly in the rear were Company I, 1st Ohio Light Artillery under Capt. Dilger, and the 13th New York Independent Battery under Lt. William Wheeler.[48]

By the time O'Neal's men stepped off to the assault, the XI Corps troops were visible moving across the open field east of Oak Hill. Before shifting to the right, one veteran from the 3rd Alabama recalled seeing "the waving Flags plainly marking the battle lines of the infantry about half mile distant." The scene proved just as impressive for another soldier from the 12th Alabama. "It was a grand sight to see the line advancing, with the Stars and Stripes and State banners floating over the green fields," he remarked in a letter to his mother. "Our General told us, 'Boys, there is the 11th Corps, if you want them they are yours' and immediately gave the command, 'forward.'"[49]

Enthusiasm notwithstanding, O'Neal's attack bogged down quickly when withering volleys of small arms fire from the Federal troops stationed along the Mummasburg Road poured into the advancing lines. The 88th Pennsylvania's Private Vautier reported that "Baxter quickly dressed his line and received the Confederate fire as their line of battle covered by a cloud of busy skirmishers, came driving through the woods to the right of the Mummasburg Road." The entire line commenced firing once the Alabama troops stepped into what Vautier labeled "easy range." The private continued: "with the sharp crack of muskets a fiery cloud of smoke rolled down the front of the brigade, and the Minie balls zipped and buzzed with a merry chorus toward the Southern line."[50]

Only after it became apparent that the three regiments under O'Neal's direct command were "making no impression upon the enemy" did Rodes order the withheld 5th Alabama, about 270 officers and men, to their support. The men of the 5th moved forward on the far left of the brigade line at the bottom of the ridge but were too late to alter the result of the initial attack. Soon

---

48 *OR* 27, pt. 1, 734.

49 "War Memories by an Old Hornet," 100; "Extract of a letter from a member of the 'Southern Foresters,' 12th Alabama Regiment, to his mother," July 8, 1863, *Mobile Evening News*, July 24, 1863.

50 John Vautier, "At Gettysburg," *Philadelphia Weekly Press*, Nov. 19, 1886; *OR* 27, pt. 1, 310.

after it entered the fight, the 5th Alabama was also stopped and forced back when Schimmelfennig's infantry and the artillery of Dilger's and Wheeler's batteries ripped through its left flank. Like their comrades, the men of the 5th Alabama were soon scrambling for whatever cover they could find.[51]

Among the Alabama troops caught in the deadly crossfire were soldiers from Private Pickens' company. Just before reaching a fence short of the Mummasburg Road, wrote Pickens in his diary, he and some of his comrades took shelter in the nearby McLean barn where they encountered "some N.C. sharp-shooters . . . who had shot away all their cartridge." After making it to the safety of the barn, the Alabamians "kept up pretty brisk firing at the Yankees, but it seemed as if we could do very little execution as they were so far off & behind a fence in the woods, though they made the bullets whistle over us."[52]

The most destructive Federal fire came from the 45th New York, which had moved into position just east of the Moses McLean farm. "The left wing of our regiment at once gave fire at very short distance (50 or 100 yards) with such terrible effect that, in result with the combination of the fire from the extreme right of the First Corps, the whole of the enemy's line halted, gradually disappeared on the same spot where they stood," Lt. Col. Adolphus Dobke from that regiment declared in his official report. Dobke noted that "the remainder, finding they could not retrace their steps, surrendered, partly to the First Corps, and a great number to the Forty-fifth Regiment."[53]

The four companies of skirmishers under Capt. Irsch pursued O'Neal's men as far as the McLean barn. Within a short time, they gathered up about 80 Confederate prisoners. The two Federal artillery batteries, meanwhile, kept up a steady fire directly into the ranks of O'Neal's retreating troops. "At about the same time the First Corps, which was on our left, succeeded in driving the enemy along the slope of the hill, and we scared them well as they ran," wrote Lt. Wheeler of the 13th Independent New York Battery.

Under covering fire from Wheeler's battery, Capt. Dilger limbered his artillery pieces and moved them forward into a wheatfield, where he unlimbered them and opened fire. From there, he had a clear field of fire toward

---

51 *OR* 27, pt. 2, 553; Busey and Martin, *Regimental Strengths*, 166. For the position of O'Neal's regiments see Paul Clark Cooksey, "They Died as if on Dress Parade: The Annihilation of Iverson's Brigade and the Battle of Oak Ridge," *Gettysburg Magazine*, 20 (January 1999), 99-100.

52 Pickens Diary, Entry for July 1, 1863, in Hubbs, *Voices From Company D*, 182.

53 *OR* 27, pt. 1, 734.

the Confederates swarming around the eastern slope of Oak Hill. "At this moment everything looked auspicious, and Captain Dilger told me that he would move his Battery, under cover of mine, about five hundred yards further forward, in order to give his guns better play, and then that I should follow him and support him," Wheeler reported, adding that "as soon as he commenced firing, I limbered up and followed, again taking position on his right."

By this time, Carter's Virginia battery had shifted to the eastern side of Oak Hill to support Page's and Reese's embattled batteries in repulsing the Federal threat against that flank. According to Lt. Wheeler, once Dilger moved forward, the Confederate batteries opened "a dreadful fire" on him. "I had the chief benefit of this as I moved up after him. All the shots fired too high for him fell into my Battery," Wheeler later reported. "[O]ne struck a driver of a gun and swept him and his two horses away." Despite the heavy return fire from Lieutenant Colonel Carter's three batteries, the Federal skirmishers and the two batteries managed to hold their positions just east of the McLean farm.[54]

Meanwhile, soldiers from the 157th New York in Schimmelfennig's brigade, who had been held in reserve, also moved forward in line of battle toward the McLean barn. Their advance overwhelmed skirmishers hidden in the tall grass along their front. After sending a number of prisoners to the rear, the New York troops pushed on to within a short distance of the barn. From there, they poured a volley of gunfire into the main body of the 5th Alabama. Their attack forced the Alabama troops to retire in disarray toward the rear.[55]

As the bulk of the 5th Alabama fell back in confusion, the company of Alabama infantry fighting around the McLean barn moved to rejoin the main body of the regiment. "After the Brig. passed on we ran out of the barn & through an open field where the bullets were flying thick & went down on the left to a lane where the Regt. was," a private recalled. "I never saw troops so scattered & in such confusion." According to the Southerner, they "were under a heavy fire from the front & a cross fire from the left & pretty soon had to fall back to a fence where the Brig. was rallied by Col. O'Neal & Gen. Rodes."[56]

---

54 William Wheeler to Dear Grandmother and Aunt, July 26, 1863, in *In Memoriam: Letters of William Wheeler of the Class of 1855, Yale College* (Cambridge, MA: n.p., 1875), 409-411; OR 27, pt. 1, 752-753.

55 R. L. Murray, "The 157th New York Volunteers at Gettysburg," *Gettysburg Magazine*, 40 (January 2009), 34.

56 Pickens Diary, Entry for July 1, 1863, in Hubbs, *Voices From Company D*, 182.

The situation farther west along O'Neal's front was no better and was in some ways even worse. Colonel Samuel B. Pickens' 12th Alabama advanced on the brigade's right flank and "suffered severely in this attack." As Pickens admitted, "We attacked them in a strong position." The intense fire poured against his front and left flank, devastating the Alabama troops. "It was impossible for us to hold the position we had gained any longer without being cut to pieces or compelled to surrender, the enemy having advantage of us in numbers and position," Pickens reported. His regiment broke and streamed rearward. "I rallied my regiment about 300 yards in the rear and formed a new line," he added. The colonel estimated that the bloody and "desperate fight" did not last long and may have been as short as "fifteen minutes."[57]

Although the fighting was relatively brief, all four regiments that participated in the attack sustained substantial losses before pulling back. "My company had all of its officers wounded and about half its men," reported Lt. Park of the 12th Alabama. "Every officer, except Captain Thomas, on the right wing of the regiment, was either killed or wounded." Lieutenant Taylor of the 6th Alabama told his wife that "Col. Lightfoot & Maj. Culver & several of our Company Officers" were wounded in the attack. The heaviest losses by far were suffered by the 5th Alabama. Private Jeremiah M. Tate noted in a letter to his sister that they lost more casualties than the rest of the brigade put together.[58]

According to O'Neal, the Federals opposing his attack were "strongly posted and in heavy force, and, after a desperate and bloody fight of about half an hour, we were compelled to fall back." Rodes later placed most of the blame for this bungled attack directly on O'Neal's shoulders. The Alabama brigade, he reported bluntly and perhaps with a bit of embarrassment since it was his former command, "moved with alacrity (but not in accordance with my orders as to direction) and in confusion into the action." The division leader also expressed surprise that "Colonel O'Neal, instead of personally superintending the movements of his brigade, had chosen to remain with his reserve regiment." The final result, continued Rodes, was that the entire brigade, with the exception of the Third Alabama, was "repulsed quickly, and with loss."[59]

---

57 OR 27, pt. 2, 601.

58 Park Diary, Entry for July 1, 1863, in Park, "War Diary," 13; Taylor to Wife, July 17, 1863, Taylor Papers; OR 27, pt. 2, 596; Jeremiah M. Tate to Dear Sister, Aug. 6, 1863, Gilder-Lehrman Collection, New York Historical Society, New York, New York.

59 OR 27, pt. 2, 553, 592, 595, 601.

Chapter Ten

The Yankees Crossed Fired on Us a Good While

The bloody repulse of Edward O'Neal's disjointed attack signified the prelude of the heavy and difficult fighting Rodes' Division would perform that warm July afternoon.

If Alfred Iverson's report is any indication, Rodes' offensive plan in general—and for Iverson's command in particular—was not well spelled out or understood. Before any attack began, Iverson received "instructions from General Rodes to advance gradually to the support of a battery he intended placing" on the southern slope of Oak Hill. These orders left him confused and frustrated. "[Not] understanding the exact time at which the advance was to take place, I dispatched a staff officer to him, to learn at what time I was to move forward, and received instructions not to move until my skirmishers became hotly engaged," wrote Iverson in his report.

A short time later, Iverson obtained some clarification from Rodes: "I received an order from him to advance to meet the enemy, who were approaching to take the battery." The division commander instructed Iverson to coordinate his actions with O'Neal on his left and to call on Junius Daniel for any needed support. Iverson "immediately dispatched a staff officer to inform Brigadier-General Daniel that I was about to advance, and one to notify my regiments, and to observe when the brigade on my left [O'Neal] commenced to move."[1]

In a rare display of tactical ineptness, Rodes had completely misread the situation confronting him. The Federal troops that he believed were threatening his batteries turned out to be nothing more than a heavy skirmish line. Iverson, however, set up for the attack without deploying any additional skirmishers along his own front line because the enemy troops Rodes ordered him to assault were visible in the field—and nothing appeared to be between them and the Tar Heel line of battle. The sharpshooter detachment remained just west of the McLean farmhouse, assigned to protect the left flank of the brigade. The domino effect of these decisions would soon have terrible ramifications far beyond what anyone could have imagined.[2]

By the time Iverson was in position, Federal skirmishers had halted well short of the Confederate lines and showed no inclination to attack the Oak Hill batteries. "The enemy did not advance as he was expected to do, but in a few minutes an order was received to follow up any movement of the Brigade on our left," Capt. Benjamin Robinson of the 5th North Carolina wrote Governor Zeb Vance. "Just then the Brigade of Col. O'Neal commenced to march forward." Instead of waiting for clarification of the situation, Iverson responded to his orders by launching his regiments across the field.[3]

While the Confederates were preparing to attack, Henry Baxter realigned his men to meet the impending threat against his left flank. After repulsing O'Neal's Brigade, the Federal brigade commander shifted the 88th Pennsylvania and the 83rd New York from their positions along the Mummasburg Road into place behind the stone wall running along the top of the ridge on the southeast side of the Forney farm field. Baxter noted that his troops "changed front to the left and moved forward to the crest of the hill" just as Iverson's men appeared along their front. Lieutenant George Grant from the 88th Pennsylvania recalled that this movement placed them in "an admirable position on the crest of the ridge behind a low stone wall."[4]

---

1   OR 27, pt. 2, 553, 579;

2   John F. Coghill to Dear Sister, July 31, 1863, John Fuller Coghill Letters.

3   Robinson to Vance, July 9, 1863, *Raleigh Daily Progress*, July 24, 1863.

4   OR 27, pt. 2, 307; Grant, "The First Army Corps," in Brady and Freeland, *Gettysburg Papers*, 1:261.

The Yankees Crossed Fired on Us a Good While

Postwar view looking northwest along the Mummasburg Road, with Baxter's position along the top of Oak Ridge in the distance on the left. *Adams County Historical Society*

The men of the 12th Massachusetts wheeled into place alongside the two regiments at the top of the ridge. The 90th Pennsylvania followed closely behind and set up on the far right of the line. To make room for the other four regiments, the troops from the 97th New York and 11th Pennsylvania on the opposite end of the line shifted to their left along the ridge. Captain Isaac Hall of the 97th New York reported that the "regiments in rear of the wall and a little back from it were hid even while standing from the observation of any force that might approach over the narrow meadow in their front."[5]

Henry Baxter's infantry were maneuvering into place while Iverson's Tar Heels pressed steadily forward without any hint of the danger looming ahead of them. According to Capt. Vines Turner of the 23rd North Carolina, the brigade

---

5 Isaac Hall, "Iverson's Brigade and the Part the 97th New York Played in Its Capture," *National Tribune*, June 26, 1884.

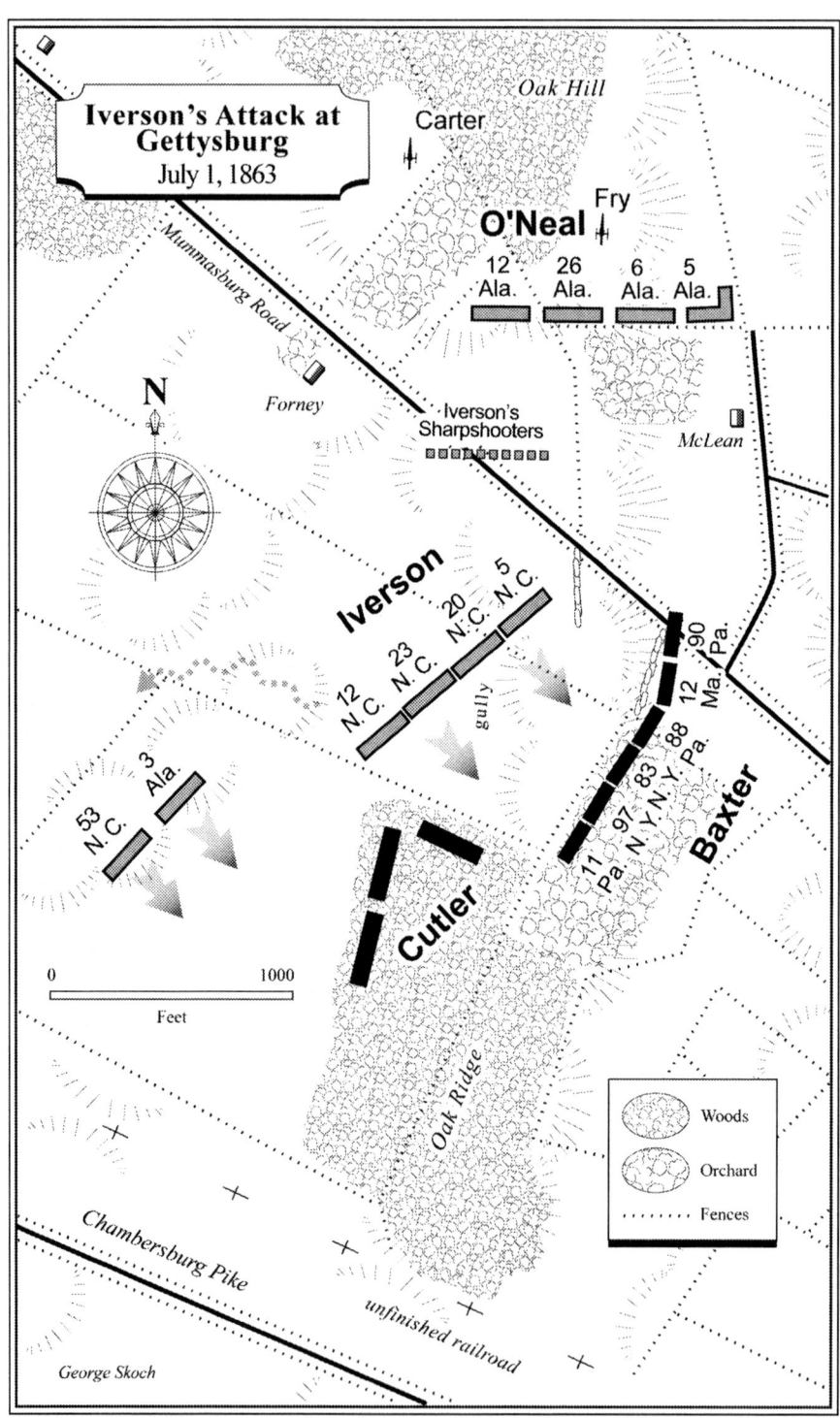

set off from the area of the Forney farmhouse "through the open grass field in gallant style, as evenly as if on parade." The 12th North Carolina's Sgt. Walter Montgomery likewise noted how coolly Iverson's soldiers advanced. The men, he recalled, "bounded forward not knowing certainly where the enemy was, for his whole line, with every flag, was concealed behind the rock wall on their right and center and a drop in the ground on their left."[6]

Not even the loss of contact with O'Neal's Alabamians on their left flank triggered any immediate concerns for Iverson's Tar Heels. Captain Robinson, who seems not to have had a firm understanding of what had taken place, reported to Governor Vance that "for some reason, O'Neal's Brigade halted, but the Brigade of Iverson had advanced with such rapidity as to have no knowledge whatever of O'Neal's movements after he commenced to advance, and consequently attacked the enemy single handed in its front." Iverson also observed the gap on his left, but mistakenly "presumed that it would soon be filled by the advancing Alabama brigade, under Colonel O'Neal." In fact, the Alabamians were already being torn apart and repulsed out of Iverson's line of sight.[7]

A similar gap opened on Iverson's right flank as his men veered left across the field. "Immediately after commencing his advance, when he had reached the open field a short distance in his front, he changed his line of direction considerably to the left, thus unmasking such of my regiments as were in his rear," Daniel explained in his report. Rodes also commented on this situation, noting that "General Daniel's gallant brigade, by a slight change in the direction of Iverson's attack, had been left too far to his right to assist him directly, and had already become engaged."[8]

The direction of Iverson's attack was further influenced by the presence of a high post-and-plank fence running through the middle of the field parallel to the Mummasburg Road. As the Tar Heels discovered to their dismay, the structure interrupted their alignment as they pressed forward during the early minutes of their assault. Unlike the other wooden fences in the field, this one was so strongly built that some of Iverson's men had to climb it because they could not easily push down the rails. Instead, most of the men swung around to

---

6 Turner and Wall, "Twenty-Third Regiment," in Clark, *NC Regiments*, 2:235; Montgomery, "Twelfth Regiment," in *ibid.*, 1:634-635.

7 Robinson to Vance, July 9, 1863, *Raleigh Daily Progress*, July 24, 1863; OR 27, pt. 2, 579.

8 *Ibid.*, 554, 566.

Postwar view looking west from the Oak Ridge tower. The Forney farm buildings are visible in the right distance. Iverson's men formed beyond those buildings and his men advanced across the intervening fields on July 1, 1863. *National Archives*

right side of this barrier as they made they their way across the field. The result was that much of the attacking force was guided by the presence of the fence line and so shuttled directly into the stone wall that ran south from the Mummasburg Road.[9]

Baxter's infantry, meanwhile, continued watching in utter disbelief as the four North Carolina regiments under Iverson tramped straight ahead toward their position behind the stone wall. The approach of the Southern line of battle presented a grand scene that none of them would forget for the rest of their lives. "The field in our front was swarming with Confederates who came sweeping on in a magnificent alignment, guns at right shoulder and colors to the front," Pvt. John Vautier of the 88th Pennsylvania observed. The most surprising thing of all was the now very obvious fact that the Tar Heels had not deployed skirmishers along their front to screen their advance across Forney field.

---

9 Statement of John S. Forney, July 1, 1884, in Hall, *History of the Ninety-Seventh Regiment*, 136-137.

The Federals remained out of view just below the crest of the ridge as Iverson's infantry approached steadily to within point-blank range. According to Vautier, the advancing Confederate infantry "reached and ascended a little gully or depression in the ground and moving on ascended the opposite slope as if on brigade drill." Even then, with long lines of Confederates already well within killing range, Baxter's waiting Federals continued to hold their fire. "Behind the stone wall, the Union soldiers, with rifles cocked and fingers in the triggers, waited and bided their time, feeling confident that they could throw back these regiments coming against them," observed the Pennsylvanian.[10]

Finally, when the Southern battle line stepped within about 80 yards of the stone wall, someone shouted a command to fire. The sudden and wholly unexpected volley of gunfire unleashed by Baxter's men tore a swath of destruction through the ranks of the unsuspecting Tar Heels. Vautier's 88th Pennsylvania, opposite the left side of Iverson's approaching brigade, was among the first to open on the advancing line. "At the command a sheet of flame and smoke burst from the wall with the simultaneous crash of the rifles, flaring full in the face of the advancing troops," recalled the private, "the ground being quickly covered with their killed and wounded as the balls hissed and cut through the exposed line." Vautier and his comrades had never experienced such an easy slaughter of the enemy.[11]

The men of the 97th New York, situated left of the 88th Pennsylvania and separated from that regiment by the 83th New York, joined in with a well executed volley of their own. "Our regiment sprang up, and as this column approached moved forward up to the wall, and was enabled to fire over the crest and attack the line in front and flank as it swung to its left into the front of the regiment," Capt. Isaac Hall remembered. He described the ridge along that part of their line as "so high before it fell off I was obliged to step forward and stretch up my neck when the yell came to see Iverson's Brigade." According to the captain, his New Yorkers were "not discovered by the brigade in consequence of this roll in the land in our front till the 97th stepped forward and fired."[12]

---

10 Vautier, "At Gettysburg," *Philadelphia Weekly Press*, Nov. 19, 1886.

11 Vautier, *History of the Eighty-Eighth Pennsylvania*, 106-107.

12 Isaac Hall to John B. Bachelder, Aug. 15, 1884, in Ladd, *Bachelder Papers*, 2:1062; Hall, *History of the Ninety-Seventh New York*, 137.

Within a handful of seconds, the entire line of Federal troops along the stone wall had unleashed a rippling barrage of gunfire. At that close range, the effect was so devastating that Iverson's men were scythed down in heaps right where they stood. An enlisted man from the 83rd New York insisted that "rarely has such a destructive volley been fired on any field of battle." The field to their front, he recalled, was instantly "strewed" with dead and wounded men. One of Ramseur's men, who had an unobstructed view of the nightmare unfolding beneath him from the top of nearby Oak Hill, acknowledged that "the death rate was terrible."[13]

In addition to the lethal barrage slicing through Iverson's ranks directly from the front, other Federals poured in a deadly fire of their own from two other directions. Brigadier General Lysander Cutler's brigade in the woods on Iverson's right front unleashed a heavy gunfire into the advancing North Carolinians. The 90th Pennsylvania and the 12th Massachusetts of Baxter's brigade, which had moved forward to a position on Iverson's left front, also opened fire. The 90th Pennsylvania was the first of these two regiments to open on the Tar Heel troops. According to Pennsylvanian Maj. Alfred J. Sellers, they "delivered such a deadly volley at very short range that death's mission was with unerring certainty."

The 12th Massachusetts' Cpl. George Kimball recalled that the soldiers from his regiment also stepped forward and "poured a volley" into the advancing troops with devastating effects. "As the Twelfth was the second regiment from the right of the brigade, our fire was left oblique," he explained. "This volley was terribly destructive." Major Benjamin Look also recalled that this "second change of front" enabled the Massachusetts regiment "to deliver a destructive enfilading fire into the advancing lines of the enemy at short range." The result was one of the most devastating few minutes of the entire war, a wide and smothering crossfire that cut down scores of Iverson's men in their tracks.[14]

---

13 George A. Hussey and William Todd, *History of the Ninth Regiment N.Y.S.M.-N.G.S.N.Y (Eighty-Third New York Volunteers)* (New York: J. S. Ogilvie, 1889), 270; Samuel D. Marshbourn, "Reminiscences," 7, Military Collections, NCOAH.

14 John P. Nicholson, ed., *Pennsylvania at Gettysburg: Ceremonies at the Dedication of the Monuments Erected by the Commonwealth of Pennsylvania*, 2 Vols. (Harrisburg, PA: William Stanley Ray, 1904), 1:488; George Kimball, "My Army Life," included in Charles Carleton Coffin, ed., *Stories of Our Soldiers: War Reminiscences*, 2 Vols. (Boston: The Journal Newspaper Co., 1893), 2:110; Look to Bachelder, Feb. 17, 1884, in Ladd, *Bachelder Papers*, 2:1021.

For most of Iverson's troops, the first realization of what they faced arrived only after the last of the Federal skirmishers withdrew from the eastern end of the Forney field. The 20th North Carolina's Lt. Joseph Oliver, advancing in the left center of the battle line, recalled that "the line in our front broke and fled back to the rock wall in their rear, from which they opened a murderous fire of musketry upon our fast thinning ranks." According to Capt. Turner of the 23rd North Carolina, one regiment to the right of Oliver, his men remained unaware of the trap they were walking into until "when we were in point blank range the dense line of the enemy rose from its protected lair and poured into us a withering fire from the front and both flanks."[15]

The effect this sudden destructive fire had on Iverson's men was simply devastating. According to Rodes, the barrage from the Federal troops posted along the stone wall was so destructive that the brigade's "dead lay in a distinctly marked line of battle." The horror of what was unfolding was almost beyond belief for those caught in the line of fire and still alive to understand what was transpiring. An enlisted man from the 23rd North Carolina who was fortunate enough to be standing in the second rank during the advance reported in a letter to his brother that he was "sprayed by the brains of the first rank."[16]

By far, the heaviest losses were sustained by the three left-most regiments—from left to right, the 5th, 20th, and 23rd North Carolina—of the advancing Southern line. In some cases, entire ranks of Tar Heels were almost wiped out *en masse*. "I was wounded by four shots and left on the field to die," recalled Pvt. James Ireland from the 20th North Carolina. "Six of my comrades in reach of my file were so wounded that five died in a few days." The remaining man in the file, he continued, survived the attack even though "six shots struck him." Ireland's wounds included shots to the abdomen, left hip, and back.[17]

Adjutant Fred Phillips from the 30th North Carolina in Ramseur's Brigade had a nearly perfect view from Oak Hill of Iverson's parade-like advance. "This force was met by a deadly fire coming from behind a rock wall which ran perpendicularly to the public road leading into Gettysburg," he recalled. Phillips noted that, "at first, it was thought to be a skirmish line of the enemy, but that it was soon discovered that a body of troops were massed there, and others were

---

15 Turner and Wall, "Twenty-Third Regiment," in Clark, *NC Regiments*, 2:235; Oliver, "Recollections," 2.

16 *OR* 27, pt. 2, 554; quoted in Kross, "That One Error," 50.

17 Ireland, "Memoirs."

seen coming through the field to the assistance of those already posted behind this solid breastwork."[18]

Although it is unclear where Iverson was during the advance and slaughter of his brigade, what is certain is that he was not at the head of his command. Just as he had done at Chancellorsville, Iverson directed the movements of his troops from a point well behind the front lines. As a result, he had only the vaguest idea of what was happening to his men on the distant end of the Forney field. "Learning that the Alabama brigade, on my left, was moving, I advanced at once, and soon came in contact with the enemy, strongly posted in woods and behind a concealed stone wall," was how Iverson described the initial meeting with the Federals his official report. He noted simply that his brigade "advanced to within 100 yards, and a most desperate fight took place."[19]

From his position someplace in the rear, Iverson attempted to secure assistance from Daniel, whose brigade was pushing forward southeast past Iverson's right flank toward Cutler's line of Federals. Daniel's long battle line included the 3rd Alabama from O'Neal's Brigade, which had taken up a position on the left end of Daniel's line. "Brigadier-General Daniel came up to my position, and I asked him for immediate support, as I was attacking a strong position," Iverson reported. "He promised to send me a large regiment, which I informed him would be enough, as the Third Alabama Regiment was then moving down on my right, and I then supposed was sent to my support."

Iverson watched as Daniel's Brigade swept past his position and "engaged the enemy some distance to my right, but the regiment he had promised me . . . did not report to me at all." Iverson had no better luck gaining help from the 3rd Alabama. With no support at hand, he tried to reestablish contact with Daniel. "I again sent Capt. D. P. Halsey, assistant adjutant-general, to ask General Daniel for aid, who informs me that he met his staff officer, and was told that one regiment had been sent, and no more could be spared," wrote Iverson.

By this time, the 53rd North Carolina, which Daniel had assigned to assist Iverson's embattled command, was already some 500 yards beyond Iverson's right flank. "I then found that this regiment had formed on the right of the Third Alabama, which was on my right, and could not be used in time to save my brigade," Iverson continued. Instead of assisting Iverson, the 53rd North

---

18 Fred Phillips to David Schenck, Oct. 27, 1891, Stephen D. Ramseur Papers.

19 *OR* 27, pt. 2, 579.

Carolina continued advancing toward the Federals posted in the woods directly north of the unfinished railroad line. Colonel William A. Owen reported that his 53rd regiment eventually "moved forward through a wheat-field to within 50 yards of some woods in front."[20]

Appended to Daniel's line of battle, the 3rd Alabama under Col. Cullen Battle followed the 53rd North Carolina on its immediate right into the attack against Cutler's brigade in the woods on Oak Ridge. As the remainder of Daniel's regiments pressed forward on their right toward the unfinished railroad bed north of the Chambersburg Pike, the Alabamians found themselves in a difficult situation. One soldier from the regiment noted that their position along the edge of the woods was "now fearfully exposed" to gunfire from two different directions. "The line in the R.R. cut was directly on our flank while those in our front was making it lively for us," he recalled. "Our Col realizing our extreme danger ordered us to fall back."[21]

Once his regiment withdrew, Battle's command was left isolated on the field without orders. "I did not know where to find Rodes or O'Neal, and as my orders were to conform to movement of Daniel I sent Private Raban of Company D to him for instructions," Battle reported. "That gallant officer said in reply to my messengers, 'Tell Colonel Battle I have no orders for him. He must act on his own responsibility.'" After receiving that response, Battle halted his bloodied regiment somewhere to the right of Iverson's position and waited for instructions from his superiors.[22]

The situation confronting the 3rd Alabama frustrated many of its members. "After some time spent in ineffectual efforts to get our regiment engaged in connection with our forces on our right, Col. Battle finally moved us by the left flank to another part of the field," one of the Alabamians wrote in a letter home. From there, the Alabama troops watched helplessly as the battle raged along the southern slope of Oak Hill and down along the front of Oak Ridge. Despite this heavy action, Capt. W. H. May complained the troops from the regiment "could not leave the field and had nothing to fight."[23]

---

20 *Ibid.*, 576, 579.

21 *Ibid.*, 579; "War Memories by an Old Hornet," 101.

22 Beck, *Third Alabama*, 83.

23 "Letter from the 3rd Ala., from a member of the Gulf City Guards," July 9, 1863, *Mobile Daily Advertiser and Register*, July 24, 1863; W. H. May, "Reminiscences of the War Between the States," GA.

While Iverson searched frantically for help in the rear, and the plight of the 3rd Alabama unfolded, the situation for the Tar Heels trapped near the stone wall went from bad to worse. The Federals continued firing at them from behind the wall while the surviving Confederates scrambled to take cover in a slight hollow that cut across the center of the Forney field. "We advanced to a gully about eighty yards in front of the rock wall," Lt. Oliver explained. "Here we halted, for by this time our ranks were so depleted it was impossible to carry the strong position in front." As a result, he added, "down into the gully we fell to carry on the unequal contest."[24]

Even in the hollow, the surviving soldiers remained vulnerable to the intense enemy fire pouring in from three directions. "We were then about eighty yards from the stone fence to the left, and somewhat further from the woods to the right, from both of which, as well as from the more distant corner of the field in our front, poured down upon us a pitiless rifle fire," Capt. Turner recalled. Caught in the crossfire, the men had nowhere to escape. "Unable to advance, unwilling to retreat, the brigade lay down in this hollow or depression in the field and fought as best it could," concluded Turner.[25]

Lieutenant Grant from the 88th Pennsylvania described the place where Iverson's troops took refuge as a "shallow bed of a dry creek about 150 yards distant." He noted that this slight depression "afforded them but poor shelter, as they could not well advance nor retreat, the ground rising gently in either direction." Private Vautier also reported that Iverson's Confederates "were compelled to fall back a couple of hundred yards to a little gully, where they rallied and maintained a sharp fire on the Union Line."[26]

The initial response from Iverson's men after the devastating early volley and retreat to the hollow caught most of the Federal troops posted along the stone wall by surprise. "Though their men were falling like leaves in a storm, they attempted to make a stand," remembered an impressed Vautier. Indeed, somehow the North Carolinians managed to return a credible fire. Private Jacob Menges from the 11th Pennsylvania, who was firing at the enemy from a prone position, recalled that the bullets from the Confederate line came pouring

---

24 Oliver, "Recollections," 2.

25 Turner and Wall, "Twenty-Third Regiment," in Clark, *NC Regiments*, 2:235-236.

26 Grant, "The First Army Corps," in Brady and Freeland, *Gettysburg Papers*, 1:261; Vautier, *History of the Eighty-Eighth Pennsylvania*, 106.

in on them so fast and thick that they actually "cut off the timothy heads above our backs."[27]

The shallow depression offered little real protection to the beleaguered regiments. "I believe every man who stood up was either killed or wounded," Lt. Oliver Williams from the 20th North Carolina declared. Captain Turner reported that the 23rd North Carolina lost "the heaviest of all in killed, as from its position in line the cross enfilading fire seems to have been the hottest just where it lay." Lieutenant Oliver from the 20th North Carolina insisted that "it was impossible to go forward and to retreat meant certain death."[28]

As the situation worsened, the 23rd North Carolina's Col. Daniel Christie decided that the only realistic course of action was to mount a charge out of the hollow. Somehow he communicated his intent to those around him and gathered up a number of men still able to fight. According to one account, he moved "rapidly forward at the head of his regiment waving his sword and cheering his men amidst a tempest of shot and shell and a hurricane of bullets." As he leaped over the embankment, Christie was struck down with severe wounds to both lungs. The remaining men in the attack fell back to the hollow in bloody disarray. Private Vautier, who witnessed the gallant efforts from a more enviable position behind the stone wall, recalled long after the war that the Tar Heels "did attempt to come forward only to be driven back to the ditch."[29]

The Federals maintained steady pressure on the men trapped in the gully along their front. According to Lt. Samuel G. Boone of the 88th Pennsylvania, Baxter's entire brigade continued to pour "some wicked firing into the mass of Confederate soldiers lying down in the field within short musket range." Lieutenant Grant from the same regiment confirmed Boone's recollection, noting that "a steady death-dealing fire was kept up, our men loading in comparative safety, and then resting rifle on shoulders before them, would fire coolly and with unerring aim."[30]

---

27 Vautier, "At Gettysburg," *Philadelphia Weekly Press*, Nov. 19, 1886; Jacob R. Menges, "Corporal's Memoirs, 1861-1865," USAHEC.

28 Turner and Wall, "Twenty-Third Regiment," in Clark, *NC Regiments*, 2:236. Oliver, "Recollections," 2.

29 "The Late D. H. Christie," *Raleigh Daily Progress*, Aug. 3, 1863; Vautier, *History of the Eighty-Eighth Pennsylvania*, 106.

30 Samuel G. Boone, "Personal Experiences," Michael Winey Collection, USAHEC; Grant, "The First Army Corps," in Brady and Freeland, *Gettysburg Papers*, 1:261.

Trapped in a slight depression by unrelenting enemy fire, the handful of surviving soldiers watched helplessly as their friends were killed and wounded around them. Private W. J. O'Daniel from the 23rd North Carolina reported to the mother of a mortally wounded comrade that her son was shot while "he was lying in a hollow in a very muddy place." He added that "all that ware badly wounded and killed was shot in this same hollow." Time seemed to stand still for those trapped in the gully. Lieutenant Oliver estimated that "this unequal contest lasted perhaps an hour or until our ammunition was about exhausted, and nearly all of our men were killed or wounded."[31]

After Christie's attack was beaten back and the firing continued for some time, the troops on the Federal side began to see signs that Iverson's men were ready to give up. Adjutant Charles C. Wehrum from the 12th Massachusetts recalled that "our fire must have taken terrible effect, for soon they laid down and a number of them tied handkerchiefs to their guns in token of surrender." The 88th Pennsylvania's Lt. Grant observed correctly that the steady fire from all along the Federal lines "was more than flesh and blood could endure, and soon hats and handkerchiefs were waved in token of surrender, but our officers hesitated, fearing a trap."[32]

About this time, the lead elements from Brig. Gen. Gabriel R. Paul's Federal brigade in Reynolds' I Corps began arriving on the field to reinforce Baxter's weary troops on Oak Ridge. Paul's brigade, part of Robinson's division, included five veteran regiments rested and ready for action. After some initial confusion, the 13th Massachusetts and the 104th New York from Paul's brigade moved into place facing north along the Mummasburg Road. At the same time, the 16th Maine, 107th Pennsylvania, and 94th New York took up position behind the wall on Baxter's left.[33]

The Federal troops on the front line were by this time running low on ammunition, and men from both Baxter's and Paul's brigades rushed forward

---

31 W. J. O'Daniel to Mrs. Torrence, July 20, 1863, in Monroe, "The Road to Gettysburg," 515; Oliver, "Recollections," 2. For additional accounts of the action along Oak Ridge, see Cooksey, "They Died As If on Dress Parade, 89-112; Krick, "Three Confederate Disasters," 129-137; Kross, "That One Error, 22-24, 48-53; Martin, *Gettysburg July 1*, 224-238; Gerard A. Patterson, "The Death of Iverson's Brigade," *Gettysburg Magazine*, 5 (July 1991), 13-18; and Pfanz, *Gettysburg: The First Day*, 145-178.

32 Charles C. Wehrum to John B. Bachelder, Jan. 21, 1884, in Ladd, *Bachelder Papers*, 2:989; Grant, "The First Army Corps," in Brady and Freeland, *Gettysburg Papers*, 1:262.

33 OR 27, pt. 1, 301.

into the field and began capturing prisoners from the hollow at bayonet point. The exact circumstances surrounding the attack into the Forney field remain clouded in the confusion of battle. A Federal officer recalled that Henry Baxter's voice could clearly be heard above the sounds of battle yelling out the command, "Up boys, and give them steel." Captain Hall remembered hearing one of the officers from his regiment shouting, "Boys of the 97th, let us go for them and capture them."[34]

The 12th Massachusetts' Cpl. Kimball insisted that the move into the field occurred without specific orders. "It was not a charge at all, only a run forward to drive in Iverson's men, who were willing enough to surrender," was how Kimball remembered the event. Adjutant Wehrum from the same regiment reported that he heard "a great deal of hollering, some to cease firing, others to charge bayonets." With nothing resembling a specific command forthcoming, Wehrum concluded that "our advance was brought about by the actions of the enemy and not by any general orders, and no special credit is due anyone in particular." The adjutant argued that "it was a spontaneous movement which everyone that did advance thought was proper."[35]

Regardless of whether the foray westward into the Forney field was triggered by an order or was spontaneously launched, the advance sealed the outcome for the remaining Tar Heels trapped in the hollow. The survivors from the 5th, 20th, and 23rd regiments on the left of Iverson's line were completely pinned down and could do little more than await their fate as the running Federal troops covered the 80 to 100 yards across the field to reach them. Memories of that terrible day were still vivid decades later for the 20th North Carolina's Capt. Lewis T. Hicks, who could hear the approach of the enemy but could not see them. "The smoke was so dense you could not perceive an object ten feet from you," he recalled. "The awful gloom of this moment is beyond the descriptions of pen." In the span of just seconds, Hicks faced a decision about what to do when the Federals finally reached them. "While we felt and heard the

---

34 Harold Adams Small, ed., *The Road to Richmond: The Civil War Memoirs of Major Abner R. Small of the 16th Maine* (Berkeley: University of California Press, 1939), 99-101; Grant, "The First Army Corps," in Brady and Freeland, *Gettysburg Papers*, 1:262; Hall, *History of the Ninety-Seventh New York*, 138.

35 George Kimball, "Iverson's Brigade, The 12th Mass. Did Join in the Charge," *National Tribune*, Oct. 1, 1885; Charles C. Wehrum to John B. Bachelder, Jan. 21, 1884, in Ladd, *Bachelder Papers*, 2:989; Charles Wehrum, "The Adjutant of the 12th Massachusetts Replies to the Captain of the 97th New York," *National Tribune*, Dec. 10, 1885.

tread of the enemy, our minds were in a tumult, whether to lie still or to yield or to die fighting."

In a letter penned to Governor Vance a little more than a week after the Forney field slaughter, Captain Robinson of the 5th North Carolina reported that "in the hottest of the fire the enemy closed in upon our lines, pouring a murderous fire into our men, and in many cases bayoneted them, when some of the wounded cried out for quarter and raised their handkerchiefs as an appeal for mercy." Captain Hicks recalled that "in the absence of white flags the wounded men hoisted their boots and hats on their bayonets to show their desperation."[36]

Within minutes, the situation had gone from desperate to hopeless. According to Lt. Oliver, "the firing from our line had about ceased when the enemy in our front advanced and captured those of us remaining." Captain Hicks barely avoided being stabbed to death, recalling that "while the very tongues of death flashed around I jumped up and found myself confronted with a bayonet of a union soldier pointed at my breast." Like most of the men caught in the gully, the captain was left with no recourse other than to give up or be killed. "I grasped the blade and reversed the handle of my sword in a twinkle and offered to surrender." The fast thinking saved Hicks' life.[37]

Federal soldiers from up and down Baxter's brigade line prodded out the lucky survivors by the score. "We fixed Bayonets and made a charge, at which time a whole Regiment of Rebels surrendered," Pvt. George Cramer of the 11th Pennsylvania boasted in a letter penned soon after the battle. "This scene rather affected me when I seen theym using white Henkerchif & Towels for Flags on theyre Guns for the Signal of Surrender." The 88th Pennsylvania's Lt. Boone observed that Iverson's troops willingly "rose singly and in groups, and came running toward us, holding their hands in token of surrender."[38]

From the sharpshooter detachment operating west of the McLean farm, Pvt. John Coghill of the 23rd North Carolina watched in disbelief as Iverson's command melted away before his eyes. The private and his detached comrades were busy "keeping the Yankes from flanking our line," but were powerless to

---

36 Robinson to Vance, July 9, 1863, *Raleigh Daily Progress*, July 24, 1863; Louis T. Hicks, "Memoirs," *Raleigh State Journal*, April 27, 1917.

37 Oliver, "Recollections," 3; Hicks, "Memoirs," *Raleigh State Journal*, April 27, 1917.

38 George Cramer to Dear Wife, July 8, 1863, 11th Pennsylvania, Union Regiment Files, GNMPC; Boone, "Personal Experiences," Michael Winey Collection.

prevent them from pulling large numbers of stunned and wounded men out of the hollow and shove them stumbling back eastward toward the stone wall and captivity. "Wee fought like tigers; The bravest stand I ever saw," he related to his family. "But the Yankes crossed fired on us a good while and then some of our men surrendered and the Yankes ran up and captured very near all of them."[39]

The sight of white flags waving from the bloody gully shook Iverson to the core. Because he was hundreds of yards from his embattled command, he did not realize what was actually taking place. The upset brigadier embarrassed himself by reporting to Rodes that an entire regiment had gone over to the enemy. "When I saw white handkerchiefs raised, and my line of battle still lying down in position, I characterized the surrender as disgraceful," admitted Iverson in his report. "But when I found afterward that 500 of my men were left lying dead and wounded on a line as straight as a dress parade, I exonerated, with one or two disgraceful individual exceptions, the survivors, and claim for the brigade that they nobly fought and died without a man running to the rear."[40]

By all indications, the men who emerged from the protection of the gully had been completely broken by their nearly hour-long ordeal. According to Wehrum of the 12th Massachusetts, "several hundred of the rebs left their arms on the ground and rushed through our lines and they were directed to run out of range as quick as possible, which they did without much urging." Corporal William H. Miller of the 83rd New York reported that the Tar Heel soldiers were "simply ordered to the rear, and I can tell you they needed no second order, but 'got up and got.'"[41]

The advance to the hollow yielded some 24 officers and more than 350 enlisted men, including many who were slightly wounded. Nearly all of the prisoners came from the left three regiments of Iverson's main battle line.

---

39 Coghill to Sister, July 31, 1863, John Fuller Coghill Letters; Coghill to Pappy, Ma and Mit, July 17, 1863, *ibid.*

40 OR 27, pt. 2, 579. The fact that Iverson felt he had to officially explain his erroneous report to Rodes is a good indication of how distraught his actions must have appeared to the division commander and others that day.

41 Wehrum to Bachelder, Jan. 1, 1884, in Ladd, *Bachelder Papers*, 2:990; William H. Miller, "They All Helped to Do It," *National Tribune*, Oct. 15, 1885. For further details on the controversy over the charge, see Isaac Hall, "Iverson's Brigade: An Old Controversy in Regard to Its Capture Renewed," *National Tribune*, Sept. 10, 1885.

About 300 of the most severely wounded were left behind and later picked up by Iverson's ambulance corps. In addition, nine officers and 106 enlisted men were killed outright on the field. At least one soldier from the 23rd North Carolina, and probably several others, eluded capture by hiding among the many bodies of the dead and badly wounded.[42]

About 1,030 officers and enlisted men were trapped in the bloody depression. Of those, no more than 230 made it to safety behind the Confederate lines once the fighting on that part of the field ended. Only the troops from the sharpshooter detachment on the left flank and the eight companies from the 12th North Carolina on the far right side of the brigade's battle line avoided the worst of the well-delivered slaughter. Private O'Daniel of the 23rd North Carolina was not far off the mark when he declared that "all that ware in the fight ware killed, wounded & captured except the s[h]arpshooters & ambulance corps."[43]

Iverson' Brigade suffered the further indignity of losing two of battle flags to the enemy. Men from the 88th Pennsylvania captured the regimental colors of the 23rd North Carolina. "Captain Joseph H. Richard of my company singled out the color bearer of the Twenty-third and had a hand-to-hand fight with him," Sgt. Edward L. Gilligan from the 88th regiment recalled. "The Confederate pluckily held on to the colors and only gave them up when I reasoned with him with the butt of my rifle." Gilligan was awarded the Medal of Honor for his efforts.[44]

On another part of the line, several soldiers from the 97th New York wrestled away the battle flag from its defenders in the 20th North Carolina. "Company C was the first at the ditch," remembered Lt. Ebenezer B. Harrington, an eyewitness and participant from the New York regiment. "Sergeant Sylvester Riley was the first to grab the Twentieth North Carolina colors and immediately handed them to me." According to Lieutenant Harrington, he "turned them over to Colonel Wheelock as soon as we had

---

42 Blacknall Memoirs, Blacknall Papers.

43 John F. Coghill to Dear Pappy, Ma and Mit, July 9, 1863, John Fuller Coghill Letters; O'Daniel to Torrence, July 9, 1863, in Monroe, "The Road to Gettysburg," 514. The casualty figures and number of men present in the hollow exclude the four officers and about 120 enlisted men from the sharpshooter detachment and the eight companies from the 12th North Carolina on the right of the line.

44 Quoted in W. F. Beyer and O. F. Keydel, Deeds of Valor: How America's Civil War Heroes Won the Medal of Honor, 2 Vols. (Stamford, CT: Long Meadow Press, 1992), 1:239.

conducted the prisoners . . . from the meadow to our former position, whence they were sent to the rear."[45]

Soon afterward, Wheelock received an order to hand over the captured flag to Gen. Baxter. "But, the colonel would not comply, saying 'my regiment captured these colors and will keep them,'" reported Pennsylvanian Lt. Grant. An angry Baxter placed Wheelock under arrest. The colonel responded by running his sword through the flag, tearing it from the staff, and waving "the torn banner" at the enemy in a "taunting manner." When an officer from a nearby company joined Wheelock in his waving of the staff, he "received a ball to the forehead and fell dead."[46]

Baxter's men were still grabbing up prisoners when gunfire erupted from Iverson's sharpshooters just north of the Mummasburg Road and from the 12th Alabama and 26th Alabama of O'Neal's Brigade, which had moved within 50 yards of the hollow. "The Alabamians fired on friend and foe," reported Confederate Capt. Hicks. "I was fronting them, and knowing the firing was coming, I turned sideways; my lieutenant, standing beside me had his head split open and his brains flew on me." Private Coghill, one of Iverson's sharpshooters, testified that the fire he helped lay down in the general direction of the Federals was so hot that he "shot every one of my cartridges away witch was 110 rounds."[47]

A captain with the 97th New York reported that the Confederate troops "who had been driven off by our skirmish line, returned and occupied the first field south of the Mummasburg road, and as skirmishers kept up a fire upon the right two regiments of our line till the approach of Iverson's Brigade in our front; and during the subsequent charge of a part of our line." According to this Federal officer, the men in his regiment "suffered from this Confederate skirmish line in the field and road to the right, and covered itself as skirmishers as best it could in rear of the wall, several men springing up in concert and firing as closely as possible whence the smoke from the Confederate fire arose."[48]

The indiscriminate firing from the Confederates near the road continued as the Federals herded their prisoners out of the gully toward their own lines. The

---

45 Ebenezer B. Harrington to Isaac Hall, April 29, 1890 in Hall, *Ninety-Seventh New York*, 141.

46 Grant, "The First Army Corps," in Brady and Freeland, *Gettysburg Papers*, 1:263.

47 Hicks, "Memoirs," *Raleigh State Journal*, April 27, 1917; John F. Coghill, Undated Portion of Letter, James O. Coghill Papers.

48 Hall, *History of the Ninety-Seventh New York*, 137.

shooting became so intense that it caused some serious problems for the men who had boldly advanced into the field. "A skirmish fire from an adjoining field on our right flank was kept up with galling effect on our line during our advance," confirmed Lt. Col. R. S. Egelston of the 97th New York. "Also, in returning, this fire was not relaxed on our left while bringing the prisoners from the field; some of whom were wounded by their own men."[49]

Vautier of the 88th Pennsylvania also recalled the flanking fire and that the Southern sharpshooters quickly rendered their exposed position on the field "too hot to hold." The rifle balls, he recalled, "were cutting the grass with a switching sound, taking effect among the Confederate prisoners as well as in our own ranks." Lt. Boone from the same regiment noted vividly that the "course of the bullets could be seen cutting the high grass as if dine by electricity." Capt. Hall reported that at least one man from his company in the 97th New York was killed and "many others were wounded by enfilading fire of this line."[50]

Lieutenant Oliver was being led away as a prisoner when the firing began. He admitted that "many of our own men were killed by bullets fired by our friends." Among the casualties were several company officers from his regiment. "Lieut. Gore from Brunswick Co.," wrote Oliver, was "shot and instantly killed by our own men as we were going to the rear." Coghill reported that this Confederate fire, which included his own 110 rounds, also killed his best friend, Pvt. Rial Stewart. "The Yankes took the best part of our Regt and Brigade and while they were carring them on to the rear we had another line of battle marched up and shot a volly into the Yankes and the prisoners and a ball hit Rial in the side," he explained in a letter home. "The ball went in one side and came out the other. He did lived some 4 or 5 hours after he was struck." According to the private, his friend "was in his right mind" until he died.[51]

Shortly after this new round of firing began, the 12th Massachusetts and several companies from the 90th Pennsylvania pushed north across the Mummasburg Road to counter the renewed threat from the 12th Alabama and the 26th Alabama and Iverson's sharpshooters. Adjutant Wehrum from the

---

49 Statement of R. S. Egelston, Feb. 16, 1889, in *ibid.*, 140.

50 Vautier, "At Gettysburg," *Philadelphia Weekly Press*, Nov. 19, 1886; Boone, "Personal Experiences," Winey Collection; Hall, *History of the Ninety-Seventh New York*, 137.

51 Oliver, "Recollections," 2; John F. Coghill to Dear Pappy, Ma and Mit, July 9, 1863, John Fuller Coghill Letters.

12th Massachusetts insisted the move was "necessary to prevent our right being turned." He recalled that the shift in their position northward "was quickly and handsomely done, by the two right regiments the 90th Penn, and 12th Mass., and were thus enabled to hold our ground against a vastly superior force for more than an hour."[52]

Major Sellers from the 90th Pennsylvania carried out the maneuver. "Although not in command, I rushed to the front, superintended the movement, and quickly established the line in its new and more advantageous position," Sellers recalled. He noted that the change in their battle line "enabled us to pour an effective fire" into the ranks of the Alabama regiments that had moved into position along the north side of the Mummasburg Road. Sellers was eventually awarded the Medal of Honor for his role in the attack north of the Mummasburg Road.[53]

The shifting Federal troops were soon joined by men from the 88th Pennsylvania who captured a battle flag from one of the Alabama regiments. Private Vautier recalled that the banner fell into their hands about the same time the men from his regiment were grabbing up the flag from the 23rd North Carolina in the nearby hollow. "To the right, Lieut. Levan and some others were scrapping for the Flag of the 26th Ala., under like conditions," Vautier wrote, adding that "a free application of a few rifle butts, with the threat of the use of the bayonet, quickly persuaded the rebels that they had no further use for those Flags."[54]

With three of Iverson's regiments nearly wiped out along the stone wall and in the hollow, only the 12th North Carolina on the far right of the line remained relatively intact as an effective fighting force. Sergeant Montgomery explained that his regiment fared "better than the others because of its being protected by a slight rise in the ground, though the loss of its left companies was severe." He further noted that "its line was slightly refused and partly sheltered by the knoll there; so that the flank fire of Cutler's brigade on the right did not strike this

---

52 Look to Bachelder, Feb. 17, 1884, in Ladd, *Bachelder Papers*, 2:1022.

53 Quoted in Beyer and Keydel, Deeds of Valor, 1:221; Thomas L. Hanna, "A Day at Gettysburg," *National Tribune*, May 23, 1901.

54 John D. Vautier, "Realities Reading Like Fiction," included in National Tribune, *National Tribune Scrapbook: Stories of the Camp, March, Battle, Hospital and Prison Told by Comrades* (Washington: National Tribune, 1909), 146. This flag is incorrectly reported as belonging to the 16th Alabama, which was not present at Gettysburg, in OR 27, pt. 1, 311.

regiment, which was also too remote to be much hurt by the union fire on the left flank of the brigade."[55]

Much of the credit for the regiment's survival belongs to its commander Lt. Col. William Davis, who reacted to the first volleys by shifting all but two of the companies from his regiment away from the stone wall to "a little bottom in a wheat field" opposite the woods north of the railroad bed. "On my left there was a gap made as far I could see," he said. "On the right there was a considerable gap between us and Daniel's Brigade." The only Federals in sight consisted of a few skirmishers from Cutler's brigade who moved along the edge of the woods just north of the railroad cut.

Although most of the 12th North Carolina remained safely away from the main killing ground, Davis was cut off from the balance of the brigade during the most crucial time in the attack. "I was left alone without any orders (our general in the rear, and never coming up), with no communication with right or left, and with only one hundred seventy-five men confronting several thousand," he declared. While the fighting continued to rage in the hollow on his left, his regiment "remained in suspense." Most frustrating of all was that "no order came from any source."[56]

By then, Iverson's only hope for saving his embattled regiments appeared to rest with the 3rd Alabama, which had halted on his right after being detached from O'Neal's Brigade early in the fight. Although no other source mentions the incident, Iverson claimed in his official report that he "endeavored, during the confusion among the enemy incident to the charge and capture of my men, to make a charge with my remaining regiment and the Third Alabama, but in the noise and excitement I presume my voice could not be heard. The fighting here," he added, "ceased on my part."[57]

---

55 William M. Robbins Journal, Entry for Sept. 12, 1897, GNMPC.

56 Quoted in Montgomery, "Twelfth Regiment," in Clark, *NC Regiments*, 1:637-638.

57 OR 27, pt. 2, 579-580.

CHAPTER ELEVEN

For a Few Minutes the Fighting was Terrific

From the moment Confederate troops stepped off Oak Hill, Rodes' effort to overwhelm the right flank of the Federal I Corps was uncoordinated and ineptly handled. The sharp repulse of Ed O'Neal's disjointed attack, coupled with the stunning disaster that had befallen Iverson's command, threatened to eliminate the advantage in terrain and position that Oak Hill offered. The Federal tactical victory, however, proved short-lived. Just as the situation appeared lost, Ramseur's Brigade, which had been held in reserve, stepped into the spreading fight on Oak Ridge.

By this point in his career, Stephen Ramseur had earned a reputation as one the best brigade commanders in the Army of Northern Virginia. Universally known by his middle name of "Dodson," the 26-year-old general was born and raised in Lincoln County, North Carolina. He attended Davidson College for a short time and earned an appointment to West Point. Following his graduation in the class of 1860, he served briefly as a lieutenant in the U.S. Army.

Ramseur resigned his commission and entered Confederate service as a captain of artillery. He was promoted to colonel of the 49th North Carolina in the spring of 1862 and sustained a severe wound in the arm at Malvern Hill. His skill and bravery earned him a promotion to brigadier general in November of 1862. The North Carolinian did not join his new brigade until mid-January of

1863, however, because of lingering problems with his wounded arm. Ramseur's star continued to ascend at the battle of Chancellorsville, where he won praise for spearheading Stonewall Jackson's bold flank attack through the heavy woods against the exposed right flank of Joe Hooker's Army of the Potomac. By the time the Southern army embarked on the march north that June, Dodson Ramseur was widely recognized as a leader destined for higher command.[1]

After witnessing the twin disasters unfold, Rodes ordered Ramseur to send two regiments to support O'Neal and two more to assist Iverson's troops. Ramseur's two left regiments, the 2nd North Carolina and the 4th North Carolina, moved promptly east to assist the Alabama effort. After advancing a few hundred yards they were recalled by Rodes and posted on Oak Hill to meet an apparent threat from Federal troops on their flank. The "threat" was likely prompted by the arrival of Paul's Federal brigade, which took up a position near the Mummasburg Road. Once it became clear the Federal troops along the road were not going to attack, Rodes ordered Ramseur's 2nd and 4th North Carolina regiments, about 440 officers and men combined, to follow their original orders and support O'Neal's effort to drive the Federals off Oak Ridge.[2]

Ramseur, meanwhile, rode with the 14th North Carolina and the 30th North Carolina, comprising some 600 veteran officers and men, as they marched into action from the area of the Forney farmhouse across the same field where Iverson's men had been slaughtered a little more than one hour before. Gabriel Paul's fresh regiments, which had replaced Baxter's troops behind the stone wall, were directly in their front.

While maneuvering his troops into position, however, a minie ball entered Paul's right temple and emerged through his left eye socket, tearing out both eyes. Despite the loss of their commander, his five regiments still represented a formidable obstacle. Their final position formed a V-shaped salient extending north in the area of the stone wall and east along Mummasburg Road. The 94th and 107th New York moved into place directly behind the wall at the crest of the ridge. The 16th Maine held a crucial position at the apex of the brigade's formation, near the junction of the wall and the road. The 104th New York and

---

1 Warner, *Generals in Gray*, 251. For a detailed account of Ramseur's career, see Gary W. Gallagher, *Stephen Dodson Ramseur: Lee's Gallant General* (Chapel Hill: University of North Carolina Press, 1985).

2 *OR* 27, pt. 2, 589.

For a Few Minutes the Fighting was Terrific 249

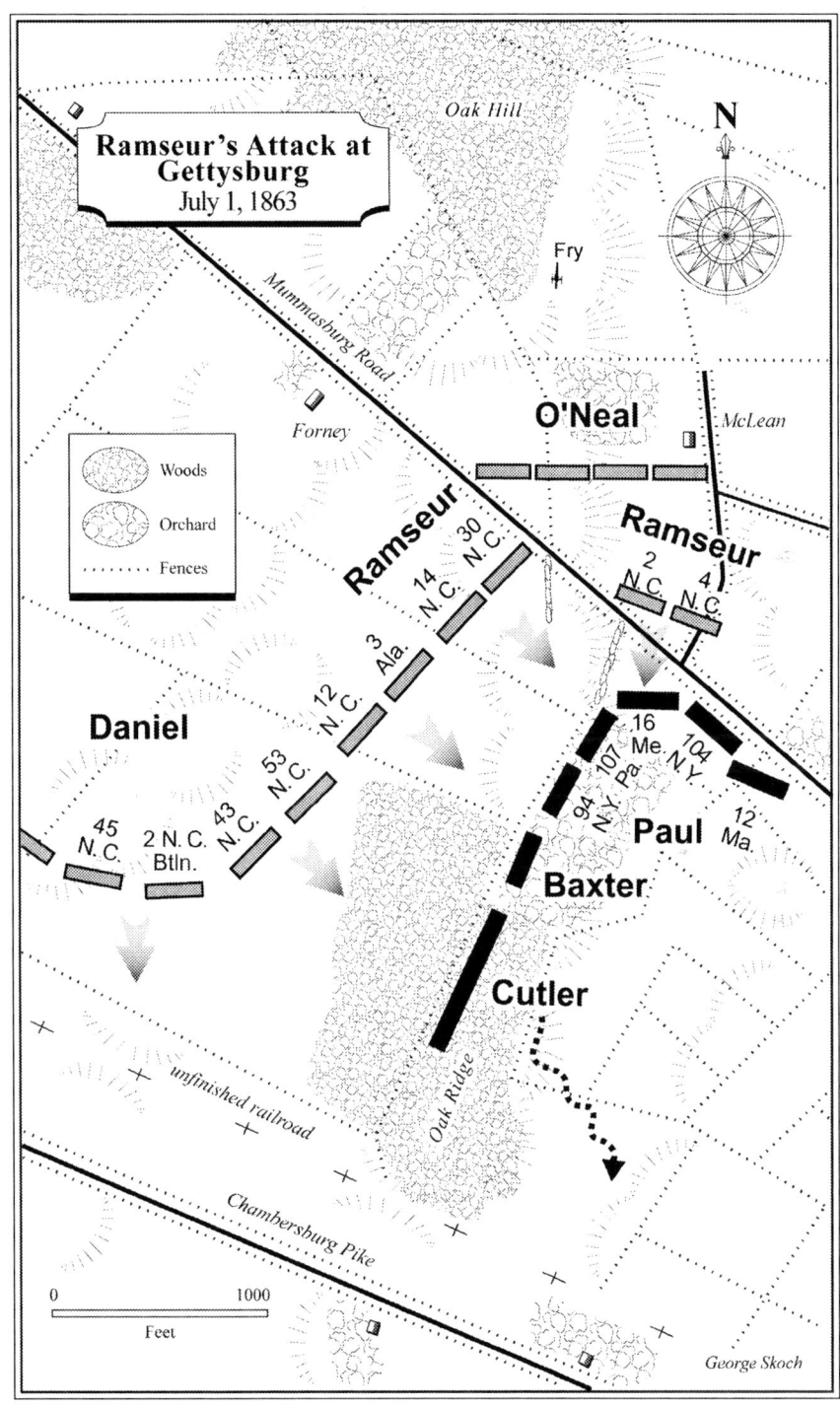

the 13th Massachusetts occupied the far right of the line along the road, fronting directly on Oak Hill.[3]

Although the earlier attacks failed miserably, Rodes expected a different outcome once his most determined fighter entered the fight. "Ramseur's Brigade, which under my orders had been so disposed as to support both Iverson and O'Neal, was ordered forward, and was hurled by its commander with the skill and gallantry for which he is always conspicuous, and with irresistible force, upon the enemy just where he had repulsed O'Neal and checked Iverson's advance," Rodes declared in his official report. Unlike Iverson, Ramseur led the way at the front of the assault.[4]

The situation his troops faced as they swept onto the field about half past three o'clock in the afternoon appeared far from promising. "I found three regiments of Iverson's command almost annihilated, and the Third Alabama Regiment coming out of the fight from Iverson's right," recalled Ramseur. "I requested Colonel Battle, Third Alabama, to join us, which he cheerfully did." According to Capt. James Harris of the 30th North Carolina, he encountered the 3rd Alabama, about 350 officers and men, just as his own regiment stepped into the Forney field. His understanding at the time was that "Rodes' old brigade did not come up to the scratch—as they ought—that day, and this Regt. by some means was cut off."[5]

Captain W. H. May recalled that men from the 3rd Alabama shouted to Ramseur for permission to attach themselves to his force as he passed nearby. According to May's account, the general replied, "N. C. will stay with you." Still frustrated by the earlier lack of response for guidance from Gen. Daniel, one of the men yelled back that "they haven't been a doing it." This time, however, the 3rd Alabama joined in the attack against the Federal position along Oak Ridge. "Away we went with him charging a stone fence," May recalled.[6]

Another 3rd Alabama soldier reported that he and his comrades "moved forward with a shout" across the field. "The enemy was in our front, behind a stone fence," he explained. "We could see them; they were 'pegging away' at us,

---

3 Busey and Martin, *Regimental Strengths*, 168. For details on the controversy over the exact positions of Ramseur's regiments, see Cooksey, "They Died As If on Dress Parade," 109-111.

4 *OR* 27, pt. 2, 554.

5 *Ibid.*, 587; Busey and Martin, *Regimental Strengths*, 166; Harris to Williford, Aug. 24, 1863, in Taylor, "A Newly Discovered Account," 31.

6 May, "Reminiscences."

like good fellows, and Gen. Ramseur said they had to be driven from there." According to the same Alabamian, "Gen. R., riding up to the front, clapped spurs to his horse, and waving his hat, cried out for us to follow him." Their advance carried them through the same hollow where Iverson's men had taken shelter during the earlier attack. "We now began to notice our men laying on the field," one veteran remarked. "Some one yells our boys have charged here and been repulsed."[7]

About the same time, Ramseur discovered on his right Lt. Col. William Davis' largely unscathed and apparently unengaged 12th North Carolina from Iverson's Brigade. He ordered Davis to "push the enemy in front." The Tar Heel's of the 12th had been holding their position in the Forney field for more than an hour without assistance. Captain Weldon Davis of the 30th North Carolina, writing without a full appreciation of how its position on the far right and the rolling terrain had saved the regiment, claimed that "the 12th Regt actually clothed itself in honor [in] this fight." He also noted that "three regiments of their brigade were taken prisoners, but the 12th kept fighting, would not surrender, and by itself held the line marked out for their whole brigade." Lieutenant Medicus Ward from the 12th North Carolina bragged to his parents that they "alone held the enemy in check until Daniel's and Ramseur's brigades came to our assistance."[8]

Lieutenant Colonel Davis responded to Ramseur's request by ordering his men to let out a yell and "charge rapidly" at the Federals in the woods opposite their position. Within minutes, they could see the enemy to their right front falling back. "So completely surprised were the enemy that they fled in confusion without firing a gun," Davis recalled with some exaggeration. What Davis did not know was that Cutler's men were running low on ammunition and had already begun pulling back to the area of the unfinished railroad bed.[9]

Farther north, Rameur's 30th North Carolina halted briefly on the field while the 3rd Alabama and 12th North Carolina moved into position. From that vantage point, Capt. Harris caught a brief glimpse of the fighting underway

---

7 "Letter from the 3rd Ala., from a member of the Gulf City Guards," July 9, 1863, *Mobile Daily Advertiser and Register*, July 24, 1863; "War Memories by an Old Hornet," 104.

8 Weldon Davis to Dear Ma, July 8, 1863, in Eaton, *Rebecca's Letters*, 68-69; Ward to Ma and Pa, July 7, 1863, *Raleigh Weekly State Journal*, July 22, 1863. Capt. Don P. Halsey, the assistant adjutant general for Iverson's Brigade, was rallying the brigade's remnants farther west.

9 *OR* 27, pt. 2, 587; Montgomery, "Twelfth Regiment," in Clark, *NC Regiments*, 1:638.

between his position and the area south of the Chambersburg Pike. "During all this time a warm engagement had been going on just to our right between the enemy, who held position in a thickety woods, and the 12th N.C. Troops," Harris recalled. He also observed that "still farther to the right Daniel's brigade was hotly engaged and further still was Pettigrew's brigade."[10]

After charging the woods, the 12th North Carolina moved to assist Ramseur's troops in the attack farther north against the stone wall. "The 12th was badly used up but a part of it joined us in the charge," explained Col. Francis M. Parker from the 30th North Carolina. "But just how many companies of the 12th went in with us I do not know. In fact, I am not sure that any organized part of the 12th N.C. was in that charge." The colonel also noted that "it was such hot and close work that a fellow had to attend pretty closely to his own business." Adjutant Fred Phillips, also from the 30th North Carolina, believed that "every man was at his post, and some of the gallant men of the 12th N.C. Regiment of Iverson's Brigade which had been driven back joined us."[11]

As Ramseur's 14th and 30th North Carolina regiments moved ahead, their orders suddenly changed. Instead of attacking due east, they were hurriedly advised to file left and strike the Federal right closer to the Mummasburg Road. The warning came from Lt. James A. Crowder of the 23rd North Carolina, who was stationed nearby with Iverson's sharpshooter detachment, and Lt. Edward M. Duguid of the 5th North Carolina, who had escaped from the deadly field on Iverson's left. Ramseur did not miss a beat. Colonel Parker recalled that the young brigadier "wheeled the line to the left and then sent us forward at the double quick, or, rather, run."[12]

The new line of attack farther north was straight ahead along the Mummasburg Road. "We were ordered to left flank, which threw us into the road leading directly into the city," an officer from the 14th North Carolina recalled. "We marched down the road through a copse of woods." At that time,

---

10 Harris to Williford, Aug. 24, 1863, in Taylor, "A Newly Discovered Account," 34.

11 Letter from Francis M. Parker, May 29, 1891, Stephen D. Ramseur Papers; Phillips to Schenck, Oct. 27, 1891, *ibid.*

12 Turner and Wall, "Twenty-Third Regiment," in Clark, *NC Regiments*, 2:237; John J. McLendon, "Memoirs," William Alexander Smith Collection, Duke; Letter from Francis M. Parker, May 29, 1891, Stephen D. Ramseur Papers. Turner and Wall identified the second officer as "Lieutenant Dugger of another regiment." This officer almost certainly was Lt. Edward M. Duguid of the 5th North Carolina.

the officer continued, they were "ordered by the right flank, which changed the direction of the Brig throwing us in rear of the Yankees behind the rock fence." From there, the Tar Heels pressed forward into the ranks of the enemy troops posted along the northern end of Oak Ridge.[13]

The brilliant tactical maneuvering was personally directed by Ramseur, who displayed remarkable courage and presence of mind throughout the attack. Phillips of the 30th North Carolina reported that the general "led the charge and he was the only officer on the field who had a horse under him." Tragedy nearly ensued when "the fine gray mare upon which he rode fell from bullet wounds within a few yards of the stone fence." Shaken but unhurt, Ramseur continued leading the assault on foot in front of the wall.

Despite mounting casualties, the men pressed ahead with a rush toward the northern section of the fence. "Col. Parker of the 30th Regiment was badly wounded in the face just as we reached the wall," Phillips recalled. "The bullet ridden flags of the 14th and 30th were planted there, and for a few minutes the fighting was terrific." Ramseur's troops from the 2nd and 4th North Carolina regiments, which had moved to support O'Neal's Alabamians, struck about the same time, moving "promptly up" against the shorter part of the L-shaped line facing northwest along the Mummasburg Road. The arrival of the Tar Heels there began to overwhelm the 104th New York and 13th Massachusetts along the road on the far right of the Federal line.[14]

The first sign that the enemy line was faltering came as welcome relief for Col. Cullen Battle from the 3rd Alabama. He admitted his regiment had been in "critical condition" until then, with a mass of Federal troops extending far beyond their position on both flanks. By all indications, the prospects for the attack were far from good. "But there was no time for hesitation," Battle reported. "'Forward Third Alabama!' was the order. Not a man flinched," he continued. "The regiment was melting away in the furnace of battle, when to my surprise, the enemy's right began to waver and fall back."[15]

Captain May recalled that the Alabama men "drove the enemy troops from the fence," forcing them to retreat by their left flank under cover of the stone wall. "This threw them to our right," he explained. "Gen. Ramseur here halted

---

13 14th North Carolina, "Memoir,"14th North Carolina File, Confederate Regiment Files GNMPC.

14 *OR* 27, pt. 2, 554, 587; Phillips to Schenck, Oct. 27, 1891, Stephen D. Ramseur Papers.

15 Beck, *Third Alabama*, 83.

the right, and threw around his left to confront them, and charged." Another member of the regiment reported that "on our right the enemy had held their ground with more stubbornness or success than in our front." He pointed out "that when we had driven them from the stone fence the line had to halt till the forces on our right could push them from a wood, from which they were enfilading us."[16]

The added support from the troops in the 3rd Alabama on Ramseur's right proved critical in driving the enemy from behind the stone wall. Ramseur credited much of their skill and bravery in the assault to the outstanding leadership of their commanding officer. Ramseur complimented Battle for his "brilliant and invaluable service" during the attack. "Attaching his regiment to my command on his own responsibility, he came in at the right place, at the right time, and in the right way," reported the brigadier. For a commander to so highly commend another commander and organization that did not even belong to his brigade was high praise indeed.[17]

As the main battle line pressed on toward the Federal position, the valiant efforts of Asst. Adjt. Gen. Don Halsey in organizing the shattered remnants of Iverson's command worked to Ramseur's advantage. "The Twelfth North Carolina, which had been held well in hand by Lieutenant-Colonel Davis," explained Rodes in his after-action report, "and the shattered remnants of the other regiments of Iverson's Brigade, which had been rallied and organized by Capt. D. P. Halsey, Assistant Adjutant-General of the brigade, made under his guidance a dashing and effective charge just in time to be of considerable service to Ramseur and Daniel, and with them pressed closely after the enemy."[18]

Ramseur declared that he met only "feeble resistance to the front attack" once the two regiments attacking from Oak Hill turned the enemy's right flank. Within minutes, the Southern troops along that part of the attack swung directly into the rear of the startled defenders. "Our gallant Brigadier, Ramseur, seeing the advantage in the face of a torrent of bullets wheeled his entire brigade to the right," wrote Capt. John Gorman of the 2nd North Carolina. "And before the

---

16 W. H. May, "First Confederates to Enter Gettysburg," *CV*, 5 (1897), 620; "Letter from the 3rd Ala., from a member of the Gulf City Guards," July 9, 1863, *Mobile Daily Advertiser and Register*, July 24, 1863.

17 *OR* 27, pt. 2, 587.

18 *Ibid.*, 554.

Yankees could think, we were pouring showers of rifle balls into their right flank and rear." Gorman went on to note that "their whole line broke and fled, and at one time I was fearful their running troops would crush our little brigade."[19]

After encountering a "severe, galling, and enfilading fire" from the strip of woods directly behind Paul's brigade, the 4th North Carolina under Col. Bryan Grimes was forced to change front to the right before attacking across the Mummasburg Road. "We then advanced upon the enemy, joining our brigade, and driving them in great confusion," Grimes reported. "And, but for the fatiguing and exhausting march of the day, we would have succeeded in capturing a very large number of prisoners." He went on to note that they still seized more enemy soldiers "by far than the number of men in the command."[20]

When the right wing along the Mummasburg Road collapsed, the Federals farther south on Oak Ridge began abandoning their position along the wall. Lieutenant William Calder from the 2nd North Carolina wrote that "when we appeared on their flank, the dark mass of the enemy could be plainly seen to waver, break and finally fly headlong toward town, as we rushed after them pouring a deadly hail of balls into their confused columns." Philips correctly observed that "the retreat of the enemy assumed the character of a rout" once the enemy emerged from the cover of the wall. "Quite as many were captured as we had in the attacking column," he declared.[21]

About this time, the repulsed regiments from O'Neal's Brigade and part of Lt. Col. Thomas Carter's artillery battalion entered the fight from the east slope of Oak Hill. "O'Neal's shattered troops, which had been assembled without order on the hill, rushed forward, still without order, but with all their usual courage, into the charge," Rodes reported. "Fry's battery, by my order, was pushed closely after Ramseur." Colonel Risden T. Bennett from the 14th North

---

19 *Ibid.*, 587; "Battles of Gettysburg," *North Carolina Standard*, Aug. 4, 1863. The source for this article is described as "a letter written by a gallant young officer of the 2nd N.C. regiment, Ramseur's brigade, to his mother in the city." A slightly different version of this same letter has been published as George Gorman, ed., "Memoirs of a Rebel: Being the Narratives of John Calvin Gorman, Captain, Company B, 2nd North Carolina Regiment, 1861-1865, Part II: Chancellorsville and Gettysburg," *Military Images*, 3, No. 6 (May-June 1982), 24-25.

20 OR 27, pt. 2, 589-590.

21 Calder to Mother, July 8, 1863, Calder Papers; Phillips to Schenck, Oct. 27, 1891, Stephen D. Ramseur Papers.

Carolina in Ramseur's Brigade recalled that he "could almost hear their bones crunch under the shot and shell" as Fry's Battery repeatedly fired into the rear of the retreating Federal troops.[22]

A soldier from the 3rd Alabama reported that they soon "had the satisfaction of seeing the whole Yankee line fleeing like frightened wild beasts toward town, followed closely by our boys," Captain May from the same regiment insisted that the attack became "almost a slaughter" as the Confederate forces pursued the Federals along the railroad embankment and through a nearby apple orchard. "This was the most murderous assault I saw during the four years," he confessed. "They were making no attempt to fight. Right there I saw five stands of Colors from first to fifth no more than 100 yards [away]." As "soon as room was made for them to run they did it."[23]

The entire Federal line was engaged in a frenzied flight for safety along the Chambersburg Pike or in the direction of town. Captain Gorman declared that Ramseur's troops "had them fairly in a pen, with only one gap open—the turnpike that led into Gettysburg—and hither they fled 20 deep, we all the while popping it to them as fast as we could load and fire." Lieutenant Ward from the 12th North Carolina bragged to his parents that their whole line "drove the enemy pell mell from their strong position beyond the town." Ramseur agreed, observing that the Federal troops "ran off the field in confusion, leaving his killed and wounded and between 800 and 900 prisoners in our hands."[24]

While Rodes' other troops were knocking the Federals off the northern and central portions of Oak Ridge, Junius Daniel's large North Carolina brigade was dislodging Col. Roy Stone's brigade from its position north of the Chambersburg Pike behind the unfinished railroad bed. Daniel's four regiments and one battalion numbered nearly 2,200 officers and men. The front line consisted of the 45th North Carolina and the 2nd North Carolina Battalion, which "engaged the enemy, very strongly posted along a railroad cut, and in the edge of the woods in rear of the cut." According to Daniel's official report, the Federal line of battle was "nearly at right angles with General Iverson's line and

---

22 OR 27, pt. 2, 554, 587; Bennett, "Fourteenth Regiment," in Clark, *NC Regiments*, 1:719.

23 "Letter from the 3rd Ala., from a member of the Gulf City Guards," July 9, 1863, *Mobile Daily Advertiser and Register*, July 24, 1863; May, "First Confederates," 620; May, "Reminiscences."

24 "Battles of Gettysburg," *North Carolina Standard*, Aug. 4, 1863; Ward to Ma and Pa, July 7, 1863, *Raleigh Weekly State Journal*, July 22, 1863; OR 27, pt. 2, 587.

supported by two batteries of artillery posted near a stone barn on the right of the railroad cut, and another on the hill to the left of the railroad."[25]

The railroad bed ran on a parallel line about 200 yards north of the Chambersburg Pike. The bed had been graded but no track had been put down. Three deep cuts had been excavated to depths between 15 and 30 feet where the line traversed Seminary Ridge and the two branches of McPherson's Ridge. The easternmost cut, which ran through Seminary Ridge, was about 200 yards long. The middle cut, behind which most of Stone's troops were posted, extended through the eastern branch of McPherson's Ridge for about half that distance. The westernmost cut traversed the main ridge line opposite the McPherson farm for nearly 100 yards at an average depth of 20 feet.[26]

The 45th North Carolina and the 2nd North Carolina Battalion continued moving forward toward the Chambersburg Pike until "within close rifle range" of the Federal position. From there, they launched a charge against the enemy skirmishers along the north side of the railroad bed. There, however, they encountered a "murderous fire" from Stone's brigade and Battery B of the 4th U.S. Artillery, posted along both sides of the railroad bed in the area of Seminary Ridge. The enfilading fire from the battery forced the North Carolinians back in confusion about 30 yards.

After regrouping, the two Tar Heel regiments resumed the advance southward. One of the men recalled that they were "ordered to charge the enemy, which was formed in three lines just in our front." When the renewed attack broke apart the Federal skirmish line and opened the way deeper into the Federal position, the 2nd North Carolina Battalion "found itself on the verge of a deep railroad cut, which was not before seen." Lieutenant Leonidas L. Polk of the 43rd North Carolina reported that his regiment on the left of the battle line also "advanced steadily across the open fields, until checked by the deep Rail Road Cut, which had hitherto been undiscovered, as it was concealed by the growing crop of small grain."[27]

---

25 *Ibid.*, 566; Busey and Martin, *Regimental Strengths*, 164. For a detailed account of the attack on Stone's Brigade from the Federal perspective, see James J. Dougherty, *Stone's Brigade and the Fight for the McPherson Farm* (Conshohocken, PA: Combined Publishing, 2001), 51-97.

26 Martin, *Gettysburg July 1*, 583.

27 Record of Events, 2nd North Carolina Battalion, Entry for July 1, 1863, in *OR Supplement*, 48:323; Leonidas L. Polk, "The 43rd N.C. Regiment During the War: Whiffs from My Old Camp Pipe," *Weekly Ansonian*, May 17, 1876.

The obstacle caught nearly everyone by surprise. "Suddenly we were on the brink of a chasm in the railroad since known as the Deep Cut, when the enemy opened on us with both field pieces and small arms," Lt. Col. Wharton Green of Daniel's staff recalled. "And before it could be prevented the men were jumping down into the Cut with the view to scrambling up on the other side, which was found to be impracticable owing to the precipitous sides encountered." According to Green, the situation became even worse when "some masked guns opened an enfilading fire, which was most destructive."[28]

Following a "bloody and protracted" fight, Daniel ordered the men around the cut to fall back "some 40 paces" behind the crest of a nearby ridge. While far from perfect, that location provided the men with some much-needed shelter from the intense enemy fire. "Our troops were then ordered to lie down, and were slightly protected by a rise of a few inches in the ground between us and the railroad cut, while a detachment was sent around to our right to enter the railroad cut and uncover the Yankees in it," Sgt. B. Frank Hall from the 43rd North Carolina recalled.[29]

After rallying his men, Daniel directed the 43rd and 53rd North Carolina regiments to cover the left and brought up the 32nd North Carolina, which had halted just short of the railroad bed, to support the right. While that was going on, the men from the 45th North Carolina and the 2nd North Carolina Battalion resumed their attack against the main line of Federal troops, many of whom had taken up position just north of the Chambersburg Turnpike inside the railroad cut. "The Forty-fifth Regiment and Second Battalion, gallantly led by their commanders and supported by the rest of the line," wrote Daniel in his battle report, "advanced at a charge, driving the enemy from the cut in confusion, killing and wounding many and taking some prisoners."[30]

Captain Van Brown of the 2nd North Carolina Battalion recalled that the enemy were soon "driven in confusion from the railroad cut across the hill into the outskirts of the town, where large numbers of them threw down their arms

---

28 Green, *Recollections and Reflections*, 175; John C. Hackett to Dear Mother, Father, and Brother, July 19, 1863, John C. Hackett Papers, Duke. Earlier in the fight that morning, men from Joe Davis' Brigade, part of Heth's Division, A. P. Hill's Corps, had made the same mistake. Hundreds were trapped inside the deep cut a bit farther west and killed, wounded, or captured.

29 B. Frank Hall, "Account of the Battle of Gettysburg, 1913," Historical Society of the Lower Cape Fear, Wilmington, North Carolina.

30 *OR* 27, pt. 2, 566-567.

and surrendered." He added that "many prisoners were also captured by the battalion and the Forty-fifth in the railroad cut." The success proved costly for the 2nd North Carolina Battalion. "Out of 240 men, exclusive of officers, nearly three-fourths had fallen," the battalion's record of events report stated. "Nearly all the officers were killed or wounded."[31]

The 32nd North Carolina under Col. Edmund C. Brabble, meanwhile, launched an attack across the railroad cut against a large stone barn on the McPherson farm just behind Federal lines. As they pushed forward, the troops encountered a fierce fire from the Federal battery posted along the railroad cut on nearby Seminary ridge. "The ground occupied by the enemy on this occasion, gave him the decided advantage, with a battery upon a hill which commanded our position and approach," one of the men observed. He also noted that the regiment "made a charge from its position under the hill and succeeded in dislodging the enemy, but being unsupported on the right and left and the batteries on the hill opening a terrific fire upon it, it fell back to a cut in the railroad."[32]

After reforming around the railroad bed, the North Carolinians attacked again from a different direction "without hindrance." From there, they soon joined up with troops from A. P. Hill's Corps to push the Federals back from around the McPherson barn. The 32nd North Carolina, wrote Colonel Brabble, "moved up beyond the barn, and, waiting a few minutes for the troops on the right, advanced near the edge of town." He added that they captured "a considerable number of prisoners" during the headlong pursuit toward town.[33]

The troops from the 45th North Carolina under Capt. J. A. Hopkins, meanwhile, charged directly into the woods just north of the railroad cut. The thrust netted them "188 prisoners in this place and several smaller squads in other places." Captain A. H. Gallaway's company in the same regiment overtook some retreating troops from Baxter's brigade near the railroad bed. After a brief scuffle, they recaptured the battle flag of the 20th North Carolina, which Gallaway turned over "to a member of that regiment."[34]

---

31 *Ibid.*, 578; Record of Events, 2nd North Carolina Battalion, Entry for July 1, 1863, in *OR Supplement*, 48:323.

32 "Thirty-Second Reg't N. C. Troops, Daniel's Brigade, Rhode's Division, Ewell's Corps, at the Late Battles of Gettysburg, Pa.," *Raleigh Weekly State Journal*, Aug. 12, 1863.

33 *OR* 27, pt. 2, 572.

34 *Ibid.*, 566-567, 575.

The troops were pouring off Oak Ridge toward town and running for their lives by the time Alfred Iverson moved to the front of the attack. Exactly what he had been doing the previous couple of hours is uncertain. According to the brigadier, he "observed that the enemy were retreating along the railroad, and immediately hastened the Twelfth North Carolina forward to cut them off." The 53rd North Carolina of Daniel's Brigade, continued Iverson, joined in the pursuit and the two regiments were the first to reach the eastern end of the railroad cut, where they gathered up droves of enemy soldiers. "Numberless prisoners were cut off by us, but I would not permit my men to take them to the rear, as I considered them safe," he explained.[35]

Daniel's other regiments also pressed forward along the railroad bed against the Federal troops making a stand on Seminary Ridge. "My own troops advanced in fine order, under a heavy fire, the Twelfth North Carolina Regiment, of Iverson's brigade, keeping abreast with my left," Daniel wrote after the campaign ended. "After severe fighting, I succeeded in taking the hill, with a very heavy loss." He wrote in his official report that "a very large number of prisoners were captured, and in the advance my troops passed over several stand of colors that had been abandoned by the enemy."[36]

The main part of the brigade pursued the Federals along the eastern slope of Seminary Ridge. Lieutenant Polk reported that, after Daniel's Brigade cleared the railroad cut and "gained the brow of the hills overlooking the town, we could see the enemy throwing down their arms by hundreds and returning to us, while the long slope which gradually ascended from the town on the other side was literally black with the flying and frightened Yankees." According to Daniel, his "command continued to move forward until it reached the outskirts of the town."[37]

On the other end of Rodes' line, the Georgians from George Doles' Brigade, together with troops from Jubal Early's Division, had overrun Oliver Howard's Federal XI Corps in the rolling plains just north of town. Rodes later reported that Doles "succeeded in driving them before him, thus, achieving on the left, and at about the same time, a success no less brilliant than that of Ramseur in the center, and Daniel on the right." Captain Shepherd G. Pryor

---

35 *Ibid.*, 580.

36 *Ibid.*, 567.

37 "From the Forty-Third Reg't. N.C.T," July 20, 1863, *North Carolina Argus*, July 30, 1863; OR 27, pt. 2, 567.

from the 12th Georgia, part of Doles' command, participated in the stunning victory that was now obvious to everyone on both sides. We shoved back the enemy nearly "two miles like chaff," recalled Pryor. Considering the credentials Doles carried to the field, the expert way in which he handled his brigade surprised no one.[38]

Despite his lack of formal military training, the 33-year-old Doles was widely regarded as an outstanding brigade commander. He spent the years prior to the war as a businessman and captain of a militia company in the Georgia state capital at Milledgeville. When hostilities broke out, he entered military service as a captain in the 4th Georgia. In May of 1862, Doles won election as colonel. After briefly serving in the region surrounding the key seaport at Norfolk, Virginia, his regiment was transferred to Lee's army near the end of the Seven Days' Battles.

Over the following months, Doles aptly demonstrated his fitness for combat command. During his first engagement under Lee's command, Doles was wounded and cited for bravery during the ill-fated attack at Malvern Hill on July 1, 1862. Following additional conspicuous displays of gallantry at both South Mountain and Sharpsburg in the Maryland Campaign, Doles was promoted to brigadier general on November 1, 1862. He once again performed brilliantly during the chaotic and horrific fighting in the woods at Chancellorsville. If anyone had any doubts about his ability to lead a brigade, his intrepid leadership on that field erased them and solidified his reputation as a hard and smart fighter.[39]

After deploying his force of 1,300 officers and men on the plain east of Oak Hill, Doles spent the early part of the afternoon protecting Rodes' left flank from a potential attack by the lead elements of Howard's Federal XI Corps. "Doles's Brigade was fully from one-half to three-fourths of a mile east of the left of the battle—the extreme left of the line engaged—occupying the attention of the Federals, who were in line along on the north side of the town," one veteran recalled. He went on to note that "the rattle of small arms was

---

38 *Ibid.*, 554; Shepherd G. Pryor to Penelope Pryor, July 16, 1863, in Charles R. Adams Jr., ed., *A Post of Honor: The Pryor Letters, 1861-1863* (Fort Valley, GA: Garret Publications, 1989), 378. For detailed accounts from the Federal perspective, see D. Scott Hartwig, "The 11th Army Corps on July 1, 1863—'The Unlucky 11th,'" *Gettysburg Magazine*, 2 (January 1990), 33-50 and Gary Kross, "The XI Corps at Gettysburg, July 1, 1863," *Blue & Gray Magazine*, 19, Issue 2 (December 2001), 6-24, 48-51.

39 Warner, *Generals in Gray*, 74.

continuous for several hours along their front, neither side seeming to gain or lose ground."[40]

The main threat to Doles' four regiments came from Alexander Schimmelfennig's brigade, which was being led on July 1 by Col. George von Amsberg of the 45th New York. Earlier in the afternoon, von Amsberg had pushed his troops forward into the area between the Mummasburg and Carlisle roads, where they helped repulse O'Neal's initial attack along the lower slopes of Oak Ridge. From their position just north of town, they stubbornly held their ground against both Doles' troops and Blackford's corps of sharpshooters. By mid-afternoon, it appeared as though the Federals were finally gaining the upper hand.

As the outcome hung in the balance, John Gordon's Brigade from Early's Division arrived from the northeast about three o'clock in the afternoon. Fortuitously for the Confederates, Gordon's all-Georgia brigade arrived at precisely the right place at the right time. "Affairs were in a very critical condition, when Major-General Early, coming up on the Heidlersburg road, opened a brisk artillery fire upon large columns moving forward against Doles's left, and ordered forward Gordon's Brigade to the left of Doles," was how Ewell explained this development in his official report. Gordon's troops appeared so suddenly that one of Doles' veterans described their arrival as coming in on the left "like a whirlwind."[41]

By this time, Federal brigades led by Brig. Gen. Adelbert Ames and Col. Leopold von Gilsa had advanced into an exposed position along Blocher's Knoll, north of the Adams County Alms House between the Carlisle and Harrisburg roads. The forward move was ordered by division commander Brig. Gen. Francis C. Barlow, who was determined to hold that piece of high ground. Barlow, however, failed to coordinate his actions with the two brigades from Maj. Gen. Carl Schurz's division on his left or even notify them of his movement.

Although the area around the knoll provided some limited tactical advantage, Barlow pushed so far forward that both of his flanks remained vulnerable to attack. Once Schurz, who was in temporary command of the XI Corps, recognized the problem, he ordered Col. Wladimir Krzyzanowski's

---

40 Busey and Martin, *Regimental Strengths*, 67; Grace, "Rodes's Division at Gettysburg," 614.

41 *OR* 27, pt. 2, 445; Grace, "Rodes's Division," 614.

brigade to Barlow's support from its position in the rear along the Carlisle Road. Before Krzyzanowski even crossed the road, however, Barlow's division was attacked by Doles on the left and Gordon on the right.

After arriving on the Harrisburg Road, five of Gordon's six regiments rushed ahead "under heavy fire" across Rock Creek directly into the Federal position along the crest of the knoll. "The enemy made a most obstinate resistance until the colors on portions of the two lines were separated by a space of less than 50 paces, when his line was broken and driven back, leaving the flank which this line had protected exposed to the fire from my brigade," Gordon reported. The brigadier pointed out that "an effort was here made by the enemy to change his front and check our advance, but the effort failed, and this line, too, was driven back in the greatest confusion, and with immense losses in killed, wounded, and prisoners."[42]

The three left regiments of Doles' Brigade joined in the attack. Along with Gordon's men, they dislodged and nearly routed Barlow's troops from their exposed position along the crest of the knoll. A gunner from Reese's Alabama battery, which had shifted into a nearby field of wheat to support the Confederate assault, recalled that his men began "giving the enemy a hot enfilading fire" just as the line finally started to crumble. The attack along that part of the field quickly "became a race, the Federals fleeing and the Confederates pursuing."[43]

Doles' regiments pressed forward in pursuit of the retreating enemy forces. Soldiers from Krzyzanowski's brigade appeared along their front just northwest of the Adams County Almshouse. The Federal advance and attack developed so quickly and was so unexpected that Doles' infantrymen faltered momentarily under the sudden pressure. With assistance from Gordon's two right regiments, Doles stabilized his line and forced the newly arrived Federal troops back in disarray. In less than fifteen minutes, Krzyzanowski's entire brigade was on the run.[44]

Krzyzanowski's troops were being defeated when a new threat appeared on the right side of Doles' line in the form of the 157th New York. The lone

---

42 OR 27, pt. 2, 492; "Twenty-Sixth Georgia Infantry," July 20, 1863, *Savannah Republican*, Aug. 5, 1863; G. W. Nichols, *A Soldier's Story of His Regiment (61st Georgia) and Incidentally of the Lawton-Gordon-Evans Brigade, Army of Northern Virginia* (Jessup, GA: n.p.,1898), 116.

43 John Purifoy, "History of Jeff Davis Artillery," ADAH.

44 J. W. B. to Mr. Editor, Aug. 12, 1863, *Augusta Weekly Chronicle and Sentinel*, Sept. 5, 1863.

regiment from Schimmelfennig's brigade had been sent forward in a desperate attempt to assist Krzyzanowski. The New Yorkers initially formed in a long column just west of the Carlisle Road. Within a few minutes, they pushed forward well past Doles' flank. The New Yorkers posed a real danger in that position. If properly handled, they could potentially drive in the exposed Confederate flank and perhaps turn the tide of battle along that part of the field north of town.

The attack caught the troops from the 21st Georgia on the far right of Doles' line so completely by surprise that they were forced back to a country lane northwest of the knoll on the Blocher farm. "Having attracted their fire, and finding their force too strong for the exposed position we then occupied, we fell back some 40 yards to a lane, where we awaited their approach," wrote Col. John T. Mercer in his official report. "By lying down, we hid ourselves from them till they had approached within a few yards, when we commenced firing, and advanced."[45]

Within minutes, the men from the 4th and 44th Georgia regiments joined in with a barrage of gunfire from their positions along the east side of the Carlisle Road. "The enemy came up to within 30 or 40 yards of us," remembered Maj. William H. Peebles, who had assumed command of the 44th Georgia after Col. Samuel P. Lumpkin fell wounded. "As soon as it was discovered that we were flanked, we made a wheel to the right, faced the new foe, and began to fire upon him." The line of Federals on their flank, continued Peebles, "faced us, and opened a severe fire upon us."[46]

As the two sides blazed away at one another at short range, the 12th Georgia under Col. Edward Willis shifted around from the left into place on the far right of the main battle line facing due south. With that move, Doles' Brigade had almost encircled the 157th New York, which was left isolated when Krzyzanowski's brigade fell back. "During the advance a portion of the enemy's troops overlapped, and I thought hardly pressed the right of the brigade," Col. Willis reported. "I moved my regiment by the right flank, and assisting the

---

45 OR 27, pt. 2, 585; Thomas M. Hightower to My Dear Lou, July 7, 1863, Hightower Letters; Sidney J. Richardson to Dear Father and Mother, July 8, 1863, Sidney J. Richardson Papers, GA.

46 OR 27, pt. 2, 586; John C. Key, "Memoir," GA; Major Key, "Reminiscences of the Civil War: And Incidents Connected With the 44th Georgia And Other Regiments," *Jasper County News*, Jan. 5, 1899.

Forty-fourth and Twenty-first Georgia regiments, the enemy was soon dislodged with heavy slaughter."[47]

Krzyzanowski's men and the 157th New York were being routed from the field when both Brig. Gen. Harry Hays' Louisiana Brigade and Col. Isaac E. Avery's North Carolina brigade, both of Early's Division, entered the fighting from the northeast. The division's artillery provided additional close-range support as they pressed forward toward the edge of town. An officer from one of the batteries recalled that the entire force "drove the enemy pell-mell over rolling wheat fields, through a grove, across a creek, up a little slope and into the town itself." He added that "the pursuit was so close and hot that, though my gun came into battery several times, yet I could not get in a shot."[48]

The entire Federal line north of Gettysburg was crumbling when all four of Doles' regiments joined in the chase. The enemy retreat turned into a wild scramble to escape the pursuing Confederates. "We met the force on the right, attacked and routed him, pursuing him across the plain in front of Gettysburg," Doles explained in his official report. "But few of his force escaped us." His Georgians, continued Doles, "then moved toward the theological College, to the right of Gettysburg, where the brigades of Generals Daniel, Ramseur, Iverson, and Colonel O'Neal were engaged with the enemy."[49]

Doles and Early's other brigades were moving in from the north while Daniel's and Ramseur's brigades pursued elements of the broken Federal I Corps from around Oak Ridge toward the western outskirts of Gettysburg. Some of Ramseur sharpshooters led the way at the front of the assault. "Into town we rushed pell-mell after them, our brigade in the advance," gushed Capt. Gorman of the 2nd North Carolina. "I was with my company in the skirmish line, in front, and when the Yankees got into town, they hid by hundreds in houses and barns, and I had the felicity of capturing any number."[50]

The stunning success was marred by the tragic loss of Lt. Frank M. Harney, the commander of one of Ramseur's sharpshooter detachments. "The sharpshooters who were in front pressed them, pursued them into the town

---

47 Francis T. Willis, "The Twelfth Georgia Infantry," *SHSP*, 17 (1889), 185; Nicholas Scott to Dear Father, July 16, 1863, Irby H. Scott Papers, Duke; Joseph J. Felder to My Dear Sister, July 18, 1863, Lavander Ray Papers, GA.

48 Robert Stiles, *Four Years Under Marse Robert* (New York: Neale Publishing Co., 1904), 210.

49 *OR* 27, pt. 2, 582.

50 "Battles of Gettysburg," *North Carolina Standard*, Aug. 4, 1863.

and fought them through streets," explained Lt. Calder. "We captured one of their colors, but lost our gallant commander Lt. Harney of the 14th who fell mortally wounded." According to Calder, "after the last one had been driven from the town, the enemy fled to a commanding hill that overlooked the town and all the surrounding country and there rallied and formed their shattered ranks."[51]

Once again, Iverson's role in this part of the fighting on July 1 remains difficult to establish. He indicated in his official report that he assisted in this part of the assault, but Ewell reported something different. Captain Halsey, explained the Second Corps commander, had "rallied the brigade and assumed command" long before this point in the fight. Except for the claims in his report, all other indications are that Iverson was more of a spectator at this time than an actual leader of combat troops. As the soldiers rushed into Gettysburg in pursuit of the beaten enemy, even Iverson was forced to acknowledge that he had lost effective control of his regiments. "Arriving in the town, and having but very few troops left, I informed General Ramseur that I would attach them to his brigade and act in concert with him," he admitted in his report.[52]

According to Rodes, his entire division pursued the enemy "closely into and through the town, Doles and Ramseur entering in such close contact with the enemy that the former, who penetrated the heart of the town first of all had two sharp, and successful encounters with the enemy in the streets." Major Eugene Blackford from O'Neal's Brigade complimented Rodes' description. As Blackford recalled the situation, it became "truly a wild scene" as the troops rushed forward "capturing prisoners by hundreds" in the streets. "A squad of us would run down a street and come to a corner just as a whole mass of frightened Yanks were rushing up another," he wrote. "A few shots made the whole surrender, and so on until we caught them all."[53]

Despite his overwhelming success, Rodes ordered his brigades to stop their pursuit in the middle of Gettysburg. "The troops, being greatly exhausted by

---

51 *OR* 27, pt. 2, 555; Calder to Mother, July 8, 1863, Calder Papers. The high ground Calder referred to was Cemetery Hill.

52 *OR* 27, pt. 2, 445, 555, 580. Ewell's use of the words "assumed command" are a strong indication that he did not believe Iverson was in charge of his brigade from that point forward. Iverson himself credited Halsey with preparing "a forward movement" earlier during the effort with the 12th North Carolina and Ramseur's attack against the stone wall.

53 *Ibid.*, 445, 555, 580; Trudeau, "5th Alabama Sharpshooters," 50.

their march and somewhat disorganized by the hot engagement and rapid pursuit, were halted and prepared for further action," was how he justified his decision. Most of the men in the division were nearly worn out by the time they reached town. "I believe I was more completely exhausted this evening than I ever was in my life," admitted Lt. Thomas Taylor of O'Neal's Brigade. "I thought I would faint. I could not shut my mouth but panted like a dog on a hot summer day."[54]

In addition to exhaustion and heavy combat losses, the men also faced the very serious problem of a lack of water. One soldier from the 12th Alabama wrote to his mother that "a great many men fainted that day from exhaustion, having been obliged to go into battle without water." An officer from Daniel's Brigade noted in his diary that "our men suffered very mutch for Water for they were marched in quick time for severel miles before they got to the Battle field & did not have the chance of getting Water in there canteens." The soldier estimated that they were forced to go without water from about ten o'clock in the morning until about five o'clock in the afternoon.[55]

While his victorious soldiers were rooting out enemy soldiers in town and trying to regroup, Rodes and Early met up with Ewell in the main town square. Both subordinates urged the Second Corps commander to press ahead with the attack against the retreating enemy, who were now gathering on the high ground just below Gettysburg. Ewell had already received instructions from Lee "to carry the hill occupied by the enemy, if he found it practicable, but to avoid a general engagement until the arrival of the other divisions of the army, which were ordered to hasten forward." Rather than acting immediately, he dispatched an officer from his staff to locate Lee and obtain clarification of his orders.

On his return, Lt. James Power Smith informed Ewell that Lee still wanted him to seize the high ground, if practical. Those orders left the Second Corps leader in a quandary about exactly what to do next. He was well aware that Rodes' Division was exhausted, had sustained heavy casualties, and remained fragmented because of its long pursuit and the manner in which it entered town. Much of Early's Division, meanwhile, also remained scattered. Both Gordon's

---

54 *OR* 27, pt. 2, 555; Taylor to Wife, July 17, 1863, Taylor Papers.

55 "Extract of a letter from a member of the 'Southern Foresters,' 12th Alabama Regiment to his mother," July 8, 1863, *Mobile Evening News*, July 24, 1863; James E. Green Diary, Entry for July 1, 1863, NCOAH.

Brigade and a Virginia brigade commanded by Brig. Gen. William "Extra Billy" Smith had been shifted about two miles east of town along the York Turnpike in response to an erroneous report that Federal troops were threatening their left flank. The late hour of the day and a lack of response from A. P. Hill to Ewell's requests for support in launching a new attack complicated the situation.[56]

Although Rodes remained ready to press ahead once his men were rested, the order from Ewell to resume the attack against Cemetery Hill never arrived. Even Ewell's substitute plan of having Edward Johnson's late-arriving division seize control of nearby Culp's Hill failed to materialize. "Receiving no orders to advance, though my superiors were upon the ground, I concluded that the order not to bring on a general engagement was still in force, and hence placed my lines and skirmishers in a defensive attitude, and determined to await orders or further movements either on the part of Early or of the troops on my right," was how Rodes explained it in his after-action report.[57]

For many of those soldiers who had served under Thomas "Stonewall" Jackson, Richard Ewell's failure to send them forward that day against the retreating enemy troops seemed nearly inexplicable. Typical of the comments were those of Ens. John A. Stikeleather from the 4th North Carolina in Ramseur's Brigade. Stikeleather recalled pointedly that "there was a little restlessness exhibited by the soldiers on account of the halt first evening of the fight, the impression seeming to obtain among them, that, had Stonewall Jackson been with us, before we slept that night, Gettysburg heights would have been ours."[58]

Whether right or wrong, Ewell's decision to halt in town without attacking Cemetery Hill caused at least some of his men for the first time to question the leadership abilities of their new corps commander—especially in comparison to the lamented "Stonewall" Jackson. Captain Gorman of Ramseur's Brigade reported about a week after the battle that they had clearly "missed the genius of Jackson" that day. "The simplest soldier in the ranks felt it, and the results have

---

56 OR 27, pt. 2, 318, 445; Jubal A. Early, "Leading Confederates on the Battlefield: A Review by General Early," *SHSP*, 4 (1877), 271-272. For a detailed account of the decision not to attack Cemetery Hill, see Harry W. Pfanz, *Gettysburg: Culp's Hill and Cemetery Hill* (Chapel Hill: University of North Carolina Press, 1993), 76-80.

57 OR 27, pt. 2, 555.

58 John A. Stikeleather, "Memoirs," 43, Military Collection, NCOAH.

An 1863 view looking southeast from Seminary Ridge toward Gettysburg. Middle Street runs left to right (west to east) through the center of the image. In the left distance is Culp's Hill, with Cemetery Hill in the center and West Cemetery Hill in the distant right. Iverson's men spent the night of July 1 along West Middle Street before moving into place on Long Lane for a planned night attack against West Cemetery Hill. *National Archives*

proven it," he grumbled in a letter home. "But, timidity in the commander that stepped into the shoes of the fearless Jackson, prompted delay."[59]

Lieutenant Calder from the same brigade insisted in a letter to his mother that Ewell's failure to take Cemetery Hill was "the great mistake" that lost all the advantage the Confederates had gained during the hard fighting on the first day at Gettysburg. "Our generals should have advanced immediately on that hill,"

---

59 "Battles of Gettysburg," *North Carolina Standard*, Aug. 4, 1863. A slightly different wording of the same comments was published in Gorman, "Memoirs," 25. Historian Gary Gallagher incorrectly attributes those comments to Ens. Stikeleather. That mistake is repeated by Darrell Collins in his biography of General Rodes. For details, see Gary W. Gallagher, "Confederate Corps Leadership on the First Day at Gettysburg, A. P. Hill and Richard S. Ewell in a Difficult Debut," included in Gallagher, *First Day at Gettysburg*, 35 and Collins, *Major General Robert E. Rodes*, 278.

he argued. "It could have been taken then with comparatively little loss, and would have deprived the enemy of that immense advantage of position that was afterwards the cause of all his success." Major Blackford from O'Neal's shattered brigade likewise declared in a letter to his father soon after returning to the safety of Virginia that "if old Jack was but here we would have been in Baltimore this day." He admitted that it was "sad to hear the men longing for him." All of these men wrote with the clarity that hindsight provides. In the event, the decision to attack or not was much more difficult to determine.[60]

When it finally became obvious that no further offensive action would take place that day, Rodes ordered Daniel back to the area of the unfinished railroad cut, where his men went into camp "under cover of an embankment." O'Neal led the troops from his brigade west of town beyond the railroad bed in the area of the Lutheran seminary. Iverson's survivors, meanwhile, joined Ramseur's and Doles' troops along West Middle Street in the center of the town, facing directly "the heights beyond Gettysburg occupied by the enemy."[61]

---

60 Calder to Mother, July 8, 1863, Calder Papers; Eugene Blackford to William M. Blackford, July 16, 1863, quoted in L. Minor Blackford, *Mine Eyes Have Seen the Glory* (Cambridge, MA: Harvard University Press, 1954), 221.

61 OR 27, pt. 2, 555, 567.

Chapter Twelve

I Told Him It Was Then Too Late

Robert Rodes' exhausted soldiers rested in town while General Lee evaluated the stunning results of of the July 1 fighting and determined how best to capitalize on them the next day. No one had expected the large meeting engagement, but the opportunity to roll up and crush the advance of the Army of the Potomac was too good to pass up once Richard Ewell's Second Corps arrived from the north squarely on the flank of the enemy. The victory that followed shattered John Reynolds' I Corps and Oliver Howard's XI Corps and drove the enemy through town. The Federals, however, had taken up new positions on the high ground below Gettysburg, where they dug in to resist further attacks.

When the fighting ended on July 1, A. P. Hill's bloodied Third Corps occupied Seminary Ridge southwest of Gettysburg. Richard Ewell's Second Corps wrapped around to the north and east through town and beyond, opposite Cemetery Hill and Culp's Hill. As a result, the Army of Northern Virginia now held a long exterior line, which was not an ideal tactical position. The question Lee faced was whether to continue the battle or maneuver his army elsewhere in search of more favorable conditions. He concluded that resuming the offensive was his best option because Maj. Gen. George Meade's

Army of the Potomac had been badly damaged and was almost certainly not fully united.[1]

With two of the three divisions from James Longstreet's First Corps now on the field, General Lee decided to launch a morning attack against what he believed was the vulnerable left flank of the Federal line running from Cemetery Hill south along Cemetery Ridge. The attack would then roll northward across A. P. Hill's Third Corps front. Lee ordered Ewell to wait for Longstreet's main assault and then "make a simultaneous demonstration upon the enemy's right [on the high ground southeast of town] to be converted into a real attack should opportunity offer." It took Longstreet much longer to march his divisions into position than Lee anticipated, and this delayed Ewell's involvement in the fighting on July 2.

Edward "Allegheny" Johnson's Division moved into position to be ready to attack Culp's Hill after Longstreet's main attack on the far right got underway. Jubal Early's Division, situated on Johnson's right, was poised to follow up with an assault against the southeastern heights of Cemetery Hill. Ewell ordered his third division under Rodes to provide support by threatening the Federal position on the western side of the hill. Ewell instructed Rodes to join the fight on Early's right "as soon as any opportunity of doing so with good effect was offered." In other words, Ewell expected Rodes to exploit any opportunity in his front.[2]

Rodes put Ramseur in *de facto* command of the operation against Cemetery Hill. Ramseur's Brigade, together with those of Iverson and Doles, made up the front line and would be guided by Ramseur's movements. The last two brigades under Daniel and O'Neal comprised a second supporting line. Iverson apparently remained in such disfavor that Rodes made no effort to inform him directly about the attack. His men remained in place until "the night of July 2, when I was informed by General Ramseur that a night attack was ordered upon the position of the enemy to the right of the town," wrote Iverson in his official report. "I had received no instruction, and perceived that General Ramseur was acquainted with the intentions of the major-general commanding, I raised no questions of rank, but conformed the movements of my brigade to that of

---

1   OR 27, pt. 2, 318-319. George Pickett's Division from Longstreet's Corps was guarding the army's trains and would not arrive until later.

2   *Ibid.*, 446-447.

Brigadier-General Ramseur." Iverson would advance with his remaining infantry but operate under Ramseur's immediate command.³

After the horrendous losses of the previous day, Iverson's entire brigade fielded no more than 30 officers and about 450 men. Seven field officers marched into the Forney farm field on July 1; only Lt. Col. William Davis and Maj. Robert Alston of the 12th North Carolina were still on duty as the troops readied for action on July 2.⁴

Longstreet's attack, which finally began about four o'clock in the afternoon, caved in the salient created by Dan Sickles' III Corps around the Peach Orchard, broke across Big Round Top, and stormed the slopes of Little Round Top. When both of his divisions were fully committed, the attack began rolling northward. Brigades from Hill's Corps joined in, storming the southern end of Cemetery Ridge. The attack broke down along this front. Hill remained strangely inactive and was probably ill. The effort was further crippled when Maj. Gen. Dorsey Pender, in command of the division on Rodes' right, fell mortally wounded "about sunset."

Rodes eventually dispatched Maj. Henry A. Whiting from his staff with a request for support with his own attack against the western side of Cemetery Hill. The message reached Brig. Gen. James H. Lane, who had assumed command of the division after Pender fell. Lane seemed unaware of the plan for the division and was unsure of how to proceed. "I did not give him a definite answer then," Lane admitted. His stance changed when a message from the Second Corps commander reached him. "On being notified, however, by General Ewell, that his whole command would move on the enemy's position that night, commencing with Johnson's division on the left, I told Major Whiting that I would act without awaiting instructions from General Hill," Lane reported.⁵

By that time, it was growing dark and Rodes' brigades were still not in position for the attack. Although Johnson was not making much headway against Culp's Hill, two of Jubal Early's brigades were already assaulting Cemetery Hill and scaling its heights. Rodes was running so late that his troops did not begin moving out of town until just before dusk. According to Doles,

---

3 *Ibid.*, 580.

4 *Ibid.*

5 *Ibid.*, 666. For a detailed account of the action on Cemetery Hill, see Pfanz, *Gettysburg: Culp's Hill and Cemetery Hill*, 235-283.

his brigade did not get underway until "about 8 p.m." Ramseur described the advance as beginning "at dark." Rodes was late. The men soon encountered difficulties navigating the crowded streets of Gettysburg. The soldiers first had to move by the right flank to the west until they cleared the outskirts of town. Once that was complete, they changed front to the left and marched south. It took more than an hour for the three leading brigades to cover the short distance to their new position.[6]

The troops in the front line eventually halted just west of a dirt road known as Long Lane, which angled from town along the western flank of Cemetery Hill. Ramseur held the right front position, with the brigades of Iverson and Doles extending the line to the left. O'Neal's and Daniel's brigades took up position about 200 yards behind them after arriving from the area around the Lutheran Seminary and the unfinished railroad bed north of Chambersburg Pike. By the time these preparations were completed, Early's pair of brigades under Brig. Gen. Harry Hays and Col. Isaac Avery had driven the defending Federals off part of the high ground and were awaiting reinforcements to exploit the stunning victory on the northeastern side of the hill.[7]

With darkness closing in, Rodes faced the daunting prospect of making a night attack against Cemetery Hill. The final confused arrangements called for the men to move forward quietly to the foot of the hill, using the cloak of darkness to approach unseen. Once everyone was in place, the main assault would commence "just as the moon arose." To avoid detection during the approach, the infantry were ordered to use only their bayonets. Major Eugene Blackford, who commanded O'Neal's sharpshooter battalion, recalled that the guns of the men assigned to this "bayonet affair" were "all inspected to see that none were loaded."[8]

Another part of the plan called for individual brigade commanders to provide their troops with passwords that would allow them to identify each other once they broke through the enemy lines. "Along with the order came the announcement that when we had driven back the enemy and had gained the crest of the hill amid the darkness and confusion in order that we might recognize friend from foe, we were to cry out 'North Carolina to the rescue,'"

---

6   OR 27, pt. 2, 556.

7   *Ibid.*

8   Trudeau, "5th Alabama Sharpshooters," 50.

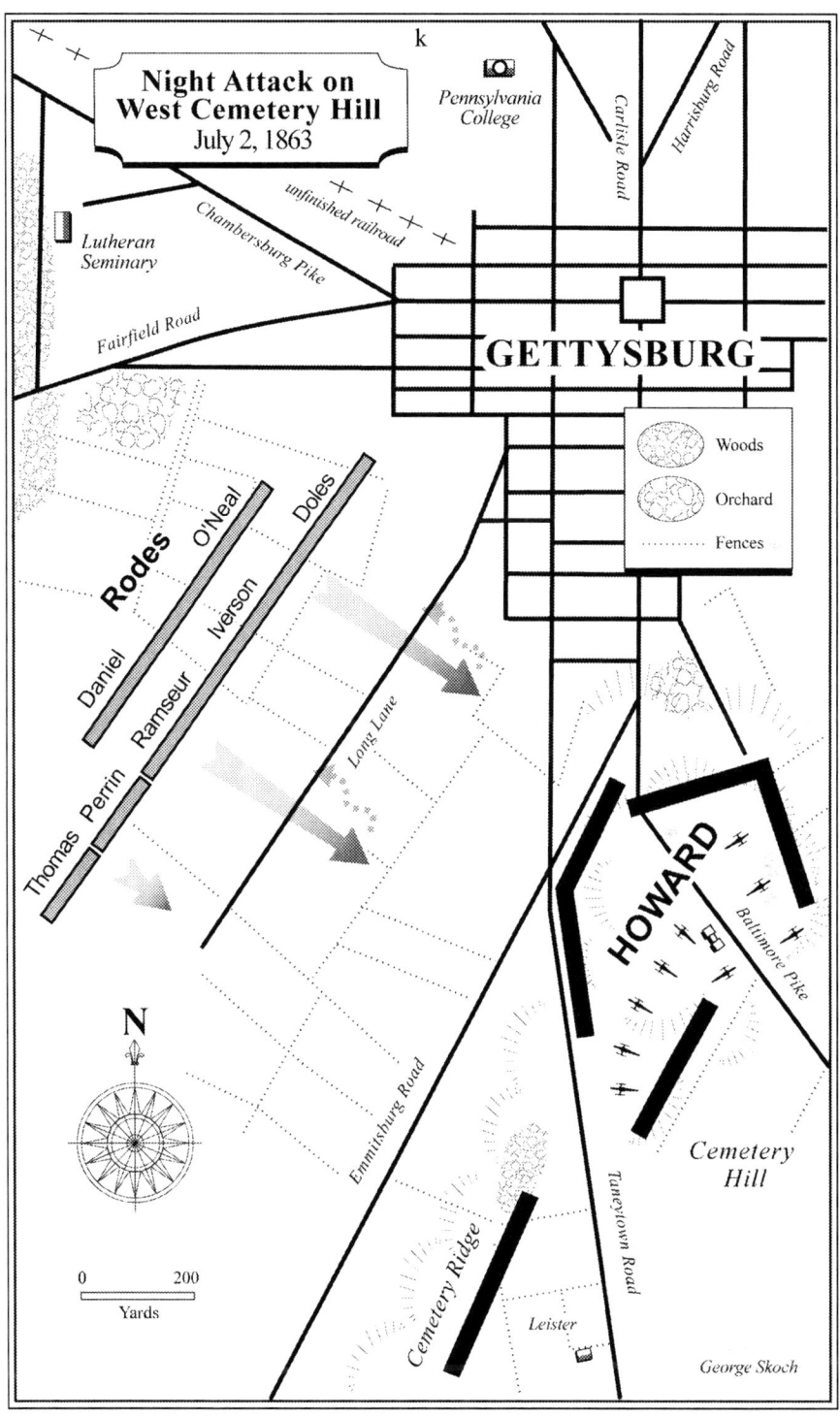

was how Lt. Edward Tripp from the 4th North Carolina recalled the instructions that night for Ramseur's Brigade. Iverson's men, who were attached directly to Ramseur's command, presumably used the same password during the attack.[9]

Despite these preparations, many of the Tar Heels manning the front ranks of the attack expressed shock when the command finally came for them to press ahead against the strong Federal lines. "I thought surely our leaders must be mad, or ignorant of the enemy's position, or else they think our little brigade of 900 can accomplish impossibilities," Capt. John Gorman of Ramseur's command confessed in a letter home. "In front of us stood this frowning eminence crowned with artillery thickly parked." The captain was justified in his deep concerns that evening. "[B]etween its base and its summit," he continued, "two long lines of stone fence ran parallel with the summit, and behind these rock walls stood two lines of battle with musket and rifle in hand awaiting our approach."[10]

Captain James Harris of the same brigade agreed. His worries about the enemy's entrenched position on Cemetery Hill were almost equaled by his concerns about how well Daniel's green troops would hold up in the night attack. Harris held out little hope for the assault's success. "Daniel was in our rear to support us," Harris told a friend. "To tell the truth, I dreaded his men equally as much or more than I did the Yankees, for the day before was the first engagement they had ever been in, and you know how much men become excited under fire in the day, much less in the night."

"It was cloudy and the moon had not yet risen, consequently it was quite dark," Capt. Harris recalled as the Confederate infantry moved slowly and quietly toward the high ground to the east. "In our front was a gently rise of some eminence, just beyond a ravine down which ran a road leading out of town and now about parallel with our lines. On either side of this road was a stone wall behind which was posted Yankee infantry." The many obstacles to success were indeed daunting, confessed the Southern captain, who added, "still after this another small hill was to cross and yet another narrow ravine

---

9 Edward Tripp, "North Carolina to the Rescue," included in Pamlico Chapter of the Daughters of the Confederacy, *The Confederate Reveille: Memorial Edition* (Raleigh: Edwards and Broughton, 1898), 41.

10 Gorman, "Memoirs," 25. Although his original account was written soon after the battle, Gorman wrongly dates the night attack as July 3.

before the hill—on which was planted the enemies batteries—could be reached."[11]

Blackford, a veteran of O'Neal's command, agreed with the pessimistic assessments. Blackford dreaded the outcome from the moment they began moving forward toward the looming hill. "When the column was formed we moved silently with bayonets fixed close up beneath the enemy's works," he recalled. "There in two lines we gave our instructions to the men. I well remember what feelings I had as I fastened my saber knot tightly around my waist. I knew well that I had seen my last day on earth." Captain William M. Norman from the 2nd North Carolina, part of Ramseur's Brigade, summarized the prevailing mood of the attackers well when he firmly declared after the war that "the idea of charging strong fortifications in the night time was an awful thing."[12]

Despite those trepidations, Iverson's and Ramseur's men continued their quiet advance until the sharpshooters out front began receiving fire from Federal troops stationed on rising ground. "Our skirmishers about 20 yards in our front have reached the summit of the first eminence and have drawn the fire of those of the enemy," Capt. Harris observed. "Our orders are to charge them—at the point of the bayonet without firing a gun and the word is 'North Carolina to the rescue.' You can just discern our skirmishers in our front." The captain added, "they have commenced firing on them away to our left the ball has opened."[13]

Corporal Benjamin B. Ross from the 4th North Carolina in Ramseur's Brigade claimed that "every man responded with a will to do or die" as they pressed forward with the attack along the west side of Cemetery Hill. One of the first obstacles they encountered was a wooden fence extending along the east side of Long Lane. "We had been ordered to make as little noise as possible in crossing this fence," Ross said. "We advanced to the crest of the hill, where the Yankees were posted with infantry and artillery." Captain Gorman, meanwhile, cautioned his men "to stick together and to pay attention to orders,

---

11 Harris to Williford, Aug. 24, 1863, in Taylor, "A Newly Discovered Account," 35.

12 Trudeau, "5th Alabama Sharpshooters," 50; William M. Norman, *A Portion of My Life: A Short & Imperfect History Written While a Prisoner of War Johnson's Island, 1864* (Winston-Salem, NC: John. F. Blair Publishing, 1959), 187.

13 Harris to Williford, Aug. 24, 1863, in Taylor, "A Newly Discovered Account," 35.

not to fire, but to make for the enemy with all possible haste as soon as ordered."[14]

Doles' Brigade on the far left of the line also pushed ahead toward the looming Federal positions on the high ground. "We advance up to the enemy's pickets and they open fire upon our skirmishers," wrote Capt. James Beck of the 44th Georgia in a letter to his hometown newspaper. "Soon a raking fire of grape and canister opened upon us. Steadily we advance. Not a thing can be seen in our front but the dark frowning hill, and the blaze of the cannons and the flash of the musket." The men from his brigade, he added, continued to "move our line until we get our proper position."[15]

Behind the main advancing line tramped the soldiers in Daniel's and O'Neal's brigades. "A little after sunset, I received orders to form in the open field in front of and below the hill and to support Generals Doles, Iverson, and Ramseur in an advance upon Cemetery Hill," Daniel explained in his official report. "With Rodes' [O'Neal's] brigade on my left, I moved in the rear of General Ramseur for a distance of about three-quarters of a mile." Captain J. A. Hopkins from the 45th North Carolina recalled that they were "a part of the time under a severe fire of sharpshooters."[16]

Once the skirmishers at the front of the main assault approached within about 200 yards of the enemy lines, Ramseur ordered a halt while he personally carried out a detailed reconnaissance of the area. "As we near the base, a low command halts us within the pale of a graveyard with marble monuments that seem typical of our fate," Captain Gorman ghoulishly recollected. "The enemy seem aware of our approach and their commands can be heard as they prepare to receive us." The men, continued Gorman, were "ordered to lie down, and our hearts thump and beat as if they would leap out of our bosoms, while noble Ramseur and scouts creep forward to reconnoiter."[17]

Iverson's and Ramseur's soldiers were now close enough to draw a steady fire from the Federal skirmishers. Colonel Risden Bennett of the 14th North Carolina, part of Ramseur's Brigade, recalled that even from his position at the

---

14 Benjamin B. Ross, "Experiences of B. B. Ross," Brake Collection; "Battles of Gettysburg," *North Carolina Standard*, Aug. 4, 1863.

15 J. W. B. to Mr. Editor, Aug. 12, 1863, *Augusta Weekly Chronicle and Sentinel*, Sept. 5, 1863.

16 *OR* 27, pt. 2, 568, 575.

17 Gorman, "Memoirs," 25.

bottom of the steep slope along the dirt road "you could almost hear the movements of the enemy's men" at the top of Cemetery Hill. The steady gunfire was enough to convince many of the troops to drop to the ground for protection. "I recall the perilous position in that road, and how we had to hug the ground," observed the colonel, who was fortunate to escape with his life. "I was shot while giving an example to my men. Standing up full height, I was shot through my hat six times—then through my left hand—then through the groin."[18]

As the men waited in "dire suspense" at the bottom of the hill, Ramseur sized up the situation facing them. The Federal batteries, he later reported, were "in position to pour upon our lines direct, cross, and enfilade fires." To his dismay, he further discovered that "two lines of infantry behind stone walls and breastworks were supporting these batteries." He concluded that the strength of the Federal position was nearly invincible and that the attack had little prospect for success. "The strength and position of the enemy's batteries and their supports induced me to halt and confer with General Doles," reported Ramseur, "and, with him, to make representation of the character of the enemy's position, and ask further instructions" from Rodes. About that time, he also received word that Early's troops had been driven off the other side of Cemetery Hill.[19]

Rodes, who was obviously not at the front with his advancing division and readily available to his brigadiers, acquiesced. Ramseur's assessment made it clear that "it was a useless sacrifice of life" to continue in the darkness against such a strong position, the division commander wrote in his report. When Ramseur received permission to cancel the attack, he withdrew "quietly to a deep road some 300 yards in rear." From there, he waited "in readiness to attack at daylight."[20]

Iverson's role at this point in the advance to Cemetery Hill remains unclear. Ramseur seems to have ignored him. His report explicitly notes only that he conferred with General Doles. Iverson's own official version of events does not claim any involvement in the decision-making at the foot of Cemetery Hill. "[P]erceiving, as I believe every one did, that we were advancing to certain

---

18 R. T. Bennett to Fred Phillips, May 28, 1891, Stephen D. Ramseur Papers.

19 *OR* 27, pt. 2, 588.

20 *Ibid.*

destruction," reported Iverson, "when other parts of the line fell back, I also gave the order to retreat."[21]

Within about ten minutes of Ramseur's return, the firing from both sides ceased. "Messengers are sent down the line, and instead of the dismal death-knell sound of 'forward,' the gladly obeyed command of 'fall back without noise' is given, and soon we are again back in our old places in line," wrote Capt. Gorman. A flood of relief swept through the ranks. "Our General saw the foolhardiness and madness of the attempt, and being unwilling knowingly to sacrifice his command, he, on his own responsibility ordered us back; and for that act there are many Carolina mothers, wives, sisters and children who should pray blessings on his head," Gorman declared. Lieutenant William Calder agreed. "After dark our division advanced to make a night attack upon the enemy but our general thought better of it and we retreated without engaging," he wrote in a letter to his mother. "It was well for us that we did for in the confusion of the darkness we would have lost nearly every man and gained nothing whatever."[22]

Captain Harris was equally pleased with the late-arriving decision to halt the night attack. He admitted that "many a heart was made glad" when the command finally came for his brigade to fall back. "A careful reconnaissance had sufficed to demonstrate the impracticability of a successful issue to our contemplated charge," he explained. "Hence the order for the retrograde movement. We dropped back about 150 yards to a small or narrow road running parallel with our lines." He went on to note that, following the halt, the soldiers "lay down on our arms, and rested for the remainder of the night."[23]

The orders to cancel the advance came as a disappointment for at least one officer in O'Neal's Brigade. According to him, the Alabama men "advanced, with empty muskets, to within three hundred yards of the enemy's works without being discovered." The officer insisted that the outlook for success remained far from hopeless. "I believe that we would have carried the heights had we gone on," he declared in a letter home. "I never saw such determination

---

21 *Ibid.*, 556, 580, 588. Doles reported that he consulted "with General Ramseur and Iverson." *Ibid.*, 582. Ramseur's report, when read with Iverson's own report, indicates that the latter officer played no active role in the conference.

22 *Ibid.*, 588; "Battles of Gettysburg," *North Carolina Standard*, Aug. 4, 1863; Calder to Mother, July 8, 1863, Calder Papers.

23 Harris to Williford, Aug. 24, 1863, in Taylor, "A Newly Discovered Account," 35-36.

as expressed by the men. Unless they were really impregnable, they would have been carried."[24]

Casualties in Rodes' aborted attack are difficult to determine conclusively because the killed and wounded were not broken out by engagement in the official report. Only three soldiers from Iverson's command, however, can be confirmed as having suffered wounds during the advance that night, one of them mortally.[25]

Whether justified or not, Rodes' failure to support Jubal Early's attack in a timely manner played a critical role in the repulse of Harry Hays' and Isaac Avery's brigades after their successful storming of Cemetery Hill from the northeast. Early's men had been told to expect reinforcements, but none arrived. "Approaching within 100 yards, a line was discovered before us, from the whole length of which a simultaneous fire was delivered," Hays wrote in his official report. "I reserved my fire, from the uncertainty of this being a force of the enemy or of our men, as I had been cautioned to expect friends both in front, to the right, and to the left." Captain William J. Seymour, who served on Hay's staff, recalled that they "anxiously waited to hear Rodes' guns co-operating with us on the right, but unfortunately no such assistance came to us."[26]

Major Samuel McDowell Tate from the 6th North Carolina of Avery's Brigade informed Governor Vance soon after the battle that "it was manifest that I could not hold the place without aid, for the enemy was massed in all the ravines and adjoining heights, and were then fully half a mile from our lines." After finally retreating down the hill, Tate demanded angrily "to know why we had not been supported." Captain Neill Ray from the same regiment felt much the same way, noting that "no one who has never been in a similar position can understand how anxiously we looked for re-inforcements." The captain added that "none came, however, and before long orders came for us to fall back to our original position."[27]

---

24 "Private Letter from an Officer of the Fifth Alabama Regiment," Aug. 20, 1863, in William B. Styple, ed., *Writing and Fighting from the Army of Northern Virginia: A Collection of Confederate Soldier Correspondence* (Kearny, NJ: Belle Grove Publishing Co., 2003), 262-263. The writer places these events on the third day of the battle, but he is clearly referring to the night attack on July 2.

25 OR 27, pt. 2, 580.

26 *Ibid.*,480-481; Jones, *Civil War Memoirs of William J. Seymour*, 75-76.

27 OR 27, pt. 2, 486; Neill W. Ray, "Sixth Regiment," included in Clark, *NC Regiments*, 1:314.

Early arrived at Rodes' position to urge him forward in support of his embattled troops even before the attack from the west was canceled. "I found him getting his brigades into position so as to be ready to advance, but he informed me that there was no preparation to move on his right, and that General Lane, in command of Pender's division, on his immediate right, had sent him word that he had no orders to advance, which had delayed his own movement," reported Early. Still, he noted that Rodes "expressed a readiness to go forward if I thought it proper, but by this time I had been informed that my two brigades were retiring, and I told him it was then too late."[28]

Rodes' lack of action so upset Early that he complained directly to Ewell. "Gen. Early's indignation was great," confirmed Lt. Thomas Turner of Ewell's staff. "He rode to Gen. Ewell's Headquarters bitterly commenting on Rodes' failure to fulfill his promise to support him." During a hurried conference between the three generals, Rodes blamed his failure to coordinate the attack with the two brigades from Early's Division on the long distance he had to move his troops from town and the failure of Lane to support him on the right.

Rodes also used Ramseur's reconnaissance report as another explanation for halting the attack. Lieutenant Turner was not persuaded, noting almost sarcastically that one of "his excuses for not advancing was that Genl. Ramseur, one of his brigadiers had objected to the attack on account of the number of guns in his front." Early blamed Rodes for the failure to capture and hold Cemetery Hill when he wrote in his official report that his own assault had failed because "no attack was made on the immediate right, as was expected, and not meeting with support from that quarter, the brigades could not hold the position they had attained."[29]

After he cancelled his forward movement, Rodes placed his troops in a position that would allow them to renew the attack the next day. "Instead of falling back to the original line, I caused the front line to assume a strong position in the plain to the right of the town, along the hollow of an old road-bed," he reported. "This position was much nearer the enemy, was clear of the town, and was one from which I could readily attack without confusion,"

---

[28] Jubal A. Early, *Autobiographical Sketch of the War Between the States* (Philadelphia: J. B. Lippincott Co., 1912), 274.

[29] "Copy of a portion of Capt. Turner's Memorandum relating to Gettysburg written before Col. Walter Taylors book either in '76 or '77," in Jones, *Campbell Brown's Civil War*, 322; OR 27, pt. 2, 470.

adding that "the second line was placed in the position originally held by the first."

About 10 o'clock that night, O'Neal's and Daniel's brigades were ordered back into town. "Everything was gotten ready to attack at daylight," Rodes explained. "But a short time after assuming this new position, I was ordered to send without delay all the troops I could spare without destroying my ability to hold my position to re-enforce Major-General Johnson." Because his front line was "much more strongly posted" than the troops in the rear, he selected the two brigades from the second line to support Johnson's command in front of Culp's Hill.[30]

One of O'Neal's soldiers reported that it was almost midnight by the time his regiment finally reached town and "stacked arms" in the street. Instead of resting for the night as he expected, the men formed ranks about an hour later for the journey to Culp's Hill, marching "down on the left wing to a ridge of mountains, where the enemy were strongly entrenched." Another Alabamian confirmed the recollection, noting that the brigade moved "around the left, and behind the town, finally halting at the foot of the mountain on which the enemy had fortified himself." West of Cemetery Hill, meanwhile, Iverson, Ramseur, and Doles remained in position along the narrow country lane throughout the night of July 2.[31]

Unable to coordinate his July 2 attacks against both ends of the Union line, Lee finally decided on the third day of the battle to call upon troops from Longstreet's and Hill's corps to assault the left center of the Federal line along Cemetery Ridge. The attack was placed under Longstreet's command. The plan called for Edward Johnson's reinforced division to carry out an attack against Culp's Hill on the far left, while the rest of the men from Ewell's Second Corps remained in position to exploit any breakthrough. The plan went awry before dawn when the entrenched Federals on Culp's Hill launched a spoiling attack, triggering a bitter seven-hour struggle long before the main attack against the Federal center could get underway. Johnson's men, augmented by Daniel's and

---

30 *Ibid.*, 556, 593.

31 "Extract of a letter from a member of the 'Southern Foresters,' 12th Alabama Regiment to his mother," July 8, 1863, *Mobile Evening News*, July 24, 1863; "Letter from the 3rd Ala., from a member of the Gulf City Guards," July 9, 1863, *Mobile Daily Advertiser and Register*, July 24, 1863. For details on the fighting on Culp's Hill, see William H. Terrell to John Terrell, July 16, 1863, William H. Terrell Letters, ADAH and Hackett to Mother, Father, and Brother, July 19, 1863, Hackett Papers.

O'Neal's brigades, could not make any headway. The fighting petered out late that morning.[32]

Rodes' three brigades along Long Lane did not play a direct role in the fighting on July 3, but his men were under fire for hours and their position was by all accounts unenviable. "The gallant men and officers of this line held their new position all day on July 3, under a sharp and incessant fire from the enemy's sharpshooters and an occasional artillery fire," recalled Rodes. "The enemy made, during the day several ineffectual efforts, by advancing heavy lines of skirmishers, equal almost, if not fully, to my main line, and using their artillery, to dislodge them from their position."

Iverson's and Ramseur's brigades, situated along the road, endured the steady barrage of rifle fire from enemy skirmishers lurking on the nearby hill. Private Thomas J. Watkins of the 14th North Carolina, part of Ramseur's Brigade, observed that the Federal sharpshooters "took a shot at every man that showed himself above our temporary breastworks." Enemy persistence notwithstanding, Southern casualties were negligible. Losses in Iverson's already severely diminished brigade from the artillery fire and skirmishing on July 3 amounted to only two men mortally wounded, one man wounded, and another man captured.[33]

While the men endured this irksome fire, Confederates elsewhere prepared for the day's offensive action farther south. Rodes, however, was apparently not directly informed that three divisions comprising what became popularly known as "Pickett's Charge" would be trying to break through the Union center. Indeed, his notification of the major assault arrived with the opening of the massive bombardment preceding it. "On the 3d, my orders were general, and the same as those of the day before," wrote Rodes in his campaign report, "and accordingly, when the heavy cannonade indicated that another attack was made from the right wing of our army, we were on the lookout for another favorable opportunity to cooperate."

With the cannonade underway, Rodes completed preparations for his three brigades to move forward in support of the infantry attack sure to follow. "This attack was accompanied, preceded, and succeeded by the fiercest and grandest

---

32 *OR* 27, pt. 2, 320.

33 Thomas J. Watkins, *Notes on the Movement of the 14th North Carolina Regiment* (Wadesboro, NC: Anson County Historical Society, 1991), 15-16; John J. McLendon, "Memoirs," William Alexander Smith Collection, Duke.

cannonade I have ever witnessed," exclaimed the division leader. Captain Norman from Ramseur's Brigade agreed, labeling the the barrage as the largest he witnessed during the entire war. "The atmosphere seemed to be as full of cannon balls, bomb shells, and flying missiles of death as a South Carolina millpond ever was of tadpoles," he declared.[34]

When the gunfire along Cemetery Ridge reached its crescendo, Rodes sent word to Ewell that "in a few moments I should attack, and immediately had my handful of men, under Doles, Iverson, and Ramseur, prepared for the onset." Captain Harris watch intently as rows of infantry "as far as the eye can reach" advanced out of the woods into the field on his right. "It was a grand sight, never did men move in better lines—never did a flag wave over a braver set of men," he informed a friend. "The Yankees saw them as plainly as we did, and all the way down the inclined plane they threw shell into their lines with as much precision as if in 100 yards. But still undaunted," continued Harris, "they move steadily forward."

As he observed the grand spectacle unfolding on his right, Harris naturally assumed that Rodes' entire division would join in the advance across the open field. "I expected when they got on the line with us that we would move forward with them, but I was mistaken." Harris continued watching as the line of troops pressed forward against the Federal positions along Cemetery Ridge. "On they went, and we retained our position," he wrote. "I presume it was well enough—scarcely had they passed our lines a hundred yards—when they commenced falling back by the hundred[s] wounded I suppose."[35]

Other men from the two Tar Heel brigades remained primed to join in the attack against the Federal forces on the distant ridge line. Private Watkins from Ramseur's Brigade recalled that he "expected every minute to be ordered forward and every man seemed to steel himself for the ordeal." Despite this anticipation, Rodes noted that "before the troops on my immediate right had made any advance or showed any preparation therefor, and just as the order forward was about to be given to my line, it was announced, and was apparent to me, that the attack had already failed."

Later that evening, the three brigades finally pulled all the way back to the area west of town alongside the unfinished railroad cut. The men from O'Neal's

---

34 OR 27, pt. 2, 556; Norman, *A Portion of My Life*, 187.

35 OR 27, pt. 2, 557; Harris to Williford, Aug. 24, 1863, in Taylor, "Newly Discovered Account," 37-38.

and Daniel's brigades joined them there after returning from their disastrous experience attacking Culp's Hill. "During the night of the 3rd, my division fell back to the ridge which had been wrested from the enemy in the first day's attack," wrote Rodes, "and, being united, was posted so that the railroad divided it about equally. Expecting to give battle in this position, it was strengthened early on the morning of the 4th."[36]

By the time Iverson's troops withdrew from the position in front of Cemetery Hill, the division surgeons had been working for more than two full days at the gruesome task of treating the hundreds of wounded men from the first day's fighting. Most had been transported from the battlefield along Mummasburg Road to the nearby Hankey and Schriver farms. Those two properties, which together served as the primary site for the division hospital, were located in close proximity to each other, about a mile and a half northwest of the Forney field.

The farm owned by 51-year-old David Schriver stood closest to the battlefield. The major buildings on his 150-acre property included a stone house situated on the north side of the road and a barn directly across on the other side. David's daughter was married to John S. Forney, who was also one of their closest neighbors. In his post-battle claim for damages, Schriver testified that his farm "was occupied by the rebel army and was held by them until July 5." The Southerners, he added, "established a hospital in and about the house and barn and they had a large number of wounded men there."[37]

The wooden-frame farmhouse on the 230-acre property owned by the heirs of Jacob Hankey was located less than a quarter-mile west of the Schriver farm on the south side of Mummasburg Road. A large stone barn P. D. W. Hankey used for his cattle business stood adjacent to the house. According to one local resident who took refuge there, the Hankey family "had on their farm a hospital of one thousand wounded Confederates . . . for whom they were compelled to supply milk and bake bread of their own flour and made full use of all their own crops and all their farm produce."[38]

A black maidservant who sought shelter at the Hankey farm recalled that "the place was thronged with Rebels" by the time she reached it. After receiving

---

36 Watkins, *Notes on Movement*, 16; OR 27, pt. 2, 557.

37 Quoted in Gregory A. Coco, *A Vast Sea of Misery* (Gettysburg, PA: Thomas Publications, 1988), 129.

38 Elizabeth M. McClean, "The Rebels are Coming," *Gettysburg Compiler*, June 8, 1908.

assurances about her safety, she spent the entire night cooking and baking for the wounded soldiers. "By morning we were pretty near dead," she explained. "There was no chance to sleep, and I couldn't have slept anyway for hearing the miserable wounded men hollering and going on out in the yard and in the barn and the other buildings." She recalled vividly the agony of the injured: "They moaned and cried and went on terribly. Oh! Take me home to my parents, they'd say."[39]

Before reaching the division hospital, most of the wounded received some form of treatment, however rudimentary, on the field from members of the regimental ambulance corps, which consisted of two litter bearers from each company. Many of the men discovered that serving as a litter bearer was even more arduous than duty along the front line. "At every step one meets with his dead and wounded comrades, and so powerful is the effect upon the nerves that many men who have done well in line of battle, falter in this position," observed an Alabama soldier from O'Neal's Brigade in a letter to his hometown newspaper.[40]

The ambulance corps in each regiment operated under the supervision of the assistant surgeon, who was tasked to follow closely behind the troops during any offensive operation. Regulations expressly forbid the surgeons from devoting their exclusive attention to any single wounded man and from leaving the battlefield to escort wounded men to the rear. Two junior officers from the line companies were detailed to oversee the activities of the ambulance corps at the brigade level. Lieutenants Marcus Sylvanus Deal from the 12th North Carolina and John Philopidus Leach from the 23rd North Carolina served in that position for Iverson's Brigade during the fighting around Gettysburg.[41]

The soldiers at the front also had strict orders against assisting their injured comrades. Anyone who dropped out of formation to care for one of his friends without permission was subject to severe punishment. "We had not gotten more than 50 paces when Norman of our company fell dead by my side," Pvt.

---

39 Clifton Johnson, *Battleground Adventures* (Boston: Houghton Mifflin Co., 1915), 192-193.

40 James Cooper Nisbet, *Four Years on the Firing Line* (Jackson, TN: McCowat-Mercer, 1963), 78; Confederate States of America, *Regulations for the Army of the Confederate States* (Harrisburg, PA: National Historical Society, 1980), 34, 241, 253; H. M. J. to Editor, May 30, 1863, *Clark County Journal*, June 18, 1863.

41 H. H. Cunningham, *Doctors in Gray: The Confederate Medical Service* (Baton Rouge: Louisiana State University Press, 1958), 114-115; "Iverson's Brigade, List of Officers Under Fire, Killed, Wounded, and Missing," Record Group 109, NA.

Louis Leon from Daniel's Brigade recorded in his diary on the first day of fighting. "Katz was going to pick him up. I stopped him, as it is strictly forbidden for anyone to help take the dead or wounded off the field except the ambulance corps."[42]

After being carried out of danger by the litter bearers, wounded men were first treated at makeshift battlefield aid stations. At least some of Iverson's men received assistance just behind the battle lines at the nearby Forney farmhouse. The 23rd North Carolina's Maj. Charles Blacknall recalled that, after being wounded early in the attack, he was transported to the Forney house and treated for his wounds there. After the war, Forney reported that his home "was occupied as a field hospital," and that his house and barn had been "greatly damaged by shells."[43]

From the aid stations, the wounded soldiers were eventually transferred to the division hospital on the Hankey and Schriver farms. The hospital operated under the direct supervision of the division's medical director, Dr. William S. Mitchell. All of the immediate medical chores fell to the regimental surgeons who were assigned there during the battle. One of the regimental surgeons, who was not relieved from duties with his own command, filled the position of brigade surgeon. Robert Hicks from the 23rd North Carolina was in charge of overseeing the other regimental surgeons in Iverson's Brigade.[44]

Hicks was 32 years old in July of 1863. He graduated from the University of Pennsylvania eight years earlier. He enlisted in 1861 from Granville County and served thereafter as regimental surgeon. He was appointed as the brigade surgeon in 1862 while serving under Samuel Garland. Hicks retained that position when Iverson took over the brigade later that year. One officer described Hicks as "a man of medium stature, good personal appearance, a long but rather squarely shaped head, a straight nose, rather long face, very short chin, prominent forehead, dark grey eyes." The young doctor, he continued, was "a man of much research and general knowledge."[45]

---

42 Leon Diary, Entry for July 1, 1863, in Leon, *Diary of a Tar Heel*, 34.

43 Blacknall Memoirs, Blacknall Papers; Coco, *Vast Sea of Misery*, 128.

44 OR 27, pt. 2, 560.

45 Medical Society of the State of North Carolina, *Provisional Record of Confederate Medical Officers* (Raleigh: n.p., 1890), 19; Albert Moses Luria Journal, Entry for Dec. 7, 1861, NCOAH. Kent Masterson Brown incorrectly lists Simon Branch as the chief surgeon for Iverson's Brigade. Branch's compiled service record consists of only a single entry, which lists him as a prisoner at

The nine members of the 20th North Carolina band joined the surgeons at the hospital, where they served as nurses and attendants. Other musicians and light-duty men from the line companies provided additional assistance to the surgeons. As was common practice throughout the army, band members were often assigned to similar hospital duties during the course of the war. "These faithful men cheered our hearts and beguiled many a weary hour, and were kind to many a wounded comrade," one veteran officer of the regiment recalled.[46]

Although the route to the hospital was supposed to be clearly marked by red flags, a slave owned by Sgt. Walter Montgomery of the 12th North Carolina could locate it only by following the trail of ambulances to the rear. "Sometimes he almost abandoned the idea of going any further because of the cries of the wounded in the ambulances as they jolted along the rough roads, and the number of dead and wounded lying in the fields, the latter hailing every passer-by with piteous cries for water and help, and blood everywhere and on everything—all so appalling and terrifying," admitted Montgomery.[47]

Finding the division hospital proved just as complicated for Pvt. Samuel Pickens from O'Neal's Brigade, who reached it only "after a long walk & a deal of difficulty." When he finally arrived there, he was overcome by what he witnessed around the Schriver barn. "The scenes about the Hospital were the most horrible I ever beheld," he exclaimed in his diary. "There were the poor wounded men lying all over the yard, moaning & groaning, while in the barn the terrible work of amputating limbs was going on, and the pallid limbs lying around presented a most disagreeable sight."[48]

Lieutenant Colonel Wharton Green from Junius Daniel's staff, who had been struck down early in the fight, recalled that the ground at the field hospital on the Hankey farm was also "covered by the wounded and mangled, while three of the Medical Staff . . . were hard at work, their coats off and sleeves

---

Gettysburg. This card is a garbled reference to Surgeon Simon Baruch of the 3rd South Carolina. See Brown, *Retreat from Gettysburg*, 102 and Simon Branch, CSR, M 270, R 293.

46 Toon, "Twentieth-Regiment," in Clark, *NC Regiments*, 2:113.

47 Montgomery, "Memoirs," 13, Montgomery Collection.

48 Pickens Diary, Entry for July 1, 1863, in Hubbs, *Voices From Company D*, 182. For additional details on the treatment of the wounded at the Schriver farm, see Major Key, "Reminiscences of the Civil War and Incidents Connected With the 44th Georgia and Other Regiments," *Jasper County News*, Jan. 12, 1899; Park Diary, Entry for July 1, 1863, in Park, "War Diary," 13; Betts Diary, Entry for July 1, 1863, in Betts, *Confederate Chaplain*, 39; Parker Letter, May 29, 1891, Stephen D. Ramseur Papers, NCOAH.

rolled up, to stem the torrent of death, having a couple of impromptu tables for operating purposes." Green was amazed at how hard and long the medical staff were able to remain at their labors. "[F]or two or three days ensuing there was no relaxation, or let up, in their gruesome work, if even a slight snatch of sleep," he wrote. The doctors simply continued working day and night, even though "the pile of amputated limbs were rapidly increasing in size."[49]

Most of Iverson's wounded officers received treatment for their injuries inside the Hankey farmhouse. One veteran from the 23rd North Carolina remembered that the inadequate supply of water from the single available pump added greatly to the misery of the officers in the building. "The well in the Hankey porch was soon pumped dry by thirsty soldiers," he recounted years later. "But still they came working the pump, jarring the house and adding to the tortures of the suffering officers inside." The soldier also recalled that the officers' agonies ended only after a soldier with a fixed bayonet was posted outside the house as a guard for the pump.[50]

The area around the house was also filled with a huge number of enlisted men from the brigade, many of whom had endured devastating injuries before being rescued from the hollow. Private W. J. O'Daniel from the 23rd North Carolina reported that one soldier from his company had his left arm amputated "above his elbow" after being shot three times through the body and twice in the arm. Another comrade suffered terribly after sustaining a severe wound to his "wright wrist." O'Daniel noted that a third company member also had "his left thigh [hit and] it was cut off."

One of the most difficult tasks for the private was telling Sarah Torrence that her son, Leonidas, would almost certainly die from the two severe wounds he sustained during the fighting in the bloody hollow in front of the stone wall on July 1. "He was wounded in the head & thigh," he explained in a letter to her with perhaps more detail than any mother would want to read. "His thigh was not broke but I could not tell what way the [shot] went. The ball in his head went in between his eye and ear. I think that it stopped some place near his brain." Your son, he continued, "came to his cences & told me he was going to die & gave me all his things except his testament and pocket handkerchief."[51]

---

49 Green, *Recollections and Reflections*, 176.

50 Backnall Memoirs, Blacknall Papers.

51 O'Daniel to Torrence, July 9, 1863, in Monroe, "The Road to Gettysburg," 514-515.

Private John Coghill from the same regiment found it just as difficult to inform his family about the death of his best friend. "He was in his right mind untill he died," Coghill wrote in a letter home. "He seamed to be willing to die. I was grieved to think that he was killed for I loved him as a brother." Making matters even worse was that his friend's belongings had been looted on the field. Coghill explained that "some one had taken his watch and his monney before he was found by any of his company but I have got his pocket book and two of his rings witch I will take good care of them untill I can send them home to those that loved him."[52]

The fighting had been so ferocious that many of the men who emerged unharmed credited their escape to nothing less than divine intervention. "I am happy to say I am all right now and with my Company and ready to give them another trial," Sgt. Montgomery from the 12th North Carolina, who had sustained only a slight wound to his knee, wrote to his father a few days after the battle. "God has certainly been with me in this great trial and I am truly grateful to Him, for preserving my life this far, and my prayer is for him to continue his blessing towards me and keep me safely. But if I should fall may I be prepared to meet death with a smile."[53]

Little more than a mile from the field hospital, however, Forney field remained littered with the broken bodies of nearly 100 men from Iverson's Brigade who had fallen in the fateful July 1 attack. A gunner from a Confederate battery left a chilling description of the "sickening and heart-rending" scene that confronted him in front of the stone wall on the morning after the fight. "There were in a few feet of us, by actual count, seventy-nine (79) North Carolinians laying dead in a straight line," he remembered. "I stood on their right and looked down their line. It was perfectly dressed." He noted that "three had fallen to the front, the rest had fallen backward; yet the feet of all those dead men were in a perfectly straight line."[54]

By the time the burial details from Rodes' Division completed their work, many of the bodies scattered along Oak Ridge had already been exposed to the elements for three long hot days. "No fighting to-day, but we are burying the

---

52 Coghill to Pappy, Ma and Mit, July 17, 1863, John Fuller Coghill Letters.

53 Walter A. Montgomery to Dear Father, July 8, 1863, *Raleigh State Journal,* July 29, 1863.

54 Henry R. Berkeley Diary, Entry for July 2, 1863, in William H. Runge, ed., *Four Years in the Confederate Artillery: The Diary of Pvt. H. R. Berkeley* (Chapel Hill: University of North Carolina Press, 1961), 50.

dead," Pvt. Leon of Daniel's Brigade wrote in his diary on July 4. "They have been lying on the field in the sun since the first day's fight; it being dusty and hot, the dead smell terribly." He went on to note that "the funny part of it is, the Yankees have all turned black." The Pioneer detachment eventually buried a large number of Iverson's men in four large trenches on the Forney farm that for years afterward were known locally as "Iverson's pits."[55]

For most of the dead, the exact site of their graves was not recorded. Ninety-two buried corpses from Iverson's command were eventually located on the Forney farm in the years following the war. Even more bodies from other brigades in Rodes' Division were laid to rest in the area around the field hospital at the Hankey and Schriver farms. Including those who died after the Federal troops took over the Confederate hospitals on July 5, about 145 men were buried on the property surrounding the two farms. Yet another 19 bodies were located on the McLean farm at the foot of Oak Hill.[56]

The losses suffered by Iverson's Brigade were simply staggering. Although the 12th North Carolina suffered fewer losses than did the other regiments, at least 70 of the 235 enlisted men who entered the fight in the main battle line or with the sharpshooter detachment were struck down in the area around the Forney field. These casualties included a dozen men who were killed outright or who later succumbed to their injuries. Lieutenant Benjamin Mosely Collins remained on the field until late in the attack despite being shot three times. Only three of the 23 officers who entered the battle that day, however, suffered wounds.[57]

The toll was much worse in the three regiments that had been trapped in the bloody hollow. The 5th North Carolina on the far left of the battle line entered the action with about 446 officers and men under the command of a captain. In just a little more than one hour, the regiment sustained 260 officers and men killed, wounded, and captured. Private Daniel Moose reported in a letter home that his company "went into the fight at Gettysburg with 51 men and came [out] with 12 men unhurt, six men killed dead in the field." He

---

55 Leon Diary, Entry for July 4, 1863, in Leon, *Diary of a Tar Heel*, 37; Turner and Wall, "Twenty-Third Regiment," in Clark, *NC Regiments*, 2:235.

56 Edward G. J. Richter, "The Removal of the Confederate Dead from Gettysburg," *Gettysburg Magazine*, 2 (January 1990), 117, 120.

57 Montgomery, "Twelfth Regiment," in Clark, *NC Regiments*, 1:639; Benjamin Mosely Collins, "Reminiscences," SHC.

lamented that "my best friends are all killed or wounded in the regiment or nearly so."[58]

Of the 29 officers in the 5th regiment, only six left the field unscathed. All four of the captains present with the regiment suffered wounds, although two of them returned to duty within a few days. The casualties also included Adjt. Fabius Haywood, who was severely wounded on the first day of the fighting. Especially lamented among the mortally wounded officers was Lt. Theodore D. Deems, the promising young son of Reverend Charles Force Deems. The wounded officer seemed on his way to a full recovery from a "flesh wound in both thighs." He took a sudden turn for the worse, however, and died in the Federal field hospital at Gettysburg on July 17.[59]

In the weeks immediately following the battle, Reverend Deems made repeated efforts to find out exactly what had happened to his son. Like so many other Southern families, all he knew for sure was that Theodore had been wounded during the fighting at Gettysburg. "The most conflicting rumors came to the family: that the wounds were slight, that they were fatal, that Lieutenant Deems had been seen in a Northern prison, and so on until the family were harassed beyond measure," another of the minister's sons recalled. More than two agonizing months passed before the family learned with certainty that the young lieutenant had succumbed to his wounds in a hospital near the battlefield.

During his time at the hospital, Deems received compassionate treatment from a man and his wife working with the Christian Commission at Gettysburg to care for the wounded. After learning that he was the son of a well-known minister, they visited with him almost daily. The couple even took a lock of his hair so that they could send it home to his family. Following his death, they carefully marked the location of his grave. The information they provided allowed the Deems family to retrieve his body soon after the war for a proper burial in a cemetery near Wilmington.[60]

Deems' death was also a severe blow to his 21-year-old fiancée Mary Hinton Carraway, who lived just outside of Goldsboro. This accomplished

---

58 Daniel M. Moose to Dear Father-in-law, Aug. 20, 1863, in Troxler and Barrier Auciello, *Dear Father*, 138.

59 OR 27, pt. 2, 287; "List of Officers Under Fire," NA; "Fifth North Carolina Regiment," July 14, 1863, *Raleigh Daily Progress*, July 21, 1863.

60 Edward M. Deems and Francis M. Deems, *Autobiography of Charles Force Deems*, 186.

young woman graduated from college at the age of 15 and had already spent several years working as a teacher. She became close to Reverend Deems and his family after he presented her with a gold medal at her graduation from college. The loss of her intended husband left Mary so saddened that she did not marry until 10 years later, and then only as a matter of social convenience to a man 16 years older than herself.[61]

Losses were even more extensive in the 20th North Carolina, which entered the Forney field just to the right of the 5th North Carolina. Aside from the sharpshooters, fewer than 40 men from the regiment made it out of the bloody field unharmed. One veteran from the Confederate Grays of Company E, which included many of the former cadets from the Franklin Military Institute, insisted that "every one of the thirty members of the company then present that went into the fight were either killed, wounded or captured except William Barfield, and he went in with the sharp shooters and not with the regular lines." According to the soldier, only nine of those men "were captured unhurt."[62]

The overall toll in the regiment included all but two of the 24 officers who participated in the attack that afternoon. Among the casualties were both Lt. Col. Nelson Slough and Maj. John Brooks. "Col Slough & my self was both soon wounded in the left arms," the more fortunate Brooks wrote to his father soon after the battle. "My wound is between the elbow & wrist. The surgeon says that no bones are injured." Command of the regiment eventually fell to Adjt. John F. Ireland, who had reached the field from a stay at a Richmond hospital after the first day's fight had ended.[63]

The list of officers killed in the attack included Capt. Oliver Mercer and his best friend, Lt. Thomas Fullwood. After recovering from his wound, Major Brooks faced the regrettable duty of writing a letter to Mercer's sister in North Carolina. "By far the most valuable relic I have to forward you is the assurance to which hundreds will bear me witness that your brother always did his duty nobly and cheerfully, was honest, upright and brave in all his dealings and that

---

61 Tempie Parker Harris Prince Collection, Heritage Place, Lenoir Community College, Kinston, North Carolina.

62 "List of Officers Under Fire," NA; Oliver, Hicks, and Carr, *History of Company E*, 20.

63 John S. Brooks to Dear Father, July 12, 1863, Brooks Letters; Oliver, "Recollections," 2; John F. Ireland to Samuel R. Ireland, June 16, 1863, Elizabeth Rudder Fearrington Croom Collection, ECU.

Col. Daniel Harvey Christie of the 23rd North Carolina in a heavily retouched photograph. Christie was being treated at the Hankey farm for severe wounds when he pledged that he would never forgive Alfred Iverson for what he had done at Gettysburg.
North Carolina Museum of History

his untimely death was sincerely lamented by his many friends in the army," he consoled her.[64]

Despite the receipt of the sad letter, Sarah Mercer continued to hold out a faint sense of hope that her beloved brother might still be alive. "I would think

---

64 John S. Brooks to Sarah Mercer, November 15, 1863, in Wyatt, *The Reeves, Mercer, Newkirk Families*, 274-275.

sometimes that there must be a mistake and that he was taken prisoner and would come home again sometime," she confided to her diary. Even that remote possibility, however, was firmly extinguished a few months later when Chaplain Alexander Betts from Ramseur's Brigade, who had been the family's local minister before the war, sent Sarah a letter describing how he found her brother's body on the field of battle. "His letter caused the last spark of hope that I had entertained of ever seeing dear Buddy on earth again, to go out," she lamented.[65]

The news from Gettysburg proved just as devastating for the families of the soldiers in the 23rd North Carolina, the last of the three regiments driven back into the bloody gully and nearly eliminated there. Of the estimated 22 officers and 262 enlisted men from the regiment trapped in the depression before the stone wall, only one officer and about 16 enlisted men made it out of the July 1 fight without injury. The casualties included the adjutant and all three of the field officers. Adjutant Junius B. French succumbed to his injuries on the day after the fight. Lieutenant Colonel Robert Johnston suffered wounds to his jaw, neck, and right clavicle during the wholly preventable fiasco in the Forney field. Colonel Daniel Christie barely clung to life after being shot in both lungs while leading his men in the desperate but short-lived charge out of the hollow.[66]

Major Blacknall also suffered a severe wound during the fighting on the first day of the battle. Blacknall was struck down by a bullet early in the attack as he tried to climb over a mortised fence running through the center of the field. While not life threatening, his injuries proved incredibly painful. During the retreat, Lt. Col. Green noticed that Blacknall spoke "with some difficulty of articulation as he had had a pretty rough operation of dentistry two days before, a musket-ball entering one side of his jaw, taking out a half-dozen of his teeth, and coming out on the other."[67]

The losses proved just as heavy among the men in the line companies. Private O'Daniel counted 28 casualties in his company alone, including both officers who were present on the field. "Our Company suffered dreadfully," he

---

65 Sarah Mercer Diary, Entry for April 24, 1864, in *ibid.*, 240.

66 "List of Officers Under Fire," NA; "The Late D. H. Christie," *Raleigh Daily Progress*, Aug. 3, 1863. For details on the career of Adjt. French, see John Lipscomb Johnson, *The University Memorial: Biographical Sketches of the Alumni of the University of Virginia Who Fell in the Confederate War* (Baltimore: Turnbull Brothers, 1871), 485-487.

67 Blacknall Memoirs, Blacknall Papers; Green, *Recollections and Reflections*, 178.

wrote a few days after the battle. "Their was three killed dead on the field. Three that was mortally wounded that died shortly after the fight was over that time. Two died before night and one in the night." According to O'Daniel, four others were "seriously wounded and ware still living when I left them on Saturday." The total also included several soldiers with more minor wounds and 11 unwounded men who were captured in the hollow.[68]

The outcome was almost as bad in Pvt. Coghill's company, which suffered 27 casualties. Lieutenant Charles William Champion, the only commissioned officer present with the company, was killed outright. The company lost one enlisted man killed, seven wounded, seven more who were both wounded and captured, and 11 unwounded men captured when the hollow was stormed by the Federals. Private Robert K. Turner was among those few who escaped capture by hiding among the piles of bodies in the gully.

Even the return of the slightly wounded men to duty did little to improve the situation. More than a week after the battle, Coghill informed his family that there still were fewer than 45 men present for duty in the entire regiment. Including the cooks, clerks, litter-bearers, and other detailed men, he counted no more than 80 men. About the same time, O'Daniel reported that only eight soldiers were present in his entire company. "We have no officer, neither Commissioned or non commissioned," he wrote. "Four Lieut[s] is all the officer[s] in the regiment."[69]

According to one veteran, Colonel Christie was so angry and distraught over the needless devastation suffered by his regiment that he summoned the survivors to the Hankey farmhouse on the morning of July 2. The scene that unfolded was one eyewitnesses never forgot. As the handful of men from the 23rd North Carolina gathered around the porch, the colonel lifted himself up in the litter that ultimately would later double as his death bed to proclaim "with much feeling" that "he might never live to again lead them in battle but he would see that 'the imbecile Iverson never should.'"[70]

---

68 O'Daniel to Torrence, July 9, 1863, in Monroe, "The Road to Gettysburg," 514. O'Daniel wrote down a nominal list of the casualties from the company on the back of his letter, which can be found only on the original copy in the Leonidas Chalmers Glenn Papers, SHC.

69 Portion of Letter, July 1863, James O. Coghill Papers; Coghill to Pappy, Ma and Mit, July 9, 1863, *ibid.*; Blacknall Memoirs, Blacknall Papers; O'Daniel to Torrence, July 9, 1863, in Monroe, "The Road to Gettysburg," 514.

70 Blacknall Memoirs, Blacknall Papers.

The mortally wounded Christie was not alone in his feeling of bitterness toward the brigade commander. Many others also expressed outrage at Iverson's failure to personally lead his troops into the fight. "Iverson's part in the heroic struggle of his brigade seems to have begun and ended with the order to move forward and 'Give them hell,'" Capt. Vines Turner complained. He further argued that the attack had failed because "our brigade commander (Iverson) after ordering us forward, did not follow us in that advance, and our alignment soon became false." Lieutenant Joseph Oliver agreed, commenting bitterly that "Gen. Iverson gave the order to forward and went back in the woods and left his brigade to take care of itself."[71]

For others, Iverson's decision to remain in the rear during the attack was cause for even harsher and more personal criticism. Stories soon began circulating that he had failed to accompany his troops onto the field because he was a coward. "Rumor had it that he not only remained in the rear but that a big chestnut log intervened between him and the battle and that more than once he reminded his staff that for more than one at a time to look over was an unnecessary exposure of person," an enlisted man in the 23rd North Carolina explained to Maj. Blacknall's son years later.[72]

The accounts of Iverson's cowardice on July 1 caught fire and spread quickly throughout the division. Among those who heard the stories was Sgt. Alexander S. "Sandie" Murdock from the 2nd North Carolina in Ramseur's Brigade. "Iverson was nowhere to be found on the battlefield," he explained in a letter to his brother about one month after the battle. "It is said that he took his position behind a tree about 1/2 mile from it." Murdock readily admitted that the news came to him as a secondhand account, noting simply that "such is the report."[73]

Major Campbell Brown, Ewell's stepson and observant staff member, also referred in his journal to "the well-known cowardly behavior of Iverson." According to Brown, the source of his information was hearsay from Generals Daniel and Rodes and from some of the survivors of Iverson's own brigade. The only account to support the widely held—but weakly sourced—belief that

---

71 Turner and Wall, "Twenty-Third Regiment," in Clark, *NC Regiments*, 2:235, 239; Oliver, "Recollections," 2.

72 Blacknall Memoirs, Blacknall Papers.

73 Alexander S. Murdock to My Dear Brother, Aug. 10, 1863, Raymond J. DeStefano, Private Collection, East Williston, New York.

Iverson was drunk that day surfaced several decades after the war from another soldier in Ramseur's Brigade. "General Ivison, who was drunk, I think, and a coward besides, was off hiding somewhere, while his brigade . . . was being beaten by the Yankees," he declared in his reminiscences.[74]

For his fellow officers, however, the most damning aspect of the sorry affair appeared in Iverson's own report to Rodes. In it, the brigadier reported that his line of battle in the hollow had gone over to the enemy which, wrote Iverson, "I characterized . . . as disgraceful." Although both Rodes and Ewell largely refrained from criticizing his actions in their official accounts of the fighting, his obvious panic in the middle of the battle, far removed from the front line, proved impossible to ignore. "The unfortunate mistake of General Iverson at this critical juncture in sending word to Major-General Rodes that one of his regiments had raised the white flag and gone over to the enemy might have produced the most disastrous consequences," Ewell announced in his official campaign report.[75]

Even before Ewell issued his official rebuke, Capt. Benjamin Robinson from the 5th North Carolina sent a detailed letter to Governor Vance strongly disputing the claim that his regiment had surrendered. "That charge I denounce as an infamous falsehood and malicious slander," Robinson declared. "No surrender was authorized; no order was given for a cessation of the fire; our colors were brought in triumph from the field, pierced with fifteen balls and the staff shattered into pieces." Vance responded by turning the message over for publication in a Raleigh newspaper.

In that same letter, Robinson vigorously denied the allegation that a large number of unwounded men from his regiment had been captured in the hollow. Instead, he insisted that nearly all of them continued to fight rather than surrender. "The pale bloody corpses of its noble men who lie sleeping on the hill sides near Gettysburg, the shrieks of its wounded on that field; the mangled bodies of its officers and soldiers, attest in tones of mighty eloquence to the gallantry of our Regiment on that occasion," he declared, "and stamp as a falsehood the ungenerous aspersions that have been leveled at its fair fame."[76]

---

74 Campbell Brown Journal, in Jones, *Campbell Brown's Civil War*, 207; Hufham, "Experiences of a Veteran," 454.

75 *OR* 27, pt. 2, 444.

76 Robinson to Vance, July 9, 1863, *Raleigh Daily Progress*, July 24, 1863.

Chapter Thirteen

We Have an Awful Night of It

General Lee began planning for the army's retreat to Virginia soon after the failure of Pickett's Charge on July 3. One of his primary concerns was providing adequate protection for the extensive wagon trains.

Lee summoned cavalry commander Brig. Gen. John D. Imboden to is headquarters about one o'clock in the morning on July 4 and ordered him to use his brigade and an artillery detachment to escort a wagon train of wounded. Organizing the huge endeavor took more time than expected, and the train did not begin rolling out of the Gettysburg area until about four o'clock that afternoon. All told, the line of wagons stretched some 17 miles and held 12,000 wounded men. Imboden's wagon train traveled west down the Chambersburg Pike through Cashtown Gap. After clearing the mountains, it turned southwest through Greencastle, proceeded south to Hagerstown, and moved on toward the Potomac River. Most of the injured who filled the wagons were from James Longstreet's and A. P. Hill's corps.

Two hours before Imboden's wagons began moving out of the area, the survivors from Iverson's Brigade were detached from the division and assigned to escort Richard Ewell's wagons on the long retreat across the mountains. In his diary, Surgeon William Marston recalled the men received orders "to change our position to follow our wagon train which is moving on the Hagerstown road." Sergeant Edward G. Butler from the brigade ordnance department explained that "our sadly depleted brigade was serving as van guard to the army, going in front of a wagon train several miles long the army at large acting as rear guard."[1]

Ewell's main column of wagons was ordered to take a more direct route southwest from Gettysburg through the town of Fairfield. The train would continue over the mountain gap along Maria Furnace Road before finally linking up with the Emmitsburg Turnpike just north of the Maryland border near Monterey Pass. From there, the wagons would follow the macadamized turnpike west to nearby Waynesboro before again turning south in the direction of Hagerstown and on to the major river crossing at Williamsport.[2]

Besides huge quantities of supplies, the vehicles assigned to the evacuation carried about 2,000 wounded men from Ewell's Second Corps, including a large number of injured from Rodes' Division. The most severely wounded were not well enough to make the difficult journey, and there was no choice but to leave them behind in the field hospitals. "During the night of the 4th, all the wounded who could walk or be transported in wagons and ambulances were sent to the rear . . . but nearly one-half of them, say about 760, were left in the hands of the enemy," reported Rodes. "This painful result was, of course, unavoidable."[3]

In Iverson's Brigade alone, five officers and about 240 sick and severely wounded men were left in the field hospital. One regimental surgeon, two assistant surgeons, two hospital stewards, and 17 others agreed to remain with their suffering comrades. Leaving friends behind proved especially difficult for some men to accept. "You doo not have any idea how bad that I hated to leave Lon," Pvt. W. J. O'Daniel of the 23rd North Carolina lamented to Sarah Torrence. "I asked the Doctor to let me stay with him but he would not." Of those who stayed, 47 officers and men, including Private Torrence, eventually died from their injuries while in Federal hands.[4]

---

1 Marston Diary, Entry for July 4, 1863, Emory; Edward G. Butler, "Soldier Reminiscences," 3, Military Collection, NCOAH.

2 OR 27, pt. 2, 326-327; Eric J. Wittenberg, "This Was a Night Never to Be Forgotten: The Midnight Fight in the Monterey Pass, July 4-5, 1863," *North & South Magazine*, 2, No. 6 (August 1999), 50-52.

3 OR 27, pt. 2, 557; "The Wounded at Gettysburg," *Raleigh Weekly Register*, Aug. 11, 1863.

4 W. J. O'Daniel to Mrs. Torrence, July 20, 1863, in Monroe, "The Road to Gettysburg," 516. For a detailed list of casualties in Iverson's Brigade, see Appendix 2.

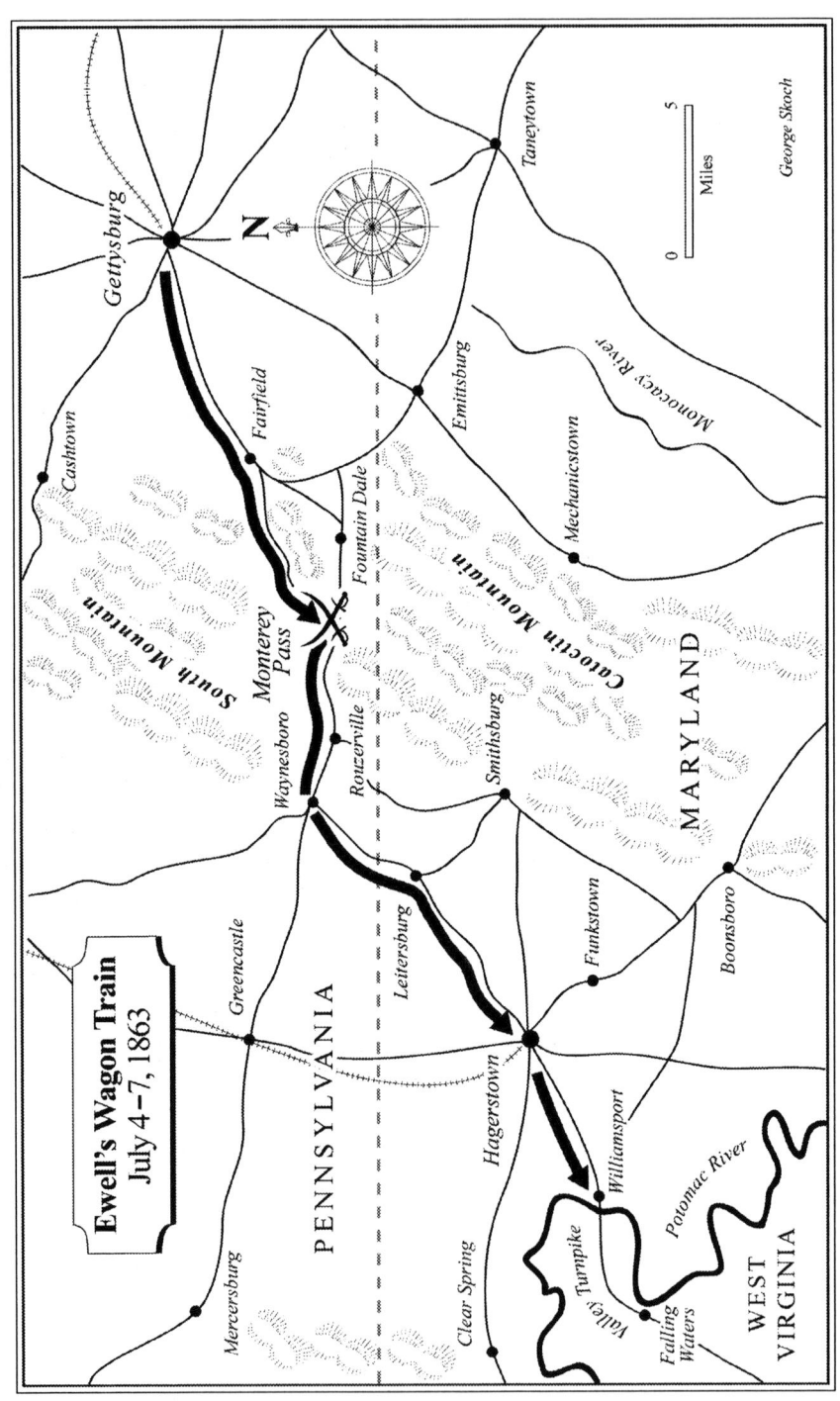

Most of the injured who could stand the trip were transferred initially to a temporary field hospital on the 184-acre farm owned by Jacob Plank. Among them were nearly 150 wounded officers and men from Iverson's Brigade. The property was located just west of the battlefield along the south side of the Fairfield Road. According to the owner, the Confederates used his "entire premises for Hospital purposes." In his postwar claim for damages, Plank pointed out that "there were 500 wounded in and on the premises, they took possession of the wheatfield, oatfield, and other fields, and part of an orchard for hospital purposes."[5]

Some of the vehicles full of wounded began moving out in the morning on July 4, but the wagon train was so long that it took much of the day to get the entire column underway. "Wagons, horses, mules, and cattle captured in Pennsylvania, the solid advantages of this campaign, have been passing slowly along this road (Fairfield) all day," explained Lt. Col. James Fremantle, who was visiting America from the British Army as an unofficial observer of the conflict. Fremantle went on to note that "so interminable was this train that it soon became evident that we should not be able to start till late at night."[6]

During the many hours it took to load the wounded into the wagons, the weather began to show signs of changing for the worse. By early evening on July 4, a major storm engulfed the area. One of the cavalrymen assigned to escort the train remembered that "just as the sun was going down, dark ominous clouds came trooping up from the west with thunder and lightning, and it was not long before the whole heavens were covered and rain was falling in torrents." Within a few hours, the heavy rain transformed every major road leading from town into a muddy quagmire.[7]

The large of number of wounded soldiers from the division carried by the vehicles in the retreating column added to the myriad of problems. Lieutenant Robert Park from O'Neal's Brigade was one of the few men who secured a place in a regulation army ambulance before the column finally got underway.

---

5 Quoted in Coco, *A Vast Sea of Misery*, 153; Kent Masterson Brown, *Retreat from Gettysburg: Lee, Logistics, and the Pennsylvania Campaign* (Chapel Hill: University of North Carolina Press, 2005), 107.

6 Arthur James Lyon Fremantle Diary, Entry for July 4, 1863, in Walter Lord, ed., *The Fremantle Diary: Being the Journal of Lieutenant Colonel Arthur James Lyon Fremantle, Coldstream Guards, on His Five Months in the Southern States* (Short Hills, NJ: Burford Books, 1954), 220.

7 Luther W. Hopkins, *From Bull Run to Appomattox: A Boy's View* (Baltimore: Fleet McGinley Co., 1908), 104.

"All able to walk were sent towards Maryland, and the badly wounded were hauled away," Park recorded in his journal. "Dr. Whitfield was very kind and placed me in the first ambulance, driven by Sam Slaton, in company with Lieutenant Wright and Captains Ross and Hewlett."[8]

Both the number and quality of the regulation ambulances left much to be desired. During the course of the war, the standard allocation had been reduced to only two ambulances per regiment. These small wagons were pulled by a single team of two horses or mules. Another difficulty was the lack of even the most basic accommodations for the injured men. "The ambulances were plain spring wagons without cushions, the bedding of the wounded men being such straw or hay as the driver was able to collect in the emergency," recalled a medical officer.[9]

Many of the other vehicles used to transport wounded from Gettysburg were even worse. Lieutenant Colonel Wharton Green from Junius Daniel's staff, who had been shot in the back of the head during the fighting on the first day, recalled that "Those who were able to stand the trip on wheels proceeded to do so, including Captain Bond of the Staff and myself, our friends having impressed a little one-horse team for the occasion." Colonel Risden Bennett from Ramseur's Brigade, suffering from a wound in the groin, reported that he and Col. Francis Parker endured the agonizing trip in a small buggy.[10]

Although nursing a painful injury to his jaw, Maj. Charles Blacknall gave up his spot in an ambulance and joined the retreat on the back of a horse. His decision drew a sharp protest from one of his relatives, who also served in his regiment. "I opposed this for he was too weak to ride," complained the 23rd North Carolina's Pvt. Tom Yancey to Blacknall's son after the war. "But he had his way. There was much delay in starting and many long wearying halts in the pouring rain." Yancey pointed out that the mortally wounded Col. Daniel Christie and Lt. Col Robert Johnston "went along with us driven in a light hack." Another small wagon carried Lt. Col. Nelson Slough and Maj. John Brooks, both of the 20th North Carolina.[11]

---

8 Park Diary, Entry for July 4, 1863, in Park, "War Diary," 14.

9 Donald B. Koonce, ed., *Doctor to the Front: The Recollections of Confederate Surgeon Thomas Fanning Wood, 1861-1865* (Knoxville: University of Tennessee Press, 2000), 66-67.

10 Green, *Recollections and Reflections*, 177; Bennett to Phillips, May 28, 1891, Stephen D. Ramseur Papers.

11 Blacknall Memoirs, Blacknall Papers.

Maj. Charles C. Blacknall was one of three wounded field officers from the 23rd North Carolina in General Ewell's wagon train on the long retreat through Monterey Pass. *North Carolina Office of Archives and History*

The long column of wagons also included about 3,400 Federal prisoners guarded by the remnants of Maj. Gen. George Pickett's Division. The situation was further complicated because many of the prisoners were suffering from wounds. "They could not care for their own wounded or ours, every ambulance was full," explained Capt. Frank E. Moran from the 73rd New York, one of the prisoners making the journey south. Moran, who had sustained an ankle injury, recalled that he "greatly preferred to limp and stumble with my comrades through the lakes of mud, than to ride in those terrible wagons and listen to the groaning wounded, many of whom were eloquently begging to be let out."[12]

The trip proved just as harrowing for the wounded Confederates carried in the wagons. "Night came on, the rain poured down," remarked Hospital Steward John Apperson, who was riding in one of the ambulances. "The road was very narrow, and in a very narrow pass. A stream dashed along, first on one side then on the other. Our train was loaded with wounded who shrieked often from the jolting of the vehicles." One of the artillerymen accompanying the wagons recalled that every time an ambulance hit a rock he could hear "the pitiful groans of the wounded."[13]

By the time the train approached the Maryland border near Waynesboro, the scene of misery was almost beyond comprehension. "I do not remember how long it was in passing, but it was miles and miles of horror," a local resident named Lida Welsh remembered years later. Welsh recalled vividly that she "could hear the groans and shrieks of agony as the heavy springless wagons jolted over the rough pike, mingled with the shouting and swearing of the drivers as they urged their jaded horses to greater speed—a huge aggregation of agony, despair, and death, hurrying back to the waiting arms of loving mothers, wives, sisters, and sweethearts."[14]

Amid the torrential downpours, the road was often blocked for miles by the heavy wagon traffic. "A pelting rain was making the mud and things in general worse every moment," Musician Jacob Nathaniel Raymer of the 4th North Carolina reported to his hometown newspaper. "But there [we] were, and had been for two hours waiting for the wagons to get out of the way." Raymer went

---

12 Charles T. Loehr, "The 'Old First' Virginia at Gettysburg," *SHSP*, 32 (1904), 40; Frank E. Moran to John S. Bachelder, Jan. 24, 1882, in Ladd, *Bachelder Papers*, 2:782.

13 Apperson Diary, Entry for July 4, 1863, in Roper, *Repairing the March*, 488; George M. Neese, *Three Years in the Confederate Horse Artillery* (Dayton, OH: Morningside House, 1988), 190.

14 Lida Welsh Bender, "Civil War Memories," *Waynesboro Record Herald*, Jan. 12, 1961.

on to note that "the men were getting impatient—wagon masters were galloping about whooping and hallowing, swearing at the drivers and hurrying them up, but it did no good."[15]

The pounding all-night thunderstorms spooked the teams of horses pulling the wagons and the huge droves of livestock herded along the road and made them nearly impossible to manage. "We had with us a good many cattle with which to feed the army," one of the cavalrymen escorting the column reported. Some of the cattle "got loose in the mountains and hills covered with timber, and between their constant bellowing and the flashes of lightning and crashing thunder the night was hideous in the extreme."[16]

The problems encountered by the wagon column began to affect the progress of the three infantry corps following along in the path of the train. "The night was very bad—thunder and lightning, torrents of rain—the road knee-deep in mud and water, and often blocked up with wagons 'come to grief,'" remarked British observer Lt. Col. Fremantle, who was traveling with Longstreet's Corps. "I pitied the wretched plight of the unfortunate soldiers who were to follow us." The progress up and down the line, he continued, "was naturally very slow indeed, and we took eight hours to go as many miles."[17]

When pursuing Federal cavalrymen threatened the safety of the wagon column, Jeb Stuart assigned Brig. Gen. William E. "Grumble" Jones to protecting it as it wound its way through the mountains. "The evening of July 4," Jones reported, "when it was reported the enemy were advancing in force on the Emmitsburg and Waynesborough road, I saw that General Ewell's train . . . was in danger, and asked to go with my command to its protection." His primary mission was to hold off the Federal cavalry until Iverson's Brigade and other infantry reinforcements arrived.

While nearly everyone acknowledged Jones to be a hard fighter and the best man in the army for outpost duty, the cavalry leader had only a small force of horsemen at his disposal that night. When his orders arrived, he set off to locate the train with the 6th and 7th Virginia Cavalry from his brigade and a section of two guns from the Ashby Battery of horse artillery commanded by Capt. Roger Preston Chew. The 7th Virginia Cavalry was soon called back and replaced by

---

15 "From the 4th North Carolina," July 20, 1863, *Carolina Watchman*, Aug. 3, 1863.

16 Hopkins, *From Bull Run*, 104-105.

17 Fremantle Diary, Entry for July 5, 1863, in Lord, *Fremantle Diary*, 221.

the 4th North Carolina Cavalry from Brig. Gen. Beverly H. Robertson's Brigade, which was already deployed in the vicinity of Fairfield Road.

The two regiments were joined by Companies B and D from the 1st Maryland Cavalry Battalion under Capts. George M. Emack and Warner G. Welsh. Company A from that battalion under Capt. Frank Bond remained well in the rear to watch for any enemy activity in the vicinity of Gettysburg and did not move to the front of the column until the following day. Opposing this meager defensive force were three full brigades of cavalry under the command of Brig. Gen. Judson Kilpatrick. His mission was to intercept and destroy Ewell's wagon train.

From the beginning, Jones encountered significant difficulties in just reaching the main part of the column. "This narrow and difficult way, rendered doubly so by heavy rain just fallen, was so blocked by wagons as to render it wholly impracticable to push the artillery or even the cavalry," he explained in his official report. Accompanied only by his staff, Jones hastened ahead "to rally all the stragglers of the train to support of whatever force might be guarding the road."[18]

Private John C. Donahue from the 6th Virginia Cavalry noted in his diary that, because the road was "very narrow and rough," the horsemen could make "but little headway and when we overtook the train our march became more difficult still and to add to the confusion the wagons were stopping every few yards." Another trooper in the same regiment described the "narrow mountain road" as so choked with wagons that "it was impossible for artillery to pass, and the cavalry only with great difficulty, only one horseman at a time being able to work his way through."[19]

The ordnance officer from Jones' Brigade recalled that the men from Chew's battery often slowed almost to a halt because the road was "badly cut up" by deep ruts. As he described it, "At many points where mountain streams crossed the road the weaker teams would stall and block the way. Through the mud and darkness, the artillery floundered along." Adding to the problems were the huge number of disabled vehicles along the road. He took note that "wagons with broken axles abandoned by their drivers had to be passed, and

---

18 OR 27, pt. 2, 752-753; Bond, "Company A, First Maryland Cavalry," 79.

19 John C. Donahue Diary, Entry for July 1863, Library of Virginia, Richmond, Virginia; John N. Opie, *A Rebel Cavalryman With Lee, Stuart, and Jackson* (Chicago: W. B. Conkey Co., 1899), 173.

sometimes broken-down ambulances filled with wounded were encountered."[20]

With the Confederate defenses spread so thinly along the road, individual acts of heroism protecting the train became almost commonplace. In the most critical action, Capt. Emack, together with fewer than 20 dismounted troopers and a single artillery piece, blocked Kilpatrick's main body of cavalry from reaching the column of wagons. Despite these nearly impossible odds, Emack and his small group maintained a stubborn resistance for more than five crucial hours along the turnpike directly east of the popular resort hotel known as the Monterey House.

The handful of troopers threw back repeated enemy attacks as the fighting escalated around Monterey Pass during the hours after midnight. "The enemy now increased their fire until it seemed as if nothing could stand before it," the captain recalled. "Still these men lay there under it coolly, awaiting an opportunity to strike another blow. The enemy's skirmishers at last walked into my line, and I was told that one of them actually trod on private Key who killed him on the spot. The enemy was again driven back." Emack pointed out that their "ammunition was entirely exhausted and some of my men actually fought with rocks; nor did they give back an inch."

About three o'clock that morning, Kilpatrick managed to advance his cavalry within 20 yards of Emack's position and gave the order to charge. Within minutes, the handful of defenders were forced back west of the Monterey House, where the remainder of his company had been held in reserve. "A running fight now ensued amid wagons and ambulances," reported Emack. "As we passed out of the mountain we met Captain Welsh's company of the 1st Maryland Cavalry at the junction of another road." Kilpatrick's troopers were "held in check for a moment, but they soon swept us aside, and on they went until they had captured all the wagons found in the road."[21]

As Emack pulled back, a Federal battery moved into place on a nearby hill, unlimbered, and began firing shells into the Southern column. "They bursted and whizzed and sparkled about uncomfortably near, which, some how, impressed on the minds of the wagoners the idea that the atmosphere was

---

20 William N. McDonald, *A History of the Laurel Brigade* (Baltimore: Sun Job Printing, 1907), 157.

21 Quoted in Henry B. McClellan, *The Life and Campaigns of Major-General J. E. B. Stuart* (Boston: Houghton-Mifflin Co., 1885), 353-355.

unhealthy—and such an everlasting getting away never was heard tell of," a musician from Ramseur's Brigade wryly observed. "It is well that the train was not loaded with glass ware." He went on to note that "the horses were whipped into a gallop, and the wagons seemed to bounce half a rod without touching the ground."[22]

The shells from the enemy battery also created a major obstacle for the troopers from the cavalry escort, who were just arriving on that section of the road. "The cavalry which was stretched along the wagon train was ordered to the front," Pvt. Luther Hopkins from the 6th Virginia Cavalry recalled. "It was with great difficulty that we could get past the wagons in the darkness, and hence our progress was slow." The Southern troopers eventually "dismounted and formed in line as best we could on either side of the road among the rocks and trees and then moved forward in an effort to drive the battery away from its position so we could resume our march."

As the men maneuvered into position, the only light they had to guide them came from the lightning and the "vivid flashes" from the enemy's cannons. Despite their proximity to the Federal battery, the result was ineffective. "Their firing did not do much execution, as they failed to get a proper range," observed a grateful Hopkins. "Besides, we were so close to them they were firing over our heads, but the booming of the guns that hour of night, with the roar of the thunder, was terrifying indeed, and beyond description." He recalled that the Confederates "would wait for a lightning flash and advance a few steps and halt, and then for a light from the batteries and again advance."[23]

Private Donahue from the same regiment encountered similar difficulties from the Federal artillery posted on the hill overlooking the road. "We dashed on at a gallop when the enemy opened upon us with a battery of artillery which completely commanded the road upon which we were advancing," he remarked in his diary. Another trooper from the 6th Virginia Cavalry recalled that the enemy artillery "poured an incessant fire of grape and canister in our direction; but, as there happened to be a bend in the road where we were halted, we suffered no injury."[24]

---

22 "From the 4th North Carolina," July 20, 1863, *Carolina Watchman*, Aug. 3, 1863.

23 Hopkins, *From Bull Run*, 107.

24 Donahue Diary, Entry for July 1863, Library of Virginia; Opie, *A Rebel Cavalryman*, 173.

A wounded officer from Junius Daniel's Brigade riding in the wagon train reported that Col. Dennis D. Ferebee eventually led part of the 4th North Carolina Cavalry into the fight near Monterey Pass. "He did so as promptly possible, but considerable difficulty was encountered in passing the wagons, as they entirely blocked up the road," the soldier remembered. "He found the enemy already in position and at work on our train" What he described as "a spirited fight ensued, but our men being overpowered were compelled to retire with some loss of prisoners."[25]

Despite the welcome addition of "some 60 or 70" Tar Heel troopers, the Confederates were still heavily outnumbered. Their arrival did little to change the precarious situation facing Emack's men along the road leading through the mountain gap. "The 4th North Carolina Cavalry now made its appearance at the junction of the two roads in my rear, and after General Jones and his staff had exhausted every means to get them to my assistance, I finally succeeded in getting a lieutenant and about ten men to dismount and advance to my line," Capt. Emack recalled.[26]

Grumble Jones, meanwhile, had been making slow but steady progress toward the scene of the Monterey Pass night fighting. After picking their way through the debris along the road, Jones and members of his staff reached the area just as the Federal cavalry began swarming into the column of wagons. "We got so mixed up with the enemy's cavalry that night that it was almost impossible to distinguish friend from foe," recalled one trooper. Although the situation was chaotic, Jones and his men pushed straight forward into the midst of the melee.[27]

Despite the best efforts of the Southern cavalrymen, the Federal attack proved so overwhelming that it swept the entire force of defenders before it. "The led horses, wagons, straggling infantry, and camp followers were hurled down the mountain in one confused mass," admitted Jones. "Ineffectual efforts were made for a rally and resistance, but without avail, until at the foot of the mountain a few joined Captain Welsh's Company of the Maryland Cavalry stationed at this point, and drove back the advance of the enemy." The cavalry general acknowledged, however, that the final stand was not strong enough and

---

25 "From the Forty-Third Reg't N. C. T.," July 20, 1863, *North Carolina Argus*, July 30, 1863.

26 OR 27, pt. 2, 753; Emack quoted in McClellan, *Campaigns of Stuart*, 355.

27 Hopkins, *From Bull Run*, 106-107.

that "this mere handful of men had to yield to the increasing numbers of the enemy."[28]

In the face of such odds, the troopers found it nearly "impossible to do anything." Many of the cavalrymen along that part of the road withdrew into the surrounding hills to await the appearance of Iverson's infantry and other reinforcements. "We remained all night in the mountains, the rain falling in torrents, during which time we had to listen to the rumbling of our wagons as the enemy carried them off without being able to do anything towards recapturing them," a private complained to his diary.[29]

All the while, the men suffering the most remained trapped in the wagons, which were repeatedly attacked by the Federal cavalry. The most dangerous moments occurred when the column was forced to halt. "It was a bright moonlight night, about ten o'clock, when . . . a heavy ordnance wagon loaded with damaged guns, in attempting to pass our little wagon took off a wheel and dropped us in the middle of the road," remembered staff officer Lt. Col. Green. "On the instant, a score of blue-coated cavalry were upon us with their revolvers leveled almost in touch." Green, together with his companions in the wagon, were now prisoners of war.[30]

The enemy troopers seized several other nearby wagons filled with wounded officers from Junius Daniel's Brigade. For a short time during the swirling chaos, all three of the wounded field officers from the 23rd North Carolina in Iverson's Brigade were captured. Confederate cavalry managed to rescue Colonel Christie and Lieutenant Colonel Johnston but could not reach Major Blacknall. The next day, however, the intrepid injured major decided on an escape plan. He threw a rubber raincoat over his gray uniform and boldly rode away. Luck was with him for awhile. Just before he reached safety, however, Blacknall "fell in a stupor" from the morphine he had taken for his wounds and was recaptured.[31]

---

28 OR 27, pt. 2, 753.

29 Donahue Diary, Entry for July 1863, Library of Virginia.

30 Green, *Recollections and Reflections*, 177-178.

31 Blacknall Memoirs, Blacknall Papers. For additional details on the capture of the officers from Daniel's Brigade, see Charles F. Bahnson to My Dear Father, July 10, 1863, in Chapman, *Bright and Gloomy Days*, 69 and Henry E. Shepherd, "Wounded and Captured," included in C. E. Graham, ed., *Under Both Flags: A Panorama of the Civil War* (Chicago: Monarch Book Co., 1896), 76.

Throughout the night, swarms of Federal troopers continued to probe for weaknesses up and down the line of wagons. "The night was a dark, dreary, rainy one," Lt. Park from O'Neal's Brigade explained. "At 1 o'clock A. M. we started after a long halt on Fairfield road, towards Hagerstown, riding over an execrable mountain road. We were suffering, wet and anxious." He noted that "the Yankee cavalry attacked our train and took several of our wagons, including the third one in our rear." Colonel Bennett from Ramseur's Brigade, together with Col. Parker, escaped the Federal cavalry on another part of the road only "by their very eyelids."[32]

The nightmare in the mountain pass made it clear to everyone involved that the only real chance to save Ewell's large Second Corps wagon train was if the four infantry regiments in Iverson's Brigade reached it in time. The journey proved to be much more difficult than any of Iverson's men expected when they set off from Gettysburg earlier that day. According to one officer from the 5th North Carolina, he and his men "marched nearly all night over a dark mountain road through a severe rain." Another soldier from the 12th North Carolina reported in a letter home that the roads were "so bad that we could scearcely get a long." Surgeon Marston from the same regiment summed up the exhausting and frustrating ordeal by noting simply, "we have an awful night of it."[33]

During the difficult journey the infantry slogged past a wagon driven by a slave owned by the late Col. Isaac Avery of the 6th North Carolina. He was hauling his master's body home for a proper burial. According to Sgt. Walter Montgomery of the 12th North Carolina, the servant was repeatedly "assailed" with orders to bury the body along the road because of the "increasing offensiveness" of the corpse. "He was cursed and beaten with pieces of fence rail by some of the troops; but he remained faithful to his trust," Montgomery recalled with some admiration. "With several other North Carolina soldiers, I came to the old negro's rescue, and enabled him to carry his charge to a place of safety." The black driver managed to transport the body only as far as

---

32 Park Diary, Entry for July 4, 1863, in Park, "War Diary," 14; Bennett to Phillips, May 28, 1891, Stephen D. Ramseur Papers. For another account of the attack on the train, see John T. Gay to My Dear Wife, July 10, 1863, Nix-Price Collection.

33 OR 27, pt. 2, 581; Company K, 5th North Carolina, Record of Events, July-August, 1863, Record Group 109, NA; Varda Hallman to C. C. Durham, Aug. 6, 1863, in Thompson, *North Carolina Confederate Letters*, 1:82; Marston Diary, Entry for July 4, 1863, Emory.

Williamsport, where Avery, who was mortally wounded in the evening assault against East Cemetery Hill, was laid to rest in a local cemetery.[34]

The problems for Iverson's men mounted as they approached the area around Monterey Pass. Because the wagons in the column had started out well ahead of his troops, Iverson "did not overtake it till midnight, at which time I learned that it been cut in two by the enemy at the turnpike." Iverson "hastened forward all my troops" on a journey through the mountains that was "the most fatiguing march I ever witnessed." Despite their proximity to the fighting, his men soon found it nearly impossible to make their way any farther due to the darkness and the heavy wagon traffic.[35]

As Iverson's infantry did their best to reach the wagons, the ambulance carrying Hospital Steward Apperson arrived within about three miles of the intersection with the turnpike to Waynesboro. To his dismay, large numbers of men were escaping in every direction. "Here it became very evident that the enemy was at work on the train," Apperson recorded in his diary. "The cannon was firing still on our left. Screamed orders could be heard ahead. Wagon Drivers came back with their trains." The few Southern cavalrymen, he added were "wandering and skulking through and like the drivers were making for the rear."

By midnight, the road was so clogged with wagons that Apperson could go no farther. Iverson's leading troops had also been forced to a standstill. The congestion along Maria Furnace Road was so bad that the steward "heard Gen. Iverson say that nothing could be done until daylight." Along with many others, Apperson continued to hold in place just short of the junction with the turnpike leading to Waynesboro. Several hours passed before "the remnant" of Iverson's Brigade was "sent up to protect the train."[36]

Iverson's troops finally reached the scene of the fighting just after dawn on July 5 and promptly engaged the enemy. Lieutenant Henry Rudisill from the 12th North Carolina recalled that his regiment "formed a skirmish line on each side of the road." Captain Yancey M. Wilfong took command of the men on the left of the road, while Rudisill supervised those on the right. From there, they engaged the Federal troopers attacking along that section of the road. Rudisill

---

34 Montgomery, "Memoirs," Elizabeth Montgomery Collection.

35 *OR* 27, pt. 2, 581.

36 Apperson Diary, Entry for July 4, 1863, in Roper, *Repairing the March*, 488.

remembered that "as the enemies Cavalry charged the rear wagons we captured about a dozen of them."[37]

A single section from Chew's Confederate battery of horse artillery joined the infantry along the turnpike. Within minutes, the gunners unlimbered their pieces and prepared for action. "Got a place for one gun and sent a few shots," one of them recorded in his diary. "Was out on the pike as day broke and opened fire. They have fallen back after cutting down a few wagons." From there, the gunners took up position directly alongside Iverson's troops. "There are two regiments of infantry supporting us, they threw up a fine breastwork in an hour," wrote an artillerist, who seemed surprised anyone could produce defensive works so fast while so tired. "The firing has been incessant and this has been the most horrible night I have ever spent."[38]

Within a short time, Iverson's infantry shoved back Kilpatrick's cavalry from the wagon train. "In passing through the mountain gaps, the enemy's cavalry attempted to halt and destroy the train, which would have been done if our brigade had not pressed forward and drove them off," Sgt. Adolphus Pitcher from the 12th North Carolina declared in his company's official record of events. Pitcher was right. Without the involvement of the infantry, many more wagons would have been lost. Iverson reported his men captured a few prisoners and eventually got "the remnants of the train" back onto the turnpike leading west.[39]

About this time Brig. Gen. Ambrose R. Wright's Georgia Brigade from A. P. Hill's Third Corps arrived from Fairfield to support Iverson's troops. "About daylight, I came upon the rear of the train upon the top of the mountain, but found the road so completely blocked up as to prevent my further progress," Wright recalled. The Georgian halted his command and rode to the front by himself. "I found General Iverson near Monterey, and not far from the Waynesborough turnpike," reported Wright, "and from him learned

---

37 George W. Hahn, *The Catawba Soldier of the Civil War* (Hickory, NC: Heritage Printing Co., 1908), 95.

38 Charles W. McVicar Diary, Entry for July 4, 1863, in Ada Bruce Desper Bradshaw, ed., *The Civil War Diary of Charles William McVicar* (Hampton, VA: n.p., 1977), 18; Charles W. McVicar to Dear Sister Kate, July 11, 1863, Charles William McVicar Papers, Steward Bell Jr. Archives Room, Handley Regional Library, Winchester, Virginia.

39 *OR* 27, pt. 2, 581; Company F, 12th North Carolina, Record of Events, July-August, 1863, Record Group 109, NA. For an overview of the fighting at Monterey Pass, see Wittenberg, "This Was a Night," 44-54.

that all the danger to the train had passed, and I directed him to move on in the direction of Waynesborough as rapidly as possible, so as to enable our troops to get through the mountain pass."[40]

Evidence of the chaos during the night remained visible all along the road as more Confederate troops tramped through the area after sunrise. A gunner from Chew's horse artillery noticed that "some of the wagons were chopped to pieces and others were burned." The fighting had left "debris, such as skillets, frying pans, camp kettles, and all sorts of camp furniture scattered all along the road." Jubal Early's 15-year-old nephew, who was traveling with the main column, "passed heaps of burnt and burning wagons."[41]

Signs of the heavy toll suffered among the already wounded men in the train were also visible. Many of the injured had been crushed to death when their wagons fell into the steep ravines along the route. "The firing among the horses attached to the wagons that had gone out on the open pike frightened them to such an extent that they were stampeded, and we saw the next morning as we rode along that some of the wagons had tumbled over the precipice on the right, carrying with them the horses; also the wounded soldiers that were riding in the wagons," wrote a private from the cavalry escort.[42]

Fortunately for Iverson's Tar Heels, their losses during the early morning fighting were not of the killed or wounded variety. Only one officer and four enlisted men among the brigade's wounded were captured during the Federal attacks. An additional eight men were lost among the teamsters and other detailed men assigned to the wagons. The worst indignity for many was the seizure of their personal baggage by the marauding troopers. "I am feeling awful today," Marston complained in his diary. "I have lost all my belongings—having been captured by the Yankees." The Federal troopers also captured "about 150 to 200 wagons from us & a great many wounded men."[43]

After being relieved by the lead regiments from Hill's Third Corps, Iverson's troops pushed on a few miles before going into camp for the night. On the following day, July 6, they continued escorting Ewell's wagon train

---

40 OR 27, pt. 2, 625.

41 Neese, *Three Years in the Confederate Horse Artillery*, 192; Early, "Southern Boy's Experience," 422.

42 Hopkins, *From Bull Run to Appomattox*, 107.

43 Marston Diary, Entry for July 5, 1863, Emory.

We Have an Awful Night of It 317

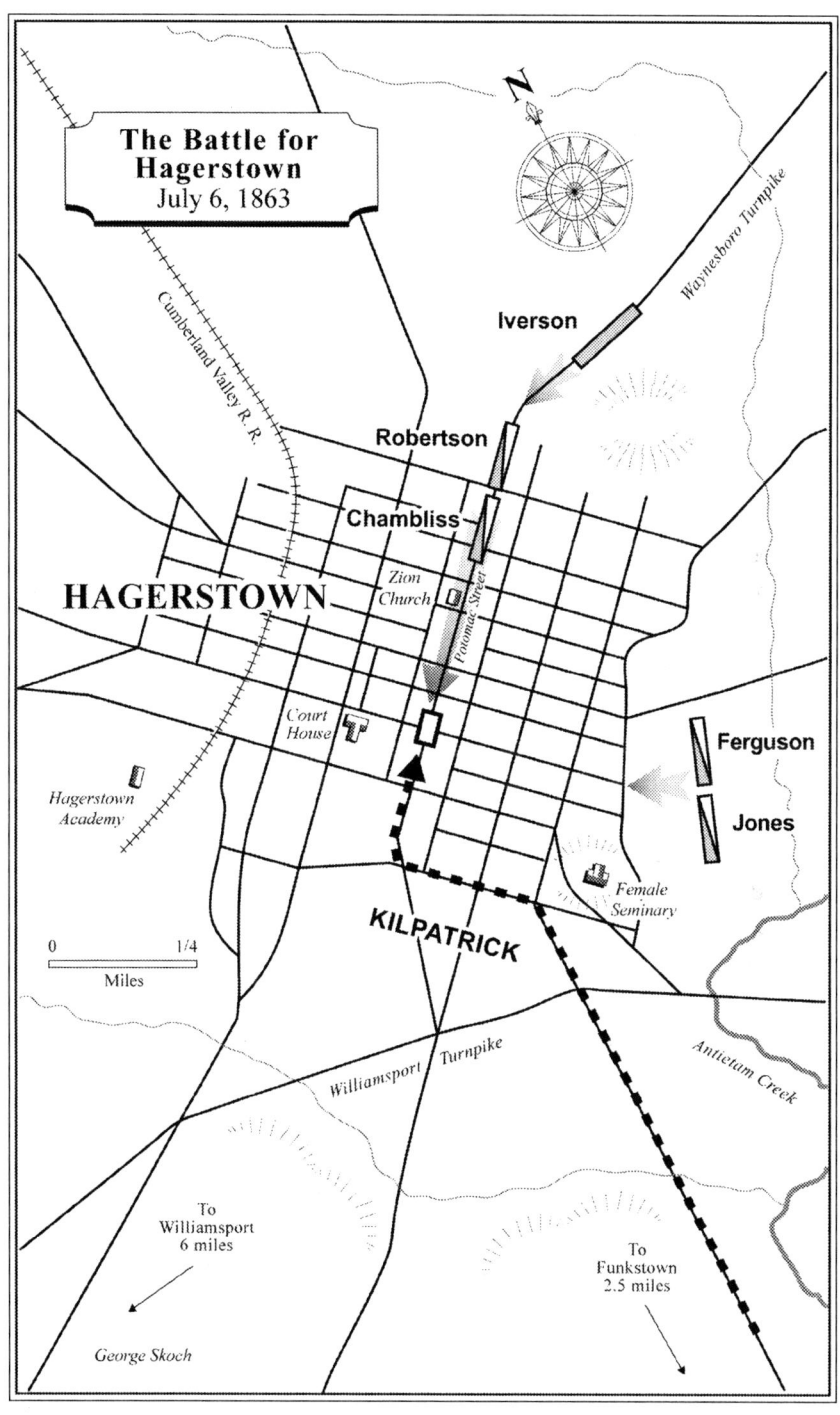

along the road toward Williamsport. The Tar Heels and wagons made it as far as Hagerstown early that afternoon, where they once again confronted raiding Federal cavalrymen. The fighting there began about noon when leading elements from Kilpatrick's division thundered into town from the south and surprised several Confederate cavalry regiments resting in the streets.

Within a short time, brigades commanded by Col. John R. Chambliss and Beverly Robertson were in full retreat. Following a flurry of hand-to-hand combat in the streets of Hagerstown, the Confederate cavalry eventually made a determined defensive stand in the northern part of town near the Zion Reformed Church. About that time, Albert Jenkins' cavalry brigade, under the temporary command of Col. Milton J. Ferguson, together with part of the horse artillery, joined the action from east of town. Iverson's men arrived about three o'clock in the afternoon, providing the first infantry reinforcements on the scene.[44]

After sending "the train back to the rear," Iverson quickly deployed his skirmishers at the northern end of town in support of the two beleaguered cavalry brigades. According to Sgt. Butler, the "sharpshooters were in line looking for trouble" from the moment they took the field, and "it did not take long to find it." With his skirmishers in the lead, Iverson's pushed his troops forward into the center of town along North Potomac Street. From there, they engaged in a significant fight in the vicinity of the central square.[45]

Some of the most dangerous gunfire came from Federal troopers posted in nearby buildings. At least one of Iverson's men who had strayed too far in front of the main skirmish line was felled in this manner. "He was in my squad of men, and just persisted in being a few yards ahead of the line," Sgt. Miles O. Sherrill from the 12th North Carolina recalled. "I called to him, and on this occasion had warned him of the danger." Seconds later and just a few yards away "from a basement door . . . a soldier fired and killed him." The Federal made good his escape despite efforts to locate him.[46]

Within a few minutes, Iverson's men gained the upper hand in the fight. Along with troopers from Jenkins' Brigade, they began forcing the Federals

---

44 Ted Alexander, "Ten Days in July: The Pursuit to the Potomac," *North & South Magazine*, 2, No. 6 (August 1999), 16-18.

45 *OR* 27, pt. 2, 581; Butler, "Reminiscences."

46 Miles O. Sherrill, "At Gettysburg in 1863: Some Reminiscences of One of the Participants in the Famous Battle," *Charlotte Daily Observer*, July 22, 1912.

back from the center of town to the south along Potomac Street. Private John Coghill reported in a letter home to his family that "when wee got there the Yankes had possession of the town but wee sharp shooters soon had the town and the Yankes before us running; so we whiped them at that place." Casualties included Capt. Massilon F. Taylor from the 12th North Carolina, who was mortally wounded in the Hagerstown skirmish.[47]

While Kilpatrick's main body began evacuating to the west, Col. Nathaniel P. Richmond from the 1st West Virginia Cavalry remained behind to cover the withdrawal. The two sides were soon engaged in another fight on the edge of town that spread along both sides of the turnpike. "More than once the deployed lines wavered—each side gaining ground only to lose it soon after," observed a Confederate sergeant. "Once when we pushed them a little further than before they assembled and took refuge behind a stone farm dwelling." Iverson's troops "were about a hundred and fifty yards away, lying behind a rail fence—on their side of it was tangled clover stretching from the fence to the dwelling."

Iverson's sharpshooters finally routed the enemy from their position with one swift assault. "Immediately some one shouted, 'Boys let's charge 'em,'" remembered Sgt. Butler. "There was prompt response to this appeal—and the clover was still more tangled. When half way to the house we saw that they were scampering as fast as their legs could carry them." This unexpected result "renewed both our zeal and speed." According to one Southern private, he and his comrades "ran after them about three miles."[48]

By early evening, the last of the Federal cavalrymen were in full retreat from the vicinity of Hagerstown. Despite catching Jeb Stuart's troopers by surprise in the initial attack into town, Kilpatrick's men sustained 19 killed, 50 wounded, and nearly 200 captured or missing. A Federal colonel admitted in his official report that "the majority of the casualties in this engagement were occasioned by the fire of the enemy's infantry, who posted in almost every house, poured in a most destructive volley on our men as they charged through."[49]

---

47 Coghill to Pappy, Ma and Mit, July 17, 1863, John Fuller Coghill Letters; John F. Coghill, Undated Portion of Letter, James O. Coghill Papers.

48 Butler, "Reminiscences"; John F. Coghill, Undated Portion of Letter, James O. Coghill Papers.

49 OR 27, pt. 1, 193, 1,006. For detailed accounts of the fighting at Hagerstown, see Brown, *Retreat from Gettysburg*, 219-233 and Eric J. Wittenberg, J. David Petruzzi, and Michael F.

After the bloody fiasco in the Forney field on July 1, the well-executed defense of the train and the successful Hagerstown fight pleased Iverson's men. A company commander in the 5th North Carolina proudly noted how they "arrived at Hagerstown about 3 o'clock P.M. when and where the enemies cavalry made a dash on the wagon train but was repulsed handsomely." He bragged that "not one man of the charging squadron escaped to tell the tale." A sergeant from the 12th North Carolina proclaimed that "with the assistance of Gen Stuart's Cavalry we succeeded in driving them off." Surgeon Marston joined in, declaring that "we were attacked at Hagerstown by the Yankee cavalry but we completely rout them & drive them before us on the Hagerstown road." Iverson was also pleased. "I believe [we] killed, wounded, and captured as many of the enemy as I had men," he reported.[50]

Iverson's conduct during the fighting won strong praise from Rodes in his official report on the campaign. "By a forced march, he arrived at Hagerstown soon after the passage of the train, and found a heavy force of the enemy's cavalry driving back our cavalry through the streets," wrote Rodes. "Making a hasty but skillful disposition of his troops, he soon routed them, capturing a considerable number." Rodes acknowledged that "great credit is due Brigadier-General Iverson for the handsome and prompt manner in which this affair was managed."[51]

The success at Hagerstown cost the brigade three men killed, seven wounded, and two captured. Of the wounded, one officer and three enlisted men died from their injuries. Most of the losses were suffered by the 12th North Carolina. Lieutenant Ward of that regiment admitted in a letter to his parents that the duty of escorting the wagon train "was conferred on us, as we were so badly cut up, but it has proved no favor."[52]

With the route to the Potomac once again open, the brigade escorted the wagons to within about two miles of the wide river before halting for the night.

Nugent, *One Continuous Fight: The Retreat from Gettysburg and the Pursuit of Lee's Army of Northern Virginia, July 4-14, 1863* (New York: Savas Beatie, 2008), 107-122. *One Continuous Fight* is the first in-depth military study of the entire retreat.

50 Company H, 5th North Carolina, Record of Events, July-August, 1863, NA; Company F, 12th North Carolina, Record of Events, July-August, 1863, *ibid.*; Marston Diary, Entry for July 6, 1863, Emory.

51 OR 27, pt. 2, 558.

52 "Casualties in the Battle of Hagerstown," *Raleigh Weekly Register*, Aug.12, 1863; Ward to Ma and Pa, July 7, 1863, *Raleigh Weekly State Journal*, July 22, 1863.

Iverson's men were on the move again early the next morning on July 7. After reaching Williamsport later in the day, Iverson finally relinquished control over the wagon train and began to enforce order among the mostly leaderless troops who clogged the streets. "Seeing great confusion," he explained, "I assumed the duties of provost-marshal, and used my brigade for several days as guards, &c."[53]

Despite the safe arrival of the wagon train, the bulk of Lee's Army of Northern Virginia remained stuck in Maryland. The heavy rain had swollen the river to a depth of more than 13 feet at Williamsport, rendering the fords along that part of the Potomac completely impassable. Further retreat was impossible until the water level dropped considerably and the pioneers rebuilt the pontoon bridge across the river a few miles downstream at Falling Waters. Especially worrisome was the likely prospect that the bulk of Meade's Army of the Potomac, which was moving in pursuit, would trap the Confederates with their backs against the river.[54]

The outcome of the campaign was still to be determined, but Alfred Iverson's tenure as a brigade commander under Robert Rodes was over. Iverson's costly failures at Gettysburg on July 1 were so egregious that General Lee issued an order relieving him as head of the brigade on July 10. Iverson's regiments were attached to Ramseur's Brigade and instructed to rejoin the main army outside Hagerstown. The erstwhile brigade commander, meanwhile, was directed to take control of Williamsport as provost marshal. No official reason was provided for the dismissal, but Ramseur confided in a letter to his fiancée that Iverson "has been relieved from the Command of his Brigade for misconduct at Gettysburg."[55]

Following his removal from command, Iverson served as provost marshal at his headquarters in the Taylor House Hotel on Potomac Street. He remained on duty at Williamsport until late in the evening on July 13. "When I got up this morning I found that Genl. Iverson, who is provost marshall of this place and who is stopping at the same hotel was gone," a regimental surgeon assigned to a hospital in the same building wrote in his diary the following day. The general "had left during the night and there was no one left in Williamsport

---

53 OR 27, pt. 2, 581; Brown, *Retreat from Gettysburg*, 284.

54 "Gen. Lee and His Sick and Wounded," *Selma Morning Reporter*, Aug. 1, 1863.

55 OR 27, pt. 3, 993; Stephen D. Ramseur to Ellen Richmond, July 29, 1863, in Letter Extracts, Stephen Dodson Ramseur Papers.

except the wounded who could not be removed, a few stragglers from the army, and myself."[56]

After making his way safely into Virginia, Iverson was formally relieved from all duties with the Virginia army on July 16 and directed to report to Richmond for further orders. In a move that surely surprised many, Lee revoked the order just three days later and assigned Iverson to the temporary command of a Louisiana Brigade in Johnson's Division. Its commander, Brig. Gen. Francis R. T. Nicholls, was severely wounded at Chancellorsville and additional casualties amongst its field officers at Gettysburg had left the brigade bereft of experienced leaders.[57]

The decision to reinstate Iverson came as no surprise for Ewell's staff officer Campbell Brown, who was privy to much of the inside information circulating in the upper echelons of the Second Corps. Brown remained firmly convinced that Iverson's powerful friends in the Confederate government at Richmond had once again stepped in to save him from disgrace. Although there is no direct evidence to support his claim, Brown wrote in his journal soon after the war that Iverson "was relieved at once & sent back to await trial— but— being forwarded to Richmond, got off scot-free.[58]

After turning over control of Williamsport to Pickett's Division, the troops from Iverson's former brigade marched back to Hagerstown and assisted in erecting a series of defensive breastworks around the town. With the swollen river behind them, nearly everyone in the army anticipated that a major enemy attack was only a matter of time. "My opinion is that another great battle will be fought before we leave Maryland," Lieutenant Ward of the 12th North Carolina wrote to his parents. Sergeant Montgomery tried to remain upbeat when he insisted in a letter to his father that "we will whip the enemy, I have no doubt." He argued that "we whiped them in Pennsylvania, and we are going to Sharpsburg to complete our victory and change our front."[59]

On the morning of July 13, however, Iverson's former troops once again fell back toward Williamsport and set up pickets on Clear Springs Road. Later

---

56 James B. Clifton Diary, Entry for July 14, 1863, NCOAH. Clifton served as surgeon for the 53rd Georgia in Semmes' Brigade from McLaws' Division.

57 *OR* 27, pt. 3, 993, 1025; Warner, *Generals in Gray*, 224.

58 Campbell Brown Journal, in Jones, *Campbell Brown's Civil War*, 207.

59 Ward to Ma and Pa, July 7, 1863, *Raleigh Weekly State Journal*, July 22, 1863; Montgomery to Father, July 8, 1863, *Raleigh Weekly State Journal*, July 29, 1863.

that evening, they were recalled and ordered to cross the receding Potomac into Virginia. "We took our stand and two days wated for the Yankes to attack us but they did not come so we recrossed the river," Private Coghill explained. Surgeon Marston observed that his regiment "retired at 1 'clock in the night and ordered to cross the river that the balance of our brigade had crossed."[60]

The slow process of evacuating Rodes' Division got underway about sundown near the point where Conococheague Creek flows into the Potomac. "It was very dark, raining, and excessively muddy," Rodes recalled. "The men had to wade through the aqueduct, down the steep bank of soft and slippery mud, in which numbers lost their shoes and down which many fell." The water, he noted, "was cold, deep, and rising; the lights on either side of the river were dim, just affording enough light to mark the places of entrance and exit."[61]

Iverson's former Tar Heel's, together with Ramseur's regiments, began crossing just after midnight about 100 yards upstream from the aqueduct. "On we went in the dark through mud and water nearly up to our knees," Lt. William Calder reported to his mother. "It was only six miles to the river, yet day had lighted up the east before we reached this side. The fording was a very ticklish business." The river "was so deep it came up to our armpits, and we had to catch hold of each other's hands to prevent being swept away." According to Marston, the last of Iverson's men did not make it to the other side of the river until "about ten o'clock in the morning."[62]

Despite the difficult problems they encountered, Rodes' exhausted men carried out the evacuation across the rain-swollen river with almost complete success. "We crossed without the loss of a single man, but I regret to say with the loss of some 25,000 or 30,000 rounds of ammunition, which were unavoidably wetted and spoiled," Rodes explained in his official report for the campaign. "After crossing I marched, by orders, a short distance beyond Falling Waters, and then bivouacked; and there ended the Pennsylvania campaign, so far as this division was concerned."[63]

---

60 Company F, 12th North Carolina, Record of Events, July-August, 1863, NA; Coghill to Pappy, Ma and Mit, July 17, 1863, John Fuller Coghill Letters; Marston Diary, Entry for July 13, 1863, Emory.

61 OR 27, pt. 2, 558-559.

62 William Calder to Dear Mother, July 17, 1863, Calder Papers; Marston Diary, Entry for July 13, 1863, Emory.

63 OR 27, pt. 2, 558-559.

The close of the campaign could not have come soon enough for most of the men in Iverson's former brigade. Of the 127 officers and 1,528 enlisted men who were present at Carlisle on June 30, only about 50 officers and 658 enlisted men made it back unscathed to the Virginia shore two weeks later. Battle casualties at Gettysburg alone amounted to 70 officers and 790 men killed, wounded, and captured. Additional losses to desertion and fighting during the retreat swelled the final total for the campaign to 77 officers and 870 enlisted men.[64]

Despite that tremendous toll, Iverson's survivors remained remarkably sanguine about the future course of the war. "I had hoped that this campaign would end the war, but fear it will prove of but little effect, but let us hope on and trust in God, and our enduring army for final success," Lt. Ward wrote home. Sergeant Montgomery proved even more defiant. "Do not feel uneasy about your son and the balance of our Brave Boys," he told his father. "We will come out all right." We had indeed endured much, he continued, but "there is no such thing as discouragement in this army."[65]

---

[64] For numbers and losses in Iverson's Brigade, see Appendix 2.

[65] Ward to Ma and Pa, July 7, 1863, *Raleigh Weekly State Journal*, July 22, 1863; Montgomery to Father, July 8, 1863, *Raleigh Weekly State Journal*, July 29, 1863.

Epilogue

The Glory it Had is Now Passed Away

Once the survivors returned to the relative safety of Virginia, Alfred Iverson's former brigade consolidated temporarily into a pair of regiments under the command of Col. Thomas Miles Garrett from the 5th North Carolina. If he was hoping for something more permanent, Garrett was soon disappointed. Early that September, Col. Robert D. Johnston from the 23rd North Carolina assumed command of the shattered brigade. Johnston's arrival at the brigade's camp, however, was delayed for almost two months while he recovered from the severe wounds he suffered at Gettysburg. According to one account, the appointment pleased the brigade's survivors. The 5th North Carolina's Capt. Jacob Brookfield noted in his diary that the men in the ranks gave him "a cordial welcome" when he rejoined the brigade on November 16.

Cordial welcome aside, Johnston's selection as the new brigade commander came as a surprise to the men in its ranks. The 26-year-old Johnston had only recently been promoted to colonel following the death of Col. Daniel Christie. A graduate of the University of North Carolina, Johnston studied law at the University of Virginia and became a prominent lawyer in Lincoln County, where he helped organize a local militia company as the conflict with the North approached. After entering the service as a captain, he

The selection of Col. Robert D. Johnston from the 23rd North Carolina as Brig. Gen. Alfred Iverson's replacement in September of 1863 stirred considerable controversy. *Cook Collection, Valentine Museum*

was elected lieutenant colonel in May of 1862 and suffered severe wounds on two occasions, once at Seven Pines and again at Gettysburg.[1]

Johnston's appointment as Iverson's replacement soon drew the ire of Governor Zeb Vance, who had favored Garrett's promotion. Once again, the dispute centered on the issue of pre-war politics. Vance noted that Johnston had openly supported secession as the war approached, unlike Garrett who

---

1 Stephen Dodson Ramseur to Ellen Richmond, Aug. 15, 1863, in Letter Extracts, Ramseur Papers; Warner, *Generals in Gray*, 162-163; Brookfield Diary, Entry for Nov. 16, 1863, NA.

took a moderate stance on leaving the Union. When several other former moderates on secession were passed over for promotion, Vance complained directly to President Davis that there "seemed to have been a studied exclusion of all once termed anti-secessionists" from promotion in the army.

Most of all, Vance disputed strongly the president's claim that his appointments were based on military considerations alone. "Now does it not seem strange, when it is remembered that two-thirds of the people of this State were opposed to secession until Lincoln's proclamation, that God should have endowed the remaining one-third with all the military talents; that 'military considerations' should divest two-thirds of our citizens, however brave, patriotic, and intelligent, of the capacity to serve their country except in the ranks or as subordinate officers?" Vance seethed.

The governor supported his charges by observing that Iverson and Johnston were selected for promotion over Duncan McRae and Garrett. As far as Vance was concerned, both cases clearly demonstrated that they had been strongly favored by President Davis because of their open support for secession in the months leading up to the outbreak of war. "I make no complaint against any of these gentlemen, but only wonder at the passing strangeness of this singular freak of nature in so partially and arbitrarily distributing the military capacity of the country," Vance wrote Davis.[2]

Vance was still grappling with President Davis over the issue of promotions when Johnston moved to retain Capt. Don Halsey as assistant adjutant general. Despite his earlier involvement with the dispute in the 20th North Carolina, Halsey had earned the respect of the entire brigade by his heroic actions on July 1 in the fighting at Gettysburg. He also won high praise from those in higher command in the army. Generals Ewell, Rodes, and Iverson all cited him for gallantry in rallying the the brigade's shattered troops in the bloody hollow just before the successful attack into the town.[3]

In recognition of Halsey's "meritorious service," Johnston recommended him that November for promotion to major. This action was necessary because the rank of major was normally reserved only for officers serving as assistant adjutant general on the division or corps staffs. Although both Rodes and Ramseur added their endorsements, the War Department denied his promotion. Early in 1865, Halsey transferred reluctantly to the division

2 *OR* 51, pt. 2, 831.

3 *Ibid.*, 451, 559, 580.

commanded by Brig. Gen. Gabriel C. Wharton, where he served until the end of the war in a staff position with the rank of major.⁴

Despite being passed over in favor of Johnston, Colonel Garrett remained more determined than ever to gain his promotion to general during the months following Gettysburg. In late September, he sent a letter of protest to Samuel Cooper in Richmond blaming Rodes for his failure to receive command of the brigade. "If the recommendation of Col. Johnston was based upon meritorious service or superior qualifications, I have only to ask that the judgment of some one else than the Major Genl Commanding may be invoked in determining the matter," he pleaded.

While his sense of duty made it difficult for him to resign, Garrett demanded to have his grievances heard by the authorities in Richmond. He even called for a full-scale investigation into the selection of Johnston. "I am content to bear all the other numerous hardships of the service, but this I cannot bear in silence," Garrett complained. He took pains to point out that "Col. Johnston is my junior in rank, age, and experience, and I respectfully ask that an inquiry may be instituted to determine whether injustice has not been done me, and whether it cannot even now be repaired."⁵

Garrett's complaints failed to draw any meaningful support from the Confederate War Department. Despite the rejection of his pleas, Garrett continued to pursue his dream of promotion with reckless abandon. Just prior to the battle of May 12, 1864, at Spotsylvania Court House, the disgruntled Garrett is said to have remarked that he "would come out of the fight a brigadier-general or a dead colonel." Less than 15 minutes after going into action, he was killed instantly by a bullet to the head during the fighting around the area known as the "mule-shoe."⁶

The same months-long period was also filled with frustrations for Col. Duncan McRae. Following McRae's resignation, Governor Vance appointed him as a special envoy to Halifax, Nova Scotia, with orders to secure badly

---

4   Robert D. Johnston to James A. Seddon, Nov. 17, 1863, Complied Service Record of Don Peters Halsey, M 275, R 115, NA; Robert E. Rodes to James A. Seddon, March 11, 1864, *ibid.*; Stephen Dodson Ramseur to James A. Seddon, March 10, 1864, *ibid.*; Yancey, *Lynchburg and Its Neighbors*, 121.

5   Thomas M. Garrett to Samuel Cooper, Sept. 21, 1863, Letters Received, Confederate Adjutant and Inspector General's Office.

6   Powell, *NC Biography*, 2:279; quoted in Hamilton, "Diary of Thomas Miles Garrett," 73; McRae and Busbee, "Fifth Regiment," in Clark, *NC Regiments*, 1:289.

needed war supplies in exchange for North Carolina cotton. Amid considerable controversy, McRae decided instead to carry out this assignment in southern Europe. After returning home, he ran unsuccessfully for a seat in the Confederate Congress. From 1864 until the end of the war, McRae published a newspaper in Raleigh that strongly supported both the Vance and Davis administrations.[7]

Like Garrett, McRae had not easily given up his hopes for attaining the rank of brigadier general. During late 1863, the entire North Carolina Congressional delegation petitioned President Davis for his "favorable consideration" of McRae for appointment as general. In support of their request, they enclosed letters of endorsement from Gens. Jubal Early, D. H. Hill, and James Longstreet. Although Longstreet described him as "one of our most efficient colonels and well worthy of promotion," McRae never gained the rank he had coveted for so long.[8]

Events unfolded even less favorably for Lt. Col. Peter Sinclair following his resignation. During late August, he complained about his mistreatment in a letter to President Davis. "Your excellency will perceive that my promotions were very rapid," he explained. "In consequence of this was a feeling of jealousy among my brother officers, my senior in years tho junior in rank." He further noted that Colonel McRae, "with whom I never got along very pleasantly for reasons that need not be stated here, when he determined to leave the army made mention of this jealousy among my junior officers to prevent my promotion to the command of the Regiment."[9]

From the time he left the regiment, Peter Sinclair faced the further taint to his reputation caused by the actions of his brother. James Sinclair was born in Scotland and immigrated to the United States. He graduated from the Western Theological Seminary in Pennsylvania and became the minister of the Presbyterian Church in Smyrna, North Carolina. In 1861, James was elected colonel of the 35th North Carolina following reports of his gallant conduct at First Manassas while serving as chaplain of the 5th North Carolina. "Those rumors, believed at the time, though false in fact, doubtless had some influence in securing his election," concluded a veteran from that regiment.

---

7   Powell, *NC Biography*, 3:189; Krick, *Lee's Colonels*, 258.

8   North Carolina Congressional Delegation to Jefferson Davis, Dec. 23, 1863, McRae Service Record.

9   Sinclair to Davis, Aug. 22, 1863, Sinclair Service Record.

Following the battle at New Bern in March of 1862, James was relieved of duty and charged with cowardice before a court of inquiry. Although the charges were later dropped, he failed to win re-election as colonel during the regiment's reorganization in early May. One of his few public supporters was Governor Vance, who had served alongside him in the battle while commanding the 26th North Carolina. Vance regarded the Scottish-born Sinclair as "an injured man" and continued to defend his actions throughout the following months. Despite the governor's steadfast support, the former colonel later deserted to the North and served as a chaplain with the Federal forces.[10]

As his brother's problems continued to mount, Lt. Col. Peter Sinclair requested special permission from the secretary of war for his own family "to pass the lines" to the safety of his father's home in Pennsylvania. He argued that the move resulted from his inability to support his family since resigning his commission in the 5th North Carolina. "No government under the skies can desire of me to let my family suffer," he insisted. When his pleas for justice were rebuffed, Sinclair reluctantly resumed publication of his newspaper in the town of Fayetteville.[11]

For the remainder of the war, Sinclair used the newspaper as a platform for criticizing Governor Vance and calling for all-out conflict with the North to the bitter end. "War is necessary—war with a base, unprincipled, inhuman, brutal and ruthless foe," he declared in an editorial in the spring of 1864. "Let the war be waged with energy; let it be 'war to the knife and the knife to the hilt.'" He argued that the people of the state should resist the enemy's advance by any means possible. Sinclair called upon them to "not only do this but punish the insolent foe for his presumption."[12]

Lieutenant Colonel Henry Coleman, meanwhile, continued to press his case for a promotion as colonel of the 12th North Carolina. In early August, he wrote a letter to Secretary of War James Seddon arguing that his appointment should be confirmed because all the proper paperwork had been sent to the

---

10 Krick, *Lee's Colonels*, 345; William H. S. Burgwyn, "Thirty-Fifth Regiment," included in Clark, *NC Regiments*, 2:592-593; Zebulon B. Vance to James Sinclair, Feb. 17, 1863, in Mobley *Papers of Vance*, Vol. Two, 58. For James Sinclair's account of his ongoing problems with Confederate authorities, see James Sinclair to W. W. Holden, Dec. 24, 1863, *North Carolina Weekly Standard*, Jan. 6, 1864.

11 Peter J. Sinclair to James Seddon, Oct. 26, 1863, Letters Received, Confederate Secretary of War; Krick, *Lee's Colonels*, 345.

12 *Daily North Carolinian*, March 30, 1864.

adjutant general's office. "In consequence of the papers having been mislaid in A.G.'s office, the appointment was not forwarded to the Senate," Coleman explained. He insisted that he should have been immediately ordered to command of the regiment once the papers were located and sent to President Davis for action.[13]

Following a review of the case, the Richmond War Department finally approved Coleman's promotion to colonel of 12th North Carolina on August 11, 1863. Predictably, the decision did not sit well with Lt. Col. William Davis, who penned a scathing letter of protest to General Cooper. Davis argued that it was "contrary to both law and justice to promote a citizen over officers in the service who are regularly entitled to the promotion unless they waive their claims or are incompetent." Davis further demanded that "Col Coleman be assigned to some other command or that the matter be investigated and justice done me in revoking the order."

In his endorsement to the letter, General Ramseur noted that "Lt Col Davis deserves much credit for the gallantry of himself & regiment at the battle of Gettysburg." Ramseur offered high praise of Davis' combat leadership abilities, emphasizing that he was "one of the best tacticians & disciplinarians in his brigade." Rodes, who also clearly favored Davis, admitted by that point there was little that could be done to change the outcome because of Davis' apparent failure to protest Coleman's appointment during the officers' meeting the previous December. Rodes went on to noted that Davis was "so efficient and gallant and so good an officer generally that I regret that his silence at the meeting alluded to has placed him and Col Coleman in their present positions."[14]

It did not take long after Coleman joined the 12th North Carolina regiment for him to become embroiled in disputes with the officers under his command. During the following spring, several of them filed formal charges accusing him of cowardice and drunkenness on duty. Soon afterward, Coleman sustained a severe wound to the head at Spotsylvania Court House. While home in Virginia recovering from his injuries, he joined a small force defending a nearby bridge on the Staunton River on June 25, 1864. During the fighting that ensued,

---

13 Coleman to Seddon, Aug. 8, 1863, Coleman Service Record.

14 Davis to Cooper, Aug. 21, 1863, Letters Received, Confederate Adjutant and Inspector General's Office.

Coleman suffered another wound, this one to the knee. The result was a citation for gallantry.[15]

Although the severe knee injury left him disabled for further field duty, Coleman had the final satisfaction of being vindicated by General Johnston. After conducting "a full and thorough investigation," Johnston reported to Coleman that "there is no foundation" for the charges against him. "On the contrary, the evidence adduced proves beyond question, that Col. Coleman has ever discharged his duty with courage upon the battle-field, and with a conscientious regard for the rights of his subordinates in camp."[16]

Lieutenant Colonel Davis, however, refused to serve under Coleman's direct command in the months following his promotion. "General Ramseur... came to me of his own accord and begged me not to resign, although I had said nothing about resigning, and said to me: 'I will see to it that you shall never be under Coleman,' and I never was," Davis recalled. "When Coleman assumed command of the Twelfth I was ordered to take command of the Twenty-third Regiment." Davis further noted, "when Coleman, for any reason was not present with the Twelfth, I was put back in command." Davis later lost his arm during the fighting at Cedar Creek in October of 1864 and resigned from his command soon afterward.[17]

The fighting at Gettysburg proved the most tragic of all for the 23rd North Carolina's Col. Daniel Christie. Despite being severely wounded in both lungs during the brief charge he led out of the bloody hollow in the Forney farm field, he survived the punishing trip in Ewell's wagon train and was admitted to the hospital in Winchester. While he lingered near death, the doctors summoned his wife Lizzie from North Carolina. Several more days of agony followed before Christie succumbed to his wounds on July 17. "His wife, whom he so longed to see, and who had hastened to him, arrived a few hours after he was buried," Capt. Vines Turner sadly reported.[18]

---

15 Charges and Specifications Against Colonel Coleman, April 1864, Coleman Service Record; Krick, *Lee's Colonel's*, 96; "Sketch of Colonel Henry Eaton Coleman," Henry Eaton Coleman Papers.

16 Robert D. Johnston to Henry E. Coleman, Nov. 5, 1864, Robert D. Johnston Papers, Duke.

17 Quoted in Montgomery, "Twelfth Regiment," in Clark, *NC Regiments*, 1:643; Krick, *Lee's Colonels*, 114.

18 Turner and Wall, "Twenty-Third Regiment," in Clark, *NC Regiments*, 2:238-239; Krick, *Lee's Colonels*, 91.

Measured against his tactical brilliance at Chancellorsville, Robert Rodes' performance at the head of his division at Gettysburg on July 1 was clearly disappointing. Neither O'Neal nor Iverson handled their brigades with any reasonable degree of competence, but Rodes must share in the blame for the disjointed attack off Oak Hill. After he arrived on the hill, Rodes let two hours slip away before launching his assault against the Federal position on Oak Ridge. He made O'Neal's attack that much more difficult by detaching the 3rd Alabama from his brigade. Rodes also assumed, mistakenly, that the Federal skirmish line in the Forney farm field was preparing to attack his artillery firing on the slope of the hill. He compounded this error by allowing Iverson to advance his brigade into the field without a screen of skirmishers covering his front.

Rodes' effort on July 2 was no better when he failed to arrange his command properly for the attack against the western face of Cemetery Hill. According to Maj. Cambell Brown, both Generals Ewell and Early "thought Rodes had been too slow" in attacking the heights that evening. In later years, Early described Rodes' failure to carry through on the attack against Cemetery Hill as "the solitary instance of remissness on the part of any portion of the corps in the battle." Ewell, it was reported, held Rodes "fairly censurable" for not launching his assault on time. Despite later distinguishing himself as one of the best division commanders in the army, Rodes seems never to have been considered seriously as a potential corps commander.[19]

One possible explanation for Rodes' uncharacteristically poor tactical performance at Gettysburg was his health. At least one eyewitness from Jubal Early's staff reported that Rodes was noticeably ill and flushed with fever during a meeting late in the afternoon on July 1. That assessment was confirmed by Early's 15-year-old nephew, John Cabell Early, who arrived in camp with the hope of being assigned as an aide on his uncle's division staff. According to the recollection of the younger Early, Rodes was "so sick that he was compelled to ride in an ambulance whenever practicable."[20]

As controversy continued swirling through his old division, Iverson was finally relieved from duty as a caretaker commander in General Lee's army with the Louisiana brigade on October 6, 1864. He was reassigned to the home guard

---

19 G. Campbell Brown to Henry Jackson Hunt, May 7, 1885, in Jones, *Campbell Brown's Civil War*, 329; Early, "Leading Confederates," 280.

20 Collins, *Major General Robert E. Rodes*, 280, 284; Early, "Southern Boy's Experience," 418.

forces in Georgia at the request of Maj. Gen. Howell Cobb. The new appointment and command seemed to revive Iverson's flagging spirits. He served in that post with Cobb's complete satisfaction until the following spring of 1864, when the term of enlistment for the home guards expired. Soon afterward, Iverson transferred yet again, this time to the Army of Tennessee to assume the command of a Georgia cavalry brigade under Maj. Gen. Joseph Wheeler.[21]

Iverson became embroiled in controversy almost from the moment he took over the brigade. When he arrived in camp, he learned the brigade's temporary commander, Col. J. J. Morrison of the 1st Georgia Cavalry, had already filled some of the staff positions with his own men. In particular, Iverson raised "most decided objections" to the appointment of Maj. N. J. Reynolds as brigade quartermaster. Reynolds had served as quartermaster of Morrison's regiment and received his official appointment to the new brigade staff in early February.

When Reynolds attempted to retain his position, Iverson charged that he was unfit for duty. "Since his first reporting to me I have taken the pain to enquire who he was and learned from truthful and reliable men that he was the proprietor of a gambling and drinking establishment in Rome Ga and is himself in the habit of drinking a great deal," Iverson declared in a letter to General Cooper in Richmond. Although Reynolds was later dropped from the staff rolls, Iverson's actions angered and alienated many of the officers in his new brigade.[22]

Despite Iverson's rocky start, his men performed well on July 30, 1864, in repulsing an attack near Macon, Georgia, by a Federal raiding force of 2,200 cavalrymen commanded by Maj. Gen. George Stoneman. Iverson's troopers, along with two other brigades of Kentucky and Alabama cavalry, confronted Stoneman's men again the next day just a few miles from Iverson's birthplace in Clinton. "We met at a place called Sunshine Church," recalled Pvt. O. P. Hargis of the 1st Georgia Cavalry. "General Iverson then attacked him at once. Stowman tried to break our lines by charging us mounted, but he failed to do so, then he dismounted his men and we had it hot and heavy." According to the

---

21 *OR* 29, pt. 2, 775; *OR* 38, part 3, 957; Howell Cobb to Samuel Cooper, March 3, 1864, Letters Received, Confederate Adjutant and Inspector General's Office.

22 Alfred Iverson Jr. to Samuel Cooper, April 17, 1864, *ibid.*; Alfred Iverson Jr. to Samuel Cooper, June 17, 1864, *ibid.*; J. J. Morrison to Samuel Cooper, Feb. 22, 1864, *ibid.*

private, "we pushed our line on him and driving him back until he made his last stand."[23]

Just as he had done at Gettysburg, Iverson directed the three brigades in the attack from well behind the lines. Private J. A. Wynn, who also served in the 1st Georgia Cavalry, attributed most of their success to the leadership displayed by the 2nd Georgia Cavalry's Col. Charles C. Crews, who assumed temporary command of Iverson's Brigade. "Stoneman had dismounted his men and put them behind breastworks in an old field," Wynn wrote. "Col. Crews dismounted us and ordered a charge. We had only 600 men all told." Wynn pointed out that "thirty-eight of our boys were killed and wounded in the charge, among them was 1st Lieutenant Jesse Crabb in command of our company."[24]

By tricking the Federal commander into thinking he was surrounded by a superior force, Iverson's troopers routed the main raiding party and captured Stoneman himself and more than 500 of his men. "My horse shot, my command was driven off the field except the Artillery and Portion of one brigade—which I held together to cover the rest of the force," Stoneman wrote to his wife the following day. "This & myself were forced to surrender after having used up our ammunition." Stoneman, who had once served alongside Iverson in the 1st U.S. Cavalry, was the highest-ranking Federal officer captured during the war.[25]

The extent of Iverson's participation in the battle remains difficult to decipher. Private Hargis reported that "General Iverson was sick and not on duty" when the Federal officers finally gave up. He also claimed that the honor of capturing Stoneman went to Col. Crews, who temporarily led the brigade. "When we got over the little hill there the Federals stood in line with their guns stacked in front of them and General Stowman sitting on his horse," recalled

---

23 O. P. Hargis, *Thrilling Experiences of a First Georgia Cavalryman in the Civil War* (Rome, GA: n.p., n.d.), 22. For accounts of the Battle of Sunshine Church, see Richard W. Iobst, *Civil War Macon: The History of a Confederate City* (Macon, GA: Mercer University Press, 1979), 316-324 and John Randolph Poole, *Cracker Cavaliers, The Second Georgia Cavalry under Wheeler and Forest* (Macon, GA: Mercer University Press, 2000), 142-145. It has been widely reported that Iverson was selected to pursue Stoneman because of his familiarity with the area around his birthplace of Clinton. His nephew, Alfred Iverson Branham, however, wrote that "General Iverson never visited Clinton after he left the town as a child until the day of the battle of Sunrise church." For details, see Alfred Iverson Branham, "Letters to the Telegraph," *Macon Telegraph*, Nov. 20, 1929.

24 J. A. Winn Memoirs, Civil War Miscellaneous Personal Papers, GA.

25 Quoted in Bryan, *Confederate Georgia*, 160.

Hargis. "Colonel Cruise [Crews] rode up and saluted General Stowman." Stoneman, continued the private, "preferred to surrender to General Iverson, but was refused by Colonel Cruise."[26]

An account by the 1st Georgia Cavalry's Pvt. R. T. Logan confirmed Hargis's version of events. Iverson, wrote Logan, was "ill and in the rear" throughout the fighting, and it was Colonel Crews who "was in command, and to him Stoneman surrendered." Private Wynn likewise recalled that it was Crews rather than Iverson who accepted the surrender at Sunshine Church. "After several hours fighting I saw a fellow with a white flag, dressed in blue, come galloping down to Col. Crews and I said, 'Boys that is good news.' He soon hurried back and in a short time I saw Gen. Stoneman and his staff ride down to where Col. Crews and his staff were and the terms of the surrender were agreed upon in about 40 minutes."[27]

Whatever Iverson's exact involvement, Sunshine Church was regarded across the Southern Confederacy as a significant victory. In his official report, General Wheeler described Stoneman's capture as the "most ignominious defeat and destruction" of any cavalry operation during the entire war. "As was acknowledged by the brigade commanders captured, their plan was to unite these columns on the railroad north of Macon, destroy the railroad, then move rapidly upon and release the 30,000 prisoners of war we held at Andersonville," he declared. Stoneman, continued Wheeler, "was thoroughly thwarted at the cost of about 5,000 men, with their horses, arms, equipments, colors, cannon, &c."[28]

During late 1864, Iverson assumed temporary command of a division consisting of two cavalry brigades operating along the front of the Federal army outside Atlanta. Regardless of whatever position he held, Iverson could not escape disputes with subordinates. His latest problem began in September when Capt. Giles S. Cecil was assigned to detached duty and replaced as the brigade commissary by Iverson's personal courier, who was only a private. After repeated protests without satisfaction, Cecil submitted his case for an investigation by the Adjutant and Inspector General's Department in the Army of Tennessee.

---

26 Hargis, *Thrilling Experience*, 22.

27 R. T. Logan, "My Experiences as a Confederate Soldier," in *Confederate Reminiscences and Letters*, 9:83; Winn Memoirs, Civil War Miscellaneous Personal Papers.

28 *OR* 38, pt. 3, 957.

Iverson responded by arguing that Cecil had totally misstated the situation out of personal spite. "I think from what I know of old Capt Cecil that he had a mania for making complaints and was very anxious to get back to his home in East Tennessee," Iverson alleged in his reply to the board of inquiry. A full investigation established that Iverson had exceeded his own authority in making the changes in the commissary department. The final report concluded that "such an order was irregular, and Capt. Cecil was justified in objecting to it."[29]

Iverson's troopers, meanwhile, harassed enemy forces in what essentially amounted to guerilla warfare as William T. Sherman's Federal armies swept eastward through his home state of Georgia. "Wheeler's cavalry has a bad name through the country they passed," Lt. Lavender Ray, who served as the acting ordnance officer in Iverson's cavalry division, admitted in a letter to his father. "They have done many villanous things and some deserve to be shot, but they were somewhat excusable as they were ordered to destroy everything in the route of the enemy." However, the lieutenant continued, "unfortunately the Yankees did not come [along] the route on which we destroyed the subsistence."[30]

During much of this time Alfred's half-brother, John F. Iverson, also served with the Army of Tennessee in a brigade commanded by Brig. Gen. John King Jackson. The younger Iverson was born in 1837 and received a military education at the Georgia Military Institute in Marietta. He enlisted for service in April of 1861 as a captain of a volunteer company from his hometown of Columbus. During the course of the war, he rose to lieutenant colonel in the 5th Georgia and participated in a number of campaigns, including Murfreesboro, Chickamauga, Chattanooga, and Atlanta.

In October of 1864, Iverson's regiment was transferred to Florence, South Carolina. There, Iverson was assigned as commander of the nearby military prison. The new prison had only recently been built to hold prisoners transferred after the fall of Atlanta from a facility in Andersonville, Georgia, which was known officially as Camp Sumter. Iverson was selected for the position because of ongoing concerns about the terrible conditions in the Florence prison and the need for better management of the stockade. Iverson's

---

29 Investigation Report, Feb. 10, 1865, Compiled Service Record of Giles S. Cecil, M275, Roll 51, NA; Alfred Iverson Jr. to John G. Devereaux, Jan. 28, 1865, *ibid.*

30 Lavender Ray to My Dear Father, Dec. 5, 1864, Lavender Ray Papers.

Iverson's half-brother, Lt. Col. John F. Iverson from the 5th Georgia, confronts prisoners at the Florence Military Prison in South Carolina during late 1864. *Library of Congress*

good intentions notwithstanding, the situation failed to improve during his time in command of the prison.[31]

Although Lieutenant Colonel Iverson served as the post commandant, his staff inspector, Capt. Thomas G. Barrett, handled most of the the day-to-day activities inside the main compound. "The prisoners complained greatly of the harsh and brutal treatment they received from Captain Barrett and Lieutenant Wilson, who had charge of the interior of the prison," a Federal officer declared following an in-depth postwar investigation. "They charged these officers with cruel and undeserved punishments, such as lengthened confinement upon bread and water in the guard-house for trivial offenses." According to the former captives, "some deaths were reported as the result of their brutality."[32]

---

31 Evans, *Confederate Military History*, 6:28; "Georgia Grays," *Daily Columbus Enquirer*, April 20, 1861; "Death of Colonel Iverson," *Columbus Enquirer-Sun*, May 31, 1887.

32 OR 8, Series 2, 766. For details on Barrett's brutality, see Warren Lee Goss, *The Soldier's Story of His Captivity at Andersonville, Belle Isle, and Other Rebel Prisons* (Boston: Lee and Shepard

At least one officer involved in the inquiry openly called for both Iverson and Barrett to "be arrested and brought to trial" for their mistreatment of the prisoners at Florence. "The testimony fixes upon them not only a series of the most cruel and inhuman acts of neglect, abuse, assault, robbery, &c., but a considerable number of well-established homicides," he asserted. "In these Barrett was the principle agent, but Iverson as his commanding officer, was clearly no less criminal." By this time, Barrett had already fled the country, and no formal charges were ever brought against either officer.[33]

While his half-brother was stationed at Florence, Alfred continued at the head of his cavalry division in the increasingly desperate fight against Sherman. By the beginning of 1865, Iverson's command had fallen back to the area north of Savannah near the border with South Carolina. General D. H. Hill, who had taken over command of the District of Georgia, openly expressed dismay about the continued misconduct of Joe Wheeler's cavalry. "The whole of Georgia is full of bitter complaints of Wheeler's Cavalry," Hill wrote Iverson in late February. "I hope that your stout and gallant resistance will redeem the odium cast upon the command."[34]

Hill urged Iverson to use every means possible to slow down the Federal advance by fighting the enemy each step of the way. To his consternation, Hill discovered that Iverson had "retired so very precipitately" from one of the positions he had been ordered to hold that the Federal troops threatened to break through deeper into the real estate held by the shrinking Confederacy. Iverson's withdrawal occurred after Hill sent him "a peremptory order" not to fall back. "If you are in communications with Iverson please impress upon him the great importance of checking the Yankees," Hill directed Joe Wheeler. "This falling back without a fight ought to be stopped; it will ruin the bravest men in the world and make them timid."[35]

Hill became so frustrated that he took up his complaints about Iverson directly with Lt. Gen. William J. Hardee, who commanded the Department of South Carolina, Georgia, and Florida. Despite orders to the contrary, grumbled

---

Publishers, 1866), 226 and Charles Fosdick, *Five Hundred Days in Rebel Prisons* (Bethany, MO: Clipper Book and Job Publishing, 1887), 87.

33 OR 8, Series 2, 783; "Death of Colonel Iverson," *Columbus Enquirer-Sun*, May 31, 1887. After the war, John F. Iverson ran an insurance business in Columbus. He died in 1887 at age 50.

34 OR 47, pt. 2, 1,047.

35 *Ibid.*, 1,054.

Hill, Iverson had repeatedly withdrawn without fighting. "I have never known anything like it in my life," declared Hill. "It has caused me great annoyance and embarrassment." For the combative Hill, the situation was deeply frustrating. "There is something terribly wrong in our cavalry organization," he observed. "They never think of delaying the Yankees by fighting them. The simple business is to get out of their way."[36]

As the front collapsed around him, Iverson somehow found time to forward his favorable comments to General Cooper in Richmond about Joe Wheeler's new book about cavalry tactics. "I have examined Major Gen Wheeler's Cavalry Tactics and regard it as the best book on Cavalry tactics in existence," declared Iverson. "The construction of commands, combination of movements, and single rank formation are peculiarly adapted to the nature of Cavalry service in this country." He went on to note that, in his opinion, it would be "advisable that these tactics be adopted by our Government as the standard work."[37]

Although the situation remained nearly hopeless, Iverson led his troopers on a raid deep behind enemy lines. "The people would find out where we were camped and cook a basket full of rations and bring them to us, and we would get feed for our horses from them," explained Lt. Ray. "We would do all the harm to the railroad that we could then we would go back into Hall County and recruit up our horses, then we would make another raid to the railroad." The lieutenant continued: "when inside the line, we would tear up the railroad, cut telegraph wires, throw off trains, and do all we could to block transportation of army supplies for Sherman's army."[38]

After returning from the raid, Iverson received orders in early March to cross into South Carolina. By then, the fighting along their front had taken a terrible toll on soldiers and civilians alike. "You cannot imagine the immense devastation I have witnessed," one officer informed his brother. Most of all, he expressed outrage at the "inhuman" conduct of the Federal troops against the civilian population in the wake of Sherman's advance through Georgia and South Carolina. "[W]e have captured many marauding Yankees," he admitted,

---

36 *Ibid.*, 1,056.

37 Alfred Iverson, Jr. to Samuel Cooper, Jan. 11, 1865, Letters Received, Confederate Adjutant and Inspector General's Office.

38 Lavender Ray to Dear Brother, Jan. 20, 1865, Ray Papers; Lavender Ray to Dear Sister, undated letter, *ibid.*

"but the men are so indignant that they generally shoot them immediately without bringing them to Gen. Iverson."[39]

In one of his last acts before the close of the war, Iverson penned a poem entitled "It Is Ended" into the pages of his journal. "I've hung up the sword," he wrote. "Let it rust and decay, through the changes of time, and the slumber of years; the glory it had is now passed away." By the time Lee's Army of Northern surrendered in early April and Joe Johnston's command capitulated later that same month, Iverson was nearly inconsolable. He steadfastly refused to take the Oath of Allegiance and settled into a life of relative obscurity in Macon, Georgia.[40]

The former general turned his attention to rebuilding a relationship with his two young daughters. Throughout the war, they had been raised by his sister-in-law Mary Octavia Smith and her husband, Charles Henry Smith, of Rome, Georgia. As late as 1874, when his daughter Minnie graduated from the Marietta Female College, his in-laws were still listed as her guardians. By then, Smith had become nationally known under the pen name of Bill Arp. After the war, Smith began writing a series of humorous letters from a Southern point of view. The letters were featured regularly in the *Atlanta Constitution* newspaper. The publication of several books of his collected letters and essays made him one of the most widely read humorist in the country.[41]

Finding a suitable career proved much more difficult for Iverson. He embarked on an elaborate scheme to convert part of the former Macon Armory building into a factory for the manufacture of household ice-making machines. After several years, he obtained a U.S. patent for a prototype model. The business venture failed because of the high cost of the machines, which put them outside the budget of all but the richest families. Thereafter, he worked for a time as a contractor during the construction of a large cotton-knitting mill in the same building.[42]

While Alfred searched for viable employment, his father continued practicing as an attorney in Columbus, Georgia, which had escaped much of the destruction Sherman's army had inflicted during his March to the Sea. After his

---

39 Lavender Ray to Dear Brother, March 9, 1865, *ibid.*

40 Iverson Journal, Iverson Papers, Emory.

41 For a detailed study of Smith's career, see Parker, *Alias Bill Arp*.

42 Bridges Smith, "How General Alf. Iverson Worked on a Big Ice Idea," *Macon Daily Telegraph*, Nov. 1, 1914; "The New Factory," *Georgia Weekly Telegraph*, Nov. 8, 1870.

retirement in 1868, the former senator relocated to a plantation a few miles east of nearby Macon. There, he remained mostly out of public view and took up a variety of agricultural pursuits. The senior Iverson died on March 4, 1873, at the age of 74 and was laid to rest in Linwood Cemetery in his hometown of Columbus.[43]

The younger Iverson remained in Georgia until 1877, when he moved to central Florida and purchased a 12-acre orange grove near the small town of Maitland in Orange County. The following year he wed 45-year-old Adela Branham, whose brother was married to Iverson's older sister Julia. He later took a one-half share interest in another 40-acre orange grove. For a time, it looked as though the former Confederate general had found a comfortable and happy life. He even built a large Spanish-style home known as Greenwood Lodge on Lake Faith.

When a freeze in 1895 damaged most of his orange trees, Iverson moved to Shingle Creek near what would become the town of Kissimmee. His wife Adela, who was a musician and educator, converted their former home into a girl's school. When his orange groves were completely wiped out in another major cold spell four years later in February 1899, the disaster left him in financial ruin. With his inheritance gone, Iverson survived for a time on his Mexican War pension of only eight dollars a month. The paltry sum made it nearly impossible to hold onto his small homestead in Florida. After several failed attempts, he managed to have the pension increased to $20 a month in 1907. Soon afterward, he qualified for a Confederate veteran's pension from the state of Florida, which provided him with an additional income of $150 per year.[44]

A series of personal tragedies during this period overwhelmed the financially-strapped Iverson. His older sister, Julia Iverson Branham, died in 1900, as did his wife Adela in 1904. He suffered another major blow when his eldest daughter, Julia Iverson Patton, died the following year. Broke and alone,

---

[43] American Council of Learned Societies, *Dictionary of American Biography*, 9:517-518; Coleman and Gurr, *Dictionary of GA Biography*,1:509-510; "Death of Hon. Alfred Iverson," *Macon Weekly Telegraph*, March 11, 1873.

[44] William Fremont Blackman, *History of Orange County Florida* (DeLand, FL: E. O. Painter Printing Co., 1927), 198; Jim Robison, "Lake Faith Lured General to Build His Florida Home," *Orlando Sentinel*, Dec. 7, 1997; Alfred Iverson Jr., Mexican War Pension Record, Records of the Adjutant General's Office, Record Group 94, NA; Pension Certificate Number 5061, Nov. 2, 1909, Kross Private Collection.

Epilogue: The Glory it Had is Now Passed Away

Alfred Iverson relaxes on the porch at his home near Kissimmee, Florida, about a year before his death in 1911. *Gary Kross*

The veterans at the reunion of the 20th North Carolina in Duplin County during 1904 included Joseph B. Oliver, James D. Ireland, and E. Faison Hicks. *North Carolina Office of Archives and History*

the former general returned to live with his youngest daughter, Minnie Iverson Randolph, in her home on Peach Tree Circle in Atlanta, Georgia. Surrounded by his surviving family members, he succumbed to the infirmities of old age on March 31, 1911, and was buried a few days later at the famed Oakwood Cemetery in Atlanta. He was 82.[45]

Although Alfred Iverson's obituary ran the next day in major newspapers across much of the South, the survivors of his brigade had long before rendered their opinion of his legacy. The passing of years had done nothing to soften their verdict. "And, unwarned, unled as a brigade, went forward Iverson's deserted band to its doom," lamented Capt. Turner of the 23rd North Carolina nearly four decades after the July 1 disaster at Gettysburg. "Deep and long must the desolate homes and orphan children of North Carolina rue the rashness of that hour."[46]

---

45 Kross, "That One Error," 52-53; Coleman and Gurr, *GA Biography*, 1:511; "Died in Florida," *Macon Weekly Telegraph*, Feb. 9, 1904; "Gen. Alfred Iverson Called by Death," *Columbus-Enquirer Sun*, April 1, 1911. Besides his daughter Minnie, he was survived by four grandchildren: Richard Patton, Priscilla Patton, Minnie Patton, and Beverly Randolph [male]. Two other grandchildren, Alfred Iverson Patton and Julia Octavia Patton, died as infants. Iverson's daughter Minnie Randolph lived until July 2, 1953.

46 Turner and Wall, "Twenty-Third Regiment," in Clark, *NC Regiments*, 2:235.

Alfred Iverson, circa 1900. Miller, *Photographic History*

Appendix 1

Iverson's Brigade Order of Battle on July 1, 1863

Sharpshooters[1] (West of McLean farm)

Engaged: 4 officers and 120 enlisted men
Casualties: 4 officers and 20 enlisted men
Percentage Loss: 19%

5th North Carolina
(Facing stone wall)

Engaged: 28 officers and 387 enlisted men
Casualties: 22 officers and 238 enlisted men
Percentage Loss: 62%

20th North Carolina
(Facing stone wall)

Engaged: 23 officers and 263 enlisted men
Casualties: 21 officers and 226 enlisted men
Percentage Loss: 87%

---

1 The sharpshooter detachment consisted of one officer and about 30 men from each regiment. Capt. Benjamin Robinson, Co. A, 5th North Carolina, was in command of the sharpshooters. The other regimental detachments were likely led by Lt. Nathan S. Moseley, Co. F, 12th North Carolina; Lt. Oliver Williams, Co. C, 20th North Carolina; and Lt. James W. Crowder, Co. A, 23rd North Carolina. Casualties for this unit are estimated, based on 20 casualties reported for O'Neal's sharpshooter detachment, which was similarly engaged. *OR* 27, pt. 2, 598.

23rd North Carolina
(Facing stone wall)

Engaged: 22 officers and 262 enlisted men
Casualties: 21 officers and 246 enlisted men
Percentage Loss: 94%

12th North Carolina (Companies B and D)[2]
(Facing stone wall)

Engaged: 4 officers and 41 enlisted men
Casualties: 1 officer and 24 enlisted men
Percentage Loss: 56%

12th North Carolina (Companies, A, C, E-K)
(Opposite railroad woods)

Engaged: 19 officers and 168 enlisted men
Casualties: 1 officer and 41 enlisted men
Percentage Loss: 22%

On the Field and Under Fire

Brigade Staff: 4 officers and 1 enlisted man

Ambulance Corps: 6 officers and 89 enlisted men[3]

---

2   Companies B and D sustained the highest casualties in the regiment and probably were the two companies reported engaged in front of the stone wall.

3   The ambulance corps consisted of 20 men from each regiment. The unit operated under the overall command of Lt. Marcus Sylvanus Deal, Company A, 12th North Carolina, and Lt. John Philopidus Leach, Company C, 23rd North Carolina. The four regimental assistant surgeons directly supervised activities of the litter bearers on the field. The nine members of the 20th North Carolina regimental band likely served with the ambulance corps on the field and later in the field hospital.

Appendix 1: Iverson's Brigade Order of Battle on July 1, 1863

Behind the Battle Lines[4]

5th North Carolina: 3 officers and 24 enlisted men

12th North Carolina: 2 officers and 24 enlisted men

20th North Carolina: 2 officers and 31 enlisted men

23rd North Carolina: 2 officers and 24 enlisted men

Brigade Field Hospital: 4 officers and 8 enlisted men[5]

Brigade Staff: 3 officers and 14 enlisted men

Brigade Pioneers: 1 officer and 19 enlisted men[6]

Wagon Trains: 0 officers and 49 enlisted men[7]

---

[4] The quartermaster and assistant commissary for each regiment were not engaged. The 5th North Carolina had one company line officer sent to the rear sick. For enlisted men, the ordnance sergeant, the commissary sergeant, the quartermaster sergeant, and the colonel's orderly in each regiment were not engaged. The total also includes cooks and other men present but unfit for combat.

[5] The brigade field hospital was manned by the brigade surgeon, the other three regimental surgeons, four regimental hospital stewards, and four regimental surgeon's orderlies.

[6] The pioneer corps was commanded by Lt. George H. Heileg, who was detailed from Company K, 5th North Carolina.

[7] The wagon train included 17 teamsters assigned to the brigade wagons and ambulances and eight teamsters with each of the regimental trains.

APPENDIX 2

Numbers and Losses in Iverson's Brigade for the Gettysburg Campaign

	Present June 30[1]	Present July 1[2]	Engaged (Estimated)	Battle Casualties
	Officers & Enlisted Men	Officers & Enlisted Men	Officers & Enlisted Men	Officers & Enlisted Men
Brigade Staff	10+51	10+51	4+1	0+0
5th NC	34+479	34+471	29+417	23+243[3]
12th NC	28+289	28+289	24+235	3+70[4]
20th NC	28+363	28+363	24+293	22+226[5]

1 Totals based on the rosters in Manarin and Jordan, *NC Troops,* 4:116-255, 5:106-274, 6:425-529, 7:133-244 and the Complied Service Records for the 5th, 12th, 20th, and 23rd North Carolina, M 270, R 145-156, R 201-210, R 269-277, R 293-302, NA.

2 The total in this column reflects an adjustment for eight enlisted men in the 5th North Carolina who straggled and were captured on the march to Gettysburg on July 1.

3 A nominal list of casualties in the 5th North Carolina was published in the *Raleigh Daily Progress,* July 16, 1863. The list was reprinted in the *Raleigh Weekly State Journal,* July 22, 1863. A corrected list for companies B, F, and H was published in the *Fayetteville Observer,* Aug.17, 1863.

4 A nominal list of casualties in the 12th North Carolina was published in the *Raleigh Weekly Register,* Aug. 12, 1863.

5 A nominal list of casualties for Company F was printed in the *Wilmington Daily Journal,* July 16, 1863. The list was reprinted in the *Fayetteville Observer,* July 20, 1863. A nominal list of casualties for Company I was printed in the *Fayetteville Observer,* July 27, 1863.

Appendix 2: Numbers and Losses in Iverson's Brigade 351

23rd NC	27+ 346	27+346	23+292	22+251[6]
Total[7]	127+1528	127+1520	104+1238	70+790

Percentage Losses: 65%

	Gettysburg Battle Losses: July 1					
	Killed	Mortally Wounded	Missing	Wounded	Wounded & Captured	Captured
	Officers & Enlisted Men	Officers & Enlisted Men	Officers & Enlisted Men	Officers & Enlisted Men	Officers & Enlisted Men	Officers & Enlisted Men
Brig. Staff	0+0	0+0	0+0	0+0	0+0	0+0
5th NC	3+33	1+26	0+0	15+62	3+66	1+53
12th NC	0+6	0+6	0+0	3+29	0+27	0+1
20th NC	4+26	0+11	0+2	8+25	1+69	9+92
23rd NC	2+41	3+14	0+1	6+40	6+81	5+72
Total	9+106	4+57	0+3	32+156	10+243	15+218

---

6 A nominal list of casualties was published in the *Charlotte Western Democrat*, July 28, 1863. The list was reprinted in the *Fayetteville Observer*, Aug. 3, 1863.

7 Thirteen officers in the 5th North Carolina are known to have been present but their presence or absence is not stated on the muster rolls. Adding these 13 officers to the 114 officers reported present for duty on June 30 in OR 27, pt. 2, 564, brings the total present to 127.

Gettysburg Battle Losses: July 2

	Killed	Mortally Wounded	Missing	Wounded	Wounded & Captured	Captured
	Officers & Enlisted Men	Officers & Enlisted Men	Officers & Enlisted Men	Officers & Enlisted Men	Officers & Enlisted Men	Officers & Enlisted Men
Brig. Staff	0+0	0+0	0+0	0+0	0+0	0+0
5th NC	0+0	0+1	0+0	0+0	0+0	0+0
12th NC	0+0	0+0	0+0	0+1	0+0	0+0
20th NC	0+0	0+0	0+0	0+0	0+1	0+0
23rd NC	0+0	0+0	0+0	0+0	0+0	0+0
Total (3)	0+0	0+1	0+0	0+1	0+1	0+0

Gettysburg Battle Losses: July 3

	Killed	Mortally Wounded	Missing	Wounded	Wounded & Captured	Captured
	Officers & Enlisted Men	Officers & Enlisted Men	Officers & Enlisted Men	Officers & Enlisted Men	Officers & Enlisted Men	Officers & Enlisted Men
Brig. Staff	0+0	0+0	0+0	0+0	0+0	0+0
5th NC	0+0	0+2	0+0	0+1	0+0	0+1
12th NC	0+0	0+0	0+0	0+0	0+0	0+0
20th NC	0+0	0+0	0+0	0+0	0+0	0+0
23rd NC	0+0	0+0	0+0	0+0	0+0	0+0
Total (4)	0+0	0+2	0+0	0+1	0+0	0+1

Appendix 2: Numbers and Losses in Iverson's Brigade

	\multicolumn{6}{c}{**Gettysburg Battle Losses: July 1-3**}
	Killed	Mortally Wounded	Missing	Wounded	Wounded & Captured	Captured
Total (860)	9+106	4+60[8]	0+3	32+158	10+244	15+219

Gettysburg Non-Combat Losses

	\multicolumn{6}{c}{**Stragglers and Deserters: July 1-3**}
	Killed	Mortally Wounded	Missing	Wounded	Wounded & Captured	Captured
	Officers & Enlisted Men	Officers & Enlisted Men	Officers & Enlisted Men	Officers & Enlisted Men	Officers & Enlisted Men	Officers & Enlisted Men
Brig. Staff	0+0	0+0	0+0	0+0	0+0	0+0
5th NC	0+0	0+0	0+0	0+0	0+0	0+20
12th NC	0+0	0+0	0+0	0+0	0+0	0+4
20th NC	0+0	0+0	0+0	0+0	0+0	0+4
23rd NC	0+0	0+0	0+0	0+0	0+0	0+4
Total (32)	0+0	0+0	0+0	0+0	0+0	0+32

---

[8] Of the 61 men listed as mortally wounded, 47 of them were captured and died of their wounds while in Federal hands.

Left Behind Sick: July 5

	Killed	Mortally Wounded	Missing	Wounded	Wounded & Captured	Captured
	Officers & Enlisted Men	Officers & Enlisted Men	Officers & Enlisted Men	Officers & Enlisted Men	Officers & Enlisted Men	Officers & Enlisted Men
Brig. Staff	0+0	0+0	0+0	0+0	0+0	0+0
5th NC	0+0	0+0	0+0	0+0	0+0	0+2
12th NC	0+0	0+0	0+0	0+0	0+0	0+0
20th NC	0+0	0+0	0+0	0+0	0+0	0+0
23rd NC	0+0	0+0	0+0	0+0	0+0	0+1
Total (3)	0+0	0+0	0+0	0+0	0+0	0+3

Left Behind to Attend to Wounded: July 5[9]

	Killed	Mortally Wounded	Missing	Wounded	Wounded & Captured	Captured
	Officers & Enlisted Men	Officers & Enlisted Men	Officers & Enlisted Men	Officers & Enlisted Men	Officers & Enlisted Men	Officers & Enlisted Men
Brig. Staff	0+0	0+0	0+0	0+0	0+0	0+0
5th NC	0+0	0+0	0+0	0+0	0+0	1+5
12th NC	0+0	0+0	0+0	0+0	0+0	0+3
20th NC	0+0	0+0	0+0	0+0	0+0	1+3
23rd NC	0+0	0+0	0+0	0+0	0+0	1+6

9 Total for 5th North Carolina includes one surgeon, one hospital steward, and four privates; for 12th North Carolina includes one hospital steward and two privates; for 20th North Carolina includes one assistant surgeon and three privates; for 23rd North Carolina includes one assistant surgeon and six privates.

Appendix 2: Numbers and Losses in Iverson's Brigade

Total (20)	0+0	0+0	0+0	0+0	0+0	3+17

Total non-combat losses (stragglers, sick, left behind)						3+52

Additional Combat Losses: July 4-14

	Wagon Train Fight: July 4-5[10]					
	Killed	Mortally Wounded	Missing	Wounded	Wounded & Captured	Captured
	Officers & Enlisted Men	Officers & Enlisted Men	Officers & Enlisted Men	Officers & Enlisted Men	Officers & Enlisted Men	Officers & Enlisted Men
Brig. Staff	0+0	0+0	0+0	0+0	0+0	0+0
5th NC	0+0	0+0	0+0	0+0	0+0	0+2
12th NC	0+0	0+0	0+0	0+0	0+0	0+2
20th NC	0+0	0+0	0+0	0+0	0+0	0+0
23rd NC	0+0	0+0	0+0	0+0	0+0	0+4
Total (8)	0+0	0+0	0+0	0+0	0+0	0+8

10 In addition, two wounded enlisted men from the 20th North Carolina and one wounded officer and two wounded enlisted men from the 23rd North Carolina were captured during the wagon train fight.

Hagerstown: July 6

	Killed	Mortally Wounded	Missing	Wounded	Wounded & Captured	Captured
	Officers & Enlisted Men	Officers & Enlisted Men	Officers & Enlisted Men	Officers & Enlisted Men	Officers & Enlisted Men	Officers & Enlisted Men
Brig. Staff	0+0	0+0	0+0	0+0	0+0	0+0
5th NC	0+1	0+1	0+0	1+0	0+0	0+2
12th NC[11]	0+2	1+0	0+0	1+1	0+0	0+0
20th NC	0+0	0+2	0+0	0+0	0+0	0+0
23rd NC	0+0	0+0	0+0	0+0	0+0	0+0
Total (12)	0+3	1+3	0+0	2+1	0+0	0+2

Williamsport: July 9

	Killed	Mortally Wounded	Missing	Wounded	Wounded & Captured	Captured
	Officers & Enlisted Men	Officers & Enlisted Men	Officers & Enlisted Men	Officers & Enlisted Men	Officers & Enlisted Men	Officers & Enlisted Men
Brig. Staff	0+0	0+0	0+0	0+0	0+0	0+0
5th NC	0+0	0+0	0+0	0+0	0+0	0+0
12th NC	0+0	0+0	0+0	0+1	0+0	0+0
20th NC	0+0	0+0	0+0	0+0	0+0	0+0
23rd NC	0+0	0+0	0+0	0+0	0+0	0+0
Total (1)	0+0	0+0	0+0	0+1	0+0	0+0

11 A nominal list of casualties in the 12th North Carolina at Hagerstown was published in the *Raleigh Weekly Register*, Aug. 12, 1863.

Appendix 2: Numbers and Losses in Iverson's Brigade

| Total Add'l Combat Losses | 0+3 | 1+3 | 0+0 | 2+2 | 0+0 | 1+10 |

Additional Non-Combat Losses: July 4-14

Stragglers and Deserters

	Hagerstown: July 5					
	Killed	Mortally Wounded	Missing	Wounded	Wounded & Captured	Captured
	Officers & Enlisted Men	Officers & Enlisted Men	Officers & Enlisted Men	Officers & Enlisted Men	Officers & Enlisted Men	Officers & Enlisted Men
Brig. Staff	0+0	0+0	0+0	0+0	0+0	0+0
5th NC	0+0	0+0	0+0	0+0	0+0	0+0
12th NC	0+0	0+0	0+0	0+0	0+0	0+2
20th NC	0+0	0+0	0+0	0+0	0+0	0+0
23rd NC	0+0	0+0	0+0	0+0	0+0	0+0
Total (2)	0+0	0+0	0+0	0+0	0+0	0+2

	Killed	Mortally Wounded	Missing	Wounded	Wounded & Captured	Captured
Williamsport and Falling Waters: July 13-14						
	Officers & Enlisted Men	Officers & Enlisted Men	Officers & Enlisted Men	Officers & Enlisted Men	Officers & Enlisted Men	Officers & Enlisted Men
Brig. Staff	0+0	0+0	0+0	0+0	0+0	0+0
5th NC	0+0	0+0	0+0	0+0	0+0	0+5
12th NC	0+0	0+0	0+0	0+0	0+0	0+1
20th NC	0+0	0+0	0+0	0+0	0+0	0+3
23rd NC	0+0	0+0	0+0	0+0	0+0	0+0
Total (9)	0+0	0+0	0+0	0+0	0+0	0+9
Total Additional Combat Losses	0+0	0+0	0+0	0+0	0+0	0+11

Total Brigade Losses: July 1-14

Total Brigade Losses	9+109	5+63	0+3	34+160	10+244	18+292

Total Brigade Losses for the Gettysburg Campaign from all causes: 947

Bibliography

NEWSPAPERS

Alabama Beacon (Greensboro, Alabama)
Albany Patriot (Albany, Georgia)
Atlanta Southern Confederacy (Atlanta, Georgia)
Augusta Weekly Chronicle and Sentinel (Augusta, Georgia)
Baltimore Sun (Baltimore, Maryland)
Biblical Recorder (Raleigh, North Carolina)
Carlisle American Volunteer (Carlisle, Pennsylvania)
Carolina Watchman (Salisbury, North Carolina)
Charlotte Daily Bulletin (Charlotte, North Carolina)
Charlotte Journal (Charlotte, North Carolina)
Charlotte Daily Observer (Charlotte, North Carolina)
Charlotte Western Democrat (Charlotte, North Carolina)
Clark County Journal (Grove Hill, Alabama)
Columbus Enquirer (Columbus, Georgia)
Columbus Enquirer-Sun (Columbus, Georgia)
Columbus Times (Columbus, Georgia)
Cumberland Valley Journal (Mechanicsburg, Pennsylvania)
Daily National Intelligencer (Washington, D.C,)
Daily North Carolinian (Fayetteville, North Carolina)
Fayetteville Observer (Fayetteville, North Carolina)
Franklin Repository (Chambersburg, Pennsylvania)
Georgia Telegraph and Republic (Macon, Georgia)
Georgia Weekly Telegraph (Macon, Georgia)
Greencastle Pilot (Greencastle, Pennsylvania)
Greensborough Patriot (Greensboro, North Carolina)
Hillsborough Recorder (Hillsborough, North Carolina)
Lancaster Daily Express (Lancaster, Pennsylvania)
Macon Daily Telegraph (Macon, Georgia)
Macon Weekly Telegraph (Macon, Georgia)

Mobile Daily Advertiser and Register (Mobile, Alabama)
Mobile Evening News (Mobile, Alabama)
New York Times (New York, New York)
North Carolina Argus (Wadesboro, North Carolina)
North Carolina Presbyterian (Fayetteville, North Carolina)
North Carolina Standard (Raleigh, North Carolina)
North Carolina Weekly Standard (Raleigh, North Carolina)
Raleigh Daily Progress (Raleigh, North Carolina)
Raleigh Register and North Carolina Gazette (Raleigh, North Carolina)
Raleigh Semi-Weekly Register (Raleigh, North Carolina)
Raleigh State Journal (Raleigh, North Carolina)
Raleigh Weekly State Journal (Raleigh, North Carolina)
Richmond Daily Dispatch (Richmond, Virginia)
Richmond Enquirer (Richmond, Virginia)
Savannah Republican (Savannah, Georgia)
Selma Morning Reporter (Selma, Alabama)
Sprit of the Age (Raleigh, North Carolina)
The Countryman (Turnwold, Georgia)
Valley Spirit (Chambersburg, Pennsylvania)
Wilmington Journal (Wilmington, North Carolina)

MANUSCRIPT SOURCES

Adams County Historical Society, Gettysburg, Pennsylvania
   Photograph Collection

Alabama Department of Archives and History, Montgomery, Alabama
   John Purifoy, "History of Jeff Davis Artillery"
   Thomas S. Taylor Papers
   William H. Terrell Letters
   John S. Tucker Diary

Allison-Antrim Museum, Greencastle, Pennsylvania
   Charles Hartman Diary Typescript

Baltimore and Ohio Railroad Museum, Hays T. Watkins Research Library, Baltimore, Maryland
   Photograph Collection

Catawba County Museum of History, Archives and Library, Newton, North Carolina
   Gibson Papers

Cumberland County Historical Society, Carlisle, Pennsylvania
    Civil War Collection Files
    Robin Stafford Collection

Davidson County Historical Museum, Lexington, North Carolina
    Badgett Papers

Raymond J. DeStefano Private Collection, East Williston, New York
    Alexander Murdock Letter

Dickinson College, Waidner-Spahr Library, Carlisle, Pennsylvania
    Thomas Miller Griffith Papers
    James Henry Morgan Presidential Papers

Duke University, William R. Perkins Library, Durham, North Carolina
    Mary Ann Boyles Papers
    William H. Brotherton Papers
    James O. Coghill Papers
    John C. Hackett Papers
    Edward Harden Papers
    Archibald Erskine Henderson Papers
    Gertrude Jenkins Papers
    Robert D. Johnston Papers
    John Thomas Nichols Papers
    Isaac V. Reynolds Papers
    Irby H. Scott Papers
    William Alexander Smith Papers
    Louis Redmon Wells Papers

East Carolina University, J. Y. Joyner Library, Greenville, North Carolina
    Elizabeth Rudder Fearrington Croom Collection
    Nathan R. Frazier Papers
    Hugh Harrison Mills Collection

Emory University, Robert W. Woodruff Library, Atlanta, Georgia
    Confederate Miscellany Collection
    Iverson Family Papers
    David Read Evans Winn Papers

Fredericksburg & Spotsylvania National Military Park Collection, Fredericksburg, Virginia
    John C. Ussery Letter

Steve French Private Collection, Hedgesville, West Virginia
    Photograph Collection

Georgia Archives, Morrow, Georgia
    Civil War Miscellaneous Personal Papers
    Thomas M. Hightower Letters
    John C. Key, "Memoirs"
    W. H. May, "Reminiscences of the War Between the States"
    Lavender R. Ray Papers
    Sidney J. Richardson Papers

Gettysburg National Military Park Collection, Gettysburg, Pennsylvania
    Gregory A. Coco Collection
    Confederate Regiment Files
    William M. Robbins Journal
    Union Regiment Files

Greensboro College, Brock Historical Museum, Greensboro, North Carolina
    Portrait Collection

Greensboro Historical Museum, Archives Division, Greensboro, North Carolina
    Photograph Collection

Handley Regional Library, Steward Bell Jr. Archives Room, Winchester, Virginia
    Charles William McVicar Papers

Historical Society of Lower Cape Fear, Wilmington, North Carolina
    B. Frank Hall, "Account of the Battle of Gettysburg, 1913"

Jackson County Public Library, Ripley, West Virginia
    Addison Austin Smith, "A Story of the Life and Trials of a Confederate Soldier and the Great Loop He Made in Three Years"

Gary Kross Private Collection, Gettysburg, Pennsylvania
    Iverson Family Papers

Lenoir Community College, Heritage Place, Kinston, North Carolina
    Tempie Parker Harris Prince Collection

Library of Congress, Washington, D.C.
    Photograph Collection

Library of Congress, Manuscript Division, Washington, D.C.
    Richard Stoddert Ewell Papers
    Jedediah Hotchkiss Papers

The Library of Virginia, Richmond, Virginia
    John C. Donahue Diary

Mariner's Museum, Library, Newport News, Virginia
    William R. Cheek Letter
    Henry Eaton Coleman Papers

Museum of the Confederacy, Eleanor Brockenbrough Library, Richmond, Virginia
    Confederate States Army Bound Volumes
    Kate Mason Rowland Collection

National Archives, Washington, D.C.
    Photograph Collection

National Archives, Record Group 94, Washington, D.C.
    Complied Service Records, Mexican War, Adjutant General's Office
    Mexican War Pension Records, Adjutant General's Office

National Archives, Record Group 109, Washington, D.C.
    Jacob Brookfield Diary
    Compiled Military Service Records for Confederate Army Volunteers
    Diary and Account Book of Colonel John Lea
    General and Special Orders, 23rd North Carolina
    Letters Received, Confederate Secretary of War
    Letters Received, Confederate Adjutant and Inspector General's Office
    Letters Sent, Confederate Secretary of War
    List of Officers Under Fire, Killed, Wounded, and Missing, Iverson's Brigade
    Orders and Circulars, Department of North Carolina, 1861-1865
    Record of Events, 5th North Carolina
    Record of Events, 12th North Carolina

Navarro College, Pearce Civil War Collection, Corsicana, Texas
    Alexander Murdock Papers

New Hanover County Library, North Carolina Room, Wilmington, North Carolina
    Cowan and Denson Family Papers
    Melinda Ray Diary

New York Historical Society, New York, New York
    Gilder-Lehrman Collection

New York State Military Museum, Albany, New York
    New York Civil War Newspaper Clipping Files

North Carolina Division of Archives and History, Private Collections, Raleigh, North Carolina
    Oscar W. Blacknall Papers
    Henry Toole Clark Governor's Letter Book
    Henry Toole Clark Governor's Papers
    J. B. Clifton Diary
    Fred C. Foard Papers
    Gales Papers
    James E. Green Diary
    John T. Gregory Papers
    Bryan Grimes Papers
    Edward Jones Hale Papers
    Daniel Harvey Hill Papers
    Joseph B. Jones Letter
    Albert Moses Luria Journal
    Elizabeth M. Montgomery Collection
    William Clark Ousby Papers
    Isaac E. Pearce Papers
    Photograph Collection
    Adolphus R. Pitcher Diary
    Stephen D. Ramseur Papers
    Richardson Family Papers
    John F. Shaffner Diary and Papers
    Anna Pierce Stafford Collection
    Thomas F. Toon Papers
    Zebulon Baird Vance Papers
    Zebulon Baird Vance Governor's Papers
    Webb Collection
    Williams-Dameron Family Papers

North Carolina Division of Archives and History, Military Collection, Raleigh, North Carolina
    Edward G. Butler, "Reminiscences"
    B. B. Carr, "Sketch of the Battle of Chancellorsville"
    J. D. Ireland, "Memoirs"
    Samuel D. Marshbourn, "Reminiscences"
    J. B. Oliver, "My Recollections of the Battle of Gettysburg"
    John A. Stikeleather, "Recollections"
    J. L. Wallace, "Reminiscences"

North Carolina Museum of History, Raleigh, North Carolina
   Photograph Collection

Pennsylvania State Archives, Harrisburg, Pennsylvania
   Moore Family Papers

R. Carol McLean, Private Collection, Rockingham, North Carolina
   Photograph Collection

Rice University, Woodson Research Center, Fondren Library, Houston, Texas
   Americas Collection

Sampson County History Museum, Clinton, North Carolina
   Photograph Collection

Troup County Archives, LaGrange, Georgia
   Nix-Price Collection

United State Army Heritage and Education Center, Carlisle, Pennsylvania
   Robert L. Brake Collection
   Carlisle Barracks Collection
   Civil War Miscellaneous Collection
   Civil War Times Illustrated Collection
   Harrisburg Civil War Roundtable Collection
   Lewis Leigh Collection
   Jacob R. Menges, "Corporal's Memoirs, 1861-1865"
   Michael Winey Collection

University of Georgia, Special Collections Division, Hargrett Library, Athens, Georgia
   Mary Barnard Nix Collection

University of Michigan, Schoff Civil War Collection, William L. Clements Library, Ann Arbor, Michigan
   David Ballenger Letters

University of North Carolina at Chapel Hill, Southern Historical Collection, Chapel Hill, North Carolina
   Edward Porter Alexander Papers
   Archibald Hunter Arrington Papers
   William Beavans Diary and Letters
   John Stanley Brooks Letters
   Burwell Family Papers
   Calder Family Papers
   Carrie H. Clack Papers

John Fuller Coghill Letters
Benjamin Mosely Collins, "Reminiscences"
Ferebee, Gregory, and McPherson Family Papers
Leonidas Chalmers Glenn Papers
Hatrick Family Papers
Leak and Wall Family Papers
William Gaston Lewis Papers
John McRae Papers
Edward Asbury O'Neal Papers
John R. Peacock Papers
Peek Family Papers
William Nelson Pendleton Papers
Polk, Brown and Ewell Family Papers
Leonidas L. Polk Papers
Stephen Dodson Ramseur Papers
Thomas Ruffin Papers
Peter J. Sinclair Papers
Preston H. Turner Papers
Lewis Henry Webb Collection
George Whitaker Wills Letters

University of Notre Dame, Rare Books and Special Collections, Notre Dame, Indiana
　　Sillers-Holmes Family Correspondence

University of South Carolina, Manuscripts Division, South Caroliniana Library, Columbia, South Carolina
　　Papers of the Means and McFadden Families
　　Watson Family Papers

University of Virginia, Alderman Library, Charlottesville, Virginia
　　John Warwick Daniel Papers
　　Reid Family Papers
　　Micajah Woods Papers

Valentine Museum, Richmond History Center, Richmond, Virginia
　　Cook Collection

Virginia Historical Society, Richmond, Virginia
　　Confederate Memorial Association Collection
　　Lee Family Papers
　　Liebermann Family Papers
　　Portrait Collection

Virginia Military Institute, Lexington, Virginia
  Henry Eaton Coleman Alumni Files

Warren County Heritage Society, Front Royal, Virginia
  Charles Eckhardt Diary

Yale University, Manuscripts and Archives Library, New Haven, Connecticut
  Diaries Miscellaneous Collection

PUBLISHED PRIMARY SOURCES

Articles

Ardrey, William E. "Civil War Account From the Diary of the Great-Grandfather of Alliance Residence," *The Pamlico News,* Sept. 2, 1992 and Sept. 9, 1992.

Barry, Louise, ed. "With the First U.S. Cavalry in Indian Country, 1859-1861: Letters to the Daily Times, Leavenworth," *Kansas Historical Quarterly,* 24 (1958), 257-284, 399-425.

Bender, Lida Welsh. "Civil War Memoirs," *Waynesboro Record Herald,* Jan. 12, 1961.

Bennett, R. T. "Fourteenth Regiment," included in Walter Clark, ed., *Histories of the Several Regiments and Battalions from North Carolina in the Great War 1861-'65.* 5 Vols. Goldsboro, NC: Nash Brothers, 1901, 1:704-732.

Betts, A. D. "The Chaplain Service," included in Walter Clark, ed., *Histories of the Several Regiments and Battalions from North Carolina in the Great War 1861-'65.* 5 Vols. Goldsboro, NC: Nash Brothers, 1901, 4:597-621.

Bond, Frank A. "Company A., First Maryland Cavalry," *Confederate Veteran,* 6 (1898), 78-80.

Bowers, William S., ed. "William Heyser's Diary," *Kittochtinny Historical Society Papers,* 16 (1970-1978), 1-88.

Branham, Alfred Iverson. "Letters to the Telegraph," *Macon Telegraph,* Nov. 20, 1929.

Burgwyn, William H. S. "Thirty-Fifth Regiment," included in Walter Clark, ed., *Histories of the Several Regiments and Battalions from North Carolina in the Great War 1861-'65.* 5 Vols. Goldsboro, NC: Nash Brothers, 1901, 2:591-628.

Burnett, Edmund Cody, ed. "Letters of a Confederate Surgeon: Dr. Abner Embry McGarity, 1862-1865," *Georgia Historical Quarterly,* 24 (1945), 159-189.

Cantwell, John L. "A Capture Before the War," included in Walter Clark, ed., *Histories of the Several Regiments and Battalions from North Carolina in the Great War 1861-'65.* 5 Vols. Goldsboro, NC: Nash Brothers, 1901, 5:23-28.

Cree, Jemima K. "Jenkins' Raid," *Kittochtinny Historical Society Papers,* 5 (1905-1908), 92-99.

Denson, C. B. "The Corps of Engineers and Engineering Troops," included in Walter Clark, ed., *Histories of the Several Regiments and Battalions from North Carolina in the Great War 1861-'65.* 5 Vols. Goldsboro, NC: Nash Brothers, 1901, 4:409-432.

Early, John Cabell. "A Southern Boy's Experience at Gettysburg," *Journal of the Military Service Institution of the United States,* 48 (1911), 415-423.

Early, Jubal A. "Leading Confederates on the Battlefield: A Review By General Early," *Southern Historical Society Papers*, 4 (1877), 241-281.

———. "Comments on the First Volume of Count of Paris' Civil War in America," *Southern Historical Society Papers*, 3 (1876), 140-154.

Elkins, William Franklin. "In the Junior Reserves," *Confederate Veteran*, 40 (1932), 171.

Gorman, George, ed. "Memoirs of a Rebel: Being the Narratives of John Calvin Gorman, Captain, Company B, 2nd North Carolina Regiment, 1861-1865, Part II: Chancellorsville and Gettysburg," *Military Images*, 3 (1982), 21-25.

Grace, C. D. "Rodes's Division at Gettysburg," *Confederate Veteran*, 5 (1897), 614-615.

Graham, W. A. "Nineteenth Regiment," included in Walter Clark, ed., *Histories of the Several Regiments and Battalions from North Carolina in the Great War 1861-'65*. 5 Vols. Goldsboro, NC: Nash Brothers, 1901, 2:79-109.

Grant, George. "The First Army Corps on the First Day at Gettysburg," included in Ken Brady and Florence Freeland, eds. *The Gettysburg Papers*. 2 Vols. Dayton, OH: Morningside House, 1988, 1:249-270.

Green, Fletcher M., ed. "A People at War: Hagerstown, Maryland, June 15-Aug. 31, 1863, *Maryland Historical Magazine*, 40 (1940), 251-259.

Hall, Isaac. "Iverson's Brigade and the Part the 97th New York Played in Its Capture," *National Tribune*, June 26, 1884.

———. "Iverson's Brigade: An Old Controversy in Regard to Its Capture Renewed," *National Tribune*, Sept. 10, 1885.

Halsey, Don P., Jr. "A Sketch of Capt. Don P. Halsey," *Southern Historical Society Papers*, 31 (1903), 193-197.

Hamilton, John Bowen, ed. "Diary of Thomas Miles Garrett at The University of North Carolina, 1849," *North Carolina Historical Review*, 38 (1961), 63-93, 241-262, 380-410, 534-563.

Hanna, Thomas L. "A Day at Gettysburg," *National Tribune*, May 23, 1901.

Hege, Henry B. "The Civil War Unvarnished—Henry B. Hege to Henry G. Hege, July 12, 1863," *Mennonite Research Journal*, 5 (1964), 19.

Hicks, Lewis T. "Memoirs," *Raleigh State Journal*, April 27, 1917.

Hill, Daniel H. "The Battle of South Mountain, or Boonsboro" included in Robert U. Johnson and Clarence C. Buel, eds., *Battles and Leaders of the Civil War*. 4 Vols. New York: Castle Books, 1956, 2:559-583.

Hodam, James Harrison. "The Hodam Manuscript: Reminiscences of a Confederate Soldier," included in Brian Stuart Kesterson, *Campaigning With the 17th Virginia Cavalry*. Washington, WV: Night Hawk Press, 2005, 274-307.

Hufham, J. D., Jr. "Gettysburg: Being an Account of the Experiences of a Veteran, Told By Himself," *Wake Forest Student*, 16 (1897), 451-456.

Johnston, Hugh Buckner, Jr., ed. "The Confederate Letters of Ruffin Barnes of Wilson County," *North Carolina Historical Review*, 31 (1954), 75-99.

Johnston, James F. "The Garland-Iverson-Johnston Brigade," included in Walter Clark, ed., *Histories of the Several Regiments and Battalions from North Carolina in the Great War 1861-'65*. 5 Vols. Goldsboro, NC: Nash Brothers, 1901, 4:520-526.

Key, Major. "Reminiscences of the Civil War: And Incidents Connected With the 44th Georgia and Other Regiments," *Jasper County News,* Jan. 5, 1899.

Kimball, George. "Iverson's Brigade, The 12th Mass, Did Join in the Charge," *National Tribune,* Oct. 1, 1885.

———. "My Army Life," included in Charles Carleton Coffin, ed., *Stories of Our Soldiers: War Reminiscences,* 2 Vols. Boston: The Journal Newspaper Co., 1893, 2:77-116.

Landon, William, ed. "The 14th Indiana Regiment in the Valley of Virginia: Letters to the Vincennes Western Sun," *Indiana Magazine of History,* 30 (1934), 275-298.

Loehr, Charles T. "The 'Old First' Virginia at Gettysburg," *Southern Historical Society Papers,* 32 (1904), 33-40.

London, Henry A. "Thirty-Second Regiment," included in Walter Clark, ed. *Histories of the Several Regiments and Battalions from North Carolina in the Great War 1861-'65.* 5 Vols. Goldsboro, NC: Nash Brothers, 1901, 3:521-550.

Mattes, Merrill J., ed. "Patrolling the Santa Fe Trail: Reminiscences of John S. Kirwin," *Kansas Historical Quarterly,* 21 (1955), 559-587.

May, William H. "First Confederates to Enter Gettysburg," *Confederate Veteran,* 5 (1897), 620-621.

McClean, Elizabeth M. "The Rebels Are Coming," *Gettysburg Compiler,* June 8, 1908.

McRae, Duncan K. "Battle of Williamsburg, May 1862," *The William and Mary Quarterly,* Second Series, 2 (1922),195-197.

———. "The Battle of Williamsburg—Reply to Colonel Bratton," *Southern Historical Society Papers,* 7 (1880), 360-372.

McRae, James C. and C. M. Busbee. "Fifth Regiment," included in Walter Clark, ed., *Histories of the Several Regiments and Battalions from North Carolina in the Great War 1861-'65.* 5 Vols. Goldsboro, NC: Nash Brothers, 1901, 1:280-292.

Miller, William H. "They All Helped to Do It," *National Tribune,* Oct. 15, 1885.

Monroe, Haskell, ed. "The Road to Gettysburg: The Diary and Letters of Leonidas Torrence of the Gaston Guards," *North Carolina Historical Review,* 36 (1959), 509-517.

Montgomery, Walter A. "Twelfth Regiment," included in Walter Clark, ed., *Histories of the Several Regiments and Battalions from North Carolina in the Great War 1861-'65.* 5 Vols. Goldsboro, NC: Nash Brothers, 1901, 1:605-652.

Moore, Samuel Scollay. "Through the Shadows: A Boy's Memories of the Civil War in Clarke County," *Proceedings of the Clarke County Historical Association,* 24 (1989-1990), 1-98.

Myers, William Starr, ed. "The Civil War Diary of General Isaac Ridgeway Trimble," *Maryland Historical Magazine,* 17 (1922), 1-20.

Nelson, William N. "Capturing an Ex-Dictator," *The Southern Magazine,* 10 (1872), 241-245.

Park, Robert E. "War Diary of Captain Robert Emory Park," *Southern Historical Society Papers,* 26 (1898), 1-31.

Peck, Robert Morris. "Recollections of Early Times in Kansas Territory: From the Standpoint of a Regular Cavalryman," *Collections of the Kansas State Historical Society,* 8 (1904), 484-507.

Piston, William Garrett, ed. "The Rebs Are Yet Thick About Us: The Civil War Diary of Amos Stouffer of Chambersburg," *Civil War History,* 38 (1992), 210-231.

Plater, Richard C., Jr., ed. "Civil War Diary of Miss Matella Page Harrison of Clarke County, Virginia, 1835-1898," *Proceedings of the Clarke County Historical Association,* 22 (1982-1983), 3-79.

Polk, Leonidas L. "The 43rd N.C. During the War: Whiffs from My Old Camp Pipe," *Weekly Ansonian,* May 17, 1876.

Purifoy, John. "With Ewell and Rodes in Pennsylvania," *Confederate Veteran,* 30 (1922), 462-464.

———. "With Jackson in the Valley," *Confederate Veteran,* 30 (1922), 383-385.

Ramsey, N. A. "Sixty-First Regiment," included in Walter Clark, ed., *Histories of the Several Regiments and Battalions from North Carolina in the Great War 1861-'65.* 5 Vols. Goldsboro, NC: Nash Brothers, 1901, 3:502-514.

Ray, Neill W. "Sixth Regiment," included in Walter Clark, ed., *Histories of the Several Regiments and Battalions from North Carolina in the Great War 1861-'65.* 5 Vols. Goldsboro, NC: Nash Brothers, 1901, 1:293-359.

Robinson, W. Stitt, ed. "The Kiowa and Comanche Campaign of 1860 as Recorded in the Personal Diary of Lt. J. E. B. Stuart," *Kansas Historical Quarterly,* 23 (1957), 382-400.

Root, George A., ed. "Extracts from Diary of Captain Lambert Bowman Wolf," *Kansas Historical Quarterly,* 1 (1932), 195-210.

Rowland, Kate Mason, ed. "Letters of Major Thomas Rowland, C.S.A.," *William and Mary College Quarterly Historical Magazine,* 26 (1917), 225-235.

Schuricht, Hermann. "Jenkins' Brigade in the Gettysburg Campaign: Extracts From the Diary of Lieutenant Hermann Schuricht, of the Fourteenth Virginia Cavalry," *Southern Historical Society Papers,* 24 (1896), 339-351.

Shepherd, Henry E. "Wounded and Captured," included in C. E. Graham, ed., *Under Both Flags: A Panorama of the Civil War.* Chicago: Monarch Book Co., 1896, 76-77.

Sherrill, Miles O. "At Gettysburg in 1863: Some Reminiscences of One of the Participants in the Famous Battle," *Charlotte Daily Observer,* July 22, 1912.

Taylor, Michael W., ed. "Ramseur's Brigade in the Gettysburg Campaign: A Newly Discovered Account By Capt. James I. Harris," *Gettysburg Magazine,* 17 (July 1997), 26-40.

Toon, Thomas F. "Twentieth Regiment," included in Walter Clark, ed., *Histories of the Several Regiments and Battalions from North Carolina in the Great War 1861-'65.* 5 Vols. Goldsboro, NC: Nash Brothers, 1901, 2:112-127.

Trimble, Isaac R. "The Battle and Campaign of Gettysburg," *Southern Historical Society Papers,* 26 (1898), 116-128.

Tripp, Edward. "North Carolina to the Rescue," included in Pamlico Chapter of the Daughters of the Confederacy, *The Confederate Reveille: Memorial Edition.* Raleigh: Edwards and Broughton, 1898, 40-42.

Trudeau, Noah Andre, ed. "5th Alabama Sharpshooters: Taking Aim at Cemetery Hill," *America's Civil War,* 14, No. 3 (July 2001), 46-53.

Turner, V. E. and H. C. Wall. "Twenty-Third Regiment," included in Walter Clark, ed., *Histories of the Several Regiments and Battalions from North Carolina in the Great War 1861-'65.* 5 Vols. Goldsboro, NC: Nash Brothers, 1901, 2:180-268.

Vautier, John D. "At Gettysburg," *Philadelphia Weekly Press,* Nov. 10, 1886.

———. "Realities Reading Like Fiction," included in National Tribune. *National Tribune Scrapbook: Stories of the Camp, March, Battle, Hospital and Prison Told by Comrades.* Washington: National Tribune, 1909, 146-148.

Wall, H. C. "In Their Own Words, 23rd Regiment Infantry (13th Regiment N.C. State Troops), Bits of War History," *Raleigh News and Observer,* April 11, 1897.

———. "The 23rd North Carolina Infantry, Organized in 1861 as the 13th Regiment of Volunteers, Historical Sketch," *Southern Historical Society Papers,* 25 (1897), 151-176.

Wehrum, Charles. "The Adjutant of the 12th Massachusetts Replies to the Captain of the 97th New York," *National Tribune,* Dec. 10, 1885.

Williams, R. S. "Thirteenth Regiment," included in Walter Clark, ed., *Histories of the Several Regiments and Battalions from North Carolina in the Great War 1861-'65.* 5 Vols. Goldsboro, NC: Nash Brothers, 1901, 1:653-687.

Willis, Francis T. "The Twelfth Georgia Infantry," *Southern Historical Society Papers,* 17 (1889), 160-187.

Wilson, Gary, ed. "The Diary of John S. Tucker: Confederate Soldier from Alabama," *Alabama Historical Quarterly,* 43 (1981), 5-33.

Wilson, George W. "First Fighting in Pennsylvania," *Confederate Veteran,* 31 (1913), 70.

Wood, Wayne, ed. "From Montgomery to Gettysburg: War Letters from Alabama Soldier Henry B. Wood," *Alabama Heritage Magazine,* 15 (1990), 26-45.

Books

Adams, Charles R., Jr., ed. *A Post of Honor: The Pryor Letters, 1861-1863.* Fort Valley, GA: Garret Publications, 1989.

Alghrary, Rebecca Ikerd, ed. *A Confederate Remembers Northern Virginia: George Rabb, Catawba County Soldier.* Newton, NC: Catawba County Historical Society, 1994.

Arp, Bill. *Bill Arp from the Uncivil War to Date, 1861-1903.* Atlanta: Hudgins Publishing Co., 1903.

Ashby, Thomas A. *The Valley Campaigns: Being the Reminiscences of a Non-Combatant While Between the Lines in the Shenandoah Valley During the War of the States.* New York: Neale Publishing Co., 1914.

Avary, Myrta Lockett, ed. *A Virginia Girl in the Civil War 1861-1865: Being a Record of the Actual Experiences of a Wife of a Confederate Officer.* New York: D. Appleton and Co., 1903.

Baer, Elizabeth R., ed. *Shadows on My Heart: The Civil War Diary of Lucy Rebecca Buck of Virginia.* Athens: University of Georgia Press, 1997.

Beach, William H. *The First New York (Lincoln) Cavalry.* New York: Lincoln Cavalry Association, 1902.

Beck, Brandon H., ed. *Third Alabama!: The Civil War Memoirs of Brigadier General Cullen Andrews Battle, CSA.* Tuscaloosa: University of Alabama Press, 2000.

Betts, A. D. *Experience of a Confederate Chaplain: 1861-1864.* Greenville, SC: n.p., 1907.

Blackford, L. Minor. *Mine Eyes Have Seen The Glory.* Cambridge, MA: Harvard University Press, 1954.

Blackford, Susan Leigh, ed. *Letters from Lee's Army*. New York: Charles Scribner's Sons, 1947.

Bleser, Carol, ed. *Tokens of Affection: The Letters of a Planter's Daughter in the Old South*. Athens: University of Georgia Press, 1996.

Bradshaw, Ada Bruce Desper, ed. *The Civil War Diary of Charles William McVicar*. Hampton, VA: n.p., 1977.

Chapman, Sarah Bahnson, ed. *Bright and Gloomy Days: The Civil War Correspondence of Charles Frederic Bahnson*. Knoxville: University of Tennessee Press, 2003.

Chappell, Frank Anderson, ed. *Dear Sister: Civil War Letters to a Sister in Alabama*. Huntsville, AL: Branch Springs Publishing Co., 2002.

Chattahoochee Valley Historical Society. *War Was The Place: A Centennial Collection of Confederate Soldier Letters*. Chambers County, AL: Chattahoochee Valley Historical Society, 1961.

Civil War Centennial Committee. *Treadwell Smith's Diary of the Civil War, October 17, 1859-April 20, 1865*. Berryville, VA: Berryville and Clarke County Chamber of Commerce, 1965.

Confederate States of America. *Regulations for the Army of the Confederate States*. Harrisburg, PA: National Historical Society, 1980.

Crist, Lynda Lasswell, ed. *The Papers of Jefferson Davis*. 10 Vols. Baton Rouge: Louisiana State University Press, 1981-1997.

Curtis, Newton Martin. *From Bull Run to Chancellorsville: The Story of the Sixteenth New York Infantry Together With Personal Reminiscences*. New York: G. P. Putnam's Sons, 1906.

Curtis, Walter Gilman. *Reminiscences of Wilmington and Smithville—Southport, 1848-1900*. Southport, NC: Herald Job Office, 1905.

Deems, Edward M. and Francis M. Deems, eds. *Autobiography of Charles Force Deems*. New York: Fleming H. Revell Co., 1897.

Early, Jubal A. *Autobiographical Sketch of the War Between the States*. Philadelphia: J. B. Lippincott Co., 1912.

Eaton Jr., Lafayette Claud, ed. *Rebecca's Letters: A Saga of a Confederate Family*. Vallejo, CA: n.p., 2000.

Freeman, Douglas S., ed. *Lee's Dispatches: Unpublished Letters of General Robert E. Lee*. New York: G. P. Putnam's Sons, 1957.

Gardiner, Mabel Henshaw and Ann Henshaw Gardiner, eds. *Chronicles of Old Berkeley: A Narrative History of a Virginia County from Its Beginning to 1926*. Durham, NC: The Seeman Press, 1938.

Georgia Division, United Daughters of the Confederacy. *Confederate Reminiscences and Letters 1861-1865*. 18 Vols. Atlanta: Georgia Division, United Daughters of the Confederacy, 1995-2000.

Glisan, Rodney. *Journal of Army Life*. San Francisco: A. L. Bancroft, 1874.

Goss, Warren Lee. *The Soldier's Story of His Captivity at Andersonville, Belle Isle, and Other Rebel Prisons*. Boston: Lee and Shepard Publishers, 1866.

Green, Wharton Jackson. *Recollections and Reflections: An Auto of Half a Century and More*. Raleigh: Edwards and Broughton Printing Co., 1906.

Hall, Isaac. *History of the Ninety-Seventh Regiment New York Volunteers: The Conkling Rifles*. Baltimore: Butternut and Blue, 1991.

Hargis, O. P. *Thrilling Experiences of a First Georgia Cavalryman in the Civil War.* Rome, GA: n.p., n.d.

Hassler, William W., ed. *One of Lee's Best Men: The Civil War Letters of General William Dorsey Pender.* Chapel Hill: University of North Carolina Press, 1999.

Hewitt, Janet B. et al., eds. *The Supplement to the Official Records of the Union and Confederate Armies.* 95 Vols. Wilmington, NC: Broadfoot Publishing Co., 1995-2000.

Hodam, Robert P., ed. *The Journal of James Hoddam.* Eugene, OR: Western Printing, 1995.

Hoge, Peyton Harrison, ed. *Moses Drury Hoge: Life and Letters.* Richmond: Whittet and Shefferson, 1899.

Hoke, Jacob. *The Great Invasion of 1863.* Dayton, OH: W. J. Suey, 1887.

———. *Reminiscences of the War In and About Chambersburg.* Chambersburg, PA: M. A. Foltz, 1884.

Hoole, William Stanley, ed. *History of the Third Alabama Regiment by Col. Charles Forsyth.* University, AL: Confederate Publishing Co., 1991.

Hopkins, Luther W. *From Bull Run to Appomattox: A Boy's View.* Baltimore: Fleet McGinley Co., 1908.

Hubbell, Raynor, ed. *Confederate Stamps, Old Letters and History.* Griffin, GA: n.p., 1959.

Hubbs, G. Ward, ed. *Voices From Company D: Diaries by the Greensboro Guards, Fifth Alabama Infantry Regiment, Army of Northern Virginia.* Athens: University of Georgia Press, 2003.

Hussey, George A. and William Todd. *History of the Ninth Regiment N.Y.S.M.-N.G.S.N.Y (Eighty-Third New York Volunteers).* New York: J. S. Ogilvie, 1889.

In Memoriam, Letters of William Wheeler of the Class of 1855, Yale College. Cambridge, MA: n.p., 1875.

Johnson, Clifton. *Battleground Adventures.* Boston: Houghton Mifflin Co., 1915.

Johnston, Frontis W., ed. *The Papers of Zebulon Baird Vance, Vol. 1.* Raleigh: North Carolina Division of Archives and History, 1963.

Jones, Terry L., ed. *Campbell Brown's Civil War: With Ewell and the Army of Northern Virginia.* Baton Rouge: Louisiana State University Press, 2001.

———. *The Civil War Memoirs of William J. Seymour.* Baton Rouge: Louisiana State University Press, 1991.

Koonce, Donald B., ed. *Doctor to the Front: The Recollections of Confederate Surgeon Thomas Fanning Wood, 1861-1865.* Knoxville: University of Tennessee Press, 2000.

Kundahl, George G. *The Bravest of the Brave: The Correspondence of Stephen Dodson Ramseur.* Chapel Hill: University of North Carolina Press, 2010.

Ladd, David L. and Aubrey J. Ladd, eds. *The Bachelder Papers: Gettysburg in Their Own Words.* 3 Vols. Dayton, OH: Morningside House, 1994.

Leon, Louis. *Diary of a Tar Heel Confederate Soldier.* Wilmington, NC: Broadfoot Publishing Co., 1992.

Lord, Walter, ed. *The Fremantle Diary: Being the Journal of Lieutenant Colonel Arthur James Lyon Fremantle, Coldstream Guards, on His Five Months in the Southern States.* Short Hills, NJ: Burford Books, 1954.

Marcy, Randolph B. *Prairie Traveler: A Handbook for Overland Expeditions.* Washington: United States War Department, 1859.

McClellan, Henry B. *The Life and Campaigns of Major-General J. E. B. Stuart.* Boston: Houghton-Mifflin Co., 1885.

McDonald, Archie P., ed. *Make Me a Map of the Valley: The Civil War Journal of Stonewall Jackson's Topographer.* Dallas: Southern Methodist University Press, 1973.

McDonald, William N. *A History of the Laurel Brigade.* Baltimore: Sun Job Printing, 1907.

McKim, Randolph H. *A Soldier's Recollections: Leaves from the Diary of a Young Confederate.* New York: Longman, Green, and Co., 1910.

Mobley, Joe A., ed. *The Papers of Zebulon Baird Vance, Vol. 2.* Raleigh: North Carolina Division of Archives and History, 1995.

Mohr, James C., ed. *The Cormany Diaries: A Northern Family in the Civil War.* Pittsburg: University of Pittsburg Press, 1982.

Moore, Frank E., ed. *The Rebellion Record: A Diary of American Events.* 12 Vols. New York: D. Van Norstrand, 1863-1865.

National Tribune. *National Tribune Scrapbook: Stories of the Camp, March, Battle, Hospital and Prison Told by Comrades.* Washington: National Tribune, 1909.

Neese, George M. *Three Years in the Confederate Horse Artillery.* Dayton, OH: Morningside House, 1988.

Nichols, G. W. *A Soldier's Story of His Regiment (61st Georgia) and Incidentally of the Lawton-Gordon-Evans Brigade, Army of Northern Virginia.* Jessup, GA, n.p.: 1898.

Nicholson, John P., ed. *Pennsylvania at Gettysburg: Ceremonies at the Dedication of the Monuments Erected by the Commonwealth of Pennsylvania.* 2 Vols. Harrisburg, PA: William Stanley Ray, 1914.

Nesbitt, James Cooper. *Four Years on the Firing Line.* Jackson, TN: McCowat-Mercer, 1963.

Norman, William M. *A Portion of My Life: A Short & Imperfect History Written While a Prisoner of War Johnson's Island, 1864.* Winston-Salem, NC: John. F. Blair Publishing, 1959.

Oliver, J. B., E. F. Hicks, and B. B. Carr. *History of Co. E, 20th N.C. Regiment.* Goldsboro, NC: Nash Brothers, 1905.

Opie, John N. *A Rebel Cavalryman With Lee, Stuart, and Jackson.* Chicago: W. B. Conkey Co., 1899.

Roper, John Herbert, ed. *Repairing the March of Mars: The Civil War Diaries of John Samuel Apperson, Hospital Steward in the Stonewall Brigade, 1861-1865.* Macon, GA: Mercer University Press, 2001.

Runge, William H., ed. *Four Years in the Confederate Artillery: The Diary of Pvt. Henry Robinson Berkeley.* Chapel Hill: University of North Carolina Press, 1961.

Small, Harold Adams, ed. *The Road to Richmond—The Civil War Memoirs of Major Abner R. Small of the 16th Maine.* Berkeley: University of California Press, 1939.

Smith, William Alexander. *The Anson Guards, Company C, Fourteenth Regiment North Carolina Volunteers, 1861-1865.* Charlotte, NC: Stone Publishing Co., 1914.

Stephens, Robert G., Jr., ed. *Intrepid Warrior: Clement Ansley Evans.* Dayton, OH: Morningside Books, 1992.

Stiles, Robert. *Four Year Under Marse Robert.* New York: Neale Publishing Co., 1904.

Stowe, Steven M., ed. *Southern Practice: The Diary and Autobiography of Charles A. Hentz, MD.* Charlottesville: University of Virginia Press, 2000.

Styple, William B., ed. *Writing and Fighting from the Army of Northern Virginia: A Collection of Confederate Soldier Correspondence.* Kearny, NJ: Belle Grove Publishing Co., 2003.

Sullivan, James W. *Boyhood Memories of the Civil War, 1861-'65.* Carlisle, PA: Hamilton Library Association, 1933.

Taylor, Michael W. *To Drive the Enemy From Southern Soil: The Letters of Col. Francis Marion Parker and the History of the 30th Regiment North Carolina Troops.* Dayton, OH: Morningside House, 1998.

Thomas, Henry W. *History of the Doles-Cook Brigade.* Dayton, OH: Morningside House, 1981.

Thompson, Ann J., ed. *North Carolina Confederate Letters, 1861-1865.* 2 Vols. Shelby, NC: Broad River Genealogical Society, 2001.

Thompson, James M. *Reminiscences of Autauga Rifles.* Autauguaville, AL: n.p., 1879.

Tolbert, Noble J., ed. *The Papers of John Willis Ellis.* 2 Vols. Raleigh: North Carolina Department of Archives and History, 1964.

Troxler, Beverly Barrier and Billy Dawn Barrier Auciello, eds. *Dear Father: Confederate Letters Never Before Published.* North Billerica, MA: Auciello Publishers, 1989.

United States Congress. *The Congressional Globe*, 35th Congress, 2nd Session. Washington: Globe Printing Office, 1859.

United States War Department. *The War of the Rebellion: A Compilation of the Official Records of the Union and Confederate Armies.* 70 Vols. in 128 parts. Washington: Government Printing Office, 1880-1901.

Vautier, John D. *History of the Eighty-Eighth Pennsylvania Volunteers in the War for the Union, 1861-1865.* Philadelphia: J. B. Lippincott Co., 1894.

Wall, Henry C. *Historical Sketch of the Pee Dee Guards.* Raleigh: Edwards Broughton and Co., 1876.

Watford, Christopher M., ed. *The Civil War in North Carolina: Soldiers and Civilian Letters and Diaries, 1861-1865, Vol. 1, The Piedmont.* Jefferson, NC: McFarland and Co., 2003.

Watkins, Thomas J. *Notes on the Movement of the 14th North Carolina Regiment.* Wadesboro, NC: Anson County Historical Society, 1991.

Wyatt, Lillian Reeves, ed. *The Reeves, Mercer, Newkirk Families: A Compilation.* Jacksonville, FL: The Cooper Press, 1956.

SECONDARY AND REFERENCE SOURCES

Articles

Alexander, Ted. "A Regular Slave Hunt," *North & South Magazine,* 4, No. 7 (September 2001), 82-89.

———. "Ten Days in July: The Pursuit to the Potomac," *North & South Magazine,* 2, No. 6 (August 1999), 76-78.

Arthur-Cornett, Helen. "Cabarrus Troops in the Mexican War," *Charlotte Observer,* Aug. 21, 2005.

Beckendorf, John Peter. "The Mystery of Wallace's Horse and Saddle," *North South Trader's Civil War,* 31 (2005), 52-58.

Cooksey, Paul Clark."They Died As if on Dress Parade: The Annihilation of Iverson's Brigade and the Battle of Oak Ridge," *Gettysburg Magazine,* 20 (January 1999), 89-112.

Crist, Robert G. "Highwater 1863: The Confederate Approach to Harrisburg," *Pennsylvania History,* 30 (1963), 158-183.

Droegemeyer, James R. "The Battle of Martinsburg, June 14, 1863," The *Berkeley Journal,* 27 (2001), 53-77.

Ent, Uzal. "Rebels in Pennsylvania," *Civil War Times Illustrated,* 37, No. 4 (August 1998), 46-52, 64-66.

French, Steve. "The Battle of Martinsburg," *Gettysburg Magazine,* 34 (January 2006), 7-25.

―――. "Federals on 'Safe' Road to Trouble," *Washington Times,* Dec. 3, 2005.

―――. "Gettysburg Fatal to Unheralded Civilians," *Washington Times,* Jan. 12, 2008.

―――. "Williamsburg Shreds Rebels," *Washington Times,* March 12, 2009.

Gallagher, Gary W. "Confederate Corps Leadership on the First Day at Gettysburg, A. P. Hill and Richard S. Ewell in a Difficult Debut," included in Gary W. Gallagher, ed., *The First Day at Gettysburg: Essays on Confederate and Union Leadership.* Kent, OH: The Kent State University Press, 1992, 3-56.

Griffith, Joe. "Georgians in the War with Mexico, 1846-1848," *Journal of the Historical Society of the Georgia National Guard,* 6 (1997), 1-15.

Hall, Charles B. "The Army Is Moving: Lee's March to the Potomac, Rodes Spearheads the Way," *Blue and Gray Magazine,* 21, Issue 3 (Spring 2004), 6-22, 44-52.

Hartwig, D. Scott. "The 11th Army Corps on July 1, 1863—'The Unlucky 11th,'" *Gettysburg Magazine,* 2 (January 1990), 33-50.

Hufham, J. D. "The Faison Family and the Kenan Family Honored by Duplin County," *Raleigh News and Observer,* Jan. 16, 1898.

Krick, Robert K. "Three Confederate Disasters on Oak Ridge: Failures of Brigade Leadership on the First Day at Gettysburg," included in Gary W. Gallagher, ed., *The First Day at Gettysburg: Essays on Confederate and Union Leadership.* Kent, OH: The Kent State University Press, 1992, 129-137.

―――. "We Have Never Suffered a Greater Loss Save in the Great Jackson: Was Robert E. Rodes the Army's Best Division Commander," included in Robert K. Krick, ed., *The Smoothbore Volley That Doomed the Confederacy.* Baton Rouge: Louisiana State University Press: 2002, 117-143.

Kross, Gary. "Fight Like the Devil to Hold Your Own: General John Buford's Cavalry at Gettysburg on July 1, 1863," *Blue & Gray Magazine,* 12, Issue 3 (February 1995), 9-22.

―――. "That One Error Fills Him With Faults: General Iverson and His Brigade at Gettysburg," *Blue & Gray Magazine,* 12, Issue 3 (February 1995), 22-24, 48-53.

―――. "The XI Corps at Gettysburg, July 1, 1863," *Blue & Gray Magazine,* 19, Issue 2 (December 2001), 6-24, 48-51.

Lash, Gary G. "Brigadier General Henry Baxter's Brigade at Gettysburg, July 1," *Gettysburg Magazine,* 10 (January 1994), 6-27.

Meade, Everard Kidder. "Col. Thomas A. Carter, C.S.A.—A Sketch," *Proceedings of the Clarke County Historical Association,* 3 (1943), 41-42.

Morrison, W. B. "Fort Washita," *Chronicles of Oklahoma,* 5 (1927), 251-258.

Murray, R. L. "The 157th New York Volunteers at Gettysburg," *Gettysburg Magazine,* 40 (January 2009), 29-41.

Parker, Roy Jr. "Heroes Flag Back in NC," *Fayetteville Observer,* Dec. 26, 2002.

Patterson, Gerard A. "The Death of Iverson's Brigade," *Gettysburg Magazine,* 5 (July 1991), 13-18.

Richter, Edward G. J. "The Removal of the Confederate Dead from Gettysburg," *Gettysburg Magazine,* 2 (January 1990), 113-122.

Robison, Jim. "Lake Faith Lured General to Build His Florida Home," *Orlando Sentinel,* Dec. 7, 1997.

Smith, Bridges. "How General Alf. Iverson Worked on a Big Ice Idea," *Macon Daily Telegraph,* Nov. 1, 1914.

Voegle, Fred B. "Chronology of the Civil War in Berkeley County," *The Berkeley Journal,* 26 (2000), 1-26.

Wittenberg, Eric J. "This Was a Night Never to Be Forgotten: The Midnight Fight in the Monterey Pass, July 4-5, 1863," *North & South Magazine,* 2, No. 6 (August 1999), 44-54.

Wright, Muriel H. "Old Boggy Depot," *Chronicles of Oklahoma,* 5 (1927), 4-17.

Books

American Council of Learned Societies. *Dictionary of American Biography.* 9 Vols. New York: C. Scribner's Sons, 1928.

Bates, Samuel P. *History of Cumberland and Adams Counties Pennsylvania.* Chicago: Warner, Beers, and Co., 1886.

———. *History of Franklin County Pennsylvania.* Chicago: Warner, Beers, and Co., 1876.

Beyer, W. F. and O. F. Keydel. *Deeds of Valor: How America's Civil War Heroes Won the Medal of Honor.* 2 Vols. Stamford, CT: Longmeadow Press, 1992.

Blackman, William Fremont. *History of Orange County Florida.* DeLand, FL: E. O. Painter Printing Co., 1927.

Brown, Kent Masterson. *Retreat from Gettysburg: Lee, Logistics, and the Pennsylvania Campaign.* Chapel Hill: University of North Carolina Press, 2005.

Bryan, T. Conn. *Confederate Georgia.* Athens: University of Georgia Press, 1953.

Busey, John W. and David G. Martin. *Regimental Strengths and Losses at Gettysburg.* Hightstown, NJ: Longstreet House, 1986.

Clemens, Thomas G., ed., Carman, A. Ezra, *The Maryland Campaign of September 1862: Vol. 1: South Mountain.* New York: Savas Beatie, 2010.

Coco, Gregory A. *A Vast Sea of Misery.* Gettysburg, PA: Thomas Publications, 1988.

Coleman, Kenneth and Charles Stephen Gurr, eds. *Dictionary of Georgia Biography.* 2 Vols. Athens: University of Georgia Press, 1983.

Collins, Darrell L. *Major General Robert E. Rodes of the Army of Northern Virginia: A Biography.* New York: Savas Beatie: 2008.

Crist, Robert G. *Confederate Invasion of the West Shore - 1863.* Carlisle, PA: Cumberland County Historical Society, 1963.

Cullum, George W. *Biographical Register of the Officers and Graduates of the U.S. Military Academy at West Point, N.Y.* 2 Vols. Boston: Houghton, Mifflin and Co., 1891.

Cunningham, H. H. *Doctors in Gray: The Confederate Medical Service.* Baton Rouge: Louisiana State University Press, 1958.

Davis, William C. *The Union That Shaped the Confederacy: Robert Toombs & Alexander H. Stephens.* Lawrence: University of Kansas Press, 2001.

Dougherty, James J. *Stone's Brigade and the Fight for the McPherson Farm.* Conshohocken, PA: Combined Publishing, 2001.

Dubbs, Carol Kettenburg. *Defend This Old Town: Williamsburg During the Civil War.* Baton Rouge: Louisiana State University Press, 2002.

Duckett, Alvin Laroy. *John Forsyth: Political Tactician.* Athens: University of Georgia Press, 1962.

Evans, Clement A., ed., *Confederate Military History: Expanded Edition.* 14 Vols. Wilmington, NC: Broadfoot Publishing Co., 1987.

Ferguson, Earnest B. *Chancellorsville, 1863*: The Souls of the Brave. New York: Vantage Books, 1992.

Franklin, John Hope. *The Militant South, 1800-1861.* Urbana: University of Illinois Press, 2002.

Gallagher, Gary W. *Stephen Dodson Ramseur: Lee's Gallant General.* Chapel Hill: University of North Carolina Press, 1985.

Gold, Thomas D. *History of Clarke County Virginia and Its Connections With the War Between the States.* Berryville, VA: Chesapeake Book Co., 1962.

Hahn, George W. *The Catawba Soldier of the Civil War.* Hickory, NC: Heritage Printing Co., 1908.

Heidler, David Stephen, Jeanne T. Heidler, and David J. Coles, eds. *Encyclopedia of the American Civil War: A Political, Social, and Military History.* New York: W. W. Norton and Co., 2002.

Heitman, Francis B., ed. *Historical Register and Dictionary of the United States Army.* 2 Vols. Washington: U.S. Government Printing Office, 1903.

Iobst, Richard W. *Civil War Macon: The History of a Confederate City.* Macon, GA: Mercer University Press, 1979.

Johnson, John Lipscomb. *The University Memorial: Biographical Sketches of the Alumni of the University of Virginia Who Fell in the Confederate War.* Baltimore: Turnbull Brothers, 1871.

Jordan, Weymouth T., Jr. and Louis H. Manarin. *North Carolina Troops, 1861-1865: A Roster.* 14 Vols. Raleigh: North Carolina Division of Archives and History, 1966-1998.

Krick, Robert E. L. *Staff Officers in Gray: A Biographical Register of the Staff Officers in the Army of Northern Virginia.* Chapel Hill: University of North Carolina Press, 2003.

Krick, Robert K. *Lee's Colonels: A Biographical Registry of the Field Officers of the Army of Northern Virginia.* Dayton, OH: Morningside, 1991.

Longacre, Edward G. *The Cavalry at Gettysburg.* Lincoln: University of Nebraska Press, 1983.

Macaluso, Gregory J. *Morris, Orange, and King William Artillery.* Lynchburg, VA: H. E. Howard, 1991.

Martin, David G. *Gettysburg July 1.* Conshohocken, PA: Combined Books, 1995.

Martin, John H., ed. *Columbus Georgia, From Its Selection As a "Trading Town" in 1827 to Its Partial Destruction by Wilson's Raid in 1865*. Columbus, GA: Thomas Gilbert Printers, 1874.

Mast, Greg. *State Troops and Volunteers: A Photographic Record of North Carolina's Civil War Soldiers*. Raleigh: North Carolina Department of Cultural Resources, 1995.

McGowen, Faison Wells and Pearl Canady McGowen, eds. *Flashes of Duplin's History and Government*. Raleigh: Edwards and Broughton Co., 1971.

McKinney, Gordon B. *Zeb Vance: North Carolina's Civil War Governor and Gilded Age Political Leader*. Chapel Hill: University of North Carolina Press, 2004.

McNeil, Jim. *Masters of the Shoals: Tales of the Cape Fear Pilots Who Ran the Union Blockade*. Cambridge, MA: De Capo Press, 2003.

Medical Society of the State of North Carolina. *Provisional Record of Confederate Medical Officers*. Raleigh: n.p., 1890.

Merrill, James M. *Spurs to Glory: The Story of the United States Cavalry*. Chicago: Rand McNally, 1966.

Morgan, James Henry. *Dickinson College: The History of One Hundred and Fifty Years 1783-1933*. Carlisle, PA: Mount Pleasant Press, 1933.

Myers, Sylvester. *Myers' History of West Virginia*. 2 Vols. Wheeling WV: Wheeling News Lithography Co., 1915.

Norris, J. E. *History of the Lower Shenandoah Valley*. Chicago: A. Warner and Co., 1890.

Nye, Wilbur Sturtevant. *Here Come the Rebels!* Dayton, OH: Morningside Press, 1988.

Parker, David B. *Alias Bill Arp: Charles Henry Smith and the South's "Goodly Heritage."* Athens: University of Georgia Press, 1991.

Pfanz, Donald C. *Richard S. Ewell: A Soldier's Life*. Chapel Hill: University of North Carolina Press, 1998.

Pfanz, Harry W. *Gettysburg: Culp's Hill and Cemetery Hill*. Chapel Hill: University of North Carolina Press, 1993.

———. *Gettysburg: The First Day*. Chapel Hill: University of North Carolina Press, 2001.

Phillips, Ulrich Bonnell. *The Life of Robert Toombs*. New York: The MacMillan Co., 1913.

Poole, John Randolph. *Cracker Cavaliers, The Second Georgia Cavalry under Wheeler and Forest*. Macon, GA: Mercer University Press, 2000.

Powell, William S., ed. *Dictionary of North Carolina Biography*. 6 Vols. Raleigh: University of North Carolina Press, 1986.

Priest, John Michael. *Before Antietam: The Battle for South Mountain*. New York: Oxford University Press, 1992.

Raper, Charles Lee. *The Church and Private Schools of North Carolina: A Historical Study*. Greensboro, NC: Joseph J. Stone, 1898.

Ray, Fred L. *Shock Troops of the Confederacy: The Sharpshooter Battalions of the Army of Northern Virginia*. Asheville, NC: CSF Press, 2006.

Roberts, William Hugh. *Mexican War Veterans: A Complete Roster of the Regular and Volunteer Troops in the War Between the United States and Mexico, from 1846 to 1848*. Washington: Brentano's, 1887.

Robertson, James I., Jr. *Stonewall Jackson: The Man, The Soldier, The Legend*. New York: McMillan Publishing, 1997.

Sanderlin, Walter S. *The Great National Project: A History of the Chesapeake and Ohio Canal.* Baltimore: Johns Hopkins University Press, 1946.

Schaff, Morris. *The Spirit of Old West Point, 1858-1862.* Boston: Houghton Mifflin, 1907.

Scharf, J. Thomas. *History of Western Maryland.* 2 Vols. Philadelphia: Louis H. Everts, 1882.

Shue, Richard S. *Morning at Willoughby Run, July 1, 1863.* Gettysburg, PA: Thomas Publications, 1995.

Shyrock, Richard Harrison. *Georgia and the Union in 1850.* Durham, NC: Duke University Press, 1926.

Sprunt, James. *Chronicles of the Cape Fear River, 1660-1916.* Raleigh: Edwards and Broughton Printing Co., 1916.

Sutherland, Daniel E. *Seasons of War: The Ordeal of a Confederate Community*. New York: The Free Press, 1995.

Tagg, Larry. *The Generals of Gettysburg: The Leaders of America's Greatest Battle.* Campbell, CA: Savas Publishing, 1998.

Thomas, Emory H. *Bold Dragoon: The Life of J. E. B. Stuart.* Norman: University of Oklahoma Press, 1999.

Tyler, Lyon Gardiner, ed. *Encyclopedia of Virginia Biography.* 3 Vols. New York: Lewis Historical Publishing Co., 1915.

University of North Carolina Alumni Association. *Alumni History of the University of North Carolina.* Durham, NC: Christian and King, 1924.

Warner, Ezra J. *Generals in Gray: Lives of the Confederate Commanders.* Baton Rouge: Louisiana State University Press, 1988.

Wertenbaker, Thomas J. *Norfolk: Historic Southern Port.* Durham, NC: Duke University Press, 1931.

Wing, Conway P. *History of Cumberland County, Pennsylvania.* Philadelphia: James D. Scott, 1879.

Wittenberg, Eric J. and J. David Petruzzi. *Plenty of Blame to Go Around: Jeb Stuart's Controversial Ride to Gettysburg.* New York: Savas Beatie, 2006.

———, J. David Petruzzi, and Michael F. Nugent. *One Continuous Fight: The Retreat from Gettysburg and the Pursuit of Lee's Army of Northern Virginia, July 4-14, 1863.* New York: Savas Beatie, 2008.

Yancey, Rosa Faulkner. *Lynchburg and Its Neighbors.* Richmond: J. W. Fergusson and Sons, 1935.

Websites

Gibbons, Carolyn. Abstracts from Fayetteville Observer 1855: http://www.ncgenweb.us/richmond/1855newsabstracts.html.

Jordan, Nancy L. Iverson-Haynes Connection: http://wc.rootsweb.ancestry.com/cgi-bin/ igm.cgi?op=REG&db=:2469703&id=I524349733.

Shockley, Woodland G. A Brief History of the Families of Richard Holt, Simon Holt, Singleton Holt, and Their Descendants: http://freepages.genealogy.rootsweb.com/~caseytexas/Holt-White/Richholt.doc.

INDEX TO FOLLOW

About the Author

Robert J. Wynstra recently retired as a senior writer for the News and Public Affairs Office in the College of Agricultural, Consumer, and Environmental Sciences at the University of Illinois. He holds Bachelor's and Master's degrees in history and a Master's degree in journalism, all from the University of Illinois. Rob has been researching Alfred Iverson's role in the Civil War for more than ten years. He is finishing work on a study of Robert Rodes' Division in the Gettysburg Campaign. This is his first book.